Medieval Jerusalem

Medieval Jerusalem

Forging an Islamic City in Spaces Sacred to Christians and Jews

Jacob Lassner

University of Michigan Press

Ann Arbor

Published in the United States of America by the
University of Michigan Press
Manufactured in the United States of America
♾ Printed on acid-free paper

2020 2019 2018 2017 4 3 2 1

A CIP catalog record for this book is available from the British Library.

Library of Congress Cataloging-in-Publication Data

Names: Lassner, Jacob, author.
Title: Medieval Jerusalem : forging an Islamic city in spaces sacred to Christians and Jews / Jacob Lassner.
Description: Ann Arbor : University of Michigan Press, 2017. |
Includes bibliographical references and index.
Identifiers: LCCN 2016057154| ISBN 9780472130368 (hardcover : alk. paper) |
ISBN 9780472122868 (e-book)
Subjects: LCSH: Jerusalem—History. | Jerusalem—In Islam. | Qubbat al-òSakhrah (Mosque : Jerusalem) Classification: LCC DS109.916 .L37 2017 | DDC 956.94/42—dc23
LC record available at https://lccn.loc.gov/2016057154

Contents

Preface

With many scholarly projects it is the odd query that whets the appetite for renewed engagement with the past. In this instance, it is with a question initially posed by an earlier generation of Western Islamicists, but then set aside when consensus drained the life out of what had once been a lively debate about the history of Islamic Jerusalem. Piqued by renewed interest in the Holy Land and its holiest city, a number of archaeologists, historians, and art historians have turned once again to a question first raised by scholars of the nineteenth century: When and in what circumstances did Jerusalem, a city long venerated by Jews and Christians, become a hallowed place for Muslims? For with great reverence, Muslims came to see Jerusalem as a holy site comparable in religious importance to Mecca and Medina, the cities of Arabia that gave birth to the Prophet Muḥammad and the first Muslim community. If revisiting Jerusalem's emergence as an Islamic city were not enough to fill a scholarly docket, this book covers less traveled ground and poses a second question: Why is it that certain medieval Muslim authorities perceived the need to go against the weight of Islamic tradition and deny Jerusalem an exalted status similar to the holy cities of Arabia?

The story of how Jerusalem became a holy site for the Muslims remains puzzling even as historians are now able to wield, as never before, the tools of modern archaeology, art historical analysis, and not the least, highly sophisticated approaches to reading medieval Arabic texts. Part of the problem is the paucity of reliable evidence. Without a firm footing on which to proceed, a number of scholars have chosen to speculate freely in search of an elusive past that was—or perhaps better put, a past that might have been. In contrast, I have generally opted for modest claims that are expressed whenever possible in language marked by considerable circumspection. More often than not, the focus is on small details in the hope that examined in tandem, incidental statements extracted from medieval Arabic texts and the testimony of the epigraphic and archaeological evidence will suggest a composite picture of how Jerusalem became a Muslim *locus sacra*. In addition, the pages that follow attempt to situate Jerusalem within the larger urban landscape of medieval Islam with a decided emphasis on developments during the first three Islamic centuries, a time frame that corresponds to the seventh to ninth centuries CE.

Probing the history of Islamic cities, one invariably confronts the lingering influence of widely acclaimed authorities of the past, scholars of previous generations whose views remain firmly anchored in a burgeoning historical literature. Well into the latter part of the twentieth century, the received wisdom of historians old and new was to speak of *the* Islamic city as if all the urban centers of the medieval Near East, no matter how different their origins and growth, shared elements of a common profile. This general observation thought of in the broadest terms—for example, the accepted legal definition of a medieval Islamic town or city—remains true. According to Islamic law, at least as it was understood in the formative centuries of Islam, *all* settlements defined as towns and cities were required to have a congregational mosque (*jāmiʿ*) large enough to contain the entire populace during Friday prayers along with a state-appointed judicial authority. The presence of both these institutions, which generally required caliphal approval, distinguished legally defined urban settlements from exurban and suburban areas, rural villages, and Bedouin encampments. The legal criteria of what constitutes a town or city may characterize a generic urban landscape, but they leave unanswered all sorts of questions about specific urban environments. To paraphrase an old Arabic proverb: One can always measure a finger, but the fingers of the hand are never of equal length. The fingers of the urban hand are indeed very different from one another.

Measured by any yardstick, the physiognomy of medieval towns and cities reflects the very diversity of Islamic civilization itself. Among the urban dwellers were great dynasts and regional or local pretenders; merchants and artisans; scholars and sainted individuals; and not the least, the flotsam and jetsam of humanity that took root in cities and towns after having wandered in from the immediate countryside and places further removed. The cities and towns were extremely variegated and very complex in topographical and social arrangement. There were great cities of antiquity that Muslims came to inhabit, if at first reluctantly, and garrison towns like Basra and Kufa that evolved from military bases that sprouted at the time of the Arab conquests. In contrast to the garrison towns that grew spontaneously and without any concern for formal city planning, there were later foundations established under the aegis of a more centralized Islamic rule, cities such as Baghdad, Rafiqa, and Samarra, all built according to preconceived plans approved by the ruling authorities. The cities founded by Muslims in the seventh to ninth centuries CE were thus classified as either "spontaneous" or "created" cities, as if they were formed in two separate and distinctive molds. However, once fully examined, the individual histories of the newly minted Islamic cities reveal considerable variation in accordance with local conditions and the political climate of the moment.

Scholars should also distinguish between the small market towns serving a limited area with a social structure not all that distinct from that of its rural surroundings and the great cosmopolitan cities, centers of a distinctive urban life. There were regional administrative centers from which local rulers controlled the hinterland beyond, and capital cities from which ruling dynasts exercised imperial power over distant provinces. The vast metropolitan cities like Baghdad, Damascus, and Cairo gave rise to every kind of activity, but there were also urban sites where life was dominated by more narrowly defined purposes, places that Muslims regarded as centers of pilgrimage or religious learning. Among the latter were Mecca and Medina, the first being the shrine city that gave birth to the Prophet and Islam, the second the large oasis where the Prophet first ruled and the Islamic community took root.

The *ḥaramayn* or holy cities of Arabia, the fulcrum of Islam during Muḥammad's life and that of his immediate successors, were soon supplanted in political importance by ancient urban centers captured by Muslim armies crossing the Arabian frontier and by newly formed Muslim garrison towns that served as platforms for further Islamic expansion. West Arabia, the birthplace of Muḥammad and his faith, simply lacked the resources with which to control a rapidly expanding Islamic polity that included vast regions of the Near East and North Africa. Be that as it may, the changed geopolitics did not alter the religious significance of Mecca and Medina, cities favored by Muḥammad and his contemporaries. Nor did it diminish the unique status of these cities for Muslims performing the obligatory rites of pilgrimage (*ḥajj*).

Jerusalem and the Larger Urban Landscape

Like the holy cities of Arabia, Jerusalem lacked the necessary wealth and manpower from which to project effective political influence. But unlike the ḥaramayn, especially Medina, Jerusalem never became a major center of Islamic learning. However, given a sacred history that could be traced back the ancient kings of Israel, and a legendary past said to have begun with Creation itself, the city celebrated in Jewish and Christian tradition, and visited by pilgrims and pietists of both faiths, evolved over time into the third holy city of Islam. Jerusalem may not have been a place from which Muslim rulers could project power; but as an idealized sacred city it gripped the imagination of the Arab conquerors and Jewish and Christian converts to Islam. As with Mecca and Medina, the idea of a city holy to Muslims had political purchase even after it was all too clear that the requisite elements for executing state policy rested in places like Damascus and later Baghdad, the administrative centers of established dynastic orders.

The commanders of the faithful stationed in Syria and Iraq were well aware of the symbolic importance of Arabia's ḥaramayn and went to great lengths to ensure the support of the local inhabitants and those who celebrated the cities' sacred past. Muḥammad's kinsmen, the clan of Hāshim, especially those who remained in Arabia, were considered important to legitimizing the election of his successors. As a result, the aristocrats of Mecca and Medina were courted with lavish gifts—a bribe that most of them gladly accepted, if not always with expressions of gratitude. The leader of the yearly ḥajj appointed by the caliph was often commissioned to distribute honors all along the pilgrimage route, an act of expedient generosity combining a sacred obligation with the political interests of the state. On the other hand, some revolutionaries seeking to overthrow established authority followed the precedent of the Prophet and met with coconspirators who quietly converged upon Mecca when the city was inundated with pilgrims. Unobserved among the throngs of visitors, they set into motion plots that would lead to open rebellion. Although no successor to Muḥammad ruled from Arabia after 661 CE, that is a mere thirty years after the Prophet's death, events emanating from the holy cities continued to influence the politics of the early Islamic state.

At first glance, Jerusalem would seem to have played a more subdued role in the unfolding history of the time. Despite the claims of Muslim authorities, both medieval and modern, the ancient city held no great significance for Muḥammad and his companions. But not long after the Islamic conquest, the history of the city holy to Jews and Christians was retroactively fitted to suit evolving Muslim needs and took on, if only for fleeting moments, a political as well as religious significance similar to that of Mecca and Medina. For reasons to be explored in the pages that follow, various Umayyad caliphs (661–750 CE) sought to be invested with rule in Jerusalem, and not the holy cities of Arabia, the custom of Muḥammad and his immediate successors. The decision of the Umayyads was no doubt influenced by Jerusalem's aura as a holy city. The reverence that Jews and Christians had displayed over countless generations continued, not only among the older monotheists but also among Jews and Christians who converted to Islam. Similarly, many Arab Muslims who settled in and around Jerusalem became intoxicated by the sanctity of the city and its environs. Some scholars have gone so far as to suggest that Muʿāwiyah, the founder of the Umayyad dynasty, and like the Prophet a Meccan by birth, considered transferring the seat of his rule from Damascus to the city of the ancient Israelites nestled in the Judean hills.

If I may be permitted to crib a title from the great English writer Charles Dickens, the story of Jerusalem turns out to be a tale of two cities. On the one hand there is the holy city of Jews, Christians, and Muslims, each community inspired by its own particular vision of Jerusalem's past. But there is also a second city, which although considered sacred, resonated ever so strongly to the politics of the temporal world. Muslim rulers used the sacred history of Jerusalem to wrap themselves in symbols of legitimacy that could blunt the claims of Muslim rivals and also demonstrate to the older monotheist faiths that in allowing the Arabs to conquer their holy city, God transferred his favor from the Jews and Christians to his new chosen people, the faith community established by the Prophet Muḥammad. These observations and more will be grist for the reader's mill as this book unfolds.

The Contents

The main body of the work consists of nine chapters. Each chapter deals with specific themes that link it directly to the other segments of the text. The first chapter begins by defining the geographical space of the Holy Land as envisioned by Muslims as well as the various names by which its holiest city was known to the Arab conquerors and their successors. The chapter then discusses the discrete body of literature in praise of Jerusalem, the so-called *faḍā'il al-Quds*, a repository of mostly noncanonical Muslim traditions. The wide ranging faḍā'il accounts inform us about the history of Islamic Jerusalem, providing all sorts of information neither stated nor even alluded to in the major chronicles of the times. Most of all, the faḍā'il reveal the place of the city in the sacred imagination of the Muslim faithful.

The next eight chapters focus attention one way or another on the origins of Islamic Jerusalem, that is, the historic moment at which Muslims elevated the importance of the city and revered it as did the Jews and Christians before them. Chapter 2 deals broadly with Jerusalem as it might have been conceived by the Prophet Muḥammad and his companions, and, linked to that, the following chapter offers a detailed explication of several critical verses in the Qur'ān that Muslims understood and continue to understand as referring to Jerusalem. The object therein is to determine whether or not Muslim scripture and the formal and informal commentary to which it gave rise can be cited as compelling evidence that Jerusalem was revered by Muḥammad and his followers at the birth hour of Islam. Particular focus is reserved for Qur'ān 17:1, the famous verse describing a night journey to the "farthest place of worship," a journey that Muslim scholars regard as an actual visit of Muḥammad to the holy city.

Most Western scholars are of the opinion that the Islamization of Jerusalem begins in earnest only with the advent of the Umayyad caliphate and that the night journey to which the Qur'ān refers is a vague mystical experience rather than an actual event. As they see it, it was only after the Umayyads transformed Jerusalem into a holy city that the verse was understood to mean that the Prophet actually made his way to Jerusalem. Traditional Muslims and Orientalists agree that the Umayyad dynasts forsook the holy city of Medina, choosing instead to rule from Damascus, the capital of al-Shām, a vast province that included Jerusalem among its many towns and cities. As noted previously, some scholars maintain that the founder of the Umayyad dynasty, the caliph Mu'āwiyah b. Abī Sufyān (661–80 CE), actually planned to move from Damascus to Jerusalem. Such a move would have been transformative. The historic city of Jews and Christians would have become the fulcrum of a newly established Islamic polity, a state in all but name that ruled a territorial expanse rivaling that of the Byzantine Empire.

Chapter 4 assesses the scholarship behind these claims through a close examination of various Arabic and Hebrew sources. These texts are cited as evidence by scholars embracing the view that the first Umayyad caliph planned on elevating Jerusalem to a Muslim holy city, if not indeed the capital of his realm. Read with careful attention to the fine detail, as is the case in chapter 4, these Muslim and Jewish accounts do not provide sufficient evidence that Mu'āwiyah had a well-conceived plan to change the religious status of Jerusalem, let alone that he had any intention of abandoning Damascus in order make Jerusalem the seat of Umayyad rule. The next segment of the book takes up the more accepted view that the fifth caliph of the dynasty, the highly innovative 'Abd al-Malik b. Marwān (685–705 CE) and his son and successor al-Walīd I (705–15) transformed Jerusalem into Islam's third holiest city. The father erected the magnificent Dome of the Rock, the oldest surviving example of Islamic architecture; the son built or completed the great al-Aqṣā mosque nearby. Both buildings were situated on the platform that at one time housed the temples of Solomon and Herod, a hallowed ground that gave rise to innumerous Jewish and Muslim legends beginning with the story of Creation. The role of the two Marwanids in the development of the Temple Mount, known to Muslims as the Noble Sanctuary (*Ḥaram al-Sharīf*), is well attested in a wide variety of written sources, as well as the dedicatory inscription of the Dome of the Rock. Readers will note that chapter 5 embraces the widely accepted view that it was ʿAbd al-Malik who first promoted Jerusalem as a city most holy to Muslims and not his illustrious predecessor, the founder of the Umayyad dynasty.

Scholars who favor Muʿāwiyah as having initiated the plan to restore Jerusalem's Temple Mount are not dissuaded by accounts directly linking ʿAbd al-Malik to restoring the temple platform and erecting the Dome of the Rock and grand mosque nearby. As they see it, the later caliphs of the realm merely completed the work conceived by their famed predecessor, who planned the building activity on the Temple Mount as part of an ambitious project to imbue the city with Islamic credentials. They base this view on privileged readings of select literary accounts and on extensive archaeological activity that was undertaken following the Israeli conquest of Jerusalem's Old City in 1967. Chapters 5 and 6 critique the merits of this view by interrogating both the medieval written sources and the evidence provided by material culture, namely the remains of buildings and realia uncovered by Israeli archaeologists in the area near the southern wall of the platform. Archaeologists were quick to label the massive ruins the "Umayyad administrative center," giving credence to the view of those scholars who argue for an intended transfer of Islamic rule from Damascus to the holy city. The archaeologists appear to have been somewhat hasty in their judgment. Chapters 5 and 6 point out that the dating and interpretation of the site in the shadow of the Temple Mount are anything but certain. Neither the literary sources nor the archaeological finds offer conclusive or even presumptive evidence that Muʿāwiyah had grand plans for the holy city of the Christians and Jews.

The following chapter (7) takes up the long-standing dispute as to whether ʿAbd al-Malik built the Dome of the Rock to serve as a substitute for the Kaʿbah, the central shrine of Mecca. According to some scholars, the caliph's grand plan was to divert the Muslim pilgrimage from the holy cities of Arabia to Jerusalem, an act said to have been governed by the internal politics of the Muslim state, namely, the revolt of the Zubayrid counter-caliph who ruled from Medina. The claim linking construction of the domed building with a conscious decision to divert the Arabian pilgrimage was first advanced in the nineteenth century by the preeminent Islamicist of the time, Ignaz Goldziher. The "Great Goldziher," as he was known to his peers, based his view on an elegant reading of the then available sources. Some seventy-five years later, Goldziher's thesis, which had become the reigning wisdom among Islamic scholars, was challenged by S. D. Goitein, who denied there was any attempt to divert the annual pilgrimage to Jerusalem. A formidable historian of medieval Islam, Goitein based his conclusions on sources largely unknown to Goldziher and by a meticulous examination of well-known texts cited and not cited by his predecessor. The debate between the followers of these two towering figures has continued unabated. In an attempt to resolve the issue, chapter 7 guides readers through the tortuous byways of Arabic historiography. Those following the dense analysis will note that the evidence cited in the chapter ultimately favors Goitein and his supporters. That still leaves unanswered why ʿAbd al-Malik restored the Temple Mount and built the domed building upon it.

In chapter 8, I turn to what one leading art historian dubbed the "meaning" of the Dome of the Rock and argue that as regards form and function the building should be seen in light of Byzantine-Muslim relations and not the contentious politics of Muslim factions seeking or holding onto rule. In this matter I am much inclined to agree with Oleg Grabar, whose views, first aired some fifty years ago, still resonate strongly. Convinced as I am by Grabar's use of epigraphic evidence, I have seen fit to juxtapose his understanding of the Dome of the Rock with art-historical interpretations based on the highly stylized decoration of the building's interior. At the same time, I have sought to situate Grabar's argument within the broad setting of early Arabic historiography. With that, I believe that I have strengthened the case for seeing the Dome of the Rock and, more generally, all of the Ḥaram al-Sharīf, as a symbol of Islam's rivalry with eastern Christendom. Chapter 9 highlights the anti-Jerusalem literature in Islam and its relationship to Jewish and Christian lore and popular religious observances. The anti-faḍāʾil texts are pictured as reflecting the concerns of the more austere religious authorities, namely, that the Muslim faithful will be seduced by enticing foreign beliefs and practices. As is often the case with close religious contacts, the lure of the exotic penetrated deeply into the daily lives of people. Pre-Islamic accounts of Jerusalem's sacrality and various non-Islamic religious practices associated with the city and adjacent ancient holy sites became part and parcel of Muslim belief and behavior.

Recent Developments

In the last few decades, scholars of Jerusalem have benefited from excellent editions of hitherto unpublished Arabic manuscripts. The newly published sources belong to a genre of Arabic writing called *faḍāʾil al-Quds* or *faḍāʾil Bayt al-Maqdis*, namely "praises of Jerusalem." With these texts, Arabists interested in the history and architecture of the medieval Islamic city can peruse hundreds, if not thousands, of pithy statements echoing pasts both real and imagined, a formidable undertaking that calls for separating the 'historic' wheat from the legendary chaff. That task, more easily spoken of than accomplished with assurance, has stimulated spirited discussion and debate. The chapters that follow should be construed as an effort to participate in and contribute to these discussions. In retrospect, I imagine so much more that I might have presented in this book: references to source material not fully digested; ideas not yet fully explored; paths of investigation that remain to be traveled; and scholarly publications that came to light to late too be integrated within the body this work. There are, however, occasions when patience can be an asset and caution a scholarly virtue. And so, I refer once again to a Hebrew ballad remembered from my youth: *Ha-shir lo tam hu rak mathil*, "the song has not ended, it has just begun."

Acknowledgments

One of the easiest ways for a scholar to encumber massive intellectual debt is to write a book on Islamic Jerusalem. There is by now a vast body of monographs, articles, and archaeological reports that bear distinguished names from virtually every era since the beginnings of modern Islamic studies. Any author who engages generations of scholarship, including conversations with colleagues past and present, faces the dilemma of having to acknowledge more individuals and works than good taste or editorial license allow. Rather than pare the list and ruffle the sensitivities of friends and associates, I have decided as in the past, to forgo such accolades trusting that no one will be offended, not even those scholars of sainted memory who are debating earthly Jerusalem from the holy city on high. Suffice it to say, my debt to all of them is profound and deeply felt.

Nevertheless, I feel compelled to cite two individuals who had a decided influence on my engagement with Islamic history, more particularly my focusing on the urban landscape of medieval Islam. The first was the late Oleg Grabar, who instructed me in Islamic art when I was still an undergraduate and he a neophyte instructor plucked out of graduate school. When I completed my doctorate in Near Eastern languages and literatures, he encouraged me to attend all his seminars, thus allowing me to pursue systematically what had been for the most part a desultory study of Islamic art and architecture. Grabar cultivated an interest in virtually all aspects of artistic production. But within this broad-ranging approach to art history, Grabar was particularly drawn to exploring how individual buildings represented elements of large patterns of settlement, namely palace-complexes and urban centers. His consuming interest was Islamic Jerusalem, the holy city about which he lectured and wrote from the outset of his career until his death nearly sixty years later. Given his intellectual energy and a willingness to challenge accepted views, his writings on Jerusalem have had an enduring influence on art and architectural historians, as well as scholars like myself who attempt to link city planning and urban growth to religious and dynastic politics. As he did, I have always attempted to balance what can be learned from studying preserved monuments and ruins with information gleaned, at times surgically, from a wide range of medieval sources. I trust readers will recognize this approach when going through the pages that follow.

My greatest debt is to my *Doktorvater*, the preeminent Semitist and Islamic scholar Franz Rosenthal. Some fifty-eight years ago, he set me on a path that has guided my research and publications ever since. Aware of my desire to be a historian, but noting as well my keen interest in Islamic art and archaeology, Rosenthal advised me to focus my attention on urban development during the formative centuries of Islam. He suggested that I begin with a specific city and region and offered as a dissertation topic the topography of Baghdad in the Middle Ages. When I accepted his proposal to write about the great capital of the Abbasid caliphs, he observed that the project would be an introduction to a life's work. It was only after I had expanded my dissertation into a book that I came to fully appreciate what Rosenthal meant by his passing remark. The original project led me far beyond Baghdad and its immediate surroundings. Over the years, I turned my attention to several other urban settings in Iraq and more recently Islamic Jerusalem. Writing about a larger urban landscape, I found myself returning time and again to the concerns of my dissertation, most of all the use of problematic Arabic sources to explain the complexities of city growth and decline during the Islamic Middle Ages. As a wise Franz Rosenthal anticipated, that project completed more than a half century ago has been in every sense an introduction to a life's work.

Franz Rosenthal died in April 2003, days after his students and colleagues of the American Oriental Society sent him a large poster bearing their signatures and best wishes for a recovery that was neither expected nor for that matter possible. I do not know whether he actually received the improvised "get well card." I do know that it would have pleased him to be so honored by persons he held in esteem. Were he alive, we would have celebrated the hundredth anniversary of his birth in 2014. It is only fitting that I pen these words and dedicate this book to his memory. My fondest hope is that *Medieval Jerusalem* will earn his approval and that of all my other mentors in the celestial academy.

Author's Note on Transliteration

As readers move through the text that follows, they will encounter any number of personal names and place-names, as well as technical terms and complete phrases that have been transliterated from Near Eastern languages. The Arabic transliteration accords with one of several acceptable schemes. Place-names that are known to a general audience retain their English spelling. Hence, the holy Arabian cities Makkah and al-Madīnah are rendered as Mecca and Medina. Where the place-name reflects an unknown toponym in English, the Arabic transliteration is given. All Arabic proper names, even those easily recognized, are rendered in transliteration. For example, *Muḥammad* rather than *Muhammad* and *ʿAlī* rather than *Ali*. As the full Arabic name often includes a lengthy genealogy, the use of *ibn*, meaning "son of," is, according to an accepted convention, printed *b*. Dynastic names and the adjectives to which they give rise are, however, recorded as in English. Read *Abbasid*, as opposed to *ʿAbbāsī*. Readers unfamiliar with Arabic should have no difficulty in navigating their way through all these names. On the other hand, there is no agreed-upon system for transliterating Hebrew and Aramaic. That being the case, I have attempted to record place-names and technical terms as close as possible to their pronunciation. Places easily recognized by readers familiar with Hebrew place and proper names, such as those of biblical locations and figures, are rendered as they are found in the *Encyclopedia Judaica*; the same holds true for references to well-known religious holidays and ceremonies.

As for illustrations: The reconstruction of the (Umayyad) Place in Jerusalem is based on the drawing of B. Lalor found in and provided by courtesy of E. Mazar from her *Complete Guide to the Temple Mount Excavations* (Jerusalem, 2003). The illustrations of the Umayyad administrative center; the cross section of the Umayyad palace; and the plaster model are taken from M. Ben-Dov's *In the Shadow of the Temple* (New York: Harper & Row, 1985). I have been unable to determine the provenance of the plaster model. The reconstruction of the Noble Sanctuary and the administrative center is from D. Bahat's *Illustrated Atlas of Jerusalem* (Jerusalem, 1996). I have been unable to reach him regarding permission to use this illustration.

Abbreviations

AIEO	*Annales de l'institut des Études Orientales*
AJSR	Association for Jewish Studies Review
AO	*Acta Orientalia*
ARN	*Avot deRabbi Natan*
ARO	*Archiv Orientalni*
BGA	Biblioteca Geographorum Arabicorum
BI	*Bibliotheca Islamica*
BIE	*Bulletin de l'Institut Égyptien*
BO	*Bibliotheca Orientalis*
BSOAS	*Bulletin of the School of Oriental and African Studies*
BT	Babylonian Talmud
CBQ	*Catholic Biblical Quarterly*
CIAP	*Corpus Inscriptionum Arabicorum Palaestinae*
DOP	*Dumbarton Oaks Papers*
EI	*Encyclopedia of Islam*, 2nd edition
EJ	*Encyclopedia Judaica*
EMA	*Early Muslim Architecture*, 2nd edition
EQ	*Encyclopedia of the Qur'ān*
ET	*Encyclopedia Talmudīt*
FHA	*Fragmenta Historicorum Arabicorum*
HTR	*Harvard Theological Review*
IEJ	*Israel Exploration Journal*
IJMES	*International Journal of Middle East Studies*
IOS	*Israel Oriental Studies*
IS	*Islamic Studies*
JA	*Journal Asiatique*
JAAR	*Journal of the American Academy of Religion*
JAOS	*Journal of the American Oriental Society*
JESHO	*Journal of the Economic and Social History of the Orient*
JJS	*Journal of Jewish Studies*

JNES	*Journal of Near Eastern Studies*
JPOS	*Journal of the Palestine Oriental Society*
JQR	*Jewish Quarterly Review*
JQS	*Journal of Qur'ānic Studies*
JRAS	*Journal of the Royal Asiatic Society*
JSAI	*Jerusalem Studies in Arabic and Islam*
JSS	*Journal of Semitic Studies*
JT	Jerusalem Talmud
LOS	London Oriental Studies
MG	*Midreshei Geulah*
MR	Midrash Rabbah
MW	*Muslim World*
NEAEHL	*The New Encyclopedia of Archeological Investigations in the Holy Land*
OC	*Oriens Christianus*
OIP	Oriental Institute Publications
OSIA	*Oxford Studies in Islamic Art*
PAAJR	*Proceedings of the American Academy of Jewish Research*
PEQ	*Palestine Exploration Quarterly*
PIEO	*Publication de l'Institut d'Études Orientale*
RAAD	*Revue de l'Academie Arabe*
RB	*Revue Biblique*
REI	*Revue des Études Islamiques*
REJ	*Revue des Études Juives*
RIMA	*Revue de l'institute des manuscrits arabes*
RSO	*Rivista degli Studi Orientali*
SI	*Studia Islamica*
WHJP	*World History of the Jewish People*
WZKM	*Wiener Zeitschrift für die Kunde des Morgandlandes*
ZA	*Zeitschrift für Assyriologie*
ZDMG	*Zeitschrift der Deutschen Morganländischen Gesellschaft*

Prologue

It is now well over thirteen hundred years since Jerusalem, long venerated by Jews and Christians, was first celebrated as a holy city by Muslims. For all three faith communities, the story of Jerusalem dates to the biblical kings David and Solomon, when the ancient settlement first became the political and then spiritual hub of an emergent Israelite polity. Neither the destruction of Jerusalem's sacred temples, first by the Babylonians in 586 BCE, and then the Romans in 70 CE, nor losing sovereignty over the land promised them by God, not once but twice, diminished the importance of the holy city in the sacred imagination of Jews. Regardless of place or time, generations of pious Jews reciting their prayers have invoked memories of the holy city and beseeched God to return them from exile to its sacred Temple Mount. That accomplished, God's chosen people would reconstitute their religious and political life as in days of yore.

Christians, in turn, added their own vision of Jerusalem, both the ancient city that sat atop the Judean hills and the "New" or "Heavenly City" that came to replace it in Byzantine times. The earliest map of the Holy Land, the so-called Madaba Map, was originally laid as a mosaic floor in the transept of a sixth-century Byzantine church. While the map depicts a truly vast geographical domain, the detailed image of Jerusalem dwarfs all the other places within and adjacent the Holy Land, much as New York City dominates the landscape of urban America in that celebrated cover of *New Yorker* magazine. The *New Yorker* map is a whimsical gesture in keeping with the publication's well-deserved fame for humorous illustrations. In contrast, the Madaba Map makes a historic claim in all seriousness. The image of the magnified holy city with its numerous churches and holy sites demonstrates ever so clearly that under Byzantine rule Jerusalem had become a *locus sacra* for the followers of Christ. Despite losing sovereignty over Jerusalem to the Muslims in the seventh century, Christians, as did Jews, continued to revere the city so prominently featured in their outlook.

Not to be outdone in their enthusiasm for the holy city, medieval Muslims acknowledged the sacred character of Jerusalem with works of fulsome praise (*faḍā'il*) and by a monumental architecture that rivaled the ancient temples and grand churches of their predecessors. As did Jews and Christians, Muslims maintained that Jerusalem and an entire world assembled within it will bear witness to the final Day of Judgment after which God will restore harmony to a troubled humankind. Such belief in an impending messianic age may have receded with the advance of secularism, but the symbolic importance of the Holy Land and the holiest of its cities are still powerfully etched in the imagination of believers and nonbelievers alike. Among the various sites that grace the biblical landscape of old, Jerusalem remains, for all three Abrahamic faiths, the most revered and most studied of all.

A vast array of ancient and medieval sources has given rise in modern times to a veritable flood of academic articles and monographs supplemented by a widely consumed general literature as legions of amateur antiquarians and popular writers have joined learned scholars in resonating to the pull of the biblical past. Fortunately, there is now a vast body of critical scholarship on the Jewish Land (*Erez*) of Israel; the Christian Holy Land (*Terra Sancta*); and what modern Muslims have come to know as Palestine (*Filasṭīn* or *Falasṭīn*). The purpose of this study is to draw upon these researches and focus on Islam's early embrace of the Holy Land, and especially Jerusalem, keeping in mind that studies of the city are contested because the complex and at times conflicting source material causes fundamental differences of opinion. The technical skills required to process the relevant data are beyond the reach of most readers and all but a few highly trained scholars. Synthesizing the findings of learned philologists, archaeologists, and historians has proved elusive for authors bravely attempting to write a general narrative of Islamic Jerusalem, especially for authors seeking to attract a broad cross section of readers. Straightforward and digestible popular narratives may provide a coherent picture of Jerusalem's history, but, all too often, that picture masks a muddled reality.

This project is a modest attempt to grapple with difficult evidence and bridge the gap between a richly annotated study on how a sacred city for Jews and Christians became a Muslim city—that is, a monograph intended for learned Arabists—and a work that will be of interest to a wider audience. My intention is to draw readers from academic fields other than Near Eastern history, or simply curious individuals with scholarly interests. The task of satisfying so large a readership is daunting, to say the least. A responsible scholar has to delve into the arcane minutiae of Jewish, Christian, and Muslim traditions and then explain in considerable detail the decision tree that supports his or her general contention. Examining the relevant literary and architectural evidence can be an intricate, if not tortuous, process that resembles cross-examining recalcitrant witnesses in a court of law. There is no avoiding this difficult process for either author or audience because, unlike some court cases, there is little room for plea bargaining in an honest scholarly tribunal, especially one dealing with highly charged issues, as is the case in the pages that follow.

CHAPTER 1

The Holy Land and Jerusalem

Singing Praise to Sacred Space

What is generally known of Muslim sacred geography has been distilled into a very broad set of understandings. Most non-Muslims vaguely familiar with the outlines of Islamic civilization are aware of the reverence commanded by the holy cities of Arabia. The pilgrimage (*ḥajj*) to Mecca and Medina, one of the "five pillars of Islam," is an annual event that draws worldwide attention. The sight of throngs of worshipers inundating the sacred precincts and circumambulating the Kaʿbah, the central shrine in Mecca, is a regular feature of all film documentaries on Islam. Similarly, illustrated coffee table books on the Islamic world feature prominently photographs of the Arabian city, its great mosque, and its large rectangular shrine, which according to Muslim belief was erected on a spot first dedicated to God by the biblical patriarch Abraham and his eldest son Ishmael. In such fashion, the Muslim faithful embraced the progenitor of the Jews and along with him the story of the Israelite line born to his wife Sarah; but they favored even more the Arab peoples given life through Ishmael, Abraham's offspring via his concubine Hagar.

Muslims point out that the shrine at Mecca preceded the building of the Temple in Jerusalem by forty years.[1] This chronology is off by nearly a millennium, but the point of the Muslim tradition is well taken. When considering sacred space, Mecca took precedence over the capital of the Israelite kings, and the sanctity of Arabia transcended that of the biblical Holy Land. Be that as it may, in early Islamic times, the land revered by Jews and Christians captured the imagination of the Muslim faithful. Feelings for Jerusalem comparable to

1. Ibn Kathīr, *Qiṣaṣ* (Q), 506–7, and his *Bidāyah*, 2:226; Kisāʾī, *Qiṣaṣ*, 285; and commentaries to Qurʾān 38:25. A study of Mecca in relation to the holy settlements is found in M. J. Kister, "'You Shall Set Out Only for Three Mosques'—A Study of an Early Tradition," *Le Muséon* 82 (1969): 173–96 (additional notes in the reprint of this article in his *Studies in Jāhilīya and Early Islam*, 211–17. *Studies* is a collection of several of Kister's articles that were originally photocopied as a reader for his classes at the Hebrew University).

those for the sacred sites of Arabia took root, and despite objections from the more dour Islamic authorities, the ancient city overlooking the Judean countryside became for certain pious circles one of the three most sacred settlements in the Islamic Near East.

Aside from learned academics delving adroitly into the minutiae of early Islamic history, the manner in which Muslims embraced the biblical landscape has not attracted great notice in the Western world. This is particularly true with regard to the media and audiences given to reading popular rather than scholarly writings. Many individuals with a passing interest in the world of Islam may well be familiar with the Dome of the Rock, that exquisite example of Islamic architecture that sits atop Jerusalem's ancient Temple Mount. They may also be aware that Jerusalem is considered the third holy city of the Muslims and that the Holy Land of Jews and Christians also has a special place in the sacred geography of Islam. But these overarching views of the holy city and Holy Land do not do justice to the complex and hotly debated circumstances that characterize Islam's early engagement with the sacred space of Jews and Christians. That debate among scholars now centers on how Arab Muslims initially redefined the biblical landscape, be it in reshaping the stories of biblical persons and events or in Muslims appropriating and redefining Jerusalem's topography, the major concern of this study.

Defining the Muslim Holy Land and Holy City

For some five hundred years before the Arab conquest, the holy city and Holy Land were considered part of the ancient province of Syria, a vast area that encompassed much of the present-day Levant. The Muslim conquerors of the seventh century CE referred to Roman-Byzantine Syria as Bilād (the Land of) al-Shām, or simply al-Shām. Explaining this name, medieval Arabic lexicographers proposed various etymologies. Some explanations rooted in local custom appear, at first, eminently plausible, if not suggestive of a distant biblical past. Others linked to the milieu of the ancient Israelites are no doubt the products of a vivid imagination. In the first instance, Muslim scholars believed al-Shām to mean "The Left Hand Land," or, "The Land to the North" based on the Arabic root *sh-'-m*, which gives rise to verbs meaning "to go left" or "go north" (*tasha''ama* and *tashā'ama*). As the medieval authorities put it, if one extends an arm facing the rising sun (like Arabian Bedouins in search of their bearings) the left hand points northward (in the direction of what had been since ancient times an immense region ruled from Damascus). Some Muslim scholars supply a specific locus from which to measure geographical orientation. They report that al-Shām was so named because the province was situated to the left of the Kaʿbah, meaning it is due north of the sacred Muslim shrine in Mecca, the West Arabian settlement that was the birthplace of the Prophet Muḥammad. Another authority indicates improbably enough that the province was called al-Shām because the many bunched villages dotting its landscape resembled a series of *shāmāt* (Arabic root *sh-y-m*), facial "moles" of changing color.[2] In his *Palestine under the Moslems*, a work based largely on Arabic geographical sources, Guy Le Strange maintained that *shāmāt* referred to fields and gardens of the great province, thus conjuring up images of a multicolored Syrian landscape that is reminiscent of beauty marks gracing the face of a comely woman.[3] But, as the Arabic source cited by Le Strange mentions neither fields nor gardens, the etymology he suggests seems at face value highly conjectural. In either case, it would appear unlikely that the Arabic word for mole (*shāmah* pl. *shāmāt* and also *shām*) gave rise to the name by which Arabs identified Graeco-Roman Syria, let alone a land considered holy by three faiths.

Turning to sacred geography, Muslims "learned in the civilizations of old (*ahl al-āthār*)" refer to a biblical landscape venerated by all the Abrahamic religions. The antiquarians lead us to believe that a people descended from Noah's grandson Canaan traveled north (*tashāʾamū*) from Arabia to the province that then bore the name "The Land to the North." This statement is seemingly linked to the dispersion and settlement of Noah's progeny in the genealogical lists of the Hebrew Bible with specific reference to Genesis 10:15–19, passages that describe the origins of the various Canaanite peoples and their land. Still other Muslim scholars, also drawing upon the Bible, maintain that the province of al-Shām derived its name not from any northward trek of the Canaanites, but from Canaan's uncle Shem, son of Noah, a figure known to readers of Genesis as the distant ancestor of Abraham, the biblical patriarch whose descendants, the Israelites, would later conquer the Land of Canaan and declare it holy in the name of the one true God.[4] This labeling of biblical lands after primordial ancestors was not a unique occurrence. Referring to al-Shām, Muslim writers indicate that the subdistricts (*jund*) Filasṭīn (Palestine) and al-Urdunn (Jordan)—not to be confused with the modern entities—were named after the great-grandsons of Noah.[5] The Hebrew name Shem is rendered in Arabic as

2. For various etymologies of al-Shām and its geographical borders, see Ibn al-Faqīh, *Buldān*, 91 ff.; Muqaddasī, *Aḥsan*, 152; Ṭabarī, *Annales*, 1/3:1568; Yāqūt, *Muʿjam*, 3:239–40.

3. G. Le Strange, *Palestine, under the Moslems* (London, 1890), 14 (based on Muqaddasī, *Aḥsan*, 152). See also Yāqūt, *Muʿjam*, 3:241.

4. Yāqūt, *Muʿjam*, 3:239–40.

5. Yāqūt, *Muʿjam*, 3:240.

Sām, but this seeming discrepancy presents no problem for modern linguists who recognize that as in other Semitic languages, the letters *sh(īn)* and *s(īn)* are interchangeable in Arabic and Hebrew. Nor, for that matter, did the Arabic name Sām present a problem for medieval Arabic lexicographers. They proclaimed that at some time in the remote past, their Arab ancestors simply altered the *sīn* to *shīn* and thus referred to the land as al-Shām instead of al-Sām.[6]

Were these traditions linked to the Hebrew Bible not sufficient an explanation for the sacred etymology of the Land to the North, the geographer Yāqūt al-Ḥamawī (d. 1229 CE) turns to another account rooted in biblical times, this one allegedly found in "Persian texts that tell the story of [the Assyrian king] Sennacherib [r. 704–681 BCE]."[7] But the story told by the medieval author is of neither Sennacherib nor his time. Rather, the Muslim geographer invokes memories of events that took place more than two centuries earlier, for he goes on to describe the division of the United Israelite Monarchy into southern and northern kingdoms following the death of Solomon, a historic development that took place early in the first millennium BCE. Among his many accomplishments, Solomon, a legendary figure in both Jewish and Muslim tradition, is best known for having built the temple to Yahweh in Jerusalem. That act defined the sacred character of the city from which he and his father, King David, ruled what has been described as a vast and powerful kingdom, a polity revered by Muslims in their own history of a remote ancient past.[8]

Drawing upon events initially described in 1 Kings 14, Yāqūt tells his readers that after Solomon's death, one Israelite tribe continued to rule from Jerusalem, a reference to the southern kingdom of Judea, the domain of the Davidic line; the other tribes settled in Shāmīn, a place-name with the ending *īn*, as in

6. Yāqūt, *Muʿjam*, 3:240. See also Yāqūt, *Muʿjam*, 3:914, where the author considers the name for Palestine (according to him, originally Falashīn) to have been changed to Filasṭīn or Falasṭīn. Note the name for Palestine in the Hebrew Bible is Peleshet (Egyptian P-r-s-t; Akkadian Palashtu); that is, the land of the Philistines (Hebrew Pelishtim). Following two Jewish revolts, the first in 70 CE, the second in 135 CE, the Roman authorities controlling the truncated Jewish state, now named Judea, put an end to Jewish sovereignty, and called the ancient Land of Israel (referred to by some current scholars as 'historic' Palestine) Syria-Palaestina (later reduced to Palaestina). By the fifth century CE, the larger area was subdivided into three subdistricts known as First (Prima), Second (Secunda), and Third (Tertiae) Palestine. For the later evolution of the name Palestine and its geographical boundaries, see B. Lewis, "Palestine: On the History and Geography of a Name," *International History Review* 11 (1980): 1–12.

7. Yāqūt, *Muʿjam*, 3:240.

8. For a digest of Muslim views of Solomon's greatness, see Thaʿlabī, *ʿArāʾis*, 292–328. The *ʿArāʾis* segment on Solomon is an exegetical romp through all the references to the ancient Israelite in the Qurʾān and contains much Jewish material that filtered into Islamic tradition. The *ʿArāʾis* is the most detailed of several Arabic sources dealing with the ancient prophets (*qiṣaṣ al-anbiyāʾ*). See J. Lassner, *Demonizing the Queen of Sheba* (Chicago, 1993). A summary of how Muslims viewed the reign of Solomon can be found in *EI*, s.v. "Sulaymān b. Dāwūd." For David, see Thaʿlabī, *ʿArāʾis*, 270–92; and in summary form *EI*, s.v. "Dāwūd."

the names of other places situated in the larger area (of the province) such as Filasṭīn, Qinnasrīn, Naṣībīn, and Ḥuwwārīn. The Muslim geographer goes on to describe ancient Shāmīn as having been "a place of commerce for the Arabs (*matjar al-ʿArab*) and one in which they obtained their foodstuffs (*mīrah*)."[9] The name is almost certainly derived from Hebrew Shomron, that is, Samaria, a toponym that applied to the capital of the northern kingdom of biblical Israel as well as to the kingdom's domain.[10] We are then informed that the Arabs subsequently shortened Shāmīn to al-Shām.

How did a name that applied to the limited territory of a truncated biblical polity come to signify for the Arabs a truly vast province of the Islamic realm? Lest we be confused by Yāqūt referring to al-Shām as both the geographically circumscribed northern kingdom of Israel and the great province known among Arabs as the Land to the North, the author informs us that the original al-Shām was limited to an area within Palestine (*arḍ Filasṭīn*).[11] But it later came to designate the entire province situated immediately beyond Arabia, what in Graeco-Roman times was known as Syria, and what is now referred to in some political discussions as Greater Syria. To make matters even more clear, the geographer notes that the vast territory the Arabs came to call al-Shām was originally known as Ṣūrā. The reference is to Ṣūr, the ancient city of Tyre, which gave rise via Greek and then Arabic to *Sūriyā* or *Sūriyah*, the name applied by Arabs to the modern nation state of Syria. Whatever the lexical origins of Arabic al-Shām, the geographical boundaries of the vast Islamic province (*bilād*) clearly embraced what is today modern Syria, Lebanon, Israel, Jordan, the lands currently administered by the Palestinian Authority, and slivers of Sinai and Iraq.

As defined by medieval Muslim geographers, Bilād al-Shām, or simply al-Shām, included all the territory from the Euphrates to al-Arish. That is, its eastern limits were formed by the great river that flows from northwest Syria to the marshes of southern Iraq; its western extremity by the border settlement that separates northern Sinai from Gaza and its surroundings.[12] The scope of

9. Yāqūt, *Muʿjam*, 3:240.

10. With creation of the northern kingdom of Israel, the capital city Shomron replaced Shechem as the major Israelite settlement of the highlands north of Jerusalem (1 Kings 16:23–24). The Arab conquerors in turn settled in the vicinity of ancient Shechem and referred to their city as Nablus (Nābulus) after Neopolis, the Graeco-Roman name given the city. Present-day Israelis invoke the old biblical names when referring to the hill country of the West Bank, territory seized from the Hashemite Kingdom of Jordan in 1967. The region to the north is thus called Shomron (Samaria); that of the south including Jerusalem is referred to as Yehudah (Judea). Israelis refer to Nablus by the ancient biblical name Shechem.

11. For the boundaries of Filasṭīn according to the medieval Arab geographers, see Yaʿqūbī, *Buldān*, 116–17; Iṣṭakhrī, *Masālik*, 56–57; Ibn Ḥawqal, *Masālik*, 111–13; Yāqūt, *Muʿjam*, 3:913–14.

12. See n. 2.

the great Muslim province conjures up the geographical parameters of the holy land promised by God to Abraham's seed in Genesis 15:18: "From the river of Egypt [meaning the Wadi al-Arish of today] to the great river, the river Euphrates." Within this broad geographical landscape were places that Muslims defined as sacred space of their own, foremost among them Jerusalem, a holy city in a land declared holy by all three Abrahamic religions. Indeed, Muslims went as so far as to consider the city in the same light as Mecca and Medina, the *ḥaramayn*, or two holy cities of Arabia. The Aqṣā mosque situated on Jerusalem's ancient Temple Mount, the area called in Arabic al-Ḥaram al-Sharīf, or the "Noble Sanctuary," became the third leg of a holy tripod; the other two being the great mosques of Mecca and Medina frequented by Muḥammad and his companions and by consecutive generations of Muslims fulfilling the obligatory rite of pilgrimage.

Muslims reportedly employed seventeen Arabic names to refer to the holy city, some seemingly traced to Jewish toponyms. Among the most notable is Ūrīshalim or Ūrīshalam, also Ūrshalim, from Byzantine Greek Hierosolyma, and before that Hebrew Yerushalayim, the name given by Jews to King David's city.[13] Shortly after the Arab conquest, Muslims referred to Īliyā', originally from Aeilia Capitolina, the pagan Roman city built to supersede Jewish Jerusalem in the second century CE, and then simply Aelia, a shortened form employed by Byzantine Christians along with Hierosolyma.[14] Later, probably by the tenth century, Muslims spoke of al-Quds, seemingly derived from Aramaic

13. For a short survey of the Arabic names of Jerusalem, see the entry of S. D. Goitein in *EI*, s.v. "Al-Ḳuds." Readers of Hebrew are referred to his "On the Arabic Names of Jerusalem," in *Minhah le-Yehudah* (Jerusalem, 1950), 62–66; also in Hebrew: Z. Vilnai, *Jerusalem: The Capital of Israel* (Jerusalem, 1970), 1:152–75 (includes Jewish names for the city); and, as regards Jewish names, especially I. Katzenelbogen, "The Seventy Names of Jerusalem [Hebrew]," *Sinai* 116 (1995): 141–59 (contains extensive bibliography of earlier publications). The most recent survey of Jewish names and epithets for the holy city is that of A. Shinan, "The Many Names of Jerusalem," in *Jerusalem*, edited by L. Levine (New York, 1999), 120–32. In Jewish sources, the distinctions between the city of and the Land of Israel are sometimes blurred; for example, "Zion" may refer to both the city and the Holy Land. The same blurring occurs in Arabic. See the references below to Bayt al-Maqdis as the city and the land. The current Arabic name Ūrshalim, seemingly derived from medieval Arabic by way of Hebrew *Yerushalayim*, appears in the Akkadian Amarna letters (fourteenth century BCE). Variants of this name also appear in Assyrian texts (ninth to eighth centuries BCE).

14. The name for Roman Jerusalem combined that of the emperor Julius Aelius Hadrianus and the pagan god Jupiter, one of a triad of gods brought to the city, under the rubric Capitolina. This etymology was apparently unknown to the Muslim conquerors. They referred to the city as Īliyā', reportedly thinking that it had been named after a woman who allegedly built it (Yāqūt, *Mu'jam*, 4:592). Note, however, 1:423–24, where Īliyā' is made the descendent of Aram, son of Shem, that is, the grandson of Noah. Similarly, the other districts of Greater Syria were named after Īliyā's alleged brothers Damascus, Homs, Jordan, and Palestine. Eponymous ancestors thus served to explain for Muslims pre-Islamic geographical place-names. In written sources, the Christians generally referred to the city as Hierosalym. Goitein's suggestion that the Arabs associated Īliyā' with Elijah (Hebrew Eliyahu) seems to me ungrounded. See his article "Al-Ḳuds" in *EI*.

qudsha, "holiness" or "sanctuary," and Hebrew *'Ir ha-Qodesh*, "The City of the Holy [Sanctuary]," hence "The Holy City." Jewish sectarians writing in Arabic at the time refer to all of Jerusalem as the Bayt al-Maqdis and to the area of the Temple Mount as al-Quds. It is, however, not clear whether contemporaneous Muslims made the same distinction.[15] The Muslims also referred to Īliyā' madīnat Bayt al-Maqdis, "Īliyā' the city of the Holy Temple,"[16] Bayt al-Maqdis being a direct translation of Hebrew *Beit ha-Miqdash* and possibly Aramaic *Beit Maqidesha*, "The Holy Temple," meaning for Jews the preexilic and postexilic temples that graced the Har ha-Bayit or Temple Mount of ancient times. For Muslims, who embraced the sanctity of Jerusalem, the term Bayt al-Maqdis (also Bayt al-Muqaddas) denoted not only the specific location of the Temple Mount but the city itself and beyond that all of the Holy Land in its environs. A similar blurring of names or epithets for the Holy Land, holy city, and the Temple and Temple Mount is common in Jewish sources, suggesting thereby a possible path of influence and common understanding.[17]

When did Muslims first embrace Jerusalem as a holy city of their own and to what purpose? Put somewhat differently, at what point was the original Arabic designation of Jerusalem, namely Īliyā', the name of the pagan and then Byzantine city, superseded by Bayt al-Maqdis and then by al-Quds, the more common Arabic toponyms signifying the sacred place of the Muslim faithful? Given the highly tendentious sources at our disposal, such queries are more easily posed than answered.

Sources

Much of the available data on the Islamic city are dated two centuries and more after the Muslim conquest. Moreover, the accounts of the Arabic historians were fashioned, at times, to reflect the political and religious sensibilities of later generations. There is then the possibility, indeed probability, that some accounts of the early Islamic city and its monuments are back-projections of more recent times. The same is true for snippets of information preserved in belletristic sources. Works written by non-Muslims and in languages other than Arabic are cited by some current scholars when addressing the history of al-Shām and the first century of Islamic rule, but these sources are no less problematic than the Arabic works we possess. Were all that not sufficiently daunting, the

15. Reference to Jewish sectarians in S. D. Goitein's entry in *EI*, s.v. "Al-Ḳuds."
16. Ṭabarī, *Annales*, 1/3:2260.
17. See n. 13.

earliest preserved compilations of material devoted largely if not exclusively to Jerusalem and other places in the Holy Land, the so-called literature in praise of the city and its environs (*faḍāʾil al-Quds* or *faḍāʾil Bayt al-Maqdis*), are dated some four hundred years after the city capitulated to the Muslim invaders.[18]

The chronological gap between the later accounts and the early history of the city has been duly noted by modern authorities, among them Oleg Grabar, the Islamic art historian and archaeologist whose studies of Jerusalem and its monuments spanned half a century.[19] When Grabar first wrote over fifty years ago, the earliest surviving text of the faḍāʾil al-Quds genre dated from the fourteenth century, the others from the fifteenth and sixteenth. Writing of the Ḥaram al-Sharīf in 1959, Grabar noted that the works of later times provide us with an answer of how Muslims interpreted the sacred space of the Temple Mount following the occupation of the first Crusaders (1099–1187), but he questioned whether all the complex traditions reported about the Ḥaram al-Sharīf had already been formulated "when the area (of the Temple Mount) was

18. A most detailed treatment of this literature is O. Livne-Kafri's "The Sanctity of Jerusalem in Islam [Hebrew]," Ph.D. dissertation, Hebrew University, Jerusalem, 1985, which was reworked into various articles, ultimately appearing in his collected essays in Hebrew with the English title *Jerusalem in Early Islam* (Jerusalem, 2000). Among these Hebrew essays, see especially "Early Arabic Literary Works on Jerusalem," 1–6; also his "On Jerusalem in Early Islam," 38–40. A fuller bibliography of his and other articles on Jerusalem is found in his "Jerusalem: The Navel of the Earth in Muslim Tradition," *Der Islam* 84 (2007): 46–47 n. 1. The article in *Der Islam* is an expanded English version of an article originally published in Hebrew. See his collected essays, pp. 53–105. Note also the various articles cited in his edition of Abū-l-Maʿālī al-Musharraf b. al-Murajjā's *Faḍāʾil Bayt al-Maqdis wa-l-Khalīl wa-l-Shām* (Shfaram, 1995), viii n. 2; I. Hasson, "Muslim Literature in Praise of Jerusalem: Faḍāʾil Bayt al-Maqdis," *Jerusalem Cathedra* 1 (1981): 168–84 (part of a published symposium on the faḍāʾil al-Quds); note in that connection the response of E. Ashtor in the same volume, "Muslim and Christian Literature in Praise of Jerusalem," 187–89; a more detailed treatment of the faḍāʾil by Hasson is found in "The Muslim View of Jerusalem in the Qurʾān and Ḥadīth," in *The History of Jerusalem, 638–1099*, edited by J. Prawer and H. Ben-Shammai (Jerusalem, 1996), 349–85, esp. 365 ff. A broad assessment of different types of faḍāʾil traditions is E. Gruber's *Verdienst und Rang: Die Faḍāʾil als literarisches und gesellschaftliches Problem im Islam* (Frieburg im Brisgau, 1975). For the faḍāʾil as a repository of historical information, see M. Sharon, "The 'Praises' of Jerusalem as a Source for the Early History of Islam," *BO* 49 (1992): 56–67. See also N. Rabbat, "The Dome of the Rock Revisited: Some Remarks on al-Wasiti's Accounts," *Muqarnas* 10 (1993): 67–75. For a detailed bibliographic note on the sanctity of Jerusalem in Islamic tradition, see J. Sadan, "A Legal Opinion Regarding the Sanctity of Jerusalem," *IOS* 13 (1993): 231–32 n. 1; and O. Livne-Kafri, "Jerusalem—'Navel of the Earth' in the Muslim Tradition [Hebrew]," *Cathedra* 69 (1993): 79–105, esp. 79 nn. 1 and 4. More generally, note H. Busse, "The Sanctity of Jerusalem in Islam," *Judaism* 17 (1968): 441–68 (with additional bibliography). A detailed and thoughtful overview of the faḍāʾil texts and their early transmitters is found in A. Elad, *Medieval Jerusalem*, 1–22, esp. 6 ff. More recently, there is S. Mourad's "Did the Crusaders Change Jerusalem's Religious Symbolism in Islam," *Bulletin of Middle East Medievalists* 22 (2014): 3–8. I have not been able to obtain a copy of J. W. Hirshberg, "The Sources of Muslim Tradition Concerning Jerusalem," *Rocznik Orientalisityczny* 17 (1951–52): 314–50.

19. Many of Grabar's articles have been reprinted in his collected studies published by Ashgate in four volumes titled *Constructing the Study of Islamic Art* (Aldershot, 2005). His remarks on the holy city are found in volume 4, titled *Jerusalem*.

taken over by the Arabs," a reference to the Muslim conquest of the seventh century CE. As he put it, "[In] the early period of Islam, the religious system and spiritual life of the [Muslim] faithful were as yet too simple—or too disorganized—to allow for as definitive and complete a system of topographical associations as appears in later writing. More often than not later traditions tend to confuse rather than clarify." With that, he suggested that the late collections of Jerusalem lore, like much of medieval Arabic historiography and traditions literature (*ḥadīth*), were likely back-projections reflecting a contemporaneous rather than early moment of Islamic history, in this case the Muslim response to the invasion of the Crusaders and the imposition of Christian rule in the heartland of Islam.[20]

In a highly regarded book on Islam and the Crusades, Emmanuel Sivan depicted how Muslims absorbed the loss of Jerusalem and the subsequent creation of Christian polities ruling a significant area of al-Shām. Sivan shows that Muslim reaction to the invaders only reached great intensity as Muslim armies gained control of the battlefield. For well over a hundred years Muslims accepted the presence of the Crusaders, imagining their conflict with Islam to be an extension of the long-standing engagement with the Byzantine Empire, a war that had waxed and waned over some four centuries. In turn, the Crusaders became willy-nilly players in the complex game of internal Muslim politics. Deplorable as it was, the Christian occupation of Jerusalem was not seen by Muslims as a catastrophe comparable to the Jewish loss of the holy city, first to the Babylonians and later to imperial Rome. Jerusalem was not Mecca or Medina, the spiritual centers of the Muslim world, nor was the territory seized by the Crusaders ever the political fulcrum of Islamic rule. But when the Crusaders threatened to move beyond their toehold in the Abode of Islam and internal Muslim politics demanded a response to the Christian challenge, the Muslims declared their struggle with the unbelievers a holy war and forced them from the Islamic heartland. In retrospect, Muslims took to the pen as they had earlier to the sword and produced a significant body of literature celebrating the reconquest of the city and other sacred locations. Seen from this perspective, the faḍā'il literature was in essence a reassertion of Islam and a declaration of Muslim triumphalism.[21]

---

20. The study cited here originally appeared as "The Umayyad Dome of the Rock in Jerusalem," *Ars Orientalis* 3 (1959): 33–59. The citation here is to the reprint: Grabar, *Jerusalem*, 2. Elad, *Medieval Jerusalem*, 10, understood "when the area was taken over by the Arabs" to mean the recapture of Jerusalem from the Crusaders by Saladin in the twelfth century, but the text does not admit to Elad's interpretation.

21. E. Sivan, *L'Islam et la Croisade* (Paris, 1967). This impact of the Crusades on the imagination and politics of the Muslims is briefly stated in C. Cahen's entry in *EI*, s.v. "Crusades."

The turn of fortune that befell the Muslims with the establishment of the Crusader kingdoms became branded into the historical consciousness of the Muslim faithful, and remained there long after the Christian invaders were forced to abandon the Holy Land. When the Israel Defense Forces captured the Old City of Jerusalem in 1967, the new administration converted an area at the foot of the Temple Mount into a large plaza. By expropriating and then razing adjacent properties, the new rulers expanded what had been a narrow street astride the exposed western wall, the holiest of all sites in the Jewish world, into an open expanse that allowed for extensive Jewish worship and other ritual acts. Muslims, agitated by what they regarded as a clearly hostile gesture, responded to the loss of their sacred space as did their forebears in response to the Crusaders. They valorized the city whose religious significance was compared to that of Mecca and Medina and produced a modern literature and oral tradition similar to the faḍā'il of old. Among various efforts to establish claim to the holy city, the Muslims reissued Mujīr al-Dīn's (d. 1521) *al-Uns al-Jalīl bi-ta'rīkh al-Quds wa-l-Khalīl*, perhaps the most illustrative of the faḍā'il works. The reissued medieval text was circulated widely with a modern introduction that condemned Israel's activities. Subsequent publications compared the Israeli occupiers with the Crusaders of old, a linkage that has gained wide currency among today's Muslims.

The unification of Jerusalem also led to increased Israeli interest in the long history of the holy city. Following the reissue of Mujīr al-Dīn's work, Israeli scholars published other medieval tracts in praise of the city and various holy places of al-Shām, texts hitherto known largely from unedited manuscripts. As a result of renewed interest in Jerusalem, we now have many traditions and a massive number of variants to peruse in search of the Muslim city. Given the chronological range of these new sources, focus has shifted from looking at the faḍā'il as literary artifacts fashioned largely in wake of the Crusades, to ruminating on how these sources might have reflected the views of Muslims in earlier times, perhaps as early as the Muslim conquest of the city in the seventh century.[22] In addition, the Israel Department of Antiquities initiated a number of major projects within the Old City and its immediate environs. Among these projects was the extensive excavation of a large site abutting the southern wall of the Temple Mount. The archaeological dig revealed massive ruins dated by archaeologists to the first Islamic century.

What can be made of this new data, starting with the literary sources?

22. The early dating for the faḍā'il was first suggested by M. J. Kister in his "A Comment on the Traditions Praising Jerusalem," *Jerusalem Cathedra* 1 (1981): 185–86.

Scholars now agree that the late appearance of certain faḍā'il collections is not a compelling reason to discard each and every tradition when attempting to write the earlier history of Jerusalem. Many of the individual faḍā'il found in later sources, such as Mujīr al-Dīn, are based on more recently studied compilations stemming from the eleventh century, namely al-Wāsiṭī's *Faḍā'il al-Bayt al-Muqaddas* and al-Musharraf b. al-Murajjā's *Faḍā'il Bayt al-Maqdis wa-l-Shām wa-l-Khalīl.* Sivan, in a short article revisiting the origins of the faḍā'il genre, suggests the eleventh-century compilations were in response to the anti-Christian campaign initiated by the caliph al-Ḥākim early in the century, an unusual moment of Muslim intolerance. The caliph's policy culminated in the partial destruction of Jerusalem's Church of the Holy Sepulcher, the most celebrated symbol of Christianity's presence in the Holy Land. Once again, Sivan leads us to believe this genre of literature is an expression of Islamic triumphalism vis-à-vis the unbelievers.[23] On the other hand, Isaac Hasson contends, albeit without hard evidence, that the faḍā'il texts of the eleventh century might have been compiled and circulated among the local masses as part of a fund-raising effort to restore damaged Muslim structures on the Temple Mount. He cites a report that the cupola surmounting the magnificent Dome of the Rock, the iconic Muslim monument on the historic platform, collapsed in 1016–17 CE and speculates that funds were collected at the time to refurbish it and also the nearby al-Aqṣā mosque.[24]

Whatever the reason for the eleventh-century compilations, there is evidence that scholars may have produced truncated collections of faḍā'il as early as the tenth or ninth century, perhaps even earlier. The historian Ya'qūbī (d. ca. 900 CE) in discussing the caliph 'Abd al-Malik and Jerusalem inserts into his narrative a popular tradition often found in works praising the city, namely, that Muslims were allowed to perform the rites of pilgrimage there as well as at the holy cities of Arabia. The casual insertion of the passage suggests that such traditions circulated freely in the author's lifetime.[25] Nor is this an isolated occurrence; authors of later faḍā'il texts often cite material on Jerusalem derived from transmitters going back to the eighth century. Amikam Elad, a leading historian of medieval Jerusalem, has assiduously gone through count-

---

23. E. Sivan, "Beginnings of the Faḍā'il al-Quds literature," *IOS* 1 (1971): 263–71, esp. 269 going over familiar ground of his "Le Caractere sacré de Jerusalem dans l'Islam aux xlle–xiiie siècle," *SI* 27 (1967): 49–82. See also S. Mourad, "Did the Crusades Change Jerusalem's Religious Symbolism in Islam," 3–8, who claims that the post-Crusade authors of faḍā'il al-Quds were not from Jerusalem and its surroundings, as were the earliest listed authors, and that in response to the Crusades they introduced an apocalyptic element not previously found in the earlier traditions.

24. I. Hasson, "Muslim Literature in Praise of Jerusalem," 173, citing Mujīr al-Dīn, *Uns*, 1:268–69; Dhahabī, *'Ibar*, 3:96.

25. Ya'qūbī, *Historiae*, 2:311. This event is discussed in full in chapter 7.

less chains of transmission both in the faḍā'il texts and in Arabic chronicles containing reports that are linked or can be linked to works in praise of the holy city. He is particularly interested in identifying figures representing the earliest generation of transmitters and goes so far as to suggest that entire tracts devoted to faḍā'il of the holy city and Holy Land were composed in the eighth century, perhaps even as early as the end of the seventh.[26] Elad invokes G. H. A. Juynboll, who maintains that expressions of praise (not merely confined to Jerusalem) were among the earliest types of Islamic tradition. There are, however, no compilations devoted specifically to praising Jerusalem in this early period, nor is there any indirect evidence to confirm Elad's assumption. It is nevertheless clear that already in the eighth century there were numerous scholars who supplied later receptors with traditions to forge a discrete body of literature in praise of the holy city and Holy Land.[27]

Among the early transmitters identified by Elad are a group of scholars and/or government functionaries from the Jerusalem area and various locations of southern al-Shām, that is, a geographical region that can more or less be identified with Graeco-Roman First and Second Palestine. In Islamic terms this region represents roughly the subdistricts labeled Filasṭīn and al-Urdunn. Some transmitters were direct witnesses to events in Jerusalem, including the construction of the Dome of the Rock.[28] Among others are

'Aṭiyyah b. Qays (ca. 700)
Khālid b. Ma'dān (d. 721 or 722 CE)
Rajā' b. Ḥaywah (d. 730 CE), born in Baysān (Beit Shean) a town located near the Golan Heights in the north of what is today the State of Israel and which belonged in early Islamic times to the subdistrict of al-Urdunn
'Aṭa' b. Abī Muslim al Khurāsānī (d. 752–53 CE), died in Jericho, buried in Jerusalem
Yaḥyā b. 'Amr al-Shaybānī al-Ramlī (from Ramle, d. 765)
Ibrāhīm b. Abī 'Ablah (d. ca. 770)

26. Elad, *Medieval Jerusalem*, 14 ff. Moshe Sharon describes an inscription found in the Negev region of Israel's south that reflects a faḍā'il tradition. The inscription is dated 165 AH / 785 CE. See his "Praises of Jerusalem," 56–57.

27. Elad, *Medieval Jerusalem*, 13, calls attention to G. H. A. Juynboll, *Muslim Tradition* (Cambridge, 1983), 74, 162, 163 esp. n. 4. Some scholars argue that the faḍā'il are a literary convention that was applied broadly and in the earliest period of Islam and even during the *Jāhilīyah*, that is the pre-Islamic period when the Arabs would boast (*tafākhur*) in their poetry of the superiority of their tribes and territory (*diyār*). See E. A. Grube, *Verdienst und Rang*.

28. Elad, *Medieval Jerusalem*, 17 ff.; also S. Mourad, "Jerusalem in Early Islam," in *Jerusalem: Idea and Reality*, edited by T. Mayer and S. Mourad (New York, 2008), 86–102, esp. 91 ff.

Thawr b. Yazīd (d. 770–71 CE)
Sa'īd b. 'Abd al-'Azīz (d. 783–84 CE)
The Jersalemite 'Abd al-Raḥmān b. Muḥammad b. Manṣūr (ca. 750–800 CE)
His father Muḥammad b. Thābit (presumably transmitted faḍā'il traditions during the first half of the century)
Thābit b. Istānībiyadh al-Fārisī al-Khumsī (ca. second half of the eighth century CE), a man of Persian descent whose *nisbah*, or genealogical marker "al-Khumsī" marks him as the descendant of slaves, presumably brought to the Jerusalem area.

Oddly enough, Elad omits from his discussion an extremely important reference supporting his claim for the early provenance of traditions in praise of Jerusalem and the Holy Land, if not the early existence of complete works. The massive geographical encyclopedia of Yāqūt al-Ḥamawī (ca. thirteenth century CE) lists in its entry on Jerusalem (*al-Quds*) some sixty wide-ranging faḍā'il statements that he attributes to the early Qur'ān commentator Muqātil b. Sulaymān (d. 767), the teacher of the aforementioned transmitter Muḥammad b. Manṣūr.[29] Yāqūt cites Muqātil without noting the informants on whom the latter relied. This is not surprising, because, unlike some leading Qur'ān scholars, Muqātil tends to omit chains of transmission. However, as versions of the statements attributed to him are found throughout the literature in praise of Jerusalem, we can safely assume that a large body of these texts circulated no later than the early eighth century, that is, in the generation previous to Muqātil. Moreover, many of Muqātil's assembled statements reveal more than random information about Jerusalem and the Holy Land. Like the statements preserved by Ya'qūbī, these traditions are part of an ongoing Muslim debate regarding the sanctity of the city, a subject discussed in detail later in this work. It seems that even if no discrete compilations existed at the time, expressions of praise for Jerusalem circulated widely at given points of Umayyad rule (661–750 CE). The discovery of new texts and the editing and publication of known faḍā'il manuscripts are apt to throw considerable light on Jerusalem in the formative period of Islamic civilization. Even texts attributed to later authors can prove extremely valuable as they may reproduce early traditions as well as chains of authority leading back to the earliest sources of this genre.[30]

29. Yāqūt, *Mu'jam*, 4:591 ff.

30. A number of these manuscripts are listed by O. Livne-Kafri. See his "Jerusalem: The Navel of the Earth," 47–48 n. 4. These include Bahā' al-Dīn Ibn 'Asākir, *Faḍā'il Bayt al-Maqdis*; 'Abd al-Raḥmān b. 'Alī b. al-Jawzī, *Faḍā'il al-Quds al-Sharīf*; Muḥammad b. Shams al-Dīn al-Suyūṭī, *Itḥāf*

When Oleg Grabar became aware of the earlier provenance of various faḍā'il statements, he reconsidered his initial views of how they might inform the city's past, particularly regarding the purpose and origins of Umayyad architecture. In a short essay modestly titled "Notes on the Dome of the Rock"[31] Grabar takes stock of scholarship past and present and evaluates the enlarged corpus of literary sources as one of three tools with which to interpret Islamic Jerusalem and its monuments—the others being information obtained by excavating a given site, and visual analyses and art-historical criticism. An experienced field archaeologist, Grabar favored facts obtained on and from the ground. As regards the Dome of the Rock, he notes that art historians plying their craft have drawn the broadest conclusions based on the smallest and most isolated details, an effort he describes as having produced mixed results.[32] Turning to the literary evidence, he continues to express a healthy skepticism of how faḍā'il texts might be employed to explain the early history of the city. He points out that the positioning of "reliable" authorities in the chain of transmission does not necessarily signify the accuracy of the material transmitted. As evidence, he cites the seemingly confused state of the data obtained from Ibn al-Murajjā's eleventh-century description of the Dome of the Rock.[33]

It is difficult to disagree with Grabar that such material should not be used as if it had unquestionable scholarly purchase, certainly not to fill in essential architectural details or determine wider questions of topography. To quote the learned art historian: "[The faḍā'il] are not necessarily good sources for the architectural history of the holy places nor for the character of their forms. They are not records of a physical reality."[34] Grabar may very well be correct, at least as regards the architectural form of individual edifices and their relationship to a more inclusive building complex or urban setting. But meticulous scholars can tease out of these problematic texts useful information about how the buildings atop the ancient Temple Mount were staffed and utilized; how various rulers legitimized their claims by identifying with Jerusalem's sacred past; and, of equal weight, the place that Jerusalem occupied in the religious practices of pious visitors and holy men who sought permanent or temporary residence within its boundaries. There is, in short, more to the making of Islamic Jerusalem than its surface monuments and more to understanding the development

al-akhiṣṣā bi-faḍā'il al-Masjid al-Aqṣā (published in Cairo, 1982, 1984); Muṣṭafā As'ad al-Luqaymī, *Laṭā'if al-uns al-jalīl bi-taḥā'if al-Quds wa-l-Khalīl.* Note also al-Firkāḥ's (fifteenth century CE) *K. bā'ith al-nufūs ilā ziyārāt al-Quds* (published in *JPOS* 15 [1935]: 51–87).

31. See Grabar's collected studies, volume 4: *Jerusalem*, 217–29.

32. Grabar, *Jerusalem*, 221 ff.

33. Grabar, *Jerusalem*, 218–21.

34. Grabar, *Jerusalem*, 220.

of the city than examining its topographical features. The Muslim city was an idea as well as a reality. Whether real or imagined, the sacred history spoken of in the faḍā'il collections bears witness to how that idea was perceived. In the end, Grabar concedes as much. He indicates that whatever their limitations for reconstructing architectural history, the faḍā'il "include unique . . . memories of the past."[35] How those memories of Jerusalem's sacred space became enshrined in the collective consciousness of Muslims is a subject of interest no less compelling than the architectural history of the Temple Mount.

Jerusalem and Sacred Space

With regard to Jerusalem, sacred space refers to hallowed geographical venues. It also refers here to literary and oral traditions serving as reliquaries for sacred narratives. These narratives, whether transmitted by word of mouth or in writing, may reflect actual states of the past or, just as likely, if not more so, imagined circumstances that should have been. When closely linked religious societies embrace similar narratives or venerate in different ways the same *topographia sacra*, as with Jerusalem and its environs, vigilant guardians of the faith have a way of privileging their own sites and stories. Modern Orientalists tend to treat the official histories of faith communities with a greater sense of detachment. However, such detachment bred of Enlightenment skepticism does not lead of necessity to definitive conclusions about events and attitudes far removed from us in place and time. Given the tendentiousness of ancient and medieval sources, modern scholars have come to realize that even proposing what might have been can produce withering criticism from skeptical colleagues. The same cannot be said for pious Jews, Christians, and Muslims who regard their received versions of history as metatruths. From the perspective of true believers past and present, such imaginaries are more real than reality itself. Because whatever doubts there may be about sacred traditions of this sort, the unfolding narratives of the past reinforce a transcendent vision; an all-embracing view of the world that allows communities to cohere when threatened by heretical activity from within or by challenges from powerful external forces. Faced with compromising long-held beliefs and pious behavior, the true believers turn to hallowed traditions as their rock and salvation.

Stories like that of the biblical bush that burned on and on and by some miracle was never consumed may strike modern scholars as a convenient

35. Grabar, *Jerusalem*, 220.

literary invention, one comparable to many such stories in the compendia of universal folklore. But to this day, the priests of St. Catherine's Monastery in Sinai can lead pious visitors to that very spot of the Burning Bush and expect them to stand there in awe as did Moses. Not all sacred space is created by linking miraculous occurrences and the presence of the divine to specific locations. Truly historic events also give rise to sacred space. David's acquisition of Jerusalem and following that Solomon's construction of a house of worship to Yahweh elevated what had been a Jebusite settlement into a site considered holy by the Israelites and their successors. Even the destruction of the second Jewish temple erected by Herod could not diminish the sacrality of the Temple Mount for traditional Jews. Until this day pious Jews pray daily for rebuilding the Lord's house and reconstituting it as the fulcrum of Jewish religious practice. Christians, though not calling for reestablishing a Jewish temple, also look to Jerusalem as a city sanctified by a history commonly shared with Jews, a description of the past to which they add events in the life of Christ and his apostles. As Muslims were broadly familiar with stories of Jerusalem prior to their conquest of the Holy Land, and as they embraced the prophets and kings of Israel as did Jews and Christians, they too held the city in special regard. It is the ebullience of Muslim praise for Jerusalem that elicits curiosity. Over time, the ancient city long venerated by Jews and Christians was considered by some Muslims as not only equal, but superior in certain ways, to Mecca and Medina, the holy cities of Arabia. We are thus left with the task of providing a historical context for Muslims praising Jerusalem and more generally the Holy Land.

By most accounts, medieval or modern, Jerusalem first became a Muslim *locus sacra* under Umayyad rule. It is no coincidence that traditions in praise of the Holy Land and holy city circulated at time when the house of Umayyah, having seized the caliphate from the Prophet's family, forsook the ḥaramayn of Arabia and governed from al-Shām, the great province where the dynasty's founder Muʿāwiyah b. Abī Sufyān had been governor for some nineteen years. Similarly, the first of the Umayyads had himself formally declared successor to the Prophet in Jerusalem. Noting the political circumstances leading to such actions, we would be remiss to approach the faḍā'il as if the pithy didactic statements merely celebrate a religiosity forged on the anvil of sacred history. Upon closer examination, praise of the city reflects as well the political climate of the moment. Within the early Islamic community, the temporal world (*dunyā*) and that of religion (*dīn*) were not easily separated, if at all. Dynastic politics were often legitimized by invoking religious sensibilities drawn from a real or constructed past. Umayyad claims to legitimacy and Muslim attempts to promote the sanctity of Jerusalem were inextricably linked.[36]

The Umayyad embrace of Jerusalem forces us to ponder whether a still earlier generation of Muslims might have looked upon the ancient city as a place of veneration and if so to what purpose. Moving backward in time, the following two chapters ask if there might have been Muslim traditions praising Jerusalem and the Holy Land during the lifetime of the Prophet and the righteous caliphs, the four successors of Muḥammad who preceded the house of Umayyah. And, if that proves true, is it possible Muslims sanctified Jerusalem even before the Islamic conquest of Syria-Palaestina? In other words, could the Prophet Muḥammad and his companions have regarded the holy city of the Jews and Christians as a sacred place of their own, and, linked to that, did Muḥammad's generation compare Jerusalem to Mecca, the city of Muḥammad's birth and the spiritual center of Islam, or to Medina, the oasis where the Prophet found refuge and established the foundations of the Muslim community? To rephrase that question: Did the Prophet and his early followers declare Jerusalem to be a most holy city for the newest and quintessential community of monotheists?

The following discussion addresses this question by interrogating Muslim scripture and the foundational narratives that situate the origins of Islam in an Arabian milieu. Some modern scholars, labeled "minimalist" or "revisionist," are inclined, however, to look beyond traditional Islamic sources in defining the early community of believers; the same for their beliefs and practices. While the revisionists are not of a single mind as regards many issues, there is a broad consensus among them that most, if not indeed all of early Arabic historiography is a back-projection that reflects intellectual and political developments some 150 years removed from the alleged beginnings of Islam. Whereas most modern scholars of the West still hope to find echoes of a past that might have been in Muslim historical writing, the revisionists declare that the foundational narratives contain no discernible traces of a real history. Many even deny that events in the Hijaz, however conceived by the first Muslim historians, played a formative role in shaping the religious and political goals of the first believers.

Relying on snippets of information from non-Islamic sources, the revisionists imagine a counternarrative of Islamic origins, one that pays particular attention to developments beyond Arabia and carves out a special place for the holy city of Christians and Jews in the religious consciousness of the first

36. See chapters 4–6.

community of believers.[37] Going against the grain of accepted wisdom that identifies an Islamized Jerusalem with the Umayyad caliphs, revisionist historians have argued that the city holy to Christians and Jews played a major role early in the religious outlook of the Prophet and his community. The most recent advocate of this position is Stephen Shoemaker, the author of a learned monograph that builds on past revisionist writings to offer a new and challenging interpretation of the Islamic conquest and Jerusalem's pivotal role in the sacred geography of a nascent Islam.[38] As do many revisionists, Shoemaker declares the early Islamic community "confessionally diverse." He imagines it as welcoming a significant number of Jews and even Christians who shared a common outlook with Muḥammad and his Arab followers. In effect, the early community of believers was characterized by a sort of hybridity. At the core of their commonly held belief was the expectation of the imminent arrival of the messianic age and the Day of Judgment when God will sit on his throne and decide the fate of all humankind, past and present. The Islamic conquest is thus seen as an eclectic movement that was intended to lead to the end of historic time and the initiation of the final hour. Unfortunately, messianic expectations went unfulfilled. In need of a new ideology that differentiated their religion from normative Judaism and Christianity, the nascent community of believers forged an Islamic narrative that tied the rise of Islam to the Arabian Peninsula and tribal sensibilities. They linked the faith of an emerging empire, forged in large part by Arab tribesmen, to an invented Arabian past.

37. The "Godfather" of the minimalist school was John Wansbrough, who argued that the Islamic historical narrative of early Islam is a form of salvation history (*Heilsgeschichte*) that bore no witness to the actual events. He argued his case in two extremely learned works: *Quranic Studies* (Oxford, 1971) and *The Sectarian Milieu* (Oxford, 1978). Perhaps the most controversial of the early works of the minimalists was M. Cook and P. Crone, *Hagarism* (Cambridge, 1977), which cast doubt on the historicity of all the Arabic accounts of the first Islamic century, particularly those dealing with Islamic origins. Having rejected all traditional views of the Prophet and the rise of Islam, Cook and Crone, using highly problematic non-Muslim sources, contend that Islam derived originally from an obscure ancient civilization. Previously unknown to scholars, this imagined civilization was produced by a highly eclectic sectarian movement given to monotheist impulses borrowed in part from reworked Jewish ideas, especially an appealing form of Jewish messianism. This calque of a civilization was labeled by Cook and Crone *Hagarism*, a name suggested by references to Muslims as Hagarites in Christian sources of the times. Accordingly, Hagarism was embraced by the Arab tribesmen who gradually crossed the frontier. But a century later the Arabs sought to differentiate themselves from Jews and Christians and invented a historical narrative of their own that bears no discernible resemblance to historical realities. See also the subsequent publications of Crone: *Slaves on Horses* (Cambridge, 1980—dealing with the formation of the early Muslim military); *Meccan Trade and the Rise of Islam* (Oxford, 1987—arguing against the commercial importance of Mecca); and *God's Caliph*, with M. Hinds (Cambridge, 1986—dealing with the rise of the caliphate). A brief evaluation of the revisionist school is found in J. Lassner, *Jews, Christians, and the Abode of Islam* (Chicago, 2012), 39–44.

38. S. Shoemaker, *The Death of a Prophet* (Philadelphia, 2012). For the messianic mission of the earliest community of believers, see 118–96. For confessional identity and sacred geography in early Islam, see 197–265.

Referring to the messianic age, Shoemaker notes the centrality of Jerusalem and the Holy Land in Jewish and Christian eschatology. At the End of Days, linear history will draw to an end, giving way to a redemptive age that begins to unfold in the holy city. Assuming that such messianic traditions were well known among the earliest believers—a likely assumption given the author's view of the interconfessional nature of the original community—Jerusalem and the Holy Land were, in his opinion, almost certainly Islam's first *locus sacra*. If we were to follow Shoemaker (and indeed other revisionists) we will have to confess that we have asked the wrong question. The proper question is not when Jerusalem achieved a privileged status similar to the holy cities of Arabia, the claim of the literature in praise of Jerusalem, but the reverse. When did Mecca and Medina become sacred places comparable to the ancient and revered city in Syria-Palaestina?

I am not convinced that the received narrative of Islamic origins, told as it is in multiple versions and extraordinary detail covering thousands of pages of text, should be completely cast aside for an imagined reconstruction of the past based on fragments of information artfully pieced together. A proper response to Shoemaker's detailed and impressively argued work is certainly desirable, if not indeed necessary, but that is not my task here. For those who read on, the question still remains: When and in what circumstances did Jerusalem become for Muslims a sacred city comparable to Mecca and Medina, the holy cities of Arabia?

CHAPTER 2

Jerusalem in the Imagination of the Prophet and His Companions

Most early statements in praise of Jerusalem and the Holy Land are ultimately derived from figures representing the second or third generation Muslims. However, as some statements are attributed to the Prophet and his companions (*ṣaḥābah*), there may be a temptation to believe that Jerusalem and the area beyond merited unusual praise from the very outset of Islam. On the other hand, readers familiar with back-projections in Islamic tradition are likely to suspect that the reported testimony of Muḥammad and the early Muslims is a literary artifact of a later time designed to give the Holy Land and Jerusalem a special place from the beginning of the Prophet's mission. How the Prophet and his contemporaries actually conceived of the city and its environs remains conjecture. The one source that can be dated to the advent of Islam (although that too is held suspect or denied outright by revisionist scholars) is the Qur'ān, Muḥammad's public utterances. But Muslim scripture contains few references to specific geographical locations. Even the Hijaz, the region of Arabia that gave rise to Islam, receives scant attention. Mecca is mentioned once, Medina only a few times. Moving beyond the Arabian Peninsula, the Qur'ān refers to Egypt (*Miṣr*) alone and then only in familiar tales linked to the ancient Israelites.[1]

Muslim scripture does contain a number of indirect references to biblical geography. The Qur'ān speaks of Moses's followers on the threshold of entering *al-arḍ al-muqaddasah*, literally "the land made holy" or if you prefer "the holy land." The reference is linked to an account in the Hebrew Bible, more specifically to the impending Israelite conquest of ancient Canaan. That is clear from verses 21–26 of Sūrah 5, a segment of Muslim scripture rich in allusions to the biblical past: The text begins: "O my people! Enter the holy land (*al-arḍ al-muqaddasah*) that God has decreed (*kataba*) for you. Do not turn back, as you will then be losers [meaning you will have squandered the opportunity

1. Mecca: Qur'ān 48:24; Medina: Qur'ān 9:101 [102], 121, 63:8, possibly 33:60.

to claim the land that should be yours]" (21). There is a distinct echo here of God's promise to Abraham that his progeny will rule the land of Canaan, a promise first articulated in Genesis 15:18–20 and repeated thereafter on several occasions. Neither Abraham nor the Hebrew patriarchs to whom the Almighty renewed this promise took possession of the land. According to the Hebrew Bible, the Israelite conquest only took place many generations later after the death of Moses and those who followed him out of Egypt. The generation of the Exodus might have entered the Promised Land, but the initial plan to penetrate the border met with resistance within the Israelite ranks. Spies sent by Moses to scout the area reported observing a powerful enemy that could not be overcome. Alarmed by what they had witnessed, all but two of the spies rallied the Israelites against their leader, incurring thereby God's anger. As a result, the generation of the Exodus was destined to trek forty years in the wilderness without ever entering the bountiful land that lay within their reach. The land promised by God to Abraham and his progeny would only be conquered by the next generation.

As if echoing these circumstances, we read in 5:22: "They [the Israelites] said unto Moses: In it [i.e. the holy land] there are [giants] people of great strength (*qawm jabbārīn*). We shall never enter it until they leave it. If they leave it, we shall indeed enter." The expression "people of great strength" apparently refers to the biblical Anakites, giant-like warriors that awaited the Israelites on the other side of the Jordan. In the Hebrew Bible, the appearance of the Anakites inspires dread among Moses's followers, who then refuse to cross into Canaan and engage the natives in battle (Num. 13–14 and later mentioned in Deut. 9:1–3). But not all the Israelites opposed entering the Promised Land. Muslim scripture continues: "Two men who feared God and unto whom God delivered his grace said: Assault them at the gate when you enter it. You will indeed be conquerors. If you be believers, put your faith in God" (23). Here again there is the echo of a biblical text, in this instance the tale of Joshua and Caleb, the two spies who supported Moses and who would later initiate the long-delayed invasion of Canaan (Num. 13:6–10, 14:24, 38; and Josh. 2). Verses 24–26 reiterate in turn the initial reluctance of the Israelites to partake of such a venture, an act of rebelliousness on their part that earned God's disfavor. As in the biblical account (Num. 13:14–38), the Qur'ān's wayward generation of the Exodus was destined to endure a forty-year sojourn in the desert without reaching their final destination. For God decreed: "Indeed, it (*al-arḍ al-muqaddasah*) will be forbidden to them for forty years as they wander about the land" (26). The allusions to Jewish scripture will seem self-evident to readers of the Hebrew Bible. Countless generations of Jewish children receiving an intensive education in classical Hebrew texts have read the passages in Numbers, Deuteronomy, and Joshua by the time they were seven or eight years of age, and then reread the biblical sources and commentaries many times over. In traditional Jewish worship, the segments of the Pentateuch are divided into weekly portions and read aloud during the Sabbath service in annual or triannual cycles so that the passages discussed here have been constantly reviewed since ancient times. For Jews acquainted with the Qur'ān, or Jewish converts to Islam raised with some modicum of a Jewish education, the *arḍ al-muqaddasah* of Muslim scripture signified the land promised the progeny of Abraham and conquered by Joshua. But how did Muslim scholars identify the "holy land" mentioned in their scripture?

In accounts that echo the biblical story of Jacob's ladder (Gen. 28:13–15), two Muslim authors not known as Qur'ān scholars, nor citing 5:21, briefly mention al-arḍ al-muqaddassah in connection with the land promised Abraham's grandson and his descendants, the Israelites.[2] Similarly, Muqātil b. Sulaymān, whose *Tafsīr* is the earliest published commentary of the Qur'ān, cites 5:21, maintaining that the arḍ al-muqaddasah mentioned in the verse refers explicitly to the land promised Abraham's offspring. Then, closely following Jewish tradition, Muqātil offers a detailed variant of the biblical story alluded to in verses 22 and 23.[3] He explains that the "people of great strength" blocking the path of the reluctant Israelites are in fact fierce fighters descended from one ʿAnaq, thus identifying the jabbārīn of Muslim scripture with the aforementioned biblical Anakites.[4] The Hebrew Bible and rabbinic tradition describe the latter as warriors so giant-like as to have made the Israelites feel like grasshoppers. In time, *ʿanak* became the generic word for "giant" in Hebrew; the same was true of *jabbār* in Arabic. As did the rabbis, Muqātil goes on to speculate about the height of these Canaanites. He also offers readers other details of the spies' mission found in Jewish sources: he mentions that they brought back samples of fruit (to indicate the quality of the land that the Bible describes as "flowing in milk and honey") and identifies the Qur'ān's two unnamed God-fearing men as the biblical Joshua, son of

2. Ibn Ṭāhir al-Maqdisī, *K. al-bad' wa-l-ta'rīkh*, 4:87; Ibn al-Faqīh, *Buldān*, 96.

3. Ibn Sulaymān, *Tafsīr*, 1:463 ff. (lists 5:21 as 5:20).

4. The biblical Anak is said to be the ancestor of the (surviving) Nephilites who spread dread among the spies (Num. 13:33). Various postbiblical Hebrew scholars identify the Nephilites as "*gibborim*," understood by them as "mighty giant warriors." Note *gibborim* stemming from the root *g-b-r* = Arabic *jabbārīn*. The size and strength of the Nephilites was no doubt connected with their having originally been a crossbreed between the sons of the gods and the beautiful daughters of humankind, as reported in the Bible (Gen. 6:1–4).

Nun, and Caleb, son of Jephunneh.[5] Muqātil b. Sulaymān was clearly familiar with details of the biblical story and its rabbinic retelling. It is less certain that he fully recognized their Jewish provenance. One suspects the same may have been true for Muḥammad and his contemporaries. There is no definitive evidence to confirm what access the Prophet himself may have had to the biblical text or to the legendary Jewish material to which it gave rise.

The Qur'ān is mute regarding the geographical extent of the holy land, and, as regards that, later Muslim authorities are sharply divided. Some scholars claim al-arḍ al-muqaddasah to be the entire province of Syria (*al-Shām*); others maintain that it signifies the *jund* or "subdistrict" of Filasṭīn (the Arab/Muslim equivalent of Graeco-Roman Palaestina Prima, that is, the area of the Mediterranean coast from the Sinai border to al-Lajjūn running north-south and from the coast inland to the hill country and then desert representing Jerusalem and its environs).[6] Still others claim it refers specifically to Jericho (*Arīḥā*), the place initially conquered by the invading Israelites led by Joshua. Also mentioned are a Filasṭīn-Damascus axis and various areas east of the Jordan River, places from which the Israelites launched their campaigns against the Canaanites, and in which three Israelite tribes came to settle. There are even claims for Mount Sinai (*Ṭūr*), an interpretation favored by many scholars who identify the "holy land" in Qur'ān 5:21 as the place where the Ten Commandments were revealed and not a location in or near Canaan. Finally, a fifteenth-century Qur'ān scholar listing the various names for Jerusalem includes among them al-arḍ al-muqaddasah. It is, however, doubtful that this late authority sheds light on what these words may have meant to Muḥammad and the earliest community of Muslims.[7]

Nowhere does Muslim scripture makes specific reference to al-Shām, let alone to Jericho or any other town, city, or subdistrict within the Syro-

5. For a survey of the rabbinic legends about the Anakites and the spies sent by Moses there is L. Ginzberg, *Legends of the Jews* (New York, 1968 reprint), 1:465–68.

6. Yāqūt, *Muʿjam*, 3:914.

7. These views are found in the standard commentaries to Muslim scripture. See, for example, Ṭabarī's *Jāmiʿ al-bayān* with regard to the relevant verses. Readers should also consult the commentaries to Sūrah 2:58, which begins: "And when we said, 'Enter this town (*qaryah*) and eat from it what you wish and enter the gate, prostrating yourselves, saying *ḥiṭṭah*.'" This enigmatic verse has given rise to much commentary and has resulted in the building of a Bāb Ḥiṭṭah on the Temple Mount. Muslim scholars equate the *qaryah* of the verse with *al-arḍ al-muqaddasah* and offer a long list of places that are thought to be the "Holy Land" referred to in the Qur'ān. See also Sūrahs 4:154, and 7:161 and their respective commentaries, and H. Busse's "*Bāb Ḥiṭṭa*: Qur'ān 2:58 and the Entry into Jerusalem," *JSAI* 22 (1998): 1–17, esp. 3–5. Chapter 4 below discusses the epithet "the ruler (*ṣāḥib* or *malik*) of al-arḍ al-muqaddasah," which refers to the Umayyad caliph Muʿāwiyah and his son. The *arḍ al-muqaddasah* of the epithet is a seeming reference to al-Shām.

Palestinian region, the anvil on which ancient Israel was forged. There is no mention of Jerusalem, at least not by any of its names known to the Arabs. Are we then to assume that Muḥammad and his contemporaries, the first generation of Muslims from Arabia, had no first- or even secondhand knowledge of the holy city? There is in fact a vague reference in the Qur'ān (Sūrah 30:2–4) to the war between the Byzantine and Sasanid emperors, a conflict in which Christian Jerusalem was lost to the Persians in 614 CE (roughly the beginning of Muḥammad's mission) and then reclaimed by the emperor Heraclius some years later on the eve of Islam's triumph in the Hijaz. The text reads: "The Byzantines (*Rūm*) have been overcome (2) in the neighboring land. But they who were overcome shall [in turn] overcome [their conquerors] afterwards (3) [that is,] a few years later. The matter is in God's hands as to [what happened] before and [what will happen] later. On that day [when the Byzantines are victorious] the believers will rejoice" (4).

The Muslim Qur'ān scholars are all agreed that the sūrah is of Meccan origin (ca. 610–22 CE). Bayḍāwī, a thirteenth century CE commentator, dates it to the year before the *ḥijrah*, the Prophet's emigration to Medina (621 CE).[8] The message in the verses that follow speaks to a society that has not yet comprehended what awaits them on the Day of Judgment as they have not properly discerned God's intervention on earth and acted according to his wishes. The theme of divine reward and punishment is perfectly consistent with that of other Meccan sūrahs. But, in relating the return of the Byzantines to the holy city, the three verses in question refer to an event that took place years after the Prophet left his native abode for Medina. Muslim scholars were certainly aware that was indeed the case. The medieval commentators indicate that the expected triumph of the Byzantines coincided with the year of Ḥudaybīyah. The reference is to the treaty of that name later signed by Muḥammad with the unbelievers, a dramatic moment that signaled the beginning of the end of pagan supremacy in his native Mecca. By all accounts, the treaty was concluded in 628, the very year in which the emperor Heraclius set into motion events that would restore Christian rule in Jerusalem. In effect, the verses are a back-projection. Presented in the form of a veiled prophecy, they describe an event that had already taken place, a historic turn whose fulfillment would cause "the believers to rejoice." According to the exegetes, the polytheists at Mecca gloated upon hearing of the initial Persian triumph because the Sasanids did not believe in the God of heaven, in contrast to the Christians and Muḥammad and his followers. But the tables were destined to be turned. It would be the Muslims who rejoiced when

8. Bayḍāwī, *Anwār*, 1:533.

the Byzantines retook their lost territory and Muḥammad's prophetic credentials were confirmed by his having predicted the turn of events. It then follows that Qur'ān 30:2–4 reflects the end of the Prophet's Medina sojourn and not his earlier time in Mecca.[9]

Given the didactic purpose for which they read scripture, Muslim Qur'ān scholars were often forced to expand the literal meaning of the text. But in this instance they seem to have captured the thrust of the original revelation, a prophetic account alluding to a victory for those who believe in the God of heaven. By referring to the year of Ḥudaybīyah, they identify the rough date of the Byzantine triumph. Beyond that, they identify "the neighboring land" of scripture with al-Shām, the great province to the north. More explicitly, Ṭabarī (d. 923 CE) indicates in his commentary that the verses refer to the battle for Bayt al-Maqdis, a seeming reference not only to Jerusalem but more explicitly to the Temple Mount; as he says, "The Bayt al-Maqdis was for the Byzantines what the Ka'bah is for the Muslims." Expelling the Persians was thus the equivalent of Muḥammad's triumphant return to Mecca and the removal of the idols from its holy shrine the Ka'bah, indeed a triumph that merited rejoicing. Interestingly enough, Ṭabarī reports that emphasis should not be placed on the Christian victory but on the defeat of the Persians (Zoroastrians), a gloss that may speak to the religious principles over which Jerusalem and more importantly Mecca were contested.

For the Byzantine emperor, restoring Christian rule to Jerusalem was nothing less than an act of faith reaffirming the position of the holy city in the religious landscape of the empire. According to some scholars, Jews of the time also harbored hopes of returning to Jerusalem and rebuilding their Temple, the spiritual icon of Judaism and the concrete symbol of a Jewish sovereignty lost during Roman times. If that were indeed the case, they surely placed no such hopes on Heraclius's counteroffensive. It would have been the earlier Persian victory that stoked messianic yearnings among God's chosen but long-persecuted people. Jews presumably saw the events of 614 as replaying a memo-

9. R. Bell sees this verse as Medinian rather than Meccan in origin. He states: "It is . . . difficult to understand Muḥammad's favorable interest in the fortunes of the Byzantine Empire at this date [i.e., the loss of Jerusalem that took place while the Prophet still resided in Mecca]." He then goes on to suggest that the text be understood as referring to a Byzantine victory over the Sasanids [i.e., Heraclius's reconquest of Jerusalem, which took place when the Prophet was in Medina]. He comes to this understanding by inverting the active and passive of *ghalaba* in 30:2, "to be victorious," so that the verses initially refer to the victory of the Byzantines in 628 but forewarn that their triumph will be short-lived as the Muslims are soon to conquer them. The reading presupposes that Muḥammad had designs on the lands of the Byzantines even before the final conquest of Mecca and the rest of Arabia, a theme prominent in later apocalyptical visions. See R. Bell, *The Qur'ān* (Edinburgh, 1927), 392–93.

rable moment that had taken place a thousand years earlier when Cyrus, king of the Persians, conquered Babylon (ca. 539 or 538 BCE). That conquest set into motion a series of developments that could be described as a watershed in ancient Jewish history. A half century earlier Nebuchadnezzar had destroyed Solomon's Temple, laid Jerusalem waste, and forced the Israelites into captivity. The Persian triumph of 539/538 led to the return of the exiles from Babylonia, the resurrection of a Jewish polity in the land promised to their forefathers, and the restoration of the Temple and temple sacrifice. No small wonder that the Jews of Muḥammad's time are said to have greeted the latest Persian conquest as the onset of their long-awaited redemption.[10]

Could Muslims of the Prophet's entourage have looked to Jerusalem with comparable religious fervor? And if Muslims were inclined to regard the city as did Jews and Christians, what led them to such views? What historic memories of Jerusalem were burned into the consciousness of the Prophet and his followers? Could the earliest generation of Muslims have been familiar with rabbinic and Christian lore in praise of Jerusalem, as were later generations of Muslim scholars exposed to learned Jews and Christians as well as material related by converts to Islam? And if they had knowledge of that extensive body of literature, how might they have come by it? Above all, were Muḥammad and his companions moved to declare openly that Jerusalem was as holy for them as it was for Jews and Christians? Or is the celebrated Muslim regard for Jerusalem largely the result of religious and political considerations linked to historical events after the death of the Prophet and the success of the Arab conquerors? These are all queries easily framed but difficult to answer with any degree of assurance.

10. The possibility that the Persians actually stoked Jewish expectations of a rebuilt Temple if not indeed the onset of the messianic age was advanced by H. Graetz in his *Geschichte der Juden von den ältesten Zeiten bis auf die Gegenwart*. I have used the German edition (Leipzig, 1897–1911), 5:24–29 (text), 361–64 (annotation); the English translation titled *History of the Jews* published by the Jewish Publication Society, New York, in several editions reproduces Graetz's text (3:19–23) but omits his meticulous annotation. One can add to this discussion the *Targum Sheni* to the book of Esther, an Aramaic midrash of disputed date loosely based on the biblical tale. The most recent edition based on numerous manuscripts is that of Bernard Grossfeld. According to Grossfeld, the lexical character of the Aramaic is that of the western dialect of ancient Palestine. The midrash also displays clear evidence of Christian polemics contra Judaism and acts of persecution against the Jews of Palestine. Given Grossfeld's provenance of the text (ca. seventh century), we can speculate that the conditions described were those faced by contemporaneous Jewry under Byzantine rule. The text, a creative version of the story in the biblical book of Esther, refers as does the biblical work to the salvation of Jews. The *Targum* may thus reflect contemporaneous Jewish expectations that the Persians would once again be their salvation, as in ancient times. The Sasanids would thus have been regarded as allies, indeed as saviors, when they invaded Palestine and later captured Jerusalem. For a brief discussion of the *Targum Sheni*, see J. Lassner, *Demonizing the Queen of Sheba* (Chicago, 1993), 131–32.

If Arab traders of the Prophet's time moved back and forth across the Syrian frontier, as most scholars believe, there is no compelling reason to deny that some Muslims may have traveled beyond the caravan terminals and visited the holy city or its environs.[11] Muḥammad, who was preaching in Mecca and Medina and displayed some knowledge of biblical persons and events, could have been exposed directly or indirectly to postbiblical traditions celebrating Jerusalem, if not from Arabs who traveled to al-Shām, then by way of Jews and Christians settled in Arabia. Since the *materia biblica* in the Qur'ān are often filtered through the lenses of rabbinic sources, there is always the possibility that specific elements of Jewish (and also Christian) lore of Jerusalem might have resonated among the Prophet and his Muslim followers.[12]

Using the Qur'ān as our essential guide, what can we conclude about the earliest Muslim attitudes to the holy city? Aside from indications that Muslims originally prayed toward Jerusalem (*ūlat al-qiblatayn*), there seem to be no explicit references in Muslim scripture that Muḥammad and his companions embraced the ancient city as a locus of veneration.[13] There is Qur'ān 38:21–25, which is linked, however loosely, to the well-known Jewish tale of the biblical

11. There is a strong consensus among scholars that H. Lammens's early and influential study of the commercial life of Mecca is a gross exaggeration, but most historians of early Islam are not prepared to follow P. Crone in minimizing so thoroughly the importance of Mecca as a center of the caravan trade. See H. Lammens, "La republique marchande de la Mecque vers l'an 600 de notre ére," *BIE* 5th series 4 (1910): 23–54; P. Crone, *Meccan Trade and the Rise of Islam* (Oxford, 1987). See also M. J. Kister, "Mecca and the Tribes of Arabia," in *Studies in Islamic History and Civilization in Honor of David Ayalon*, edited by M. Sharon (Leiden, 1986), 33–57. For the controversy occasioned by Crone, see M. Bukharin, "Mecca and the Caravan Routes in Pre-Islamic Antiquity," in *The Qur'ān in Context*, edited by A. Neuwirth, N. Sinai, and M. Marx (Leiden, 2011), 115–34. The larger context of the Arabian trade networks is currently being explored by Michael Bonner of the University of Michigan. Hopefully, he will soon produce a major monograph bringing together the various papers he has presented at scholarly meetings.

12. The influence of rabbinic Judaism on the Qur'ān and early Muslim tradition dealing with the life of Muḥammad and his milieu was seriously examined first by A. Geiger in his *Was hat Mohammed aus den Judenthume aufgenommen?* (Bonn, 1833); translated by F. M. Young as *Judaism in Islam* (Madras, 1898). Geiger's pioneering work was followed by M. Grünbaum, *Neue Beiträge zur semitischen Sagenkunde* (Leiden, 1893); H. Hirschfeld, *Beiträge zur Erklärung des Koran* (Leipzig, 1986); I. Schapiro, *Die haggadischen Elemente im erzählenden Teil des Korans* (Berlin, 1907); and A. Katsh, *Judaism in Islam* (New York, 1980), which deals only with Sūrahs 2 and 3. These studies, however learned, tend to exercise considerable license in determining the actual path of Jewish influence. G. Weil's *Biblische Legende der Musselmänner* (Leipzig, 1846) and the English translation, *The Bible, the Koran, and the Talmud* (New York, 1886), are geared to a general audience and lack a critical apparatus and outlook. For a more sophisticated approach to cultural borrowing, see H. Speyer, *Die biblischen Erzählungen im Qoran* (Hildesheim, 1961 reprint); H. Z. Hirschberg, *Jüdische und cristliche lehren im vor- und früislamischen Arabien* (Kraków, 1939); S. D. Goitein, "Who Were Muḥammad's Noteworthy Teachers [Hebrew]," *Tarbiz* 23 (1953): 146–59; and Lassner, *Demonizing the Queen of Sheba*—an examination of Islamic traditions based on Qur'ān 27:15–41; see esp. 120–55. Most recently: C. Gilliot, "Les informateurs juifs et chrétiens de Muḥammad," *JSAI* 23 (1998): 84–126.

13. Qur'ān 2:142–50.

David holding court. In Muslim scripture the court is rendered as *miḥrāb*, an Arabic word generally understood by Qur'an commentators as David's "sanctuary" in Jerusalem. But that tells us little about what place Jerusalem might have had in the religious imagination of the nascent Muslim community.[14] Other verses seemingly draw attention to the ancient temples of Solomon and Herod.[15] But there is no indication that in mentioning these places holy to Jews and Christians, the Qur'ān means for them to be considered equally sacred by the Prophet and his companions. In Muslim scripture, the destruction of Jerusalem's temples signals God's punishment for the inequities of the Jews and by implication all who seek to deny him and his will. One cannot conclude that, read literally, these presumed references to Jerusalem and its temples proclaim the city sacred for the Muslims.

Whatever special status might have accrued to the holy city at the outset of Muḥammad's mission was tarnished by reorienting the direction of Muslim prayer from Jerusalem toward Mecca and, more generally, by stressing the importance of Arabia as the crucible in which monotheism was formed for the benefit of humankind. The Qur'ān relates that Abraham, the first to believe in the one and only God, and his son Ishmael (the progenitor of the northern Arabs and the direct ancestor of Muḥammad and his kin) were responsible for establishing the Ka'bah as a place of prayer and religious ritual.[16] Hence, Muslims could cite this verse to claim that Mecca is the oldest (and most important) center of monotheism. That claim for Mecca notwithstanding, the holy city of the Jews and Christians became an integral part of Islam's sacred geography, but one can argue persuasively that was well after the Prophet and his generation had come and gone. How then could the Muslim proponents of Jerusalem's sanctity make a case that their ancient city was comparable to the birthplace of monotheism and God's last prophet? Muslims seeking to justify Jerusalem's newfound importance retrofitted their veneration of the city to reflect the views of Muḥammad and his companions. The most direct and efficacious path to this reshaping of history was to exercise interpretive license, reading passages carefully selected from Muslim scripture. What better imprimatur for legitimizing the sanctity of Jerusalem than the word of God revealed through his last and quintessential messenger.

Given the absence of explicit references to Jerusalem in the Qur'ān, linking individual verses to the holy city forced Muslim scholars to tax their literary

14. For David's *miḥrāb*, see H. Busse, "The Tower of David / *Miḥrāb Dāwūd*: Remarks on the History of a Sanctuary in Jerusalem in Christian and Islamic Times," *JSAI* 17 (1994): 108–41.

15. Qur'ān 17:2–8.

16. Qur'ān 2:125–26.

inventiveness. Witness 2:114 (in other versions 108): "Who are more wrong (*aẓlamu*) than those who prohibit the mention of God's name in his places of worship (*masājid*) and strive to destroy them. They should only enter them in fear. For them, there will be humiliation (*khiz'*) in this world (*dunyā*) and great punishment in the hereafter." What did readers or audiences exposed to the recitation of scripture make of this revelation? Who were those blameworthy individuals or groups who prohibit the mention of God's name and in the very houses of worship dedicated to him? To what places of worship is the text alluding, and how is it that the unnamed wrongdoers would go so far as to destroy or despoil the sacred structures? Above all, what moral lesson should be drawn from a close reading of 2:114? The questions clearly beg for answers, but none seem apparent, especially if we restrict ourselves to a literal reading of the text.

As are modern Orientalists, the generations of Muslims following that of the Prophet were left facing a quandary. Lacking direct testimony from Muḥammad's contemporaries, they were hard pressed to recover what meaning the earliest community gave this difficult passage and others like it. Later Muslims realized that in order to fully understand the Prophet's message, or proclaim that they did, they needed to supply a historical context to individual verses. Scholars thus directed their readers to what they termed "the circumstances of revelation (*asbāb al-nuzūl*)." These efforts at recovering historical background could be no less problematic than the original text itself. As a result, Western scholars who seek to derive meaning from the Qur'ān rather than impose meaning on it often find themselves doubting, if not rejecting outright, the explanations provided by medieval Muslim authorities. Moreover, medieval Muslim Qur'ān scholars were often at odds with one another in probing scripture for its essential meaning. So it is with the aforementioned verses, a text that most, but not all, Muslim exegetes have associated with Jerusalem and the Temple Mount.[17]

A few Muslim scholars understood the verse to be rooted in events taking place during the Prophet's lifetime. For them, the "places of worship" refers to the Ka'bah and Muḥammad's birthplace. The "wrongdoers" are made out to be polytheists who either prevented the Prophet and his followers from praying in the Ka'bah, a situation reflecting the persecution of the early Muslims in Mecca, or barring the faithful from the Meccan sanctuary during the truce of Ḥudaybīyah when the Muslims sought peaceful entry into the city as pilgrims.[18]

17. See S. Bashear, "Q 2:114 and Jerusalem," *BSOAS* 52 (1989): 215–38.

18. For example, Ṭabarī, *Jāmi'*, citing Ibn Zayd and "others." One could add Rāzī's *Tafsīr* with its unique claim that 2:114 refers to the Jews who intended to destroy the Ka'bah because Muḥammad had changed the orientation of prayer from Jerusalem to Mecca. Bashear notes as well the even

However, most exegetes read the verse as though it pertained to events of an ancient past well before the rise of Islam. These scholars understood the "places of worship" to mean the Jewish temples of old that were at the heart of a sacred precinct situated atop Jerusalem's Mount Moriah.[19] The wrongdoers were in turn identified with a well-known cast of evil rulers: Nebuchadnezzar the Babylonian (who destroyed Solomon's Temple); Antiochus Epiphanes (the Seleucid who looted the rebuilt Temple in 169 or 168 BCE and then offered unclean sacrifices there to the Olympian god Zeus); and Titus (the Roman general and later emperor who destroyed and looted the Second Temple in the first century CE). There is also a mysterious Khardūs (Khardaws?), king of Babylon, whom the exegetes might have confused with Nebuchadnezzar or Nebuzaradan, the general who carried out the former's orders to destroy the city and the buildings in the Temple Mount.[20] These noteworthy figures together with other persons known from ancient sources became objects of discussion for scholars commenting on Qur'ān 17:2–8, a series of verses that was also understood as referring to the history of the great temples that graced Jerusalem.

As regards 2:114 and the destruction of the holy sites on the Temple Mount, the exegetes add to the brief against "the wrongdoers" who violated the religious purity of the Temple by trashing it, more specifically by casting carcasses into the building and using the sanctuary to sacrifice pigs (an animal deemed unclean according to Jewish and Islamic law).[21] The devastation of Jerusalem, the political fulcrum of Jewish sovereignty, and the profaning of the Temple, the cultic center of God's chosen people, are all described in ancient Jewish sources and have become stories told and retold by Jews throughout their long and checkered history.

This ancient history so well known to Jews (and also Christians), and the subject of so much biblical and rabbinic scholarship, appears confused in medieval Qur'ān commentary. Somehow, the Muslim scholars link the Qur'ān's wrongdoers to the Rūm (ordinarily meaning Romans or Byzantines), and

---

more bizarre claim of Muḥammad b. Shams al-Dīn al-Suyūṭī, the author of a fifteenth century CE work in praise of Jerusalem. Suyūṭī holds that the transgression was that of the Byzantines who prohibited the Muslims from praying in Jerusalem, a claim that would indicate Jerusalem had become a holy city for the Muslims before the fall of the city to the Muslim armies. Note his "Q 2:114," 215–16, 232 ff. citing Muḥammad b. Shams al-Dīn al-Suyūṭī, *Itkḥāf al-akhiṣṣā* (Cairo, 1982), 1:100. Clearly Suyūṭī's claim as regards the Byzantines is a later invention and is to be seen, as does Bashear, with an anti-Christian bias that pervades some of the commentary to this verse. See also the discussion of anti-Christian bias in the commentary to Qur'ān 17:2–8 in chapter 3.

19. Op. cit., 222, citing Muḥammad b. Sa'd, Ibn 'Abbās, Mujāhid, Qatādah, and Suddī; also Bayḍāwī, *Anwār*, 1:533–34; Ibn Sulaymān, *Tafsīr*, 1:132–33 (identifying the verse as 2:113).

20. See n. 19 for the trashing of the Temple. On the specific use of pigs for pagan sacrifice, see Ibn Sulaymān, *Tafsīr*, 1:132.

21. See nn. 18 and 19.

in most instances identify the "blameworthy" as Christians (*Naṣārā*). In the strange chronology of Qur'ān scholarship, the Rūm or Naṣārā are described as assisting the Babylonians of the sixth century BCE and, following that, of cooperating with Antiochus the Seleucid who ruled some two centuries before the birth of Jesus and the rise of Christianity. The Muslims also describe the Christians as active participants in the first Roman (*Rūm*) siege of Jewish Jerusalem. The reason given for the Christian-pagan alliance is that the Jews had to be punished for killing John the Baptist (who was put to death by Herod Antipas in 28 or 29 CE); or the killing of their prophets of old, an accusation found in the Qur'ān (2:61, 87, 91, 3:181, 183, 4:155, 5:70) and presumably based on various episodes reported in the Hebrew Bible and then alluded to in the anti-Jewish polemics of the New Testament. Were the murder of genuine prophets not sufficient cause for punishing the Jews, the Israelites also stand accused of disobeying their God-given laws (*aḥkām*).[22]

It would appear that when recording history Muslim scholars had reservations about the alleged role of Christians in the events leading to Jerusalem's destruction. The chroniclers referring to the catastrophe that befell Judaism's holiest shrines do not cite the problematic commentary and exegesis to Qur'ān 2.114. Instead, they turn to the oblique but clearly intended references to the ancient Jewish temples in Qur'ān 17:2–8 as well as the more ambiguous verses 2:259 and 2:11.[23] Muḥammad b. Jarīr al-Ṭabarī transmits the skewed account of Jerusalem's temples when citing 2:114 in his massive commentary on the Qur'ān. However, he omits any reference to the muddled version he and other Qur'an commentators attached to 2:114 when referring to the destruction of

22. Ṭabarī, *Jāmiʿ al-bayān*, commenting on 2:114; Bayḍāwī, *Anwār*, 1:134. The accusations that Jews killed God's prophets and forsook their own laws are Muslim literary conventions based on New Testament polemics against the Jews. Among the numerous anti-Jewish polemics of the New Testament; see Matt. 5:12, 23:30–31, Luke 11:47 (hounded and killed their prophets), and Acts 7:53 (Jews do not keep their laws). The New Testament references to Jews killing their prophets is presumably influenced by similar stories in the Hebrew Bible that were no doubt available to Muslims in one form or another. See 1 Kings 19:10, 2 Kings 9:7, Jer. 2:30 and 27:15; also other leading figures in 2 Chr. 34:17–22. For an explicit Muslim reference that Jews as a group do not obey their laws, see Qur'ān 62:5. The reference to Jews killing John the Baptist and the punishment received thereby may confuse the destruction of the Temple that Herod built with the destruction of his army at the hands of the king of Petra, an event blamed on the Jewish king for having been complicit in the death of the Baptist. See Josephus, *Antiquities*, 18.5.2. Note also the role of the Jews toward John the Baptist in the time of Nebuchadnezzar in the ahistorical commentaries to Qur'ān 17:2–8 treated in detail by H. Schützinger, "Die arabische Legende von Nebukadnezar und Johannes dem Taeufer," *Der Islam* 40 (1965): 113–41; and as regards 17:2–8, which also speaks of the perfidies of the Jews in killing their prophets, see chapter 3.

23. Qur'ān 2:259 [261]: "Or like him who had passed by a city (*qaryah*) in total ruin"; Qur'ān 21:11: "How many a city (*qaryah*) that did wrong have we ruined, leaving another people to inhabit it." Note Arabic *qaryah* = Hebrew *kiryah*, which refers to Jerusalem ravaged by the Babylonians in Lam. 2:11.

the temples in his universal chronicle. Writing as a historian, he describes Nebuchadnezzar's victory over the Israelites, the destruction of the Solomonic Temple, and the exile of God's chosen people to Babylon based on the familiar story told and retold by Jews and Christians. Put succinctly, there may have been some doubts about the prevailing commentary to 2:114 and its reported linkage to Jerusalem and its Jewish temples.[24]

That still leaves us with the need to explain why the verse gave rise to such a bizarre understanding of the past when the accepted versions of the Jewish temples and their fate were known to Muslim antiquarians in broad if not great detail. What was the true purpose of the intellectual exercise that altered the received wisdom of the other monotheist communities, and how does it affect, if at all, the question that is of immediate interest to us: Did Muslims revere the city of Jerusalem in the lifetime of the Prophet? Readers will observe there is a polemical thrust to the early and most accepted line of Muslim interpretation. We are led to believe that Jews suffered the loss of their central shrine and endured exile because of their iniquities, particularly killing their own prophets and John the Baptist. This accusation may be a veiled reference to the manner in which the Jewish tribes of the Hijaz rejected Muḥammad, warred against him, and in certain traditions went so far as to plan his death. For these later actions they suffered loss of their lands and exile (as did the wayward Israelites before them). But why stop with indicting the Jews? Given the triangularity of polemical discourse among the three monotheist faith communities, Muslim authors would have seen fit to establish a bill of particulars against the Christians as well, in this case making them the willing allies of pagans who destroyed and despoiled the Temple and exiled the inhabitants of Jerusalem. Indeed, 2:113 castigates both Jews and Christians who dispute one another even though both cite revealed scripture, and similarly impugns the polytheists who have no knowledge of the Book.

Suliman Bashear is well aware of the history presented by the Muslim exegetes, but he casts a far wider net in an attempt to provide a context for the disparities, be it the muddled chronology or the disputed venue for the events allegedly referred to in 2:114. He addresses the contradictory views of scholars, identifying the blameworthy action as having taken place in Mecca and those who relegate it to Jerusalem. With great erudition Bashear traces the development of the commentary to 2:114. He concludes that the earliest view was clearly intended as an anti-Christian (read anti-Byzantine) polemic grafted on

24. Ṭabarī, *Annales*, 1/1:643–51.

to the well-known history of the ancient Israelites.[25] But then a second view emerged; a counterclaim that denied the blameworthy acts ought to be identified with destroying the temples in Jerusalem, the killing of many of its inhabitants, and the exile of the Jews. Instead, some Muslim scholars understood the verse as promoting the importance of Arabia and particularly the Hijaz as the birthplace of Islam—hence the substitution of the Ka'bah in Mecca for the temples in Jerusalem. Certain Muslim scholars asserted the importance of the Hijaz and its holy cities, Mecca and Medina, at the expense of al-Shām and Jerusalem. The latter interpretation of the verse may thus be seen as part of a broad enquiry rooted in later disputes within the Islamic community as well as a polemical confrontation with Christians (and also Jews).

In either case, nothing that has been discussed so far is likely to convince skeptical readers that the "places of worship" in 2:114 originally meant the Jewish temples in Jerusalem. Furthermore, there is no compelling reason—at least none that I can ascertain—to believe that the Prophet and his contemporaries would have regarded the twice- or thrice-violated Jewish sanctuaries as places worthy of truly special veneration, certainly not the reverence bestowed on the Ka'bah in Mecca or sites in Medina where the Prophet's community took root. Even the commentaries that identify the *masājid* in 2:114 as the temples in Jerusalem do so as places venerated by the Jews and Jews alone. We therefore have to ask whether there is proof elsewhere in Muslim scripture that Muḥammad and his followers embraced with full conviction the sanctity of Jerusalem and the Temple Mount.

Qur'ān 17:1 and Ancient Traditions of Jerusalem and the Temple Mount

Among the various verses that allegedly refer to Jerusalem, the most noteworthy, certainly the most discussed, is the opening of Sūrah 17, a segment of scripture said to have been revealed in the Meccan or early period of the Prophet's activities.[26] The verse in question refers to Muḥammad's nocturnal journey

25. Bashear, "Qur'ān 2:114," 232 ff.

26. For an overview, see *EI*, s.v. "mi'rādj" and "isrā'"; similarly *EQ* s.v. "Ascension" and "Aqṣā Mosque." Most notably, C. Gilliot, "Coran 17, *isrā'* dans la recherche occidentale: De la critique des traditions au Coran comme texte," in *Le Voyage initiatique en terre d'Islam: Ascensions célestes et itinéraires spirituels*, edited by M. A. Amir-Moezzi (Louvain, 1996), 1–26 (surveys Western literature); also A. Neuwirth, "Erste Qibla—Fernstes Masgid? Jerusalem im horizont des historischen Muḥammad," *Zion—Ort der Begegnung: Festschrift für Lurentius Klein*, Bonner biblische Beiträge 90, edited by F. Hahn et al. (Hanstein, 1993), 227–70, and H. Busse, "Jerusalem in the Story of Muḥammad's Night Journey and Ascension," *JSAI* 14

(*isrāʾ*) to the city and his ascension to heaven (*miʿrāj*) from it, or so most Muslims gather when they read that God took (*asrā*) "His servant [Muḥammad] one night from the sacred place of worship (*al-masjid al-ḥarām* [presumably referring to Mecca]) to the furthest place of worship (*al-masjid al-aqṣā*), [a place] whose surroundings [God] blessed (*baraknā ḥawlahu*) so as to show him [Muḥammad] God's manifest signs (*āyāt*). He is All-Seeing and All-Hearing."

By the second Islamic century, Muslims interpreted the undisclosed "furthest place of worship" as referring to Jerusalem, or more specifically to the ancient mount on which the great temples of Solomon and Herod were built. Commenting on 17:1 in his *Jāmiʿ*, Ṭabarī equates the furthest place of worship with "the Temple Mount and its surroundings (*Bayt al-Maqdis wa-nawāḥīhi*)," which I take to mean all of Jerusalem. On the other hand, Ibn Iṣḥāq, the eighth-century biographer of the Prophet, identifies the furthest place of worship as the Bayt al-Maqdis of (*min*) Īliyāʾ, presumably a specific reference to the site of the Jewish temples rather than the entire city.[27]

Later Muslim authorities endowed the Temple Mount with legendary credentials. As did the Jews, they proclaimed that the temples of Solomon and Herod were built over a primeval rock whose waters slaked the entire earth (Arabic *ṣakhrah*, Hebrew *even shetiyah*).[28] The primeval rock and more generally all of Jerusalem were declared by Jews and Muslims to be the very "navel of the universe," the very center of the world. Jews described the city as the gateway to paradise; Christians as the midpoint between the "Heavenly Jerusalem" and the netherworld below.[29] The ancient rabbis maintained that the Holy Land was the center of God's creation, the center of the Holy Land was in turn Jerusalem; the center of Jerusalem was the Temple; the sanctuary was in the center of the Temple, and positioned at the center of the sanctuary was the celebrated ark that stood directly on (or before) the primeval rock.[30] The rock whose waters gave rise to the world was said to be situated on Mount Moriah, the place where Adam was fashioned by God from dust obtained from that very rock, thus initi-

(1991): 1–40; also J. Van Ess, "Vision and Ascension: Sūrat al-Najm and Its Relationship with Muḥammad's *miʿrāj*," *JQS* 1 (1999): 47–62.

27. Ibn Iṣḥāq, *Sīrah* (Beirut), 2:32.

28. Among the seventy names attributed by the rabbis to the Holy City was "Waters" (*yam*) based on Genesis 1:9: "Let the waters below the sky be gathered in a single place." See I. Katznelson, "Seventy Names of Jerusalem [Hebrew]," *Sinai* 116 (1995): 141–59.

29. For Jerusalem as the center of the world, see P. S. Alexander, "Jerusalem as the Omphalos of the World: On the History of a Geographical Concept," in *Jerusalem*, edited by L. Levine (New York, 1999), 104–19. A brief reference to rabbinic sources can be found in *ET* and *JE*, s.v. "Even Shetiyah." For a summary of the rabbinic sources, see Ginzberg, *Legends*, 5:14–16. For the reference in Tosephta, *Yom ha-Kippurim*, see S. Lieberman, *Tosefta ki-fshutah*, 4:772–73.

30. *Midrash Tanhuma* (Buber), 2:78 (based on Ezek. 38:12); see also 1 Enoch 26:1 and Jub. 8:12 for earlier views.

ating the birth of humankind.[31] It was there that the first man erected an altar to God and was expelled from Paradise. Moving forward in time, Mount Moriah is where Abraham took his son to be sacrificed as a burnt offering but an angel of God intervened and the patriarch now relieved of killing his beloved son offered a ram instead. Abraham named the place "Yahweh Yir'e (God Will See)" a toponym that gave rise, according to the biblical author, to the proverbial expression "on the mountain of God it will be seen" (*bihar Yahweh yeirue*) (Gen. 22:14). The rabbis understood this last expression as alluding to God's presence on Mount Moriah with specific reference to the Temple in Jerusalem.[32]

Another biblical tale allowed the rabbis to draw an even stronger connection between Mount Moriah and the platform upon which the great temples were built. Commenting on the account of Jacob's ladder, a nocturnal vision in which Abraham's grandson dreamed he had been brought into God's presence, the rabbis declare the event occurred (as did the binding of Isaac) on Mount Moriah. As Jacob renamed the place of his dream, then known as Luz, Bethel, "House of the Lord" (Gen. 28:19), and as he erected a commemorative stone pillar there to designate "God's [future] house" (28:18), the rabbis had no difficulty in going a step further and identifying Mount Moriah with the Temple Mount. Jacob's dream took the form of an apocalyptic vision linked to Jewish messianic expectations. He saw the tribulations of exile that were to befall his progeny. Eager that, following this misfortune, his offspring be made once again masters of the land promised them by God (and by inference restore the Temple), Jacob prostrated himself before the primeval rock and asked the Almighty to fulfill his promise, first made to Abraham and later to himself and others.[33] By referring to the recorded memories of the beloved patriarchs, the rabbis enshrined Jerusalem and the Temple Mount in Jewish history long before David acquired the city and Solomon erected the first house of worship to the Lord. As if the connection between the Temple Mount and Abraham's mountain needed any additional support, there was 2 Chronicles 3:1: "And Solomon began to build the house of the Lord in Jerusalem on Mount Moriah."

We learn from Jewish sources that once the Temple was built, the outcrop of stone could actually be seen, as a part of the rock three fingers deep protruded

---

31. JT, *Nazir* 7.2 and later MR, *Gen.* 14.8 (among other sources).

32. BT, *Pesahim* 88a and later in MR, *Gen.* 69.7. E. A. Speiser in his commentary to Genesis suggests that the intended reading was *yir'eh*, "will see," to accord with verse 8: "God will see to the sheep." See *Anchor Bible Series Genesis* (New York, 1964), 219. The rabbis reading the text in the passive voice indicate the future construction of the Temple on that very spot. See n. 33.

33. BT, *Sanhedrin* 95b. The Samaritans, whose sacred mountain is Mt. Gerizim, list among the names for that site Luz and Bethel, thus legitimizing their sacred place of sacrifice. See Z. Ben-Hayyim's Hebrew study, *A Collection of Samaritan Midrashim* (Jerusalem, 1988), 150–51.

from under the Holy Ark positioned above.[34] The ark was the receptacle that the wandering Israelites first built in the desert to house the tablets of God's law. Originally transported by Moses's followers wandering about the wilderness, and then positioned in a temporary sanctuary after the conquering Israelites settled in Canaan, the ark was given a proper home once the Jerusalem Temple was built. More specifically, the ark resided in the Holy of Holies, a circumscribed area accessible only to the high priest, and only on the Day of Atonement, when, invoking the ineffable name of God, the high priest sought forgiveness for his own sins, that of the priestly family, and finally those of all Israel. The ancient ceremony described in the Talmud remains enshrined in traditional Jewish liturgy until this very day.[35]

Jews first sanctified the rock because of its link to the history of the Israelites, beginning with David, who made Jerusalem his capital, and Solomon, who erected the house to Yahweh there. In the second century CE references to the rock were fully integrated with rabbinic visions of cosmogony.[36] This melding of biblical history and creation myths, which became a feature of Jewish and then Christian lore of the Temple Mount, also became part and parcel of Muslim traditions, especially those featured in the literature praising the merits of Jerusalem. Indeed, some faḍā'il texts are best understood when examined in tandem with their Jewish (and also Christian) antecedents. The Muslim chronicler Ibn 'Asākir (d. 1176 CE) praises the Holy Land and its holy sites in a manner unmistakably linked to the Jewish tradition in which the rock, situated at the very center of the earth, is described as the fulcrum of several concentric places of holiness. Citing Thawr b. Yazīd (ca. eighth century CE), Ibn 'Asākir maintains: "The holiest part of the earth is al-Shām; the holiest part of al-Shām is [the subdistrict] Filasṭīn; the holiest part of Filasṭīn is Jerusalem (*Bayt al-Maqdis*), the holiest part of Jerusalem is the [temple] mount (*al jabal*); the holiest part of the mount is the temple [rendered in Arabic as *al-masjid*], and the holiest part of the temple is the dome (*qubbah*)." Quite obviously, "the dome" refers to the Dome of the Rock (*Qubbat al-Ṣahkrah*), the magnificent Islamic structure said by Muslims to surmount the primeval rock.[37]

Some Muslim allusions to Jewish tradition are readily apparent, but not all the references to Jewish lore are easily identifiable, nor would they have been in times past to most Muslims. On occasion, the echoes of Jewish tradition are so

34. BT, *Yoma* 54b; see also 2 Enoch 71:35.

35. The liturgy is that of the afternoon service (*musaf*) for the Day of Atonement. The role of the high priest is taken on by the cantor, who serves as the intercessor of the entire community.

36. Mishneh *Yoma* 5.2. (tracing the link to the Temple to the time of the first prophets). On the rock and rabbinic visions of cosmogony, see Alexander, "Omphalos of the World," 115–16.

37. Ibn 'Asākir, *Ta'rīkh* (Damascus, 1951–), 1:142.

faint that few current readers, let alone medieval Muslims not learned in Judaism, could fully grasp the Jewish (or in certain cases Christian) substratum.[38] Given the difficulty of dating specific rabbinic accounts, especially fragments preserved in later anthologies, caution is called for in ascribing paths of cultural influence. We cannot assume that all of Jewish tradition regarding Jerusalem and the Temple Mount circulated when Muslim scholars first commented systematically about the meaning of specific Qur'ānic passages. That caveat aside, early Muslim authorities living among Jews and learned Jewish converts (and also Christians and Christian converts) were certainly aware of various tales about the Temple Mount and Jerusalem, whether or not they acknowledged or knew enough to acknowledge their pre-Islamic origins. In any case, Jewish and also Christian material became enmeshed with the Islamic lore of Jerusalem, perhaps not in Muḥammad's lifetime but certainly by the time of the Qur'ān scholars writing around the turn of the first Islamic century and continuing well beyond.

The historian al-Muṭahhar b. Ṭāhir al-Maqdisī (ca. tenth century CE) evokes, consciously, or otherwise, Jewish lore of the holy city.[39] He makes no mention of rabbinic cosmogony, or of Adam, Abraham, and Isaac, but begins instead with Jacob's dream at Bethel. The story related in Arabic so closely follows the account of the Bible, in many respects it might seem to be a paraphrase of the original Hebrew. Maqdisī also introduces new elements. In his extended account, an awestruck Jacob does not build a house to God on his own initiative, as in Genesis. He does so according to God's command. And so, Jacob dutifully traced (*ikhtaṭṭa*) the foundation boundaries of the Temple (*masjid*). Following him, Khiḍr, a mysterious figure of Islamic lore identified with Enoch among others, traced the lines of the cupola (*qubbah*) of Jerusalem (*Īliyā'*).[40] Returning to Jewish tradition, the author reports that David began the task of building (a temple) at the site and that it was Solomon who completed the project. Nebuchadnezzar destroyed it, Cyrus rebuilt it, and Titus, the accursed Roman (*al-Rūmī al-mal'ūn*), destroyed it once again. As opposed to the Qur'ān scholars, Maqdisī correctly outlines the received Jewish version of the Temple's history. There is then reason to believe that the Muslim author may have been served, be it directly or indirectly, by a Jewish informant, or at least by an individual knowledgeable in Jewish tradition. One notes in this respect the intrigu-

38. See, for example, J. Lassner's treatment of Qur'ān 27:40: "The 'One Who had Knowledge of the Book' and the 'Mightiest Name of God': Qur'ānic Exegesis and Jewish Cultural Artifacts," *Studies in Jewish and Muslim Relations* 1 (1993): 59–74.

39. Maqdisī, *Bad'*, 4:87–88.

40. *EI*, s.v. "Khiḍr."

ing reference to Titus as the "accursed Roman," possibly an echo of the general's rabbinic epithet "may his bones be beaten to powder," that is, "may his remains be reduced to nothing."[41] More will be said of the primeval rock in a subsequent segment of this book that deals directly with Jewish-Muslim linkages, both real and imagined.[42]

The following chapter focuses in detail on Muslim interpretations of Qur'ān 17:1, the verse that Muslim scholars read as linking the Prophet directly to a miraculous event on what they called the Noble Sanctuary. Their interpretation suggests that Muslim reverence for Jerusalem, examined here as linked to Jewish tradition, was given a distinctively Muslim gloss and firmly planted in the imagination of the Prophet and his companions. Was that indeed the case? Or is the Jerusalem revered by Muslims a later historical development, an imaginary based on a particular reading of scripture, that is, an exegetical turn that was retroactively fitted to the Prophet and the early Muslim community?

---

41. For example *ARNA*, 4.
42. See chapter 9.

CHAPTER 3

The "Furthest Place of Worship"

Muslim Tradition and Modern Scholarship

Many Muslim scholars identified the destination of Muḥammad's journey in 17:1 as Jerusalem, or more specifically its Noble Sanctuary. By identifying the "furthermost place of worship" with the legendary Mount Moriah, these exegetes conjured up vivid images of a religious history going back to the moment of Creation. Muslim commentators and exegetes then turned their attention to still another enigmatic phrase: "God's manifest signs" shown to the Prophet Muḥammad. According to Muslim scholars, this vague reference to "signs" describes the circumstances of Muḥammad's ascent to heaven, a picture of a prophetic moment not unlike that experienced by the biblical Jacob at the very same place. A series of compelling and detailed narratives relate how Muḥammad made his way to Jerusalem and then up to the celestial abode accompanied by Gabriel, the angel assigned to assisting God's prophets. With Gabriel as his guide, Muḥammad passed by the other angels and the prophets previously sent by Allah. Angels, and prophets according to rank, lined the ascending stations of Muḥammad's heavenly path (as if welcoming his arrival and paying homage to his exalted status).

Other Muslim authorities indicate that Muḥammad did not meet the ancient prophets by ascending to the heavens; rather he encountered them by visiting their places of birth and burial, a journey mostly overland.[1] In an evolving Muslim tradition, the Holy Land was revered for the numerous prophets buried there, and pilgrims frequently visited the alleged gravesites.[2] Whether the Prophet's journey was horizontal or vertical, the point of encountering God's former messengers remains the same: Muḥammad was destined to receive the recognition of those previously favored by God. How else should the prophets

1. See chapter 2, n. 26 for an overview of the literature, medieval and modern.
2. See chapter 9.

of old have reacted to Muḥammad's arrival? Both a later Qur'ānic verse and subsequent Muslim tradition maintain that each and every prophet (sent to the Jews and Christians) had made a covenant with God to recognize the authenticity of his future messenger, and to proclaim the truth thereof to their respective communities.[3] With that obligation to God fulfilled, the truth of Muḥammad's vocation entered the sacred writings and oral traditions of both faith communities.

Does the commentary to 17:1 trumpet Muḥammad's credentials as the greatest of God's messengers and leave it at that, or is their more to this reading of scripture? By presenting Muḥammad as a worthy successor to God's previous prophets—so recognized by their honored assembly at his presence in Jerusalem—the interpreters of 17:1 seemingly offer their readers a subtle polemic. With a mere dollop of imagination, we can read their comments as a brief against those who would deny Muḥammad's prophetic vocation despite undeniable references to his future coming in their sacred books and religious tradition. Understanding the thrust of any such polemic would not have been difficult for Muslims encountering the text; the failure of Jews and Christians to acknowledge the legitimacy of the Prophet is a well-articulated theme of Muḥammad's revelations in Medina. Time and again, the Qur'ān castigates the older monotheists, especially the Jews, of denying a self-evident truth they know only too well. To sum up: The Qur'ānic verse, as understood by the later Muslim scholars, underscores that Muḥammad's nocturnal journey was a confirmation of his standing among God's prophets, and as if to accentuate the point, they identify the event with Jerusalem, the place revered above all others by recalcitrant fellow monotheists. Are we then to infer, based on Muslim commentary, that Jerusalem or the Temple Mount was clearly defined in the Qur'ān as a sacred site venerated by Muḥammad and his companions, just as it had been for generations of Jews and Christians? Were that so, the capture of the holy city from the Byzantines in 638 CE might have signified more than a demonstration of Arab military prowess. The Muslim conquest of the city might have given rise to significant religious fervor when the victors arrived at the celebrated place of the Prophet's nocturnal visit and ascent to the heavens.[4]

---

3. Ibn Iṣḥāq, *Sīrah*, 1:215–16. This polemical thrust of Qur'ān 3:75 [81] and the manner in which it was interpreted by the author of the *Sīrah* is discussed in J. Lassner, "The Covenant of the Prophets: Muslim Text, Jewish Subtext," *AJSR* 15 (1990): 207–38.

4. Since the idea was first promoted by C. H. Becker, historians of the first Islamic expansion have been inclined to regard the Arab conquest as occasioned by economic causes; namely, the breakdown of centralized authority in Arabia; the subsequent displacement of local populations; and a general decline of living space, concurrent, as it were, with war weariness inspired by debilitating conflict between the Byzantine and Sasanid authorities in their provinces north and northeast of Arabia. According to this view, Arab tribesmen relieved this pressure by crossing the now

The sweeping Muslim military success certainly stoked religious sensibilities among Christians and Jews. During the previous decade the Byzantine emperor Heraclius emptied the imperial treasury to raise and equip a massive army, and went on to reclaim Jerusalem from its Persian conquerors. Now, a few years later, unbelievers had once again occupied Jerusalem. Shaken Christians sought solace from an apocalyptical literature that pointed to eventual redemption from Muslim control.[5] As for the Jews, there is reason to believe they may

---

porous frontier as in pre-Islamic times to raid in the settled territories. However, given their swift military successes, the tribesmen displaying the banners of Islam conquered vast areas beyond the frontier and settled there permanently. Unlike past occasions when they melded into the local landscape, the Arabs carved out of the conquered provinces what to all intents and purposes was to become a nascent Islamic state. The concise quintessential statement of this view can be found in Becker's essay "The Expansion of the Saracens—the East," in the *Cambridge Medieval History* (last reprint with corrections Cambridge, 1987), 2:329–89; esp. 329–55. These ideas were formulated by Becker in his detailed studies that appeared from 1924 to 1932. See his *Islamstudien* (Leipzig, 1924–32).

A later and extremely brief assessment of the conquest intended for a general scholarly audience is L. Vecca Vaglieri's "The Patriarchal and Umayyad Caliphates," in *Cambridge History of Islam* (Cambridge, 1970), 1:58–60. She endorses broadly Becker's description of events but adds, "Nevertheless, despite all these concomitant circumstances, the decisive factor in this success was Islam, which was the co-ordinating element behind the efforts of the beduin, and installed in the hearts of the warriors the belief that a war against the followers of another faith was holy war, and that the booty was the recompense offered by God to His soldiers" (60). Linking Islam to the motivation of the Arab tribesmen is more fully developed by F. Donner, who meticulously reviewed the relevant Arabic sources in his revisionist study *The Early Islamic Conquests* (Princeton, 1981) and later in "The Origins of the Islamic State," *JAOS* 106 (1986): 283–96. The question of early Muslim self-identity is a theme frequently stressed by Donner in lectures and other presentations. It is not entirely clear that Donner's revisionist view reflects the actual state of the past. Christian Arab tribes also contributed to the earliest campaigns. While Islamic authority, such as it was, could be considered the cement that held the whole enterprise together, the early campaigns were for the most part loosely coordinated and reflect the desire for quick enrichment rather than promoting the new faith. General support for Donner's point of view is found in S. Shoemaker's *The Death of a Prophet*, a most recent and provocative revisionist view of Islamic origins. Shoemaker argues that the Prophet did not die in 632 CE as indicated in the traditional Islamic narrative, but lived on to lead the early Islamic conquests with the backing of a highly eclectic community of believers including many Jews and even Christians, all seeking to initiate the messianic age. The armies led by the Prophet included other monotheists living in the disputed territories along with Arab tribesmen from Arabia. The scholarly world waits for a measured response to this challenging view of the conquest and the formation of the earliest community of believers. For a concise and thoughtful summary of the Arab conquests, see M. Bonner, *Jihād in Islamic History* (Princeton, 2006), 56–76.

5. A most recent survey of this material is S. H. Griffith, *The Church in the Shadow of the Mosque* (Princeton, 2008), 23–44; W. Kaegi, "Initial Byzantine Reactions to the Arab Invasions," *Church History* 10 (1969): 139–49 and more fully developed in his *Byzantium and the Early Islamic Conquests* (Cambridge, 1992). A brief summary of Christian and Jewish reactions to the Muslim conquest of the Holy Land and holy city can be found in G. Stemberger, "Jerusalem in the Early Seventh Century: Hopes and Aspirations of Christians and Jews," in *Jerusalem*, edited by L. Levine, 260–72; and the more detailed account of G. J. Reinink, "Ps.-Methodius: A Concept of History in Response to the Rise of Islam," in *The Byzantine and Early Islamic Near East: Papers of the First Workshop on Late Antiquity and Early Islam*, edited by A. Cameron and L. Conrad (Princeton, 1992), 149–87, based on Reinink's edition of Ps.-Methodius: *Die Syrische Apokalypse des Pseudo Methodius* (Louvain, 1993); see also P. J. Alexander, *The Byzantine Apocalyptic Tradition* (Berkeley, 1985). Alexander's study includes the European reception of Ps.-Methodius, including late medieval texts.

have viewed the onset of Islamic rule with favor, not only because it removed the yoke of recent Christian oppression. The Muslim conquest came to be seen as a prelude to the messianic age, the rebuilding of the Jewish Temple, and the ultimate salvation of God's chosen people. Such expectations, seemingly present when Persians ruled the city from 614 to 628, were reflected once again, this time in Jewish messianic texts said to originate from the time of the Islamic conquest.[6] We are still left to ponder how Muslims might have resonated to the conquest of the city most holy to Jews and Christians. Was similar reverence for Jerusalem reflected in contemporaneous Muslim views? And, as for our immediate concern, how did the Prophet and his contemporaries view the city, and how might the Prophet's night journey illuminate this question?

The suggested anti-Jewish (and also anti-Christian) polemic advanced in the commentary to 17:1 would seem to reflect Muḥammad's views during his Medinian period, a time when the Prophet was in direct conflict with the Jews and had theological issues with the Christians. But Muslim and Western scholars attribute the verse to the Prophet's earlier preaching in Mecca. One would have to conclude, therefore, that if the polemical commentary boldly ascribed here to the commentators has any reality, it was engineered by the hindsight one gains when viewing history in retrospect, a scholarly approach often practiced by later Muslim scholars whether explicating scripture or writing the history of the Prophet and his time. The same can be said for identifying the *masjid al-aqṣā* of Muslim scripture with Jerusalem and the Temple Mount. However, not all Muslim scholars accepted that the masijd al-Aqṣā of 17:1 represented Jerusalem. There was also a difference of opinion whether the Prophet's ascent to heaven, which is not mentioned explicitly in the verse, should be linked to the *isrā'* and whether it was a real event and not an awesome dream. There is also speculation as to whether Muḥammad visited the burial places of the earlier prophets interred in the Holy Land.[7] The very opaqueness of the verse in question begged for interpretive license, and Muslim scholars were more than willing to oblige.

Modern scholars of the West are skeptical of linking 17:1 to any historical or geographical reality. In their view, the Qur'ānic passage refers not to Jerusalem but to an imagined place, the final destination of a mystical journey.[8] A

6. Stemberger, "Jerusalem in the Early Seventh Century," 266–71. For a detailed analysis of the Jewish apocalyptical traditions, see chapter 4; also chapter 2, n. 10, for the possible linkage between the Sasanid conquest of Jerusalem and Jewish messianic expectations.

7. References to these diverse opinions can be found inter alia in Ṭabarī's Qur'ān commentary (*Jāmi' al-bayān*) discussing 17:1.

8. For a review of Western literature on Qur'ān 17:1, see Gilliot, "*Isrā'* dans la recherche occidentale," 1 ff.

miraculous undertaking would not have been unique for one truly invested with a prophetic calling. Nocturnal visions have been the stock and trade of those receiving God's revelation since the most ancient of times. Not surprisingly, some Orientalists have linked the *isrā'* and *mi'rāj* with the account of the biblical prophet Ezekiel, who experienced a vision that he was miraculously transported from Babylon to one of Jerusalem's temple gates. There the ancient prophet relates having seen the glory of his God (Ezek. 8). Whether or not Muslims of Muḥammad's circle had some inkling of these biblical passages, let alone associated Ezekiel 8 with the accounts of the isrā' and mi'rāj, remains unanswered, if not indeed unanswerable.[9] For most modern Islamicists, the interpretation of 17:1 rendered by Qur'ān commentary and other post-Qur'ānic writings is a reflection of views first held by Muslim scholars sometime before the emergence of the second Islamic century; by no means are they thought to preserve echoes of Muslim views from the outset of Islam. Contrary to Muslim Qur'ān commentary and exegesis, the holiness ascribed to Jerusalem by the faithful postdated the age of the Prophet. To be sure, there remains the reference to Jerusalem as *ūlat al-qiblatayn*, the first place to which Muslims directed their prayers, but that practice, however it may have been understood, was abandoned during the Prophet's lifetime (Qur'ān 2:150, 143–45).[10]

Revisionist Views Connecting 17:1 with Historic Jerusalem

Charting a course different from that of most Orientalists, Uri Rubin contends that the learned Muslim exegetes captured the intended meaning of the Qur'ānic passage, and that the earliest generation of the faithful truly believed the Prophet journeyed to the real holy city, albeit with divine assistance and di-

9. There is no established reference for Ezekiel in the Qur'ān. A. Yūsuf Ali's identification of the mysterious Dhū-l-Kifl of Qur'ān 21:85 with Ezekiel is offered without any foundation. See *The Meaning of the Glorious Qur'ān*, 2nd edition (London, 1983; earlier versions published in Lahore), 965 (reference to Ezekiel in index). There are brief references to Ezekiel (Ḥizqīl) in Qur'ān commentary and exegesis, including historical sources and the Arabic literature devoted to the tales of the biblical prophets (*qiṣaṣ al-anbiyā'*), but I have found no references linking him to the famous night journey. Muslim scholars considered Qur'ān 2:243 [244], "Have you not considered those who went forth from their dwelling places in thousands in fear of death? God said to them, 'Die,' but afterward brought them back to life," as words originally spoken by Ezekiel (presumably influenced by Ezek. 27:1–14). See *EI*, s.v. "Ḥizkīl."

10. For a discussion of these verses relating to the merits of Jerusalem, see A. Neuwirth, "Jerusalem and the Genesis of Islamic Scripture," in *Jerusalem*, edited by L. Levine, 315–26. See also her "Erste Qiblah." The precise moment at which the orientation of prayer was redirected to Mecca cannot be determined.

vine purpose. The only question was whether he did so in a nocturnal vision or was transported corporeally.[11] A scholar noted for highly imaginative readings enhanced by a superb command of Arabic and Arabic sources, Rubin initially grounds his claims for this counterintuitive argument in a philological analysis of *aqṣā* (feminine *qiṣwā*), "furthest," *asrā* (verbal noun *isrā'*), "undertake a journey," and *baraknā ḥawlahu*, in reference to the place whose "surroundings [God] blessed."[12] Turning to all of Muslim scripture, he observes that *aqṣā* and the feminine form *qiṣwā* are always used to denote earthly travel rather than a journey through sacred space, as in Qur'ān 28:20, where Moses is warned by a man "coming from the furthest part of the city (*ja'a min aqṣā-l-madīnah*)," and in 36:20, where the exact same expression is employed with regard to another person giving warning. Rubin also cites a verse from the segment of the Qur'ān that deals with the battle of Badr, the first great victory achieved by the nascent Muslim community. Regarding the impending battle, the text speaks of the Muslims assembled at the nearest end of the valley (*bi-l-'udwat al-dunyā*) and the enemy at the farthest end (*bi-l-'udwat al-qiṣwā*) (Qur'ān 8:42). He also notes two second-century Muslim sources that state the Prophet, then in his eighth year at Medina, undertook a minor pilgrimage (*'umrah*) to Mecca and paused to pray at a place near Ji'rānah. Muḥammad reportedly prayed there at the masjid al-aqṣā (so named because it was) located at the "far end of the valley (*'udwat al-aqṣā*)" approaching Ji'rānah, as opposed to a second mosque, the *masjid al-adnā*, situated at the near end of the valley.[13]

As for *asrā*, "undertake a journey," and *isrā'*, "journey," Rubin indicates five places in Muslim scripture, each dealing with the history of the ancient Israelites and each referring to a biblical figure moving from one place on earth to another: Three times Moses takes the Israelites out of Egypt, and twice Lot is mentioned as fleeing Sodom with his family.[14] The last phrase in 17:1 exam-

11. U. Rubin, "Muḥammad's Night Journey (*Isrā'*) to al-Masjid al-Aqṣā: Aspects of the Earliest Origins of the Islamic Sanctity of Jerusalem," *Al-Qanṭara* 29 (2008): 147–64. See 148 n. 2 for references to earlier scholarly literature cited by Rubin and chapter 2, n. 26.

12. Rubin, "Muḥammad's Night Journey," 150–53.

13. Rubin, "Muḥammad's Night Journey," citing Wāqidī, *Maghāzī*, 3:958–59 and Azraqī, *Akhbār Makkah*, 430. Ṭabarī, *Annales*, 1/3:1669, 1670, 1674–75, and 1685 describes Ji'rānah as the place where Muḥammad defeated his enemies from Ṭā'if and divided the spoils among the Muslims (no mention of Badr). Ḥamdānī, *Ṣifat Jazīrat al-'Arab* lists Ji'rānah as being in the vicinity of Mecca; Yāqūt, *Mu'jam*, 2:85–86, places it between Ṭā'if and Mecca, closer to the latter. He refers to the distribution of booty and indicates that there was a mosque there (no indication of a second mosque). A. Guillaume, "Where Was the Masjid al-Aqṣā?," *Al-Andalus* 18 (1953): 323–36, attempts to link the mosque spoken of to the al-Aqṣā in Jerusalem, but that is not possible in light of the available sources.

14. Qur'ān 20:77 and 26:53 (referring to the Exodus from Egypt); 44:23 (with specific reference to traveling by night); 11:81 and 15:65 (referring to Lot leaving Sodom at night), thus connecting *asrā*, *isrā'* with actual travel and beyond that travel at night, as Rubin claims for 17:1.

ined by Rubin is "whose surroundings [God] blessed (*baraknā ḥawlahu*)."[15] He argues that the use of *baraknā* in the Qur'ān (with the preposition *fī*) is found four times in Muslim scripture, three in connection with the Holy Land, the other in a story about the Sabaeans of southern Arabia, a people who appear to have stayed at way stations between their home territory and "the cities God blessed." The first three verses address the Israelite conquest of Canaan, described as a land God "had [already] blessed" (7:137); the emigration of Abraham and Lot (to Canaan), "the land blessed [by God] for all people" (21:71); and Solomon's command of the strong wind (*'āṣifah*) that transported him to the "blessed land" (that is, to Canaan, which in Solomon's time was the united Kingdom of Israel, 21:81). The fourth reference (Qur'ān 34:17 [18]) reads: "We have established between them and the cities (*qurā*) upon which we have bestowed blessing towns in prominent places (*qurā ẓāhirah*) and have established them as waystations along a measured route. Travel there secure night or day." The Qur'ān commentators saw the story of the Sabaeans as alluding to Yemenite participation in international trade (*matājir*), a lucrative venture that took them to the "cities God blessed," meaning the caravan terminals of al-Shām.[15] Given Abraham's prominent links to Mecca in Islamic tradition, all these citations refer to what Rubin labels elsewhere an axis of sanctity between Arabia and the Holy Land, more explicitly between Mecca and Jerusalem. Qur'ān 17:1 is therefore but one piece in that larger picture of actual travel between Arabia and the Holy Land.[16]

15. The earliest preserved Qur'ān commentary, the *Tafsīr* of Muqātil b. Sulaymān (eighth century AH) indicates that the "blessed cities" are in *al-arḍ al-muqaddasah*, which he defines as al-Urdunn (Jordan) and Filasṭīn (Palestine), both subdistricts of al-Shām (Greater Syria). Between the blessed cities and Yemen (home to the Sabaeans) were various "cities" or "settlements" (*qurā*) with markets from which goods were transported from Syria to Yemen and back. See inter alia the citations of early Qur'ān commentary in Ṭabarī's discussion of verse 34:18–19 in his *Jāmiʿ al-Bayān*. These comments amplify Ibn Sulaymān's understanding of the "blessed" cities and the verse as a whole. As for the "blessed cities," Ṭabarī cites Qatādah and Mujāhid, who understand the verse as referring to Bayt al-Maqdis (which may signify the city of Jerusalem or its surroundings, or less likely all of al-arḍ al-muqaddasah). Ṭabarī also cites Ibn 'Abbās, who refers to the cities as al-arḍ al-muqaddasah, an ambiguous geographical label. For al-arḍ al-muqaddasah, see chapter 2. As does Ibn Sulaymān, Ṭabarī, citing various authorities, explains the function of the way stations in the conduct of long-distance trade. However, the authorities he cites (Qatādah, Mujāhid, Ibn Zayd) only speak of trade between (the caravan terminals) of al-Shām and Medina, which in the time of the Prophet and the righteous caliphs was the administrative center of the nascent Islamic state. Were that the case, their understanding of the cities "adjoining" al-Shām may well have been the settlements of the Wādī-l-Qurā that lay between the Hijaz cities and the caravan terminals of al-Shām.

16. U. Rubin, "Between Arabia and the Holy Land: A Mecca-Jerusalem Axis of Sanctity," *JSAI* 34 (2008): 345–62. In the 2016 meetings of the American Oriental Society, Nathaniel Miller argued that in Arabian inscriptions and pre-Islamic poetry claims were made by Syrian and South Arabian monarchs to project their power over long distances. For Miller the isrā' can be understood as "spiritualization of a contemporary Arabian and Hijazi notion of political power."

Based on Rubin's philological observations, the Prophet's nocturnal travel was meant to be understood as a journey to an actual place located in the historic city revered by Jews and Christians. Does Rubin tease too much out of the verses he cites in support of this view? If the key vocabulary in 17:1 is used elsewhere in scripture to denote a terrestrial locale and an actual journey to or from a given place, are we to maintain that the same words cannot be employed to reflect a mystical journey to a heavenly destination? How else could the text describe the Prophet's nocturnal travel and miraculous visit to the heavenly abode? I cannot see how the verses quoted by Rubin prove beyond doubt that when Muḥammad's companions considered "the furthest place of worship" they envisioned the holy city across the Byzantine frontier.

Even if we were to be persuaded by Rubin's philology, we would still be left to wonder what Muḥammad and his companions made of his visit to the real Jerusalem. What purpose was served by claiming that the Prophet was transported by God to the city venerated by Jews and Christians? Post-Qur'ānic writings relate that Muḥammad, after miraculously returning to Mecca in time for the next day's prayer—ordinarily a month's journey—described to his amazed listeners the extraordinary reception he received in God's heavenly abode. The Prophet's account reportedly stirred the emotion of his companions, as it reinforced belief in him and his mission, for only a true messenger of God could have been privileged to undertake such a journey. But the Qur'ānic text read at face value without the benefit of this later commentary offers no hint whatsoever as to how or why the nocturnal visit resonated with the earliest Muslims. Can the answer be found by reading the opening verse in tandem with the text that follows?

Qur'ān 17:2–8 and the Temples of Jerusalem

Read literally, 17:1 seems, at first glance, completely detached from the following verses, references to how the ancient Israelites were, according to their own scripture, destined to suffer two calamities for having been arrogantly corrupt. For given the option of "doing good and benefiting," they did the opposite and "suffered loss" in their own land not once but twice.[17] To quote from 17:7: "So

17. For an analysis of Qur'ān 17:2–8, see H. Busse's thorough treatment of the Arabic sources in his "The Destruction of the Temple in Jerusalem and Its Reconstruction in Light of Sūra 17:2–8," *JSAI* 20 (1996): 1–17. Busse also cites the extensive Christian literature that links the fate of the Jews with their sinful acts (9–12). Compare 17:2–8 with Qur'ān 2:114 (see chapter 2). The views of the early commentators are cited in Ṭabarī's *Jāmi' al-bayān* in dealing with these verses.

when the time of the last prediction comes to pass, they [your enemies] will bring evil on your leaders and enter the temple (*masjid*) a second time as they did the first, and utterly destroy what they conquered." Consciously or otherwise, the Qur'ān invokes the theology of the biblical Deuteronomist as regards rewarding good and punishing evil; castigates the Israelites for failing to heed the laws (*aḥkām*) of the Torah (stated explicitly by the exegetes); and seemingly refers, however vaguely, to the destruction of Solomon's Temple and that of Herod. Given our interests, we have to ask whether these verses inform us of how Muslims in Muḥammad's entourage resonated to Jerusalem, and above all whether they revered the city as being holy for them as it was for Jews and Christians.

The Muslim commentators with their skewed vision of the Jewish past are mired in confusion while providing verses 17:2–8 with a historical context. As they did with Qur'ān 2:114, a verse dealt with in the previous chapter, Muslim scholars embellished the ancient history of the Jews, linking historic actors and events in a most improbable fashion.[18] In addition to the villains previously mentioned, namely Nebuchadnezzar, Antiochus, Titus, and the enigmatic Khardūs (or Khardaws), king of Babylon, the commentary to 17:7 introduces other biblical personages said to have had a hand in the destruction of the Jewish Temple(s). The new accusation is broad reaching and refers to several events centered at Jerusalem, some not explicitly linked by the biblical chroniclers to the destruction of the Solomonic house of worship. Thus, Goliath is mentioned in some Arabic sources as the first to destroy the Temple, no doubt a reference to the Philistines carrying off the holy ark as the spoils of war.[19] Similarly, Sennacherib (704–683 BCE) is introduced, in this case referring to the aborted siege of Jerusalem mentioned in the book of Kings and described by the prophet Isaiah.[20] In the first instance the ark was removed from the sanctuary at Shiloh; the Temple was yet to be built. In the second, the Temple was untouched thanks to the miraculous intervention of the Almighty, who sent upon the Assyrian hosts a plague that forced them to abandon the siege of Jerusalem. Muddying the waters of the past still further, the fate of the second place of worship—presumably understood by Muḥammad's followers as Herod's Temple—is linked to Parthian and Sasanid emperors (*akāsirah* and *majūs*) who ruled long after the destruction of the building in 70 CE. And if that were not enough, adding to the earlier account of Christians collaborating with pagans in ravaging Jerusalem, Muslim scholars commenting on 17:2–8

18. Busse, "Destruction of the Temple," 2–16; H. Schützinger, "Arabische Legende," 113–14.
19. 1 Sam. 4–6.
20. 2 Kings 18:13–19:37 and Isa. 36–37; also 2 Chron. 32:1–23.

introduce other ancient peoples for whom we have no record of involvement with the historic events seemingly referred to in the Qur'ān.

Clearly, various Muslim writers took license to expand what appears to be the original message of the text, namely that the Jews acting arrogantly and in perfidious fashion brought upon themselves the wrath of God, who then sent foreign rulers acting as his agents to punish the Jews and destroy their holy city and its central shrine. The original message was probably intended as a moral pronouncement about walking in the ways of the Lord lest one run the risk of divine punishment, as did the deviant Israelites of old. As 17:8 puts it: "If you revert to your previous [arrogant and sinful] behavior, We shall return [to punishing you as before]." Because it was vague as regards place and time, this last verse opened the door to all sorts of imaginative interpretations; it enabled Muslim exegetes to move beyond the historic destruction of the temples and extend the punishment of the ancient Israelites to include the misdeeds of Jews at later moments of history. The two houses of worship explicitly mentioned in the Qur'ān as destroyed were seen as forerunners to events yet to take place, among them the recalcitrance of the Jews who would not accept the legitimacy of Muḥammad's mission, and subsequent to that the expulsion of Jews from their enclaves in Arabia, the equivalent of the two major exiles that followed the Babylonian and Roman conquests of Jerusalem.[21] The Qur'ān scholar Rāzī (ca. twelfth to thirteenth century CE), who often expresses antagonism to Jews and Christians, ascribes the first destruction to the usual suspects and for the usual reasons. But he then attributes the second to Constantine I, the Byzantine emperor who embraced Christianity and made it the official state religion. This reading of 17:7 enables Rāzī to criticize the sinful behavior of the Jews while at the same time implicating the Christians in destroying a place of worship dedicated to the one true God. Rāzī's understanding of the verse may have been colored by Constantine's effort to create a sacred space for Christians in what was termed a "New Jerusalem," the holy precinct beyond the Temple Mount, whose ancient buildings were leveled and its surface left rubble strewn. There is, however, nothing in his explication of the verse that speaks to how 17:7 might have been viewed by Muḥammad's companions.[22] They most likely understood the

21. Busse, "Destruction of the Temple," 6–7.

22. Busse, "Destruction of the Temple," 7, citing Qurṭubī, *Jāmi'*, 10:222 and Rāzī, *Tafsīr*, 20:158 ff. (an attempt to link the text to the apocalyptical mood created by the Christian loss of Jerusalem to the Sasanians in the seventh century CE). Rubin's attempt to link these verses to "the hopes (read messianic expectations) and fears of the Jews and Christians of Arabia . . . and . . . with an Islamic messianic longing for Jerusalem" seems to me more than a bit of a stretch in the absence of any tangible evidence. Although Rāzī's accusing Christians of participating in the destruction of the Jewish Temple is paralleled in several Muslim commentaries on Qur'ān 2:114, his specific reference linking Constantine to the destruction of the Temple is to my knowledge unique (perhaps these

verse as a general moral pronouncement and more particularly as reflecting the Prophet's difficult relationship with the Jewish tribes of Arabia. In any case, there is nothing in 17:2–8 that leads us to believe that early Muslims embraced Jerusalem as they did Mecca and Medina, and that the holy city of Christians and Jews stirred Muslim religious emotions as it would in generations to follow.

As with the content of many Meccan sūrahs, the verses immediately following the account of the isrā' link reward and punishment. But what link if any is there between the opening verse of the sūrah and what comes thereafter? What has Muḥammad's trip to the furthermost place of worship and the heavenly abode to do with the failure of the Israelites to follow God's path. In his *Geschichte des Qorans*, published in 1860, a puzzled Theodor Nöldeke suggested that the redactors of Muslim scripture may have omitted several verses that originally followed the opening of Sūrah 17, and in doing so obscured its intended meaning (and possible link to the verses that follow).[23] The opening section of the sūrah certainly invites informed speculation. Looking at the redacted version, the only apparent connection between the initial verse and the six that follow is reference to a masjid in both 17:1 and 17:7; the first to the mysterious masjid al-aqṣā, the second almost certainly to the Temple(s) in Jerusalem. One could establish a more direct connection between the two references to a masjid by accepting the commentary to 17:1 that declares the masjid al-aqṣā to be in the holy city, or more specifically on Jerusalem's Temple Mount. That is indeed Rubin's contention.

The positioning of individual verses and subsegments of Muslim scripture is at times difficult to fathom; the text is highly disjointed; sūrahs labeled as Meccan and Medinian are all too often composite texts of Muḥammad's preaching. Different revelations are spliced together for no apparent reason, at least none that were or can be safely determined by medieval or modern scholars. Aside from the opening sūrah and some of the very short early revelations, only the twelfth, the story of the biblical Joseph, reads as a coherent whole with a beginning, middle, and end. In that respect, Muslim scripture resembles certain prophetic works of the Hebrew Bible. Like the pronouncements of the Hebrew prophets, Muḥammad's revelations feature clipped language, intricate cadences, and highly allusive messages. Undeterred by the difficulty of elusive biblical verses, the rabbis moved beyond the literal meaning of texts—what

accounts represent an echo of changing the religious orientation of the city from the Temple Mount to the emperor's New Jerusalem). See text below.

23. T. Nöldeke, *Geschichte des Qorans*, 2nd edition (Hildesheim, 1970 reprint), 1:134; see also J. Horovitz, "Muḥammeds Himmelfahrt," *Der Islam* 9 (1918): 162 and J. Wansbrough, *Quranic Studies* (London, 1977), 68.

they termed the *peshat*—and with considerable imagination and a display of intellectual pyrotechnics, they derived a wide range of readings from scripture, the technique known as *derash*. Passages of the Hebrew Bible were inserted as proof texts within a didactic literature of the rabbis' invention. As a result, the ancient rabbis were able to expand exponentially the intent of biblical authors. As regards matters of biblical legislation, the rabbis applied a series of hermeneutic principles to given passages, a method that enabled them to expand laws that were fixed in time and place in order that they might apply to the needs of a contemporary age. Similarly, one can readily understand the need for Muslims a generation and more removed from Muḥammad to delve beyond the literal meaning of the revealed text so that it might serve as a guide for their own times.

That still leaves us with unenviable task of reclaiming the Qur'ān's *peshat*. Conscious of the need to establish a historical context that led Muḥammad to associate the "furthest place of worship" with the real Jerusalem, and with that to establish a unity for the first eight verses of the sūrah, Rubin invokes the Christian "Heavenly Jerusalem," a concept rooted in a New Testament apocalypse, where a pristine city descends from on high to replace an earthly Jerusalem marked by corruption.[24] When Constantine I (r. 306–37 CE) embraced Christianity and declared it the official religion of the East Roman Empire, the term "Heavenly Jerusalem" was applied to the Christianized earthly city. Constantine's New Jerusalem replaced pagan Aelia Capitolina, the city named after a Roman imperial family and a triad of pagan deities. The skyline of pagan Jerusalem featured a temple to Jupiter that dominated the ancient Temple Mount and a column of the emperor Hadrian mounted on horseback. The Roman city was thus meant to symbolize a total break with the Jewish past, punishment, as it were, for the ill-fated Jewish rebellions against imperial authority in the first and second century CE. Following the creation of Aelia Capitolina, only a small number of Jews continued to reside in an urban area that had once been the fulcrum of their religious and political identity. Jews, celebrating the rich history of the past, continued to visit the site of their destroyed Temple, but their hopes of rebuilding it never materialized.

When Constantine I embraced Jesus, pagan Jerusalem was, in turn, displaced by a city that valorized Christianity, a New Jerusalem for a new imperial faith. Among the numerous buildings erected by the first Christian emperor

24. Rev. 3:12, 21:2. For a general survey of Byzantine Jerusalem, see the various studies in part 3 of *Jerusalem*, edited by L. Levine, 133–274, esp. Y. Tsafrir, "The Configuration of the Christian City," 133–50 and Z. Rubin, "The Cult of the Holy Places and Christian Politics in Byzantine Jerusalem," 150–62; and more generally G. Stemberger. *Juden und Christen in Heiligen Land* (Munich, 1987).

was the magnificent Church of the Holy Sepulcher, the quintessential symbol of Christianity's recently established dominance in the region. Streams of Christian pilgrims and pietists now made their way to the Holy Land and holy city, just as Jewish pilgrims had done during the yearly festivals associated with the Temple. Many Christian visitors stayed for long periods of time, others settled permanently. The influx required the development of hostels, hospitals, and shelters. Most important was the new regime's efforts to eliminate all traces of the pagan past. Pagan buildings were demolished for building material or remodeled into places of Christian devotion. The local authorities mapped out a sacred historic topography that enabled Christians participating in newly formed liturgical processions to reenact Jesus's movements in the holy city, a precursor to the current walks along the Via Dolorosa at Easter time.[25] The release of such emotions also gave rise to an active trade in religious relics, the expression of an increasingly vibrant popular religion. The political center of the Holy Land may have remained in Caesarea and the hub of imperial rule was situated as before in Byzantium, but in the wake of these developments Jerusalem emerged for most Christians as the most sacred of sacred places in Syria-Palaestina, if not all the empire, the protestation of some anti-Jerusalemites notwithstanding.[26]

No Christian monuments were constructed where the temple to Jupiter had been positioned and before that where the temples of Solomon and Herod had stood. The Temple Mount, revered by Jews even after the destruction of the Second Temple, was to remain strewn with rubble to mark their perfidious behavior in times past and their continued recalcitrance at accepting Jesus Christ. As if to reinforce this negative perception of the Jews, the authorities permitted them to ascend the Temple Mount only on the ninth day of Ab, a day of fasting in which Jews recognized their past sins and memorialized the destruction of their holiest shrine. Constantine's Jerusalem, labeled "heavenly" by the fourth-century author Eusebius, took shape elsewhere within a larger urban environment. The lavish monuments of the "New Jerusalem" were intended to signify the ultimate triumph of Christianity over the pagan past and the continuing conflict with the Jews. The plan was to eviscerate all traces of paganism and not allow even a symbolic resurgence of Judaism. But the sacred credentials of

25. See B. Bitton-Ashkenazy, "The Attitudes of the Church Fathers towards Pilgrimage to Jerusalem in the Fourth and Fifth Centuries," in *Jerusalem*, edited by L. Levine, 188–203; J. Baldovin, *The Urban Character of Christian Worship* (Rome, 1987); R. Wilkin, *The Land Called Holy* (New Haven, 1992), 108–25. J. Wilkinson, *Pilgrims before the Crusades* (Jerusalem, 1997).

26. Z. Rubin, "The Church of the Holy Sepulcher and the Beginning of the Conflict between the Sees of Caesarea and Jerusalem," *Jerusalem Cathedra* 2 (1982): 76–106, and more generally, P. Walker, *Holy City, Holy Places* (Oxford, 1990).

the Jewish Temple Mount apparently still circulated among Jerusalemites be they Jewish or Christian. Rather than deny outright the legends that accrued to Mount Moriah, the ecclesiastical authorities adapted them to new sites, creating thereby a new sacred topography within the expanded area of New Jerusalem. Christians claimed that it was on a site within New Jerusalem that God had created Adam; that Abraham had bound Isaac; and that Jesus had been crucified and buried. The sublime Church of the Holy Sepulcher had replaced not only the pagan structure that surmounted Christ's tomb; it superseded the sacred Temple Mount of the Jews. The rock of Golgotha where Jesus was crucified and later interred had in effect replaced the rock of the Temple Mount as the foundation stone of the earth. The ancient Jewish *even shetiyah* gave way to a new Christian *lapis pertusus.*

The distinction between the Heavenly Jerusalem or New Jerusalem of the Christians and the ruined Temple Mount of the Jews gives Rubin license to link the farthest place of worship of 17:1 with the destroyed temples of 17:7. In that sense, he echoes the aforementioned Qur'ān commentary of Rāzī. But Rubin takes this link well beyond Rāzī's blank statement that the Byzantine Christians were responsible for the destruction of a second place of Jewish worship. He opines that just as Christians in late antiquity drew a line between Christian New Jerusalem and the sin-filled Jewish city of old, a line drawn in sacred sand, so to speak, the account of the isrā' draws a line of its own. By sanctifying the Temple Mount anew, Muslim scripture redeems a sacred space from the ruins occasioned by the previous sins of the Jews and the purposeful neglect of the Christians. In effect, Rubin maintains that Muḥammad's nocturnal journey signifies the rededication of the Temple Mount and the creation of still another New Jerusalem, albeit one of the Muslims.[27] If this were the original meaning of 17:1, the Islamization of Jerusalem was already an integral part of Muslim thinking from almost the very beginning of Islam. Are we then to assume that the medieval Muslim scholars were right and the Islamicists of the modern West are in error?

There is no direct or even indirect reference in Muslim scripture to the aforementioned events of the fourth century. The link between Constantine and the desecration of the Temple is mentioned in Qur'ān commentary but only in passing and only in late sources. There is no compelling need to superimpose this later interpretation of 17:7 on how the Prophet's followers understood the verse. Rubin's reading of the Qur'ānic text is highly conjectural. Be that as it may, conjecture is one of the conceptual tools with which historians of

27. Rubin, "Cult of the Holy Places," 153–55.

the murky Islamic past must work. One can hardly begrudge Rubin the highly imaginative approach he has chosen to address the questions before us. What concerns me is the lack of tangible evidence that might serve as a convenient point of entry into an elaborate argument ultimately built on questionable assumptions. On the other hand, *if* we were to accept the Qur'ān commentary to 17:1–8 as truly reflecting Muḥammad's thinking in Mecca—a most significant *if* indeed—we might, with considerable license, claim that verses 1–8 represent a single literary unit, and that this unit can best be understood as a polemic against the Jews of Medina, but with an argument that leads readers back to a well-known ancient history of Jewish malfeasance.

In this suggested reading based on Qur'ān commentary, the honor bestowed on Muḥammad by the heavenly beings and most significantly by the Israelite prophets of old is designed to prove he was a legitimate messenger of God, thus reinforcing what was written in Jewish scripture and promulgated in Jewish tradition. It then follows that if Jews, going against the grain of what they knew to be true, denied this truth, they were merely acting as did their ancestors who twice denied God's edicts and were forced to pay for their inequities. Each time their disobedience resulted in the destruction of their Temple, a building that stood on the very ground where Muḥammad's mission was validated (17:2–8). God, who is "All-Hearing and All-Seeing," was not deceived by their actions. His "manifest signs" (17:1) made known to Muḥammad were also the record of God's intervention in earthly affairs—in this case God's punishment visited upon the Jews for their sins. The Qur'ān scholars commenting on 17:2–8 list these sins as abandoning the laws of the Torah; killing a number of God's prophets, including John the Baptist; and intending to kill Jesus. These condemnable acts are referred to elsewhere in Muslim scripture and its commentary.[28]

Seeing the opening eight verses as representing a coherent unit may give explanation to a problematic text, but it rests heavily, if not almost entirely, on views promulgated a century and more after the Prophet's revelation in Mecca and reflects the anti-Jewish sentiments that emerge prominently during Muḥammad's mission in Medina. Moreover, the exegetes never explicitly claim any connection between the opening verse of the sūrah and the seven that follow. Accordingly, this second reading of 17:1–8 should be taken for what is: musing about a difficult text rather than a literary-historical analysis born of conviction. I am inclined to agree with those modern scholars who regard 17:1 to be of Meccan origins and 17:2–8 to reflect prophetic utterances

---

28. See n. 17.

by Muḥammad in Medina where he experienced rejection by the Jews.[29] Similarly, I agree with the majority of Orientalists who claim the Qur'ānic commentary on the isrā' is a back-projection of a later era, and not as Rubin suggests, the echo, however distorted, of how and why Muḥammad and his followers equated the furthest place of worship with a terrestrial Jerusalem.

I admire Rubin's embrace of Arabic philology, a discipline that has been woefully neglected among the linguistically challenged, but it remains to be seen whether his brief, which lacks a convincing historical context, will be accepted by the current fraternity of Western scholars. Unlike Rubin, the latter tend to regard linking the Qur'ān's "furthest place of worship" with a real Jerusalem as dating no earlier than several decades after the onset of the Islamic conquest. Most modern scholars see the commentary on the isrā' and mi'rāj as a deliberate attempt to enhance the religious importance of the city and Temple Mount in Umayyad times, years after the death of the Prophet. Seen from this last perspective and shorn of traditional explication, Qur'ān 17:1 represents nothing more and nothing less than a reference to a vague dreamlike rite of passage that has no roots in any particular geographical setting. In short, the sum and substance of the traditions linking the Temple Mount and the Prophet's night adventure are likely to have been unknown to the Prophet's followers in Arabia. Interpreting Qur'ān 17:1 as referring to the real Jerusalem, subsequent Muslim authorities were probably influenced by older non-Muslim lore of the holy city; perhaps by the later building of a mosque on the Temple Mount; and, more generally, by the Islamization of the entire area in Umayyad times.

Although the Muslim conquerors established a place of worship somewhere on the Temple Mount (ca. 638, the year the city capitulated to the Muslims), the conversion of the entire platform into Muslim sacred space called al-Ḥaram al-Sharīf would appear to have begun in earnest only several generations after the Arab conquest. The magnificent Dome of the Rock (*Qubbat al-Ṣakhrah*) that surmounts the primeval *ṣakhrah* (hence the name of the building) was completed by the Umayyad caliph 'Abd al-Malik around 691 CE in the vicinity of the first mosque, a rather modest or even makeshift place of worship described by the Christian pilgrim Arculf some twenty years earlier.[30] Following the construction of the domed building on the Temple Mount, the caliph's son al-Walīd (r. 705–15) built or completed a vast congregational mosque nearby, presumably at the site of the original Muslim place of worship.[31] A truly mag-

29. See chapter 2, n. 10 and R. Bell, *The Qur'ān*, 1:262.

30. For this first mosque erected by 'Umar, see text below.

31. Muslim sources attribute the construction of the mosque to 'Abd al-Malik as well as his son al-Walīd. The geographer Muqaddasī and Mujīr al-Dīn, who wrote a work in praise of Jerusa-

nificent edifice, this second building, which came to be known as the al-Aqṣā mosque, lay south of the domed structure that covered the rock from which the Prophet is said to have ascended to heaven. Was the name of al-Walīd's mosque inspired by the Qur'ānic verse as it was understood in the lifetime of the Prophet according to Rubin, or rather by the commentary to that verse, which was more or less coterminous with the Umayyad development on the Temple Mount? Faced with choices of this sort, Muslims are wont to say: *wa-Allāhu a'lamu*, "God knows better," meaning "Only God knows." Nevertheless, it seems to me that the burden of proof rests with Rubin and not the scholars who link Muḥammad's night journey to well-known tropes in the literature of prophetic calling.

Jerusalem and Its Muslim Conquerors

It would seem that Jerusalem fully enters the Muslim imagination only after the onset of the Arab conquest (632 CE), and more particularly after the siege and capture of the city (638 CE) some six years after the Prophet's death. We are informed by Muslim historians (albeit more than two centuries post facto) that 'Umar b. al-Khaṭṭāb, the second commander of the faithful (634–44 CE), went to Jerusalem to accept its surrender from the bishop Sophronius.[32] Were these accounts an accurate reflection of the past, 'Umar's journey in 638 would seem to suggest that Jerusalem was already of special importance to Muslims. Until that moment, no other city or territory surrendering to the victorious Muslim armies required the presence of a caliph to lay down the terms of capitulation. 'Umar, in going to al-Shām, became the first titular head of the Islamic community to traverse the borders that separated Arabia from the conquered lands to the north.

The terms reportedly arranged by 'Umar were addressed to the people of Īliyā', an indication, at least as reported in this account, that the old pagan name Aelia, retained by the ecclesiastical authorities in referring to Constantine's

lem and Hebron, both favor 'Abd al-Malik as building the great mosque; the Christian chroniclers Eutychius and Bar Hebraeus as well as the Muslim historians Ibn al-Athīr and Ibn Ṭabāṭabā (Ibn al-Ṭiqṭaqā) cite al-Walīd. One ought to consider that the planning for the structure or perhaps some preliminary construction might have been from the time of 'Abd al-Malik and that al-Walīd completed the project. See the brief comments of K. A. C. Creswell, *Early Muslim Architecture*, 2nd edition (Oxford, 1969), 1/2:373–74.

32. The most extensive analysis of 'Umar's role in the surrender of Jerusalem is found in H. Busse, who has thoroughly examined and evaluated all the relevant sources. See Busse's "'Omar b. al-Khaṭṭāb in Jerusalem," *JSAI* 5/2 (1984): 73–119; and his "'Omar's Image as the Conqueror of Jerusalem," *JSAI* 8 (1986): 149–68.

New Jerusalem, was still current three centuries later along with the more official Hierosolyma. What of the conquering Muslims? How did they initially refer to the city? There is a tradition that Kaʿb al-Aḥbār, an acquaintance of ʿUmar's who was reportedly a learned Jewish convert to Islam, instructed (a Muslim?): "Do not say Īliyāʾ [I would add here the gloss: *as do the local Christians*], but refer instead to Bayt al-Maqdis (the Islamic name of Jerusalem)."[33] Read as I believe it was meant to be, Kaʿb's pronouncement suggests that the transition to Islamic Jerusalem might have begun as early as ʿUmar's caliphate, a mere six years after the Prophet's passing. There are indeed numerous accounts in which the learned Kaʿb refers to Jerusalem and its sacred history; these include stories in which he discusses the city with the commander of the faithful. Were there any truth to all these reports, ʿUmar would have been broadly aware of the city's sacred status for Jews and presumably for Christians. If we accept that view, Jerusalem and its environs, an area so rich in history for monotheists in the past, could have been regarded, indeed were most likely regarded, as a sacred place by Muslims who like ʿUmar were contemporaries of the Prophet. Expressed somewhat differently, the holy city, long called Īliyāʾ/Aelia by pagans and Christians, was formally renamed during the reign of ʿUmar *Bayt al-Maqdis*, the Arabic translation of Hebrew "Holy Temple" and one of the names Muslims used to signify Jerusalem's sacred status.

A word of caution is in order. Muslims continued to refer to Īliyāʾ well after the conquest of the city. Moreover, in Islamic tradition, the historical Kaʿb, taking license to use the adjective historical, is more a figure of legend than of fact.[34] His origins rendered him useful when Muslims linked Jewish cultural artifacts to the emergence of early Islamic culture. Kaʿb's alleged pronouncements, coming as they did from a former rabbi, validated Muslim claims al-

---

33. Yāqūt, *Muʿjam*, 3:592. Another statement naming Jerusalem attributed to Kaʿb is preserved in Ṭabarī (*Annales*, 1/3:2009). In that tradition Kaʿb refers to the Holy City as "Ūrshalim," an Arabicized version of Hebrew "Yerushalayim." As the text reflects a prediction of the future Muslim victory projected backward in the form of Jewish prophetic vision, the use of the more ancient form Ūrshalim is most appropriate. A similar Jewish prophecy fulfilled by ʿUmar's conquest of Jerusalem is reported by Ṭabarī (*Annales*, 1/3:2403), where ʿUmar is confronted by a Jew from Damascus who informs him that he, ʿUmar, is (the future) master of Jerusalem. For this last tradition, see chapter 8. N. Rabbat is inclined to place greater weight on the traditions transmitted by Kaʿab and contends that other early Muslims who were not Jewish converts had direct knowledge of Jewish sources and could have been reliable transmitters of accounts concerning Jerusalem. See his "The Meaning of the Umayyad Dome of the Rock," in *Muqarnas* 6 (1990): 14.

34. A brief description of Kaʿb's life can be found in *EI*, s.v. "Kaʿb al-Aḥbār." For more details: I. Wolfensohn, *Kaʿb al-Aḥbār und seine Stellung in Ḥadīt und der islamische Legende* (Frankfurt am Main, 1933); M. J. Kister, "Haddithū ʿan banī Isrāʾīla wa-la-ḥaraja," *IOS* 2 (1972): 15–39 (citing and explicating several accounts). Also M. Perlmann, "A Legendary Story of Kaʿb al-Aḥbār's Conversion to Islam," in the *Joshua Starr Memorial Volume* (New York, 1953), 85–89, and his "Another Kaʿb al-Aḥbār Story," *JQR* 45 (1954): 48–51.

ready articulated in the Qur'ān, that Muḥammad's mission was legitimately rooted in monotheist traditions of the past. The convert's learned pronouncements thus became a vehicle for criticizing Jews who retained their faith and their opposition to Muḥammad's prophecy following the ascendance of Islam. Considering the role assigned to converts in Muslim polemics vis-à-vis the Jews, modern scholars have always to assess the tendentiousness of accounts transmitted from and about Ka'b.

Similarly, historians have also to consider whether the accounts of 'Umar and the holy city are in large part, if not altogether, the creations of later era. In some accounts, it is Abū 'Ubaydah b. al-Jarrāḥ, the commander of the Muslim forces in the field, or some less important figure, who accepts the surrender of the city, while the caliph is said to have remained at the Muslim base camp at al-Jābiyah.[35] One version attempts to harmonize these contradictions by having the caliph accept the surrender of the city in the Muslim military encampment. The terms of capitulation set forth by 'Umar are also different in various Muslim sources as well as in highly embellished Christian versions that have their own religious ax to grind. The stories of how 'Umar sought to visit the Temple Mount and Sophronius's attempt to have the caliph visit instead the Church of the Holy Sepulcher make for entertaining reading but invite great skepticism.[36]

35. Some early accounts of these events (all pre-eleventh century CE) can be found in Kūfī, *Futūḥ*, 1:296–97; Ibn Khayyāṭ, *Ta'rīkh*, 1:124; Ya'qūbī, *Historiae*, 2:167; Balādhurī, *Futūḥ*, 139–40; Ṭabarī, *Annales*, 1/3:2403–10 (several versions collected from different authorities based on the narrative of Sayf b. 'Umar). For the most detailed analysis, see the articles of H. Busse, who has investigated a wide range of sources, esp. his "'Omar as Conqueror." The historicity of the accounts of the Byzantine surrender of Jerusalem is subject to dispute. The question revolves around the reliability of the Arabic narrator Sayf b. 'Umar, whose account of events forms the basis of later historical reports. See the brief entry in *EI*,, s.v. "Sayf b. 'Umar." And for more details, E. Landau-Tessiron, "Sayf b. 'Umar in Medieval and Modern Scholarship," *Der Islam* 67 (1990): 1–26; also S. D. Goitein, "Did Omar Prohibit the Stay of the Jews in Jerusalem?" in *Palestinian Jewry in Early Islamic and Crusader Times in Light of the Geniza Documents*, edited by J. Hacker (Jerusalem, 1980), 36–42 (denies historicity); M. Gil, *A History of Palestine, 634–1099* (Cambridge, 1992), 51–56 (accepts accuracy of surrender account); M. Levy-Rubin, *Non-Muslims in the Early Islamic Empire* (New York, 2011), 52–53 (also accepts accuracy).

36. The accounts of the deliberations between Sophronius and 'Umar bear the hallmark of an invented tradition in which the caliph, acting on behalf of a victorious Islamic community, is portrayed as having changed the religious landscape of the holy city to reflect the new order. See C. Von Schönborn, *Sophrone de Jerusalem* (Paris, 1972); and esp. H. Busse, "'Omar b. al-Ḫaṭṭāb in Jerusalem," 76 ff. Busse notes that according to received reports 'Umar did not pray at the Church of the Holy Sepulcher but at the Tower of David (*Miḥrāb Dāwūd*), a place also venerated by Christians but, more importantly, a place that resonated to a pre-Christian Israelite history that Muslims could embrace in accordance with Qur'ān 38:21–26 (the account of two disputants entering the *miḥrāb* of David). Following that, 'Umar reportedly ascended the Temple Mount, long neglected by the Christians, and ordered clearing the rubble and the construction there of the first Muslim mosque in the city. See Busse, "'Omar b. al-Ḫaṭṭāb in Jerusalem," 79 ff., an account more fully developed in his "The Tower of David / *Miḥrāb Dāwūd*: Remarks on the History of a Sanctuary in Jerusalem in Christian and Islamic Times," *JSAI* 17 (1994): 142–65, esp. 150–56. There is the possibility that

Reported exchanges between Muslim luminaries and Christian religious figures are the stock and trade of Christian apologetics and Muslim polemics.[37] One also has to consider the many imaginative tales of ʿUmar's reign. Such stories allowed later Muslim chroniclers to give the caliph a role larger than life. His already substantial reputation was thus enhanced, and policies later put into effect by others were given the legitimacy that comes with historic precedents established by one of the Prophet's most illustrious companions. Still, there is no reason to doubt that ʿUmar, or some Muslim contemporary of his, ordered the first mosque built on the mount where the ancient Jewish Temple had stood. The question is, why there?

Oleg Grabar has raised the possibility that ʿUmar's mosque was erected on the Temple Mount because of the available space. At first glance, this suggestion seems plausible. The Muslims were not about to level any part of Christian New Jerusalem to replace it with a Muslim newer Jerusalem. As a rule, the victorious Arab tribesmen did not destroy existing urban structures of the vanquished, but preferred to settle nearby in cantonments of their own. The decision to build on the barren land where the great Herodian edifice once stood might have been guided therefore by pragmatism rather than a profound recognition of the site's sacred history.[38] The Byzantinist Cyril Mango also argues that in building their first mosque on the Temple Mount, the Muslims were guided by practical considerations, albeit of a nature somewhat different from those suggested by Grabar. Reviewing the relevant sources, he contends that the area was neither a rubble heap nor reduced to a rubble heap when Constantine I built the New Jerusalem. According to Mango, it had been since the building of Aelia Capitolina the site of a temple to Jupiter, a visual symbol that the holy city and political fulcrum of the Jews was no more. He surmises that with the ascendance of Christianity, the pagan house of worship had fallen into disuse and was at the time of the Muslim conquest the hollow shell of its former self. The ruined Temple could, however, serve as the infrastructure around which to build a modest mosque to serve the needs of the Muslim conquerors.[39]

---

the account of ʿUmar praying as he did at the Tower of David is part of a more extended version of events designed to demonstrate a separation between Muslims and Christians at the time the city was occupied by the Muslim warriors.

37. For examples of apologetic dialogue between Christians and Muslims, see H. Griffith, "The Monk in the Emir's *Majlis*: Reflections on a Popular Genre of Christian Literary Apologetics in Arabic in the Early Islamic Period," in *The Majlis: Interreligious Encounters in Medieval Islam*, edited by H. Lazarus-Yafeh et al. (Wiesbaden, 1999), 13–65, and his "Muḥammad and the Monk Baḥīrā: Reflections on a Syriac and Arabic Text from Early Abbasid Times," *Oriens Christianus* 79 (1995): 146–74; also J. Lassner, *The Middle East Remembered* (Ann Arbor, 2000), 341–85 (the Baḥīrā legend as a Jewish response to Muslim and Christian apologetics).

38. O. Grabar, "The Umayyad Dome of the Rock," in volume 4 of his collected studies *Jerusalem*, 12.

39. C. Mango, "The Temple Mount AD 614–638," *OSIA* 9/1 (1999): 3.

One notes that the seventh-century Umayyad mosque in Damascus was situated within the existing structure or adjoining grounds of a functioning Christian place of worship, the famous Church of St. John. In the following century, the church and its grounds were fully appropriated by the Muslims and reconfigured to serve as the great mosque of the city.[40] The pattern of fashioning mosques from non-Muslim houses of worship was repeated in al-Shām during the first Islamic century and beyond. In addition to the Church of St. John in Damascus, mosques were built in parts of grand churches in Homs, Aleppo, and perhaps Diyārbakr. The architectural historian K. A. C. Creswell is of the opinion that no mosques were built from the ground up until the reign of ʿAbd al-Malik or al-Walīd, that is, until the late seventh or early eighth century CE.[41] Practical considerations notwithstanding, neither Mango nor Grabar is prepared to dismiss entirely that the mystique of the Temple Mount affected in some way ʿUmar's decision to build a house of worship on the ancient platform. Grabar goes on to argue that the caliph was indeed influenced by the ancient lore of the site but, in the end, had no thought of making Jerusalem a visual symbol of the new order. And so, the first Jerusalem mosque was a rather modest building as described by the Christian pilgrim Arculf around 670 CE.[42] Mango suggests that the conquering Muslims may have mistaken the pagan ruins for those of the ancient Jewish structure and therefore decided to appropriate it as their mosque. Building on holy sites of old and utilizing architectural members from the ruined monuments of empires past were seen throughout the long history of the Near East as symbolic gestures that proclaimed the triumph of the new ruling order. The problem facing contemporary scholars is how to assess the historicity of medieval writings, in this instance the residual and newly invented foundation lore of Jerusalem. Modern historians of early Islam tend to regard as highly problematic the ancient and medieval texts that serve as the building blocks of their scholarship, although in a number of cases they seem all too willing accept certain sources when they seem to confirm their favorite preconceptions. Despite a justifiable skepticism regarding the recorded history of the past, one could argue confidently that the Arab Muslims came to regard Jerusalem as a place of great religious importance early in the first Islamic century, though perhaps not in ʿUmar's lifetime.

40. K. A. C. Creswell, *EMA*, 1/2:151 ff.
41. *EMA*, 1/2:17.
42. Mango, "Temple Mount," 3.

CHAPTER 4

The Islamization of Umayyad Jerusalem

The Role of Mu'āwiyah b. Abī Sufyān

Some two decades after the fall of the city, the Umayyad ruler Mu'āwiyah b. Abī Sufyān (661–80 CE), then governor of al-Shām, had himself declared caliph in Jerusalem. At the time he was entering the final phase of his rebellion against 'Alī b. Abī Ṭālib, the reigning commander of the faithful. As did Muḥammad and his three successors, Abū Bakr, 'Umar, and 'Uthmān, 'Alī, the fourth of the so-called righteous caliphs (*rāshidūn*), chose the Prophet's city Medina as his capital and the nearby shrine city of Mecca as his spiritual center. As did all his predecessors, 'Alī recognized what had been obvious to all Muslims in the formative stages of their community: the holy cities of Arabia (*ḥaramayn*) represent the sacred and political fulcrum of the Islamic realm.

Even as real political power shifted to the conquered territories, large provinces commanded by governors with formidable armies and access to vast tax revenues, the ḥaramayn remained as before, the spiritual and political center of a burgeoning Islamic state. But faced with a concurrent rebellion of Hijazi notables who had gone to Iraq to raise an army in Basra, 'Alī was forced to leave Medina and establish a base camp at Kufa, the second garrison town of Iraq. There he sought troops to augment his inadequate forces. No sooner had he raised an army and dispatched the rebels, Ṭalhah and al-Zubayr, than 'Alī faced a second and more serious crisis: Mu'āwiyah's revolt in al-Shām. The caliph never again ruled from or even returned to Arabia. And yet he felt compelled to retain Medina as the official capital of the realm. That drew no curious reaction; even non-Hijazis recognized that the ḥaramayn, linked as they were to the Prophet and the rise of Islam, demanded the respect of all Muslims.

One can understand the rebel Mu'āwiyah's dilemma as he was about to claim for himself the temporal and spiritual leadership of the Muslim community. He was on a path to supplant the old regime, but the Muslim aristocrats of the Hijaz denied him the legitimacy of being elected commander of the faithful in the Prophet's city, as were all the caliphs before him. It appears that as a counterweight to Medina (and Mecca) Muʿāwiyah decided to be acclaimed in Jerusalem, a place with a long religious history of its own. That ancient history was certainly known to Jews and Christians in al-Shām as well as their former coreligionists who embraced Islam. The extensive lore of Jerusalem might even have spoken to the evolving religious sensibilities of Arab tribesmen who crossed the frontier and settled in the various subdistricts of the great province. Interacting with the indigenous inhabitants and previous Arab settlers, the newcomers presumably assimilated elements of local culture, including a popular religion that celebrated the sanctity of Jerusalem and its environs. Visiting Christian pilgrims and pietists, with whom we associate popular religion, settled in New Jerusalem for extended periods of time, and reshaped the religious character of what had been the pagan Aelia Capitolina and before that the Yerushalayim of the Jews.

What reason would there have been for Muʿāwiyah to choose Jerusalem of all places if the sacred city's symbolic importance did not resonate among Muslims in his own province? Jerusalem was no center of political power, as it had been under the kings of Israel and the Herodians, nor would it be until the arrival of the Crusaders at the end of the eleventh century. It was not even the capital of the subdistrict of Arab Filasṭīn. That honor went to Lydda (*Lūd*) and would then be transferred to nearby Ramle (*Ramlah*) in the eighth century.[1] If he desired to project an image of raw political power, Muʿāwiyah would have been better served by declaring his caliphate in Damascus, his capital of some twenty years and the political hub of the wealthy province where he enjoyed local support unprecedented among governors of the realm. Why hold the ceremonial investiture in Jerusalem, which had become the political backwater of Damascus long before the rise of Islam? Among modern scholars, it is generally assumed that Muʿāwiyah needed a counterweight to the prestigious cities of the Hijaz, the very places recognized by all Muslims as the crucible in which their faith and community were formed, and from which all the previous heads of the Islamic state projected power. Not insignificantly, the vaunted and loyal Syrian army, the very backbone of Muʿāwiyah's rebellion, consisted in large part of Arab tribal levies that had migrated to Syria-Palaestina before the Islamic conquest. Their purpose: guarding the frontier for their Byzantine overlords. These tribesmen, some of them Christian at the time of the conquest, could well have shared the symbolic importance of Jerusalem and its environs with the indigenous Jews and Christians, most of whom had not yet converted to Islam.

1. *EI*, s.v. "Lūd" and "Ramla" for a concise history of the two locations.

This understanding of Mu'āwiyah's relationship to the holy city is in contrast with Oleg Grabar's bold contention that by going to Jerusalem to have himself invested with caliphal authority, the first of the Umayyads clearly saw himself as "a prince in the tradition of the pre-Islamic kings of the Arabian world."[2] Grabar never identifies these pre-Islamic Arab kings, nor does he indicate their political or religious conception of the world. I must confess that I cannot find any contemporaneous template of Arabian kingship that serves to explain Mu'āwiyah's political outlook. If anything, he fully understood the difficulty of imposing centralized authority on a body-politic infused with the anarchic sensibilities of Arab tribalism. Rather than a king among kings or a prince among princes, Mu'āwiyah was the very model of a tribal sheikh manipulating an assembly of lesser tribal sheikhs and their representatives with consummate skill.

We should be wary of making claims, be it for Mu'āwiyah or any of his contemporaries. As a matter of course, our understanding of early Islamic history is highly impressionistic. Current historians are obliged to tread lightly when charting the history of the Umayyad house. The available sources, all composed well after the events in question, display a pronounced bias against Islam's first dynasty, regarding them as usurpers of the Prophet's authority and the rights of his Hāshimite kinsmen. At times, there is grudging admiration for various Umayyad rulers, but even then they are praised for their political adroitness and not their religious character. With the exception of the pious 'Umar II, they are described as was Mu'āwiyah, rulers suited for the temporal world (*dunyā*) and not that of faith (*dīn*). In the end, these sources, however tendentious, are the foundation upon which we attempt to imagine a past that might have been.

With that reservation in mind, I turn to the tenth-century Arab author Ibn al-Faqīh (ca. 900 CE), who devotes a major section of his descriptive geography to the Holy Land and to the monuments and lore of Jerusalem. Among these accounts is the story of a hostile Iraqi delegation that met with Mu'āwiyah after he had been elected caliph, a tale also related by the historian Balādhurī (d. 892 CE) on the testimony of 'Awānah b. al-Ḥakam al-Kalbī (ca. eighth century).[3] This tradition, preserved in a corpus of Jerusalem lore from the late ninth century, can thus be traced to a source at least a hundred years prior to Balādhurī, still another indication of the early provenance of stories about the Holy Land and holy city. In Ibn al-Faqīh's version of events we see the commander of the faithful greeting the Iraqis with words of praise for himself and his province. After describing himself as the best caliph, Mu'āwiyah goes on to say: "You have

2. O. Grabar, "The Meaning of the Dome of the Rock," in his collected studies, *Jerusalem*, 150.
3. Ibn al-Faqīh, *Buldān*, 115; short variant in Balādhurī, *Anṣāb*, 4A:25.

come to the Holy Land (*al-arḍ al-muqaddasah*), the land in which the dead will be gathered and then resurrected (*al-mahshar wa-l-manshar*); the land in which are found the graves of the prophets (*qubūr al-anbiyā'*)."[4]

These words are stock expressions in praise of Jerusalem and its environs. They appear time and again in the extensive literature praising the holy city. What is interesting about this account is that they are attributed to Mu'āwiyah, and so suggest the caliph considered his legitimacy as being linked to the sanctity of the holy city and the Holy Land. The leader of the delegation, Ṣa'ṣa'ah b. Ṣuḥān al-'Abdī (who had been a partisan of Mu'āwiyah's rival, the former caliph 'Alī b. Abī Ṭālib), issues skillful rejoinders to each and every one of the caliph's comments. He sows doubts about the caliph's legitimacy and even denigrates the sanctity of Jerusalem and the Holy Land, claiming that more pharaohs (that is, despots) are buried in the land than prophets; and that proximity to (the so-called holy) land is no help to the unbelievers and no hindrance to the faithful, a not-so-veiled allusion to the Days of Judgment and Resurrection that are destined to take place around Jerusalem. But the most telling criticism of the caliph is embedded in his comment about the holiness of the land: "The land does not make the people holy (*tuqaddisu*); rather the people of the land declare it holy (*yuqaddisūnahā*)."[5] The point being: Who is Mu'āwiyah to claim an authority that God has not approved for him in a city and land that he has sanctified for his own political purposes?

Does this tell us anything about Mu'āwiyah's decision to be proclaimed caliph in Jerusalem? Or is the account, like many other stories about the first Umayyad, a skillful invention to discredit the able caliph and the regime he founded? As previously stated, one version of this account is reportedly traced back to the historian (*rāwī*) 'Awānah b. al-Kalbī, an authority witnessing events as they unfolded in the second half of the eighth century. At the time, there was residual sympathy for the deposed regime founded by the gifted Mu'āwiyah. Support for the house of Umayyah was particularly evident in the vast province from which he and his successors ruled. Given the circumstances, the Abbasid caliphs who replaced the house of Umayyah, as well as the Alids who had long claimed the right to command the faithful, both feared a possible Umayyad resurgence, improbable as that might have been. Abbasid and Alid propagandists circulated traditions demeaning the previous dynasts, thus justifying their own claims to the Prophet's authority while depriving the surviving Umayyad offspring any claims of present or future legitimacy.

4. Ibn al-Faqīh, *Buldān*, 115.
5. Ibn al-Faqīh, *Buldān*, 115.

The highly charged remarks attributed to the Alid partisan Ṣaʿṣaʿah b. Ṣuḥan al-ʿAbdī also give short shrift to the historic importance of the vast province from which the family of Umayyah ruled, a seeming attempt to reassert the primacy of Mecca and Medina, the anvils upon which the Prophet and his religion were forged. However cautious we should be in reading the exchange between the caliph and the Alid sympathizer—the historicity of the account as reported is surely subject to question—we can hardly rule out that Muʿāwiyah actually considered Jerusalem special and acted accordingly. In that regard, he was followed by other caliphs of the dynasty who preferred to accept the oath of allegiance there and not in Damascus, the capital of their realm, or for that matter in the holy cities of Arabia.[6]

Was Muʿāwiyah Intent on Transferring the Seat of Islamic Rule to Jerusalem?

It is one thing for Muʿāwiyah to have seized upon Jerusalem's status as a holy city and have himself declared caliph there. Some scholars would have us believe the caliph's plans for Jerusalem were far more ambitious.[7] They argue that the long-standing governor of al-Shām was prepared to abandon Damascus altogether and establish the seat of his rule in a city sacred to a broad cross section of his constituents. Proof that the caliph actually embarked on such a course, if only in principle, is, however, elusive; the evidence slim at that. Had the caliph actually initiated plans to move the seat of Islamic government to Jerusalem, we would expect to see evidence of extensive building activity, or at the least reports of ambitious city planning. Our sources make clear that Muʿāwiyah initiated a number of building projects in Mecca to cater to pilgrims and other visitors to the city.[8] One should then expect similar reports for Jerusalem. But even Amikam Elad, who has spent the better part of a lifetime studying Islamic Jerusalem, is hard pressed to find evidence that Muʿāwiyah attempted to build there on a grand scale. He admits that among the numerous Arabic authors known to him only al-Muṭahhar b. Ṭāhir al-Maqdisī indicates that Muʿāwiyah erected a building in Jerusalem and only one at that.[9] In his *K. al-badʾ wa-l-taʾrīkh* (ca. 966 CE), Maqdisī relates that Muʿāwiyah built a

6. Ibn Khayyāṭ, *Taʾrīkh*, 329.

7. A. Elad, *Medieval Jerusalem*, 23 n. 5; F. S. Peters, *Jerusalem and Mecca* (New York, 1986), 93; S. D. Goitein in his entry "Al-Ḳuds" in *EI*; Grabar, "Meaning of the Dome of the Rock," 146–48.

8. M. J. Kister, "The Battle of Ḥarra: Some Socio-economic Aspects," in *Studies in Honor of Gaston Wiet*, edited by M. Rosen-Ayalon (Jerusalem, 1977), 33–49, esp. 38, 42–44.

9. Elad, *Medieval Jerusalem*, 23–24.

mosque in the city, as did ʿUmar before him.[10] It is not clear why Elad refers to the mosque as "the al-Aqṣā Mosque"; Maqdisī gives the place of worship no name.[11] Nor is it clear what relationship may have existed between this mosque of Muʿāwiyah and the house of worship erected earlier by ʿUmar. Does Elad think there were now two mosques on the Temple Mount; or does he mean to suggest that the Umayyad building replaced (or is) the place of worship described by the Christian pilgrim Arculf around 670 CE; and how are we to link, if at all, Elad's al-Aqṣā to the great mosque of that name whose construction is attributed to the later caliphs ʿAbd al-Malik and/or al-Walīd? Should we also consider the possibility that the Umayyad mosque referred to by Maqdisī was not meant to signify an entirely new construction but ʿUmar's house of worship repaired or refurbished? Whatever the case, there is little in the Arab chronicler's account to support the view that Muʿāwiyah was actually intent on moving from Damascus to Jerusalem.

In an attempt to throw additional light on Muʿāwiyah's possible "commitment" to the holy city, Elad cites a short fragment from Hebrew apocalypses known collectively as *The Book (Sefer) of Zerubbabel*.[12] The fragment indicates that a Muslim ruler with the garbled name M-S-Y-H ben Abi S-F-U-N (read by Elad Muʿāwiyah ben [= ibn] Abī Sufyān) is destined to build the "walls of the Temple Mount (*homot ha-bayit*)" and enjoy a long life or reign (*ve-ya'rikh shanim ve-yamim*). However, there is no compelling evidence with which to corroborate either the Arabic source or the Hebrew account cited by Elad. Quite the opposite, another work of this genre, the Ben (or Bar) Yochai cycle of apocalypses, attributes the repair of the walls and the clearing and smoothing out of the (rubble strewn) Temple Mount to an unnamed ruler most easily identified as ʿUmar b. al-Khaṭṭāb, the caliph who reportedly built Jerusalem's first mosque on the temple platform. Were that not sufficient to muddy the waters, a variant in the Ben Yochai cycle cites the caliph ʿAbd al-Malik (r. 685–705 CE) as destined to repair the walls, a tradition that echoes the many Muslim

10. Maqdisī, *Bad'*, 4:87.

11. C. Mango labels the mosque of ʿUmar "surely the first Aqṣā." See his "The Temple Mount, AD 614–638," *OSIA* 9/1 (1992): 2, perhaps following the lead of K. A. C. Creswell, *EMA*, 1/1:32. There is, however, no indication that ʿUmar's mosque was referred to in that fashion by the Arab conquerors of Jerusalem. Elad's identification of Maqdisī's mosque with a first al-Aqṣā strikes me as problematic. Note also M. Rosen-Ayalon, who seems to speak of a "first al-Aqṣā" mosque replaced by that of ʿAbd al-Malik, following the medieval authors who attribute the great al-Aqṣā mosque to ʿAbd al-Malik and not his successor, al-Walīd. See her *The Early Islamic Monuments of al-Ḥaram al-Sharīf*, Qedem 28 (Jerusalem, 1989), 6. To avoid confusion it would be best to speak of the first Jerusalem mosque and leave it at that.

12. Elad, *Medieval Jerusalem*, 24 n. 8; for the passage he cites obtained from a fragment of the *Book of (Sefer) Zerubbabel*, see S. A. Wertheimer, *Batei Midrashot*, 2nd edition (Jerusalem, 1967), 2:504.

reports that attribute to that Umayyad the critical role in developing the area of the ancient temple precinct. Given the confusion created by the Ben Yochai apocalypses, it is hard to see how Maqdisī's chronicle and the fragment of the *Sefer Zerubabbel* referred to by Elad are positive proof that Muʿāwiyah intended to move his capital to Jerusalem.

Moreover, the broad range of the Jewish apocalypses consists of different and often contradictory versions. Scholars are dealing with problematic texts. For one, there are no complete manuscripts relevant to our interests; the only extant apocalypses tend to be small fragments. Some are medieval texts from the Cairo Geniza; other fragments are found mostly in later versions of legends pertaining to the messianic age, the earliest of which date from the sixteenth century. These texts then become the basis of more recent midrashic anthologies, one of which is marked by excessive editorial license. A cautious scholar perusing the printed editions of these Hebrew fragments would be hard pressed to find firm ground on which to build a speculative, let alone convincing, argument that Muʿāwiyah was inclined if not indeed determined to make Jerusalem the political center of the Islamic world, let alone a Muslim holy city comparable to Mecca and Medina.[13]

In a footnote to his larger discussion of the Umayyads and the holy city, Elad calls attention to Julian Wellhausen, who maintained, based on various Arabic reports, that Muʿāwiyah planned to transfer the pulpit of the Prophet's mosque from Medina to al-Shām, a symbolic act of immense importance.[14] The Medina mosque served as a place of religious devotion, but it was also the hub of political activity for Muḥammad and his companions.[15] The Prophet ascended his pulpit to lead prayers, but he also mounted it to deal with communal matters, announce policy, and rally the Muslims to engage in battle. Removing

13. See text above for a full discussion of these Jewish sources. In addition to the *Book of Zerubbabel*, there is the Ben or Bar Yochai cycle of apocalyptical midrashim, various accounts of the legendary Simeon Ben/Bar Yochai, who reportedly had visions of the future salvation of Israel while hiding from the Romans in a cave. Several edited versions of different Bar or Ben Yochai texts are reproduced in the anthology of apocalyptical sources edited by Yehuda Even Shemuel (originally Kaufmann) titled *Medreshei Geulah* (Jerusalem, 1954). Even Shemuel also reproduces various versions of the Zerubbabel cycle. The author's attempt to create a unified text out of the disparate accounts invites serious criticism (see above). A review of scholarly opinion on the Ben Yochai variants is found in B. Lewis, "An Apocalyptic Vision of Islamic History," *BSOAS* 13 (1949–51): 308–10. A complete reexamination of the Hebrew apocalyptical literature citing events of Islamic history and with that a renewed discussion of the various Jewish messianic movements during the formative centuries of Islam is a desideratum. For a schematic survey there is *EJ*, s.v. "Messiah and Messianism."

14. Elad, *Medieval Jerusalem*, 23 n. 5, citing J. Wellhausen, *The Arab Kingdom and Its Fall* (Beirut, 1963), 214.

15. On the architecture of the Prophet's mosque in relation to later mosques, see J. Johns, "The House of the Prophet and the Concept of the Mosque," *OSIA* 9/2 (1999): 59–112.

an evident symbol of the Prophet's authority and that of the early caliphs who followed would have given rise to considerable controversy, especially among the aristocrats of Medina, members of the Prophet's family and clan. And yet Wellhausen leads us to believe the Umayyad caliph was bent on this very path. Elad agrees that the reported event is indicative of the caliph's authentic wish and intention. In Elad's words, "It is certainly a reflection of Umayyad trends and the state of mind among them."[16] From this perspective, removing the pulpit from Medina would have been seen as signifying the transfer of power and authority from Muḥammad's Hāshimite relatives and those of his closest followers. Of this there can be no doubt. But nowhere do the Arabic reports speak of Jerusalem. Nor does Wellhausen specifically refer to the holy city.

Can we nevertheless massage these medieval statements to show that the first of the Umayyads was intent on remaking Jerusalem equal to, if not indeed more important than, the holy cities of the Hijaz? Elad, following Wellhausen, focuses on several accounts from the universal history of Ṭabarī *sub anno* 50 AH, that is, nine years into Muʿāwiyah's reign. The chronicle informs us that the caliph initiated the transfer of the Prophet's pulpit and then sought to do the same with his wooden staff (another symbol of the Prophet's authority). His stated reason: The Medinese had been the enemies and murderers of the caliph's relative, the martyred 'Uthmān b. 'Affān. Muʿāwiyah's sense of outrage notwithstanding, the action did not sit well with one of the caliph's advisors. Taking license to admonish the commander of the faithful, he asks with mocking tone whether Muʿāwiyah would also remove the Prophet's mosque. The chastened caliph then reversed course. Instead of transporting the pulpit to al-Shām, he returned it to its place, adding six additional steps so there were now eight in all. Properly humbled, he asked the notables of the city for forgiveness.[17]

Another version reports that having removed the pulpit from its place (there is no mention of the staff), the caliph witnessed a terrifying cosmic sign. There was a complete eclipse of the sun. The sky had become so dark the stars that shone at night could be clearly seen at the height of day. Overcome with anxiety and awestruck by what the heavens had wrought, Muʿāwiyah had a change of mind. No doubt, he was well aware that the Medinese were also awestruck at witnessing the sky's blackening (a portentous event for which they would have surely blamed the caliph and his scheme to tamper with Medina's holiness). Forced to explain his action, Muʿāwiyah indicated that he only wished to remove the pulpit because of possible damage from worms (eating into the

16. Elad, *Medieval Jerusalem*, 23 n. 5.
17. Ṭabarī, *Annales*, 2/1:92–93; also Masʿūdī, *Murūj*, 5:66.

wood). That very day, he restored the religious object to its proper place and draped it with a decorative (or protective) cover.

This story does not end with the first of the Umayyads. The chronicler then reports that ʿAbd al-Malik, the fifth sovereign of the ruling house, also had designs on the Prophet's pulpit. He deferred, however, to the advice of Qabīṣah b. Dhu'ayb, who warned the caliph not to remove it as it rightfully belonged to the people of Medina and reminded him of the cosmic disturbance that occurred when Muʿāwiyah was commander of the faithful. Qabīṣah then quoted a dictum attributed to the Prophet, proclaiming in effect that whoever uses the pulpit for sinful or criminal purposes prepares for a place in the fire below. The sixth caliph, al-Walīd, was similarly inclined to move the pulpit to al-Shām but in the end was persuaded not to. When al-Walīd's successor, Sulaymān, arrived in Medina during the pilgrimage, he was told that ʿAbd al-Malik and al-Walīd had initially coveted the sacred object. Sulaymān would brook no further discussion linking such an ill-advised act to his predecessors. He pointed out that the house of Umayyah had the whole of the temporal world (*dunyā*) in their hands (meaning they had no need of the Prophet's pulpit to legitimize their rule). In effect, the caliph was responding to critics who accused the Umayyad dynasts as having usurped the authority that rightfully belonged to the Prophet's clan and family.[18]

Although he is convinced that these Arabic accounts contain a kernel of historic truth, Amikam Elad is far too sophisticated a reader of Arabic texts to accept this narrative at face value. He concedes that the story told by the sources and cited by Wellhausen may have been designed to denigrate the Umayyads.[19] Accusing the Umayyads for preferring *dunyā* to *dīn* is a recurrent theme of Arabic historical writing. Also familiar is the literary artifice in which cosmic disorder—in this case the total eclipse of the sun—is used to signify God's disapproval of wayward human action. Among peoples of the Near East, the blackening of the sky is often presented as a sign of impending calamity. When the unbelieving queen of Sheba awoke and found the sun she worshiped totally eclipsed, she tore her garments as a sign of despair.[20] Similarly, when the Mongol Hulaku considered putting an end to an Islamic dynasty that had endured for half a millennium, he was initially dissuaded from doing so because such an act would cause the sun to cease shining, the rains to stop falling, and the earth from giving rise to vegetation, all manifest signs of cosmic dis-

18. Ṭabarī, *Annales*, 2/1:92–93.
19. Elad, *Medieval Jerusalem*, 23 n. 5.
20. Thaʿlabī, *ʿArāʾis*, 315.

order.[21] No wonder the Muslims became agitated following God's disapproval of Mu'āwiyah's behavior. And once they were apprised of what had happened during Mu'āwiyah's reign, it is also no wonder that 'Abd al-Malik and al-Walīd gave up thoughts of embracing their predecessor's agenda. Sulaymān in turn preferred to quash any discussion of moving the pulpit from the outset. Better to not tempt fate and be safe rather than sorry.

Recognizing that a tendentious literary convention is at the heart of these accounts does not preclude that the text is a legitimate echo of the past. A conscientious historian examines carefully the sum and substance of individual texts before throwing out the baby with the bathwater. Nevertheless, I remain unconvinced that the Umayyad caliph intended to move the pulpit and staff to the holy city and, following that, his capital from Damascus to Jerusalem. Had Mu'āwiyah intended to move to Jerusalem at the time, he surely would have mentioned the holy city by name. If there is any truth to the story related by Ṭabarī, it is most likely that the visual symbols of the Prophet's authority were to be relocated in Damascus, the city the Arabs called "the administrative center of al-Shām (*qaṣabat al-Shām*)."[22]

There is also the question of timing. The medieval sources agree that the caliph was resolved to transfer the pulpit and staff at the midpoint of the first Islamic century. That would place the event about a decade after Mu'āwiyah was invested with the caliphate in Jerusalem. One might think that if the caliph wished to move from Damascus to the holy city with the intention of legitimizing his credentials, he would have done so when he was declared commander of the faithful. It was then that he needed to be accepted as an authentic successor to the Prophet, especially by the Hāshimite aristocrats and their associates. Mu'āwiyah's caliphate was at best grudgingly acknowledged by important followers of his former enemies. Some of the Prophet's kinsmen refused at first to pay the caliph homage. In the end, Mu'āwiyah, with his superb grasp of Arab tribal politics, managed to neutralize them while stationed in Damascus. Having fought a debilitating civil war that exhausted friend and foe alike, he sought gentle methods of persuasion based on traditional tribal politics of patronage and clientage. He took insults from Muḥammad's kinsmen, the Hāshimites, with his celebrated forbearance (*ḥilm*) and flattered and bought off potential rivals among them and their allies. By showing them deference and, not the least, by showering them with favors, he prevented any serious opposition from taking root among those who thought they had a better claim to command the

21. Ibn Ṭabāṭabā, *Fakhrī*, 140 ff.
22. Yāqūt, *Mu'jam*, 3:238.

Muslims. Even the most vociferous critics of the Umayyad house were forced to admit the political astuteness of the caliph.[23]

There is simply nothing happening in 50 AH that would have compelled Muʿāwiyah to consider transferring the Prophet's pulpit and staff, be it to Damascus or Jerusalem. Why initiate an act so freighted with symbolic importance and risk compromising a policy of accommodation that had been so successful? The act was sure to provoke a reaction among the Hāshimites in Medina and elsewhere. The later caliph Sulaymān's claim "We have the temporal world in our hands" could just as easily have been spoken by the first ruler of the realm.[24] What gain was there in seeking to offend those whom Muʿāwiyah had so successfully placated. A better case could be made for the later Umayyad caliph ʿAbd al-Malik, who was confronted by a prolonged and extremely dangerous rebellion in the name of the Hijazi ʿAbdallāh b. al-Zubayr.[25] The rebel was related to the Hāshimites by way of his mother, the daughter of Abū Bakr, the first of the righteous caliphs. His mother was also sister to the Prophet's beloved wife ʿĀʾishah. ʿAbdallāh's father was one of the Prophet's earliest companions, a member of the electoral council that chose the early caliphs, and a candidate for the caliphate in his own right. As seen by the Muslims, especially the Hijazis, the rebel had impressive credentials, more impressive than those of the reigning commander of the faithful. A possible link between the rebellion and Jerusalem will be explored in a later discussion of ʿAbd al-Malik's ambitious construction on the Temple Mount. As regards the transfer of the pulpit and staff, the stories told of ʿAbd al-Malik, al-Walīd, and Sulaymān appear no more than a contrived addendum to an earlier and similarly contrived moment of Umayyad history, the account accusing the first caliph of the realm of wishing to remove the Prophet's pulpit and staff from their rightful place in Medina. In all likelihood, the tale in its present form was designed to blame the Umayyads for playing politics in not respecting the central role of Medina in the religious life of the Muslim faithful.

Elad also refers to Francis Peters,[26] whose academic career has been largely devoted to cultural interaction between the monotheistic faiths, be it in the realm of ideas or, as regards Jerusalem, the appropriation of physical space. In reference to Jerusalem, Peters writes "claims and expectations . . . had to be converted into stone and mortar; where institutions had to be housed, staffed,

23. Ibn Ṭabāṭabā, *Fakhrī*, 104–5.

24. Ṭabarī, *Annales*, 2/1:93.

25. For an extended discussion of this revolt and its possible impact on the Temple Mount of Jerusalem, see chapter 7.

26. Elad, *Medieval Jerusalem*, 24 n. 8.

and supported; and where politics and religion had to come to terms."[27] With that, Peters argues that Muʿāwiyah had a grand design to make Jerusalem the political, if not indeed the religious, center of the Umayyad realm.[28] He cannot help but note that the first Umayyad chose to rule from Damascus, but suggests that may not have been the caliph's original intent. According to Peters, Muʿāwiyah, who was "crowned" in Jerusalem, had an emotional investment in the city and apparently initiated an ambitious plan to move from Damascus to the holy city and rule the Abode of Islam from there. For Peters that plan included the construction of the residential and administrative complex that Israeli archaeologists uncovered following the June war of 1967 adjacent to the southern wall of the Temple Mount below and west of the al-Aqṣā mosque.[29] Were that not enough of a commitment to stones and mortar, Peters maintains that the caliph also envisioned erecting "the two religious buildings intended to sacralize the space atop (the platform)," a reference to the Dome of the Rock and the al-Aqṣā mosque nearby.[30]

Peters first made the case for Muʿāwiyah in a scholarly article published in 1983, and then again in a popular book on Jerusalem that appeared two years later.[31] Elad mentions the second work in a footnote but omits any reference to the earlier and more detailed work.[32] As for the book, Peters writes of Muʿāwiyah and the Islamization of Jerusalem in all of two pages and in language so guarded as to give the reader occasion to pause. I take it the author intended to present his general audience with a plausible or at least possible scenario of the past, rather than offer a thorough explanation of what actually transpired—credit Peters for that. However, in the end he fully endorses the view he articulated earlier, namely, that Muʿāwiyah was intent on transforming Jerusalem into the epicenter of Muslim rule, and beyond that laid plans for major construction on the Temple Mount, the very positions that Elad seems willing to endorse.

How does Peters justify this conclusion, and does his presentation of evidence withstand close scrutiny? The evidence from material culture is based on identifying the archaeological finds adjacent the Temple Mount as a massive Umayyad complex linked to the first caliph of the realm. Peters also endorses a view initially advanced by S. D. Goitein and Oleg Grabar. Both scholars sup-

27. Peters, *Jerusalem and Mecca*, ix.

28. Peters, *Jerusalem and Mecca*, 92 ff.

29. For an extended discussion of the archaeological discoveries near the southern wall of the Temple Mount, see chapter 6.

30. Peters, *Jerusalem and Mecca*, 92 ff.

31. F. S. Peters, "Who Built the Dome of the Rock?," *Graeco-Arabica* 2 (1983): 119–38.

32. Elad, *Medieval Jerusalem*, 23 n. 5.

posed that construction on the ancient platform widely attributed by medieval and modern scholars to ʿAbd al-Malik and al-Walīd was so massive it required considerable lead time for the design of the structures, as well as for recruiting, organizing, and supervising the labor force.[33] As Muʿāwiyah chose Jerusalem the place to have himself proclaimed caliph, Peters, like Goitein and Grabar, regards him the most likely candidate to have initiated the project. At first glance, this supposition may strike some readers as eminently plausible. What then are we to make of the epigraphic and literary evidence that links the vast construction in the temple area to ʿAbd al-Malik and al-Walīd? Peters accepts that the two Umayyad rulers had a role in transforming the Temple Mount—the evidence seems irrefutable. But he limits their responsibility to completing what had been initially conceived by the first Umayyad caliph. Peters cites no Arabic texts in support of these views. His draws attention instead to a detailed study of the aforementioned Ben Yochai cycle, so-named after its protagonist, Rabbi Simeon ben (or bar) Yochai, a witness to the failed Jewish revolt against Rome in the second century CE.

The Ben Yochai Apocalypses: A Composite Version

In these apocalyptical texts the legendary rabbi is described as escaping a Roman death sentence by hiding in a cave, where he remained cut off from the world for thirteen years.[34] After enduring this lengthy isolation, he fasted and prayed for a period of time[35] and then beseeched God to offer salvation for his oppressed people. Citing a verse from the book of Psalms, Rabbi Simeon asks: "How long will you be wrathful to the prayers of your people?"[36] Put somewhat differently: How long will Israel have to suffer because the angry Lord of the Universe is unresponsive to their pleading? Apparently touched by the rabbi's anguished words, the Almighty revealed to him the events that will give rise to the messianic age, among them the ascendance of the Muslims. This vision of the future did not relieve the rabbi's anxiety. He feared the Muslims would

---

33. See chapter 5.

34. See n. 13.

35. According to the variant known as the *Secrets* (*nistarot*) of Simeon Ben Yochai: three days and nights; see *MG*, 187. In another variant, the *Prayer* (*tefilah*) of Simeon Ben Yochai: forty days, in *MG*, 273.

36. Ps. 80:5. Following the exact wording of Psalms. The midrash that reads "your servant" (*ʿa-v-d-kh*) may be a scribal error for "your people" (*ʿa-m-kh*). In either case, the meaning is much the same. The rabbi is pleading on his own behalf and that of the people of Israel. Reciting Psalms, thereby asking God to intervene at a moment of great personal and public distress, is a well-known Jewish tradition.

simply replicate the evil rule of the Romans. But he was soon mollified. According to some versions, the archangel Metatron appeared before him and starting with a prophecy from the book of Isaiah explained that the rise of Islam foreshadowed a long-sought cataclysmic event that was in the offing. The Muslims were to pave the way for the Messiah and the accompanying salvation of Israel.[37]

Modern readers of ancient and medieval apocalypses will surely recognize that when explained in full, the angel's description of the future included thinly disguised allusions to historic figures and to events that took place long after Isaiah preached. The introduction of sage characters quoting ancient prophecies that consist of veiled references to more current events is after all a well-known literary convention of eschatological texts, be it Jewish, Christian, or Muslim eschatology. As one scholar observed, medieval apocalypses are actually "chronicles [of events passed] written in the future tense."[38] In the Ben Yochai cycle we find Metatron massaging the text of the prophet to reveal the coming of kingdoms that graced the pages of history after Isaiah and even after the Roman oppression that forced the rabbi to seek safety in his hidden cave. In what is presumably the earliest version of the cycle (ca. mid-eighth century CE), God's angel cites Isaiah 21:6–7 and then explicates the text. The prophet's text reads: "For thus said the Lord to me: Go set up a sentry. Let him make known what he sees (6). He will see [a troop of] mounted men (*rechev*), horsemen in pairs; mounted men on asses; mounted men on camels. Take heed, much heed!" (7). The original meaning of the biblical text clearly indicated Isaiah was prophesying the future destruction of Babylon; for as the Hebrew prophet explains two verses later: "And here they come, mounted men, horsemen in pairs. . . . Fallen! Fallen is Babylon and all the idols of their Gods have been smashed into the ground" (9).

Because the later verse in Isaiah (21:9) mentions only "mounted men, horsemen in pairs" and omits reference to men mounted on asses and camels (who are clearly assumed in the biblical text to be part and parcel of the larger army attacking Babylon), Metatron, exercising a literary license all too familiar to students of rabbinic literature, expands the range of the prophet's vision to include the fate of kingdoms other than Babylon—all polities that will rise and fall before the final redemption of Israel. In this instance, the apocalyptical imagination necessitated breaking down the other contingents of Isaiah's avenging army and assigning them to different ages and dynasties in order to

37. *MG*, 188.

38. P. Alexander, "Medieval Apocalypses as Historical Sources," *American Historical Review* 73 (1968): 1018.

produce the requisite number of kingdoms that will come and go, including a future Muslim caliphate. Like Babylon and its idols, all will come crashing to the ground.[39]

The angel explains to Rabbi Simeon: "Mounted men" refers to Babylon; "Pairs" refers to the Medes; "horsemen" refers to the Greeks; "mounted men on asses" refers to the Edomites (a well-known rabbinic euphemism meaning Romans and also Byzantines); "mounted men on camels" refers to the Ishmaelite kingdom (that is, the rule of the Muslims). A later version plays with the text to include the Messiah who, according to Jewish tradition, will make his appearance "lowly and riding upon an ass."[40] Following his introduction of the Ishmaelites, Metatron refers—however obliquely—to the Muslim future. He recalls events of early Islamic history: wars with the Byzantines, internal Muslim politics, innovations in governance, and, most important for us, the restoration of the Temple Mount. Once the contemporaneous reader (or listener in the case of oral transmission) connected the angel's vague prophecy with recognizable persons and events of a more recent Islamic past—confirming thereby that certain elements of Isaiah's ancient prophecy had already been fulfilled—the way was paved for accepting what God's angel said was soon to come. In effect, the reader (or listener) felt that the prophecy was authentic in all its particulars. With that, he or she was bearing witness to the onset of the end of days and the immanent salvation of Israel.

It would appear, however, that the Jewish Messiah keeps to a mysterious time schedule. Time and again the redeemer of the chosen people has failed to appear at moments of heightened expectations. And yet the belief in his ultimate arrival remained constant among Jews in Islamic lands. Redemption was inevitable, but it had to be put off for a future moment, and then another and another. This did not mean that the vision of the future related in the tale of Rabbi Simeon was a patent falsehood, only that the proof texts with their veiled allusions to events and people lacked proper explication. With neither the Messiah nor his herald arriving as expected, the predictions of an anticipated messianic age had to be adjusted to the realities of the moment. Later redactors reinterpreted the original biblical prophecies and added other additional proof texts to accommodate references to a more recent Islamic history. The apocalypse of Ben Yochai was thus brought up to date for successive generations of readers longing for the arrival of the Messiah and the salvation of God's faithful. In effect, the oblique statements that Metatron explicated in order to pre-

39. *MG*, 189 ff.

40. Zech. 9:9. The reference to the Messiah in the prophecy of Isaiah is in the *Prayer* of Simeon Bar Yochai. See *MG*, 272.

dict the future for Ben Yochai took on, with the delayed arrival of the Messiah, what may be characterized as an agglutinating literary formation. The redactors from different times and regions spliced together snippets of earlier accounts and added their own material to stretch the meaning of the original vision. In such fashion, they added material that reflected additional dynasts and regimes that were destined to rise and fall with the march of history.[41]

Newer versions of the Ben Yochai cycle referred indirectly to the times of the Abbasid and Fatimid caliphs; the Carmathians and Saljuqs; and to the Crusaders who ravaged the Holy Land and its Jewish community only to see defeat at the hands of the Muslims. The initial Muslim victories over the Byzantines, events of the seventh century referred to in the earliest Ben Yochai texts, may not have led directly to the onset of the messianic age, but the defeat of the other peoples mentioned in the later versions was surely expected to do so. These references to later polities were disguised in vague language and to the same purpose as before. Once again, the reader was presented with a puzzle that called for associating familiar names and situations of a biblical past with more or less contemporaneous rulers and events. In such fashion, Israel's anticipated redemption, as described in earliest versions of these apocalypses, was put off for several hundred years to accommodate ensuing events. Originally scheduled for the first Islamic century, a time when Muslim Arab armies forced the Byzantines from the Holy Land and neighboring regions, the salvation of the Jews was eventually made to coincide with a second Muslim victory over oppressive Christians, this time wearers of the cross who came from distant places and despoiled the Holy Land and its holiest city.[42]

41. The composite nature of the Ben Yochai cycle and the interpolation of material reflecting later moments of Jewish history was stressed by B. Lewis in his "Apocalyptic Vision," 308–38. One can add to Lewis's article, E. Urbach's study of Oxford Ms. 2339, a midrash written in Hebrew and Aramaic that interpolates into a Ben Yochai account material describing the Crusader siege of Acre in 1191 CE; the Christian attack on Egypt in 1249; and various other events of the thirteenth century. See his "A Midrash of Redemption From Late Crusader Times [Hebrew]," *Eretz Israel* 10 (1971): 58–63. See also the early study of F. Baer, "Eine jüdische Messiasprophetie auf das Jahr 1186 und der dritte Kreuzzug," *MGWJ* 70 (1926): 113–22, 155–65, esp. 162–65. See also M. Sharon, "Praises of Jerusalem," 63–64.

42. *MG*, 270 ff. The apocalypse labels the Crusaders Kenites, a people linked to the Israelites by Moses's marriage to Jethro's daughter (Exod. 3:1, 18:1. For other names of his father-in-law, see Exod. 2:18, Num. 10:29, and Judg. 1:16, 4:11). The Hebrew Bible takes an ambivalent attitude toward the Kenites. On the one hand there is a description of early friendly relations with the Israelites (Num. 10:29–32). They are nevertheless also counted among the enemies of Israel (Num. 25:6–15, 31:1–12) and are said to have been associated with the most hated of all Israel's enemies, the Amalekites (1 Sam. 15:6), the descendants of Esau who are linked to the land of Edom (see, for example, Exod. 17:6–16, 18:5, and esp. 1 Sam. 15). Over the course of generations, the name Amalek applied to the most dangerous of all the enemies of the Jews (including the Nazis). Hence by extension the label Kenite equals Amalik and Kenite equals Edom applied to hated Crusaders.

There is also reference to *Ashkenaz* (*MG*, 273), a name that first appears in the genealogical

What, if anything, does all this tell us about our original concern: Muʿāwiyah's supposed scheme to shift the political center of the Islamic realm from Damascus to Jerusalem and to make the city holy to Christians and Jews equally sacred for Muslims? Put somewhat differently, given what we know of these apocalyptical texts, can we still rely on them to inform us about the early history of Islam, and, more particularly, Jerusalem? As does Elad, can we follow Peters and employ the Ben Yochai cycle as evidence that Muʿāwiyah had grand plans for the city in which he was proclaimed commander of the faithful? The allusions to historical persons and events, especially the statements dealing with the restoration of the Temple Mount, are extremely problematic. For with the passing of time, the references to more and more persons and historic events became increasingly confused, not the least because for Jews the earlier memories of Islamic history faded quickly. As a rule, even Jews exposed to Muslim learning did not take an avid and sustained interest in Arabic historical writing. At best, the different apocalyptical versions are a reflection of how Jews might have imagined the Islamic past at diverse moments of their own existence. By no means are these apocalyptical texts the stuff with which to reconstruct an orderly vision of political developments in early Islamic times, especially when we find that the oblique references to Islamic history in the fragmented and textually unstable Hebrew sources are at variance with detailed reports found in numerous Arabic chronicles and belletristic works. The Hebrew apocalypses are not "chronicles written in the future tense" if by chronicle we mean a more or less sustained historical narrative.

Muʿāwiyah and Jewish Apocalypses

There is then every reason to approach the historicity of the Ben Yochai cycle with great caution. All the more so when the texts are cited as proof of

lists of Gen. 10:12, where Ashkenaz is identified as the grandson of Japheth, the progenitor of what modern scholars referred to as the Indo-European peoples. In Jer. 51:27 Ashkenaz came to signify a non-Semitic kingdom that opposed the Babylonian empire. This non-Semitic polity is identified by modern scholars of the ancient Near East with the Ishkuza who are said to have originated between the Caspian and the Black Sea. See S. Parpola, *Neo-Assyrian Toponyms*, Alter Orient und Altes Testament 6 (Neukirchen-Vluyn, 1970), 178. Even Shemuel identifies Ashkenaz with foreign mercenaries hired to combat the Muslim Saljuqs. See his annotation to *MG*, 273. The identification of Ashkenaz with the enigmatic Khazars of Europe seems far-fetched, as one can hardly find a dramatic role for the Khazars in the various histories of the Near East. For the Khazar connection, see A. H. Silver, *Messianic Speculation*, 47. Eventually, Ashkenaz came to represent the areas of Jewish settlement in Europe's Rhineland, the territorial enclave embracing today parts of northern France and Germany. When our writers speak of Ashkenaz, they may be referring to the crusading Europeans who wreaked havoc among the Jewish communities of Mainz, Speyer, and Worms before making their way to the Holy Land and killing Muslims and Jews there.

Muʿāwiyah's intention to make the holy city the fulcrum of Muslim power. With proper circumspection Peters relates that there may be some confirmation that Muʿāwiyah planned to rule Islamic world from Jerusalem in a Jewish apocalypse whose kernel goes back to the time of the Islamic conquest. He admits that its version of early Islamic history is more than a little disordered—an understatement that speaks volumes because by any standard of measurement, the presumed order of rulers and events linked to them in the Ben Yochai texts is often confused, at times hopelessly so. This confusion is especially noticeable as regards the earliest caliphs. Peters goes on to say that the midrash "seems to refer directly to the Temple [Mount]" (which is true) and cites a statement that "seems" to indicate (note the frequent use of seems) that Muʿāwiyah is to be identified with an unnamed "second Muslim ruler" mentioned in the text, a ruler whose identity is important, if not critical, to Peters' argument. That second ruler is described as a "lover of Israel" who is destined to restore the breaches of the Temple [platform], level the surface of Mount Moriah, and "build a mosque there over the (primeval) rock (*even shetiyah*)." Having satisfied himself that Muʿāwiyah is this second ruler, Peters maintains that ʿAbd al-Malik and his son al-Walīd "are reduced to repairing the Temple [precinct]." The implication: Muʿāwiyah was the true architect of transforming the Temple Mount and Jerusalem into a quintessential symbol of Islamic rule. The later Umayyad caliphs merely completed the long-standing project that their predecessor envisioned (in full) and initiated (in part).[43]

But can this be gleaned from the source itself? Peters cites none of the several edited versions. For access to the Hebrew apocalypse he relies entirely on Bernard Lewis, who provides him with a graceful translation and a judicious analysis of different versions drawn from the Ben Yochai cycle. Of the many scholars who attempted to situate these medieval apocalypses, Lewis was the first to fully appreciate the extent to which the different versions we possess are composed of fragmented texts. Redacted over the course of centuries, the collected accounts, all heavily coded, portray diverse moments of Islamic history that have been grafted onto original core texts that have been lost with the passing of time.[44] Despite Lewis's heroic effort at sorting out different versions and identifying the specific events to which they allude, we are still left mulling over much that is confusing. Reading Lewis, whose assertions are always tempered by scholarly caution, should have given Peters cause to reflect carefully on his own boldly stated claim that links the Hebrew apocalypse's account of restoring the Temple Mount to Muʿāwiyah. Going a step further, should we consider this

43. Peters, *Jerusalem and Mecca*, 92–93. The text can be found in *MG*, 189, 401 = *Beit ha-Midrash*, 79.

44. See n. 13.

source evidence of the caliph's alleged plan to reestablish the seat of Islamic rule in a city long venerated by Jews and Christians?

None of the passages cited by Lewis contains an unambiguous reference to Muʿāwiyah, let alone mentions him by name or ties him to the Temple Mount or the so-called administrative complex uncovered beyond the southern wall of the platform. The ruler destined to restore the breaches of the Temple, level the surface of Mount Moriah, and build a mosque over the primeval rock is identified only as the second Muslim (Ishmaelite) ruler and a lover of Israel. He is also described as engaging the Sons of Esau in combat (meaning the Edomites) and inflicting a great defeat on them, all that before dying in peace and with great honor.[45] A variant of Ben Yochai's vision describes the second Muslim ruler as a conqueror who will war successfully against the Edomites and will be a lover of Israel who goes to Jerusalem and prays there. As in the previous account, he will repair the breaches in the temple precinct (*heichal*), hew Mount Moriah, level the surface of the entire platform, and die in peace and with great honor.[46]

How then are we to determine the identity of the unnamed second ruler; the lover of Israel, and the initiator of major Muslim construction in the holy city? There is little if any reason to believe the Jewish author has Muʿāwiyah in mind. The Umayyad was the first of his dynasty, not the second. Moreover, in the texts cited by Peters, the second ruler is destined to be followed by a great king who will rule but a short time before the Sons of Kedar (meaning the Northern Arabs) will rise up and kill him. The descendants of Ishmael will then crown another ruler whose name is Marwān, and he will give rise to four descendants, the first of whom will repair the walls of the Temple Mount (a seeming reference to ʿAbd al-Malik), adding still another caliph to our list of those responsible for building activity on the ancient platform.[47] If we accept that the second ruler was Muʿāwiyah, as Peters suggests, how are we to explain what is clearly a skewed sequence of Muslim rulers? At first reading, the third ruler who is killed by revolting Arab tribesmen seemingly refers to ʿUthmān

45. Lewis translates from the *Secrets* one of the Ben Yochai texts published by Adolph Jellinick in his anthology *Beit ha-Midrash* (third printing Jerusalem, 1967), 2:77–82. The relevant passage is on p. 79 = *MG*, 401.

46. *MG*, 189, a text heavily redacted by Even Shemuel, who emends it to read, "and he will pray there [to the God of Israel]." After listing the repairs undertaken by the second ruler, Even Shmuel adds, "He [the ruler] will call upon Israel to erect a building on the sacred area (*ba-heichal*). In his day, Judah will be redeemed and the plant of (the Messiah) Son of David will sprout." The reason for the emendation is given in the introduction to the text, p. 166 n. 20, and is based on the assumption that the Jews regarded the clearing of the Temple Mount as the first step of the Muslims allowing them to rebuild the Temple. However, in the end, the ruler built a Muslim place of worship there. There is no hard evidence to support this expectation, let alone to emend the text. The other variants give no reason for the editor to have emended the text as he did.

47. Jellenick, *Beit ha-Midrash*, 2:79 = *MG*, 401.

b. ʿAffān, Muʿāwiyah's predecessor twice removed, and not the Umayyad's son and successor Yazīd. Nor did ʿUthmān rule for a brief period before his death, as did the third ruler of the apocalypse. Quite the opposite, he may have been chosen because the small band of electors thought the aged Muslim would be a short-lived commander of the faithful, but, much to their dismay, he reigned for twelve years before his murder. Nor does Muʿāwiyah's son Yazīd fit the profile of his successor as described in the Hebrew source. After succeeding his father, Yazīd lived for three eventful years before dying a natural death. And what are we to make of Marwān's son who is credited with repairing the walls of the Temple Mount, an event that could only have taken place years after Muʿāwiyah's death? The Hebrew apocalypse simply does not square with the history of the times reported by all the Arab chroniclers. As they say in Hebrew: "There are no bears, nor is there any forest." In sum, there is no reason to assume, based on the Jewish sources known to Peters, that Muʿāwiyah was the aforementioned second caliph and guiding force behind major Islamic construction in Jerusalem, let alone that the first of the Umayyads envisioned moving his capital to the holy city from Damascus. When all is said and considered, the Ben Yochai cycle does not suggest, let alone state forthrightly, that Muʿāwiyah undertook to Islamize Jerusalem on a grand scale.

We still have to consider the fragment of the *Sefer Zerubbabel* cited by Elad, the text in which a ruler with a garbled name that stands for Muʿāwiyah is credited with building the wall of the Temple Mount.[48] There is also the statement of al-Muṭahhir b. Ṭāhir al-Maqdisī that Muʿāwiyah built (or perhaps refurbished) a mosque on the platform where the ancient temples of the Jews had stood.[49] The apocalyptical fragment cited by Elad has the correct order of the Umayyad caliphs; speaks sparingly of the events of their time; and even identifies a number of them by name, including ʿAbd al-Malik, whose reported destiny was to build "the house (*beit*) of the Lord of Israel."[50] I assume this last statement is a reference to his building activity on the Temple Mount that the text considers a prelude to the messianic age, the end of days when the Temple will once again be used to give sacrifices to the God of the chosen people. Oddly enough, Peters does not refer to *Sefer Zerubbabel*, and more surprising, he does not mention Maqdisī, whose chronicle he might have used in support of his view.

Another source that Peters and others might have cited has seemingly gone unnoticed. In claiming Muʿāwiyah desired to relocate to Jerusalem and establish the city revered by Jews and Christians as the political hub of the Islamic

48. See n. 12.
49. Maqdisī, *Bad'*, 4:87.
50. Wertheimer, *Batei Midrashot*, 2:504.

realm, scholars could have turned to the earliest extant annalistic history, the *Ta'rīkh* of Khalīfah b. Khayyāṭ (d. ca. 855 CE). Ibn Khayyāṭ refers to the first Umayyad caliph as the ruler (*malik*) of *al-arḍ al-muqaddasah*, "the land made holy" or "the holy land."[51] Given the ambiguous nature of the expression *al-arḍ al-muqaddasah*, one can imagine scholars like Peters, once informed of the passage, would have taken license to declare that it referred to Jerusalem and its surroundings, or in any case to what had been the Palaestina of Graeco-Roman Greater Syria. That being the case, the text might be seen as reinforcing the view that the first Umayyad caliph had special plans for the holy city. It is clear, however, from variants cited by Ibn 'Asākir (d. 1176 CE) that the land made holy or holy land was meant in this instance to be understood as all of al-Shām and not Jerusalem and its surroundings. Moreover, in the accounts cited by Ibn 'Asākir, the caliph's son Yazīd is also labeled together with his father "ruler (*malik* or *ṣāḥib*) of al-arḍ al-muqaddasah."[52] As no one has suggested Yazīd intended to rule from Jerusalem, it seems all too clear his label like that of his father meant that both Umayyads ruled al-Shām, presumably from Damascus.

In Conclusion

The aforementioned Hebrew and Arabic sources provide no compelling evidence that Mu'āwiyah was on the verge of creating a "New Jerusalem" for Muslims. One can hardly conclude, based on the texts cited, that the first of the Umayyad line had a specific plan to shift the capital of the Islamic realm from Damascus to Jerusalem, let alone that he envisioned Jerusalem as a center of Muslim religious activity, the likes of the ḥaramayn. At most, one might suggest that Mu'āwiyah gave some thought of moving to Jerusalem, but, in the end, did not carry through with the project. The evidence, such as it is, indicates that there was never any serious thought or, for that matter, any thought at all of making Jerusalem the nerve center of Muslim political activity. As for the Islamization of Jerusalem—the deliberate effort to rank the city as a Muslim holy place by undertaking major construction on the Temple Mount—that change of status for the city first took root during the reign of 'Abd al-Malik. That was some thirty-odd years after Mu'āwiyah's death. Nevertheless, the claim that the first of the Ummayad rulers had a grand design for Jerusalem has found a place in modern scholarship, including the more popular versions of the city's history.

51. Ibn Khayyāṭ, *Ta'rīkh*, 258; see also Dhahabī, *Ta'rīkh*, 3:91.

52. Ibn Khayyāṭ, 205; also Ibn 'Asākir, *Ta'rīkh Dimashq* (Beirut), 65:408–9. I am indebted to J. Lindsay, who called this reference in Ibn 'Asākir to my attention.

CHAPTER 5

ʻAbd Al-Malik and the Temple Mount

Revisiting S. D. Goitein and Oleg Grabar

Popular histories of Jerusalem can be very seductive for readers not familiar with Arabic historiography or methods of field archaeology and art history. The writings of F. S. Peters, which are widely discussed in the previous chapter, are generally intended, or so it would seem, for a broad and highly intelligent audience of nonspecialists. Gracefully written and easily digested, they enjoy a favored place alongside the detailed scholarly works that serve as the foundation of his narrative. We can assume that Peters's writings are also a point of entry for many scholars of religion who are interested in the history of Jerusalem but who are without the requisite tools to make informed judgments of detailed archaeological reports and of data obtained from primary sources written in unfamiliar languages. While easing the general reader's burden in exploring Jerusalem's history, Peters often leaves them without sufficient awareness of the specialist's dilemma; in this instance the need to confront highly fragmentary and often contradictory evidence. Despite occasional disclaimers, the author tends as a rule to create an air of certainty for the story he tells. It is as though his feet, hence those of his audience, hover above an epistemological minefield that awaits safe crossing. His readers, specialists and nonspecialists alike, might have been better served if he had guided them through the twists and turns of that scholarly danger zone. With that, they could more fully appreciate the difficulty of seeking clarification of a murky past.

To be fair, even the most meticulous researchers, scholars whose writings are thick with footnotes to primary sources and peppered with methodological markers each step of the way, even such scholars are occasionally inclined to accept as conventional wisdom what may be described as general observations aired by an authoritative voice. For historians of medieval Islam, S. D. Goitein remains such a voice. Some scholarly works have a short shelf life, but Goitein's writings retain a prominent place at the center of many debates decades after they were written. Although deceased for nearly thirty years, he remains until this day the very model of a scholar's scholar. Among historians of the Islamic world who practiced their craft in the twentieth century, none was more rooted in primary sources than Goitein. He often referred to himself as a "sociographer," an arcane label meaning someone who describes societies of old based on written records. In his work on Islamic history, especially his magisterial study of Mediterranean society, Goitein combined superb philological skills with prodigious learning and a keen sensitivity to social history.[1] In plumbing a vast range of written sources and describing their contents, he gives the impression that he is a contemporary observer of the historic people he encounters, albeit with understandings shaped by the tools of modern scholarship. There is, however, another dimension to Goitein. This most meticulous scholar who demanded textual evidence from colleagues was often given to broad observations based on intuition—flashes of insight that he shared with listeners who then worked out the details, shaping his astute observations into articles and books. How then are we to assess Goitein when he opines that in all likelihood Muʿāwiyah was the first Muslim ruler to conceive of major construction on the Temple Mount, a view noted in his entry on Jerusalem (*al-Ḳuds*) in the second edition of the *Encyclopedia of Islam*?

Although stated with conviction, Goitein's brief comments should be taken as a reflective, rather than definitive, statement; that is, as a point of departure calling for an extended discussion among historians of Islamic Jerusalem and, more generally those of the Umayyad dynasty. In essence, the case for Muʿāwiyah presented in the encyclopedia entry is based on several assumptions, each of which can be challenged. The author notes that the first Umayyad caliph developed a number of properties in Mecca for the benefit of Muslims fulfilling the rites of pilgrimage. He seems to argue that having invested in Mecca, the caliph also would have undertaken major construction in Jerusalem, the venerable city where he was declared commander of the faithful.[2] Goitein assumes that the modest Muslim place of worship described by the Christian pilgrim Arculf (ca. 670 CE) must have taken shape during Muʿāwiyah's reign and equates this sanctuary with the *masjid* whose construction (or refurbishing?) was ascribed to Muʿāwiyah by al-Muṭahhar b. Ṭāhir al-Maqdisī.[3] Finally, he writes in the encyclopedia entry: "It stands to reason that the plan for the

1. S. D. Goitein, *A Mediterranean Society* (Berkeley, 1967–93), 6 vols. The cumulative indices in volume 6 were prepared by P. Sanders after Goitein's death. The larger study was abridged and revised in one volume by J. Lassner (Berkeley, 1999).

2. M. J. Kister, "The Battle of Ḥarra," 38, 42–44.

3. Maqdisī, *Bad'*, 4:87.

erection of the Dome of the Rock, which needed immense preparations, was already made during the protracted and orderly rule of Muʿāwiya(h)." He then goes to suggest that while ʿAbd al-Malik had good reasons to finish the project "which would show him as a great champion of Islam . . . the early years of his caliphate were hardly suited for both conceiving such an enormous undertaking and carrying it out to its very end during a comparatively short period of time." I imagine Goitein refers here to ʿAbd al-Malik's campaigns against the rebel counter-caliph ʿAbdallāh b. al-Zubayr and the latter's Iraqi allies; intermittent warfare along the Byzantine frontier; outbreaks of tribal feuds that had to be settled; the always confrontational Khārijites; and a short insurrection within the ruling house in the capital.[4]

Do these assumptions actually point us in the direction that Goitein would have us move? Muʿawiyah's projects in Mecca, noted earlier, do not necessarily suggest that he was similarly inclined to build in Jerusalem, be it on the Temple Mount or anywhere else. Nor is there any reason to believe that Bishop Arculf was describing a mosque built by Muʿāwiyah on the Temple Mount as reported by Maqdisī, or that Maqdisī's statement, which is not corroborated by any other Arabic source, indicates the first Umayyad caliph actually constructed a new mosque somewhere on the ancient site. Why should we doubt the current view that the Christian visitor to the holy city came upon the unobtrusive place of worship erected by ʿUmar for Jerusalem's first Muslim community? If Muʿāwiyah had indeed built a mosque on the Temple Mount to serve as a visual symbol of his rule, and if that were part of an ambitious plan to transfer the political center of the Islamic realm to Jerusalem, one would expect the caliph to have erected a structure far more imposing than the building described by Arculf. Even if we were to accept Maqdisī's statement that Muʿāwiyah had a hand in developing the Temple Mount, there is no compelling reason to believe that the caliph actually erected an entirely new mosque. It may be that that the author wishes to indicate that Muʿāwiyah enlarged or spruced up the original place of worship erected by ʿUmar. Could ʿAbd al-Malik have devoted the requisite planning and energy to initiate and complete a vast project on the Temple Mount? Goitein clearly believes that the turbulence of the times would have precluded any such endeavor.

Oleg Grabar, the doyen of Islamic art historians and archaeologists, reviewed Goitein's views and considered them an idea proposed in a passing remark without substantiating evidence, that is, the kind of scholarly reflections

4. For a survey of these events, see ʿA. A. ʿA. Dixon, *The Umayyad Caliphate, 65–86/684–705* (London, 1971), esp. 121–42 (Zubayrid revolt); also G. R. Hawting, *The First Dynasty of Islam* (London, 1986), 46–58.

that one finds sprinkled in Goitein's writings from time to time. Nevertheless, following Goitein's intuition, Grabar revised his own thinking on the Dome of the Rock, whose construction he had originally dated, as did others, to the reign of ʿAbd al-Malik. More than a quarter of a century after his 1959 pathbreaking publication on the domed structure, Grabar revisited the origins and meaning of the building in a public lecture at Oxford University. The lecture, which was refashioned into a reflective essay, stands as Grabar's endorsement of Goitein's revisionist history.[5] Like Goitein, Grabar, speaking in 1985, accepted that the first of the Umayyads envisioned a major building project on the Temple Mount.

In the published version of this lecture, which appeared in 1988, the famed art historian notes the wide acceptance of his original views where he maintained that the Dome of the Rock was a monument celebrating the victorious presence of Islam in a Christian city first made holy by the ancient Israelites. As did his scholarly contemporaries, Grabar originally saw the Muslim construction on the Temple Mount as part of the so-called reforms of ʿAbd al-Malik, the fulfillment of a revolutionary vision that was to transform the course of Islamic history. In addition to building the Dome of the Rock, ʿAbd al-Malik overhauled the monetary system, reduced the weight of the coins minted, and introduced for the first time Islamic coins to replace the pre-Islamic currency then in circulation. Like the domed building, the new coins, originally bearing the visage of the caliph, became a visual symbol of Islamic rule. ʿAbd al-Malik also made Arabic the administrative language of the realm, forcing the Greek functionaries inherited from the Byzantine system to adapt to a wholly new reality. In time, Arabic was employed in a wide range of situations other than administrative record keeping and scripting religious writings. Despite resistance from Persian speakers, Arabic became—within a century or two—the dominant literary language of the Islamic world, and for the conquered peoples of the Fertile Crescent and points west, a language of daily discourse. A less transcendent but certainly important accomplishment of the caliph was his successful military campaigns against the Byzantines, a sign that Muslims were likely to retain their hegemony where Christians once ruled, including Jerusalem, the city long venerated by the latter.

In the Oxford lecture and subsequent essay, Grabar holds to the main thesis of his original work and states unequivocally that ʿAbd al-Malik dedicated

5. Grabar's remarks were originally presented as the George Antonius Lecture sponsored by St. Anthony's College, Oxford. They were subsequently published as "The Meaning of the Dome of the Rock in Jerusalem," *Medieval Studies at Minnesota* 3 (1988): 1–10 and then reprinted in volume 4 of his collected writings. See *Jerusalem*, 143–58, esp. 158–51.

the building on his watch. But, as did Goitein, he altered his view. Agreeing with Goitein, he favored Muʿāwiyah as the ruler who most likely conceived and initiated the project on the Temple Mount. He notes that the first Umayyad ruler chose to be declared caliph in Jerusalem (and not Damascus). Grabar remains guarded about Muʿāwiyah's alleged plan to transform Jerusalem into the seat of the realm, an idea suggested tentatively by Goitein, but, as we have seen, enthusiastically accepted by others. Above all, Grabar agrees with Goitein that the completion of the project must have taken many years, too many for it to have been started and completed by ʿAbd al-Malik. Grabar lists the many things that would have been required before the completion of the Dome of the Rock, among them: clearing and leveling the ancient surface for the building and its platform; assembling construction material from nearby abandoned or destroyed structures; producing other needed materials locally; and setting mosaics and marble into the walls. Designing the patterns of the mosaics required the availability of expert craftsmen, and the tesserae and plaques of marble had to be brought from the workshops where they were manufactured by skilled artisans. He goes on to argue that Jerusalem "was not a major center for what nowadays might be called a construction industry, and was not a capital city bound to attract [such] craftsmen artisans seeking employment."[6] Moreover, building the Dome of the Rock would have required a huge financial investment, sizable logistical support, and a network of administrators (and he could have added security personnel) to oversee the project. He concludes that it would have taken years to initiate and complete such a venture and that the Umayyads were for a decade occupied with the extended rebellion of Ibn al-Zubayr and his Iraqi allies.

Building in Jerusalem: A Comparative Perspective

Grabar would have us believe that the handful of years it reportedly took for ʿAbd al-Malik to build the Dome of the Rock would not have been enough under the circumstances. Can he be right in assuming that so limited a time span would not have provided ʿAbd al-Malik with ample opportunity to plan and complete the building? At first glance, his assumption, like that of Goitein's, is proffered as a sensible proposal, and also like Goitein's passing comment, a proposal without substantiating evidence. How are we to assess Grabar's contention that Jerusalem and its environs could not have provided the human

---

6. Grabar, *Jerusalem*, 149.

resources and construction materials to sustain a vast effort like that developing the Temple Mount? We might wish to ask what is known of other major building efforts from the formative period of Islamic rule, and how might knowledge of these other projects enhance our understanding of developments in Umayyad Jerusalem. The best-reported and surely most massive urban project of early Islamic times is the magnificent Round City (*al-madīnah al-mudawwarah*) conceived by the Abbasid caliph Abū Jaʿfar al-Manṣūr (r. 754–75) and erected by him on a site generally referred to as Baghdad. Planned with meticulous attention to detail, the Round City was designed to serve as the fulcrum of the recently established Abbasid regime and as a visual symbol that dramatically proclaimed the legitimacy of the new dynastic order.[7]

Unlike those Muslim structures on the Temple Mount that have been preserved and frequented for a thousand years and more—to be sure with allowances for repair and modification—there are no physical traces of the Round City. Nor is it likely archaeologists will have the opportunity to recover any. The Abbasid structure that fell into ruin a thousand years and more lies deeply buried beneath the densely built up and heavily populated modern city of Baghdad. In the best of circumstances, locating the precise location of the Round City would be extremely difficult, and if located, initiating a large-scale dig would be highly impracticable. The same can be said for the suburban lands (*arbāḍ*) immediately to the east, west, north, and south of the Round City, which together with the caliphal enceinte formed the City of Peace (*Madīnat al-Salām*), the capital of the newly established Abbasid realm. As regards the site of al-Manṣūr's capital, Grabar's preference for facts on or in the ground has had no bearing so far, and it is not likely to have any in the future.

There are, however, detailed medieval accounts describing the architectural features of the Round City, the recruiting of the workforce, and how the project was supervised.[8] These sources reveal that the so-called Round City was not a true city, but an extraordinary palace complex that served as the administrative center of a far-flung empire.[9] The perfectly symmetrical structure was divided

7. See J. Lassner, *The Shaping of ʿAbbāsid Rule* (Princeton, 1980), 163–83.

8. Khaṭīb, *Taʾrīkh Baghdād* (Cairo, 1931), 1:66–79. The topographical introduction to the Khaṭīb's work was edited and translated with partial annotation by G. Salmon as *L'Introduction topographique à l'histoire de Baghdad* (Paris, 1904). See esp. 1–20; also the densely annotated translation of J. Lassner, *The Topography of Baghdad in the Early Middle Ages: Texts and Studies* (Detroit, 1970), 45–63.; Yaʿqūbī, *Buldān*, 233–40; and the section on Iraq in the complete version of Ibn al-Faqīh's *K. al-Buldān* (Cairo). The original Leiden edition published by E.J. Brill (BGA 5) is an abbreviated text (*mukhtaṣar*) that omits completely the segment on Baghdad and the rest of Iraq. The description of the Round City in the fuller text shares much in common with that of the Khaṭīb and the entries on Baghdad and its individual locations in the *Muʿjam al-buldān*, the great geographical dictionary of Yāqūt al-Ḥamawī.

9. Originally argued in J. Lassner, "The Caliph's Personal Domain: The City Plan of Baghdad

into four quadrants, each extending one Arabic *mīl* (two kilometers) along the exterior wall. The four quadrants were framed by gated arcades and featured two concentric rings of occupation: an outer ring that housed the government functionaries and four thousand troops of the palace regiment, and an inner ring that contained the offices of the caliph's government, the apartments of his young children, the arsenal, the treasury, and a kitchen. These rings in turn enclosed an enormous inner court in which the caliph's residence and communal mosque were situated, as well as the headquarters for his security service (*shurṭah*) and personal guard (*ḥaras*).[10] The palace complex covered over 450 hectares, an expanse so large that it exceeded in surface area any full-fledged city in the history of Iraq, save Ctesiphon, the capital of the Sasanid dynasty.[11]

The Dome of the Rock and the platform upon which it stood could have been comfortably placed within the inner court (*raḥbah*) that surrounded al-Manṣūr's palace and mosque. The al-Aqṣā mosque would have fit conveniently into the Abbasid palace, a large square structure originally six hundred feet to a side; the entire Temple Mount took up less space than one of the Round City's four quadrants; and all of Jerusalem could have been squeezed into the Abbasid administrative center.[12] What is significant is that the project initiated by the Abbasids, a prodigious undertaking that dwarfed the Temple Mount, took only four years to complete, including time lost when the caliph was engaged in suppressing an Alid revolt.[13] That is, building the enormous Round City required no more time than it reportedly took to construct the Qubbat al-Ṣakhrah. That does not include the area of greater Baghdad, which included military camps established beyond the city walls to the north; the splendid royal palaces built along the Tigris shore to the east; or the markets that were established to the south and southwest. The claim that 'Abd al-Malik could not have completed the Dome of the Rock within the time it took to erect these structures is worth questioning.

What of Grabar's claim that Jerusalem was not a major center of a construction industry or a capital city bound to attract citizens seeking employment? And based on that, his contention that in addition to a large financial investment, building the Dome of the Rock would have required logistical support

Reexamined," in *The Islamic City*, edited by A. H. Hourani and S. M. Stern (Oxford, 1970), 103–18 (= Lassner, *Topography*, 138–54) and later in expanded form in his *'Abbāsid Rule*, 184–241 and *The Middle East Remembered* (Ann Arbor, 2000), 153–79.

10. For the plan of the Round City, see Lassner, *Topography*, 207.

11. Lassner, *Topography*, 155–77, esp. 157–68. For Ctesiphon and the Diyala Plains, the hinterland of Baghdad in Iraq, see R. M. Adams, *Land beyond Baghdad* (Chicago, 1965).

12. See illustrations 4 and 5 in chapter 6.

13. Lassner, *'Abbāsid Rule*, 69–79; F. Omar, *The 'Abbāsid Caliphate, 132/750–170/786* (Baghdad, 1969), 223–55.

(presumably for transporting men and materials to the building site), as well as a network of administrators (to supervise construction, secure the area, and arrange for the needs of the workforce)? I have the distinct impression that Grabar was influenced by accounts of the Round City, a story with which he was thoroughly familiar, having read and then penned the preface to this author's topographical history of the Abbasid capital, a work whimsically referred to by myself and others as the "Baedecker of Medieval Baghdad." As reported by Muslim authorities, the construction of the Round City required bringing skilled and unskilled laborers from outlying regions in what is today Syria and Iraq.[14] According to one source, the number of workers exceeded one hundred thousand,[15] an exaggeration to be sure, but nevertheless an indication of the need for imported labor occasioned by the enormous scale of the project. The data on comparative wages and prices reveals that the situation at the building site was conducive to creating a boom town, precisely the surroundings that would have attracted laborers from beyond the immediate environment.[16] Planning the Round City was left to expert architects, engineers, and surveyors; supervising the immense project was the responsibility of builders (*bannā'*), in reality military officers, whose men provided the necessary security. All told, the sources describe a level of organization and activity comparable to that which Grabar claims would have been necessary for building the Dome of the Rock from conception to completion. But would that really have been the case for Jerusalem?

This situation at Baghdad, described in detail by various Arabic sources, hardly applies to 'Abd al-Malik's project on the Temple Mount. How can one compare clearing the Jerusalem site and building the Dome of the Rock with al-Manṣūr's immense project? Moreover, why was Grabar so sure that the skilled labor required for building the structure on the Temple Mount was not available locally? The Jerusalem of the Byzantine emperor Heraclius and the period of the righteous caliphs that followed may not have been the resplendent New Jerusalem of an earlier era, but it still remained a vibrant urban settlement with many magnificent buildings, the most notable being the awe-inspiring Church of the Holy Sepulcher. All these buildings, new and old alike, would have required maintenance and some restoration over time. It seems inconceivable that Jerusalem was as lacking in artisans and building material as Grabar suggests. Indeed, there is ample evidence of construction and restoration in the holy city, its immediate surroundings, and the hinterland beyond during the

14. Khaṭīb, *Ta'rīkh Baghdād*, 1:66–67; Ya'qūbī, *Buldān*, 238.
15. Ya'qūbī, *Buldān*, 238.
16. Khaṭīb, *Ta'rīkh Baghdād*, 1:70.

early Islamic period, a time span roughly defined through the ninth century CE. Major restoration of the Church of the Nativity in nearby Bethlehem, an event dated to 680 or 681, would have required all sorts of skilled workers and access to building material, as would the construction of other Christian edifices dating roughly to the same time.[17]

Even if ʿAbd al-Malik needed materials and skilled workers unavailable locally, he might very well have drawn then from nearby Damascus and other cities of al-Shām. One notes the Arabic chronicler Ibn Kathīr, who tells us that when the caliph turned his attention to the Temple Mount, he assembled workers from the far reaches of the province (*min aṭrāf al-bilād*), by which he presumably means Greater Syria.[18] A more extended version of Ibn Kathīr's account is found in manuscripts of Sibṭ b. al-Jawzī's, *Mirʾāt al-zamān*, a text long known to scholars but whose passages relevant to the construction in Jerusalem were first edited in 1992 by Amikam Elad as an appendage to a detailed article on the Dome of the Rock.[19] Elad's edited text gives readers a picture of how labor was organized by the caliph and his agents. Sibṭ b. al-Jawzī tells us that ʿAbd al-Malik left Damascus (for Jerusalem) accompanied by workers (who were to build the Dome of the Rock). Rajāʾ b. Ḥaywah and Yazīd b. Salām, clients of the caliph, were entrusted with supervising the construction. The caliph then gathered skilled craftsmen (*ṣāniʿ*) and "engineers" (*muhandis*) from regions far beyond (*āfāq*) and ordered them to trace (*sawwara*) the plan of the building before starting construction. They did that in the court of the mosque, whereupon the caliph, amazed by the outline of the building, ordered that construction to proceed along with that of seven domed prayer niches (*miḥrāb*) surrounding the Dome of the Rock and facing Mecca. The text then describes the coverings produced for the building, one for winter, another for summer, as well as the features of the interior of the structure, various ceremonies that were held

17. See G. Avni, "From Hagia Polis to al-Quds: The Byzantine Islamic-Transition in Jerusalem," in *Unearthing Jerusalem*, edited by K. Galor and G. Avni (Winona Lake, IN, 2011), 387–416; and in the same volume, J. Seeligman, "The Hinterland of Jerusalem during the Byzantine Period," 361–83. More recent is the detailed volume of Avni, *The Byzantine-Islamic Transition in Palestine: An Archeological Approach* (Oxford, 2014), which analyzes recent archaeological researches on Palestine and Jordan from the sixth to the eleventh centuries. Note also S. Blair, who sees the extended construction and repair of Christian buildings, including the Church of Nativity in Bethlehem, as having attracted a sizable workforce of Christian artisans who would then have been available to work on the Muslim Temple Mount projects, including the Dome of the Rock (S. Blair, "What Is the Date of the Dome of the Rock?" *OSIA* 9/1 [1992]: 59–88). The continuity of building activity after the Islamic conquest does not preclude substantive changes in other phases of life after the Islamic conquest. See the review of Avni's book by P. Booth in *AHR* 120 (2015): 1574–75.

18. Ibn Kathīr, *Bidāyah*, 8:280.

19. "Why Did ʿAbd al-Malik Build the Dome of the Rock? A Re-examination of the Sources," *OSIA* 9/1 (1992): 33–58 (Arabic text, 53–58).

there, and the tasks of the gatekeepers (*sadnah*) and the attendants (*khuddām*) who serviced the building on Mondays and Thursdays.[20]

That still leaves us to explain how the caliph arranged to pay for restoring the Temple Mount and building the Dome of the Rock, a project that reportedly cost the equivalent of seven years' tax revenue from the wealthy province of Egypt.[21] Given all the political disturbances of the time alluded to by Goitein, Grabar, and others, would the Umayyads have had the wherewithal to finance an undertaking that included leveling the surface of the ancient Temple Mount and restoring its walls; building the domed structure over the primeval rock; erecting the seven prayer niches; and possibly initiating construction of the al-Aqṣā mosque? As regards financing the project, Sibṭ b. al-Jawzī is most instructive. The chronicler notes that 'Abd al-Malik brought with him wealth (*māl*), presumably a reference to hard currency with which to meet a payroll and reimburse a network of suppliers. Operating from a facility (*bayt li-l-māl*) the caliph had built east of where the Dome of the Rock was soon to be erected, Rajā' and Yazīd, 'Abd al-Malik's clients, seemingly acted as paymasters to the assembled labor force and handled all other encumbrances. According to 'Abd al-Malik's instructions, Rajā' and Yazīd were to spend as freely as required.[22] With this extended description of events, those who still doubt that 'Abd al-Malik had the capacity to undertake and complete the Temple Mount project might be wise to pause and reflect.

Unlike Jerusalem and its surroundings, the area where al-Manṣūr established his capital was at the time virtually uninhabited and distant from any Islamic settlement of importance. There was only a monastery and a sprinkling of small villages nearby. There was not even a permanent market for the local

20. Sibṭ b. al-Jawzī, *Mir'āt* (Elad), 54–55. On Mondays and Thursdays Jews assembled in their synagogues to perform ritual acts and attend to communal affairs. Note that Jews were reportedly used to service the Dome of the Rock. The significance of those Jews who serviced the Dome of the Rock and the events taking place there on Mondays and Thursdays is discussed in chapter 7. A variant of Ibn al-Jawzī's account (Wāsiṭī, *Faḍā'il*, 80–81) indicates how 'Abd al-Malik arranged for construction but omits references to the activities of the Jews.

21. Mujīr al-Dīn, *Uns*, 1:241 (the expenditure on the Dome of the Rock equaled seven years' tax revenue from Egypt). No doubt the author wishes to impress us that the grand project required an enormous outlay of expenditures. Similarly Wāṣitī, *Faḍā'il*, 80–81, which indicates the two clients in charge of finances were able to return to the caliph one hundred thousand gold coins after all the expenditures had been accounted for. The figure is of course grossly exaggerated, but it reflects the grand nature of 'Abd al-Malik's undertaking. N. Rabbat's attempt to identify the Dome of the Chain (*Qubbat al-Silisilah*), a small structure that stands near the Dome of the Rock, with the *bayt al-māl*, or treasury of the project, does not seem plausible. Given its size and structure, the Dome of the Chain could not have functioned as the bank and pay station of 'Abd al-Malik's building project. Nevertheless, the small domed building might have been place where the payroll and other monies were kept. See Rabbat's "The Dome of the Rock Revisited," 70.

22. Sibṭ b. al-Jawzī, *Mir'āt* (Elad), 54. See chapter 7 for the Jews' presence in the Dome of the Rock.

inhabitants; only a weekly fair. The local population could hardly be counted upon to provide the necessary day laborers let alone the skilled craftsmen required for the grand project al-Manṣūr envisioned. Nor could the market held weekly on Tuesdays have addressed the needs of the growing workforce; it surely could not have provided the required artisanal and industrial workshops. Virtually everyone and everything had to be brought to the site, or constructed from scratch, like the brickyard that supplied building blocks for the city's massive walls and interior buildings. The construction of the Dome of the Rock, a far more modest undertaking, would have presented 'Abd al-Malik with an entirely different and certainly less difficult set of circumstances. If despite all this al-Manṣūr could complete the Round City in four years, what reason is there to believe 'Abd al-Malik could not have erected the Dome of the Rock and repaired the Temple Mount in a comparable period of time?

Of course one has to consider the various conflicts that engaged 'Abd al-Malik's attention: destabilizing feuds among the tribes; battles with the Khārijites; the Zubayrid insurrections; warfare and diplomacy with the Byzantines; and a family uprising in Damascus over the succession to rule.[23] The fighting led Goitein and Grabar to presume that 'Abd al-Malik would have been too preoccupied with his enemies to plan, initiate, and complete his signature building program within a handful of years. Again, there is an apt comparison with al-Manṣūr and Baghdad. The Abbasid caliph also faced an insurrection after work on the Round City had begun three years earlier in 762. Like the Zubayrid challenge of Umayyad times, it was a two-pronged assault by two brothers, one rebelling in the Hijaz, the other in Iraq. In the latter case, Muḥammad al-Nafs al-Zakīyah opposed the caliph from his native Medina, while his brother Ibrāhīm rallied the Alid faithful in Kufa. In wake of the Alid uprising, al-Manṣūr was forced to halt construction and left the Baghdad area, regrouping at his capital, al-Hāshimīyah.[24] The rebellion was crushed within months and the caliph resumed building his new capital according to a plan personally approved by him after seeing the Round City drawn by his architects. Al-Manṣūr moved into the Round City four years after the foundation lines were traced.[25]

23. See n. 4.

24. Ṭabarī, *Annales*, 3/1:278, 281; Mas'ūdī, *Tanbīh*, 360; Ibn Qutaybah, *Ma'ārif*, 192. The disruption of the building project at Baghdad was obliquely referred to in a prophetic tale legitimizing al-Manṣūr and his capital (Lassner, *Topography*, 124–26). The Alid revolt is discussed in detail in Lassner's *'Abbāsid Rule*, 69–79, 81–84.

25. Ṭabarī, *Annales*, 3/1:277–78; Yāqūt, *Mujʿam*, 1:682.

The Threat to the Umayyads Revisited

We are obliged to ask if ʿAbd al-Malik, facing similar adversity from rebels contesting his regime, could have finished work on the Temple Mount in an equal period of time. Admittedly, equating the respective challenges to both ruling houses can be misleading. Compared to the initial dangers the Zubayrids and others posed for the Umayyad regime, the anti-Abbasid rebels who were situated in Arabia and Iraq do not seem to have been as great a threat to al-Manṣūr—at least not at first notice. The outbreak of the Alid revolt in Medina turned out to be a quixotic affair. When informed of the uprising, al-Manṣūr turned to one of his trusted military advisors, who exclaimed: "Praise God, for [the rebel] has made his appearance in a place where there are no financial or human resources (to raise and finance an army); no weapons and no horses (with which to equip a proper fighting force)."[26] A loyalist army, eighteen thousand men strong, was dispatched from Iraq to Arabia under the command of ʿĪsā b. Mūsā, the caliph's nephew and governor of Kufa. After easily penetrating the outer defenses of Medina, the Iraqi army made short work of the rebels. By far the more serious threat to ruling authority, whether to the Umayyads or Abbasids, was that of the pretenders' brothers, Muṣʿab b. al-Zubayr and the Alid Ibrāhīm b. ʿAbdallāh b. al-Ḥasan, situated as they were in Iraq, a province of great wealth and large numbers of combat veterans.

The second stage of the Alid revolt that erupted in Iraq forced the Abbasid caliph to abandon the construction site at Baghdad. With ʿĪsā b. Mūsā and the Iraq army fighting the rebels in the Hijaz, and two other Abbasid armies, one stationed in the distant province Khurāsān, the other campaigning in North Africa, the caliph, left with only token forces, withdrew to his palace complex at al-Hāshimīyah. The existing center of Abbasid rule was situated within hailing distance of the old garrison town of Kufa, by then a sizable city where, as the caliph put it, the rebel Ibrāhīm could call upon one hundred thousand potential fighting men.[27] As a result, the caliph was forced to initiate a series of ruses that made it seem that his meager forces were far greater than they were. Faced with

26. Some medieval sources seem to indicate that major elements of the Round City were completed as early as 146 / 763 CE; the final elements (presumably the outer and inner walls and moat and interior furnishings) were put in place only in 145/766 when the caliph moved to the Round City and set up the various agencies of the government that had until then been situated in al-Hāshimīyah. See Khaṭīb, *Tar'īkh Baghdād*, 1:66; Ṭabarī, *Annales*, 3/1:281, 319; Ibn Qutaybah, *Maʿārif*, 192; Masʿūdī, *Tanbīh*, 360; Yāqūt, *Muʿjam*, 1:680; and Muqaddasī, *Aḥsan*, 122. Balādhurī, *Futūḥ*, 295 gives 147/764–65 for the completion (may refer to the inner wall as well as the interior structures). In any case, the entire administrative complex was built in no more than four years.

27. Ṭabarī, *Annales*, 3/1:223–24, 291. For a variant giving different reasons downplaying the military significance of a revolt centered in the Hijaz, see Masʿūdī, *Murūj*, 3:295.

potential disaster, al-Manṣūr exhibited all sorts of erratic behavior, fearing with good reason that if the populace in nearby Kufa declared for the rebels, he had no means of resisting them. And so the caliph took to a place of prayer, where he remained for fifty days unkempt, unwashed, and generally unresponsive to human contact. Fortunately for al-Manṣūr, the Alids exhibited the hubris that allowed them time and again to parlay possible triumphs into spectacular defeats. They did not press their advantage. When the Abbasid army returned from campaigning in Arabia, they engaged Ibrāhīm's forces in a series of short but decisive battles. After fierce fighting, the second stage of the rebellion crumbled as did the first, and al-Manṣūr resumed building the Round City.[28]

At first glance, the situation confronting the Umayyad caliph seems to have represented a more serious problem. ʿAbd al-Malik was at war with the Zubayrids in Arabia, the rebels in Iraq, and also the Khārijites and Byzantines. There was even a brief insurrection by a relative in Damascus while the caliph was away from the city. Various campaigns were fought not over several months and in short decisive battles, as in the Alid revolt, but from the outset of ʿAbd al-Malik's reign in 685 until 697, some twelve years in all. As a good deal of the fighting took place after ʿAbd al-Malik completed and dedicated the Dome of the Rock in 691 or 692, we might ask how in supposedly turbulent times he found the energy and resources to do even that in addition to initiating the various programs that are known collectively as his reforms. Can it be that the turbulence, such as it was, was not an impediment to ʿAbd al-Malik acting decisively and imaginatively and that Goitein, Grabar, and those who follow them exaggerated the challenges facing the Umayyad caliph?

Lest we forget, virtually all the fighting between the Umayyads and the rebels was confined to Arabia, Iraq, southern Syria, and the Byzantine frontier. The fact is, ʿAbdallāh b. al-Zubayr's capacity to engage the existing regime in any decisively threatening action was limited. After the defeat of the rebels at Ajnadayn in 686 CE, there was no significant threat to Jerusalem and its environs. The Byzantines were bought off with tribute and at first given a free hand to settle matters of interest to them so that the Umayyads could concentrate on the internal threats to their regime. Why should we be surprised that ʿAbd al-Malik was able to begin construction on the Temple Mount soon thereafter and complete it within a few years? The number of troops that would have been required to keep order in Jerusalem would have been minimal. If necessary, additional security forces would have been available from a large military encampment nearby. To be sure, the Iraqis, led by Muṣʿab, the brother of the

28. Ṭabarī, *Annales*, 3/1:308.

Hijazi counter-caliph, represented a potential threat of significance, but Muṣʿab squandered his resources in Iraq by reigniting an old feud with the Alids and fighting intermittently with the ever troublesome Khārijites, thus embroiling all the potential and actual enemies of the regime in a conflict that weakened them instead of doing damage to the ruling authority. Like the revolt of the Iraqi based Ibrāhīm b. ʿAbdallāh the following century, the challenge to established rule bore no fruit.

Oddly enough, Goitein originally assessed the threat of the Zubayrid rebels as I have outlined here. In an article published long before his casual remarks in the *Encyclopedia of Islam*, an article then recast in an expanded study, Goitein downplays the capacity of ʿAbdallāh b. al-Zubayr and his followers to balance the scales of power in their favor.[29] He points out the changed fortunes of Ibn al-Zubayr's counter-caliphate, which are duly noted in considerable detail by the major Arabic chroniclers, and then cites the historian Balādhurī (892 CE), who quotes ʿAbd al-Malik as saying: "If ʿAbdallāh b. al-Zubayr were a[n authentic] caliph, as they [his supporters] say, he would rebel [by initiating combat] instead of hiding his tail in the holy city Medina (*Ḥaram*)."[30] As reported, the statement was meant to demean the rebels by labeling them cowards, the most egregious insult that could be leveled at an Arab tribesman. But it also speaks to the inevitable failure of any rebellion that relies on human and financial resources found in the Hijaz region of Arabia. Goitein's brief comments in the encyclopedia are thus nothing less than a complete reversal of earlier detailed, and seemingly more correct, views.

I am puzzled therefore why Grabar, who was familiar with these earlier publications, felt compelled to revise his original view, which credited ʿAbd al-Malik with initiating and completing the major construction project on the Temple Mount and, despite clearly expressed reservations, embraced Goitein's later assumptions. Given a relatively secure environment and the limited scope of building activity on the Temple Mount—limited at least compared to the massive construction at the site of the Round City—in all likelihood, there would have been no significant obstacle to acquiring the labor force and materials with which ʿAbd al-Malik could have begun and completed the Dome of the Rock. Moreover, as was Goitein, Grabar was aware of Sibṭ b. al-Jawzī's *Mirʾāt al-zamān*, the aforementioned chronicle that details a massive building project begun and completed within four years. In sum, there is no overwhelming reason to conclude that the innovative Umayyad would have been unable to

29. For a detailed description of the military phases of the campaign, see n. 13 above.

30. S. D. Goitein, "The Sanctity of Jerusalem and Palestine," in his collected works titled *Studies in Islamic History and Institutions* (Leiden, 1966), 135–48, esp. 139–40.

promote a policy of combat and construction simultaneously, or as it might be expressed in modern parlance: a strategy of guns and butter.

If ʿAbd al-Malik rather than Muʿāwiyah were responsible for clearing the Temple Mount and planning and completing the Dome of the Rock, one could still argue that the first Umayyad caliph considered moving the seat of Islamic rule to Jerusalem. With that, the holy city of Jews and Christians would have been launched as *topographia sacra* for Muslims. For scholars holding this view of Muʿāwiyah and Jerusalem, the burden of proof would seem to rest with the meaning assigned to a series of buildings uncovered by Israeli archaeologists adjacent the southern and southwestern walls of the Temple Mount. The initial assessment, still held by many if not indeed most scholars, is that the ruins are the remains of what had been a lavish Umayyad building complex that combined the residence of the ruler and the administrative agencies of his government. We have already noted that Peters and Elad identify the cluster of buildings as representing the administrative center from which Muʿāwiyah intended to rule. Whether or not this is true remains to be seen.

CHAPTER 6

The So-Called Umayyad Administrative Center

Following the 1967 war, Israeli archaeologists began extensive digs at many locations in and around Jerusalem's Old City. Their hope was to uncover substantial evidence of different historic periods going back some three thousand years. The initial interest was in baring elements of the Graeco-Roman city astride the stone platform on which the ancient temples stood. The Temple Mount itself was off limits, as political and religious considerations precluded tampering physically with the site. However, the archaeologists were able to clear part of Solomon's Stables, an underground chamber east of the current al-Aqṣā mosque. Amid controversy, the Islamic authorities took responsibility for the site and began work of their own, converting the underground space into a place of prayer currently known as the Marwānī Mosque.

The Area South and Immediately West of the Temple Mount

Most important for our concerns are the massive ruins uncovered by archaeologists digging along the southern and southwestern walls of the ancient platform. The discovery was the beginning of a vast archaeological project sponsored by the Israel Department of Antiquities and conducted by a team supervised by the archaeologists Benjamin Mazar and Meir Ben-Dov. After a brief moment of skepticism, Mazar, the senior scholar, accepted Ben-Dov's claim that the ruins were those of the administrative center and residence of Jerusalem's Muslim rulers, a view that has been endorsed by historians of Islam and specialists in Islamic art and architecture. As noted earlier, the archaeological findings were cited by Amikan Elad and F. E. Peters to support their contention that Mu'āwiyah b. Abī Sufyān, the first Umayyad caliph, intended to transfer the seat of his realm from Damascus to the holy city.[1]

1. For Mu'āwiyah's alleged attempt to move his capital from Damascus to Jerusalem, see chapter 4.

If Muʿāwiyah actually contemplated a move to Jerusalem, erecting a residence and administrative center there would have been a priority. But the dig along the wall has yet to reveal any evidence that Muʿāwiyah or for that matter any other caliph intended to make the city the focal point of Islamic governance, let alone a sacred place comparable to the holy cities of Arabia. One can also question whether the structures adjacent to the Temple Mount were built expressly to accommodate a governor (or subgovernor) ruling or visiting Jerusalem. For that matter, it is not at all certain that all or any of the buildings, whatever their intended purpose, were actually built in Islamic times. Like the literary sources cited in the previous chapters, the physical evidence found in and above the ground is at present highly problematic. With all due respect to the technical competence of the archaeologists, scholars examining their claims would be best served if they viewed them as a subject for debate rather than established truth.

Archaeology is a science that relies on dating remains with a degree of accuracy. This is best done when there is a dedicatory inscription giving the date of completion or other relevant epigraphic evidence; where there are literary sources that describe the unearthed building or, at the least, mention the circumstances leading to its construction in time and place; where decorative motifs can be traced to a specific artistic style; and where the architectural forms, construction material, and the remains of objects found amid the debris can be linked to a well-defined period, if not a more specific moment in time. Needless to say, finding buildings in a good state of preservation allows scholars to appraise a site with a heightened sense of confidence.

In the best of circumstances, there are likely to be many unanswered questions about the form and function of individual buildings and their relationship to the surrounding area. In the end, architectural historians, no matter how skilled, produce imagined reconstructions that draw heavily on other known sites and buildings presumed contemporaneous with or similar to those of immediate interest. Anyone who has observed archaeologists agonizing over their field notes can appreciate the often messy nature of the evidence uncovered above or in the ground, as opposed to the precise plans of buildings generated by architectural historians and then rendered by skilled draftsmen or computer technicians into definitive drawings. All too often the publication of final field reports is delayed for years. And when the final reports do appear, the field notes and preliminary sketches will be filed and stored along with numerous photographs taken at the site. Most of this material will never to be seen again by interested parties. As a result, the finely crafted hand drawings and more recently the digitized reconstructions can give rise to more or less permanent understandings, what Oleg Grabar labeled "the meaning" of buildings and their surroundings.

As regards the 'Islamic' ruins adjacent the Temple Mount, there is as yet no authoritative final report, that is, no publication comparable to those of other well-known Umayyad sites. *Final Report II*, subtitled *The Byzantine and Early Islamic Periods*, is devoted almost entirely to the former; little is said of the latter.[2] No schematic floor plans exist for the Islamic level; nor are there definitive drawings of the buildings or a complete catalog and thorough discussion of the numerous items found amid the debris of the purported Islamic administrative center. In contrast careful attention is paid to the Byzantine level beneath the Umayyad structures and in the areas of Byzantine settlement beyond.

Our ability to better understand the Islamic assemblage adjacent to the Temple Mount is also compromised by what has been described as an unwieldy division of labor between principal investigators. Nevertheless, the finds in the shadow of the Temple Mount made for dramatic claims that were duly trumpeted by the media. It is often the case with archaeological discoveries that representations of the past find a broad audience well before exacting scholarly judgments can be rendered. The tendency of the media to dramatize archaeological finds is particularly true in Israel, where archaeology remains a national pastime and each new discovery is greeted with great excitement not only among scholars but the populace at large. Not surprisingly, the Israeli archaeologists were keen to go public with their spectacular finds. Following suit, historians of early Islam were quick to draw conclusions based on preliminary archaeological information and what they knew of administrative centers and palaces from the Umayyad and early Abbasid periods. An imagined reconstruction of the past thus took on the trappings of historic reality.

Referring to the Umayyad government center, the archaeologists speak of four buildings that cover a considerable expanse. An additional building uncovered near the slope leading from the easternmost section of the wall revealed an abundance of Christian religious memorabilia and was labeled a small Byzantine monastery, adjacent to which archaeologists discovered other Byzantine structures: a winery and a large building designated by them a hospice.[3] Another building directly west of the Islamic structures displayed images of four seven-branched candelabras (*menorot*), suggesting to the archaeologists that they had uncovered evidence of a building inhabited by Jews, as they put it, perhaps a synagogue from early Islamic times. It is not clear, however, why

2. E. Mazar, *Qedem* 43 (2003).
3. Mazar, *Qedem* 43, 3–67 (monastery), 68–77 (winery), 78–103 (hospice).

they should have considered the building a synagogue, nor do they offer any substantive reason why the Jewish building dates from the Islamic period, and not, say, the years of Sasanid occupation, when a Jewish presence in the holy city was apparently favored by the ruling Persian authorities. Be that as it may, the building was subsequently named by the archaeologists *Beit ha-Menorot*, "The House of the Candelabras."[4]

The ruins of two major edifices adjacent to the Temple Mount's southern wall drew particular interest from scholars focused on Umayyad Jerusalem. Remnants of clay sewage pipes that rose vertically amid the original walls indicate that the buildings situated immediately below the al-Aqṣā mosque were multistory structures. The retaining walls are not preserved, but traces of the foundation are of sufficient width (nine meters) to suggest they could have been three stories in height, tall enough in this instance to frame edifices of many chambers surrounding an open court. The excavators concluded that the buildings could have served as a palace / dār al-imārah, that is, a residence and administrative complex for the ruling authority, be it a caliph or his appointed agent.[5] It is now commonplace for most scholars to refer to the Umayyad palace.

The remains of the building along the western wall revealed a series of furnaces and flues that heated a large room designated by the archaeologists a caldarium. And so they declared the structure a bathhouse, built in this case to serve the resident rulers, their courtiers, and their guests. Having discovered an antechamber leading from the caldarium to an adjacent room, Ben-Dov opined

4. Mazar, *Qedem* 43, 163–95; also E. Mazar, "The 'Jewish Beth Ha-Menorot,' in the Temple Mount Excavations in Jerusalem," *New Studies on Jerusalem: Proceedings of the Fourth Conference*, edited by E. Baruch and A. Faust (Ramat Gan, 1996), 64–80. The proceedings of these conferences on Jerusalem were conducted and published in Hebrew.

5. For the original assessment of the finds, see M. Ben-Dov, "The Omayyad Structures Near the Temple Mount [Hebrew]," *Eretz-Israel* 10 (1971): 35–40 plus photographs; and his "Building Techniques in the Omayyad Palace Near the Temple Mount in Jerusalem [Hebrew]," *Eretz-Israel* 11 (1973): 75–91. For the ground plans and early reconstruction of the buildings by Ben-Dov see illustrations 1 and 2. There seems to have been an evolving consensus as to the reconstruction of the buildings. Contrast the early drawings of Ben-Dov and his cross sections of the Umayyad palace with the photo of a plaster-of-paris reconstruction published by him in his *In the Shadow of the Temple* (New York, 1985), 296, which represents a somewhat different series of structures. Similarly D. Bahat's drawings in *The Illustrated Atlas of Jerusalem* (Jerusalem, 1996), 81, and those by E. Mazar in *The Complete Guide to the Temple Mount Excavations* (Jerusalem, 2000), which seemingly correspond to the plaster-of-paris model (illustrations 4 and 5). Note also Y. Baruch and R. Reich, "Renewed Excavations at the Umayyad Building III [Hebrew]," in *New Studies on Jerusalem* 5 (1997), 128–40, and their "The Umayyad Buildings near the Temple Mount. Reconstruction in Light of Recent Excavations [Hebrew]," in *New Studies on Jerusalem* 8 (2002), 121–32. A concise review of the excavations written by Ben-Dov is found in the *New Encyclopedia of Archeological Excavations in the Holy Land*, edited by E. Stern et al. (New York, 1992), 2:793–95. A fifth, smaller structure (unfinished) lies directly east of the administrative building. Its function is unknown.

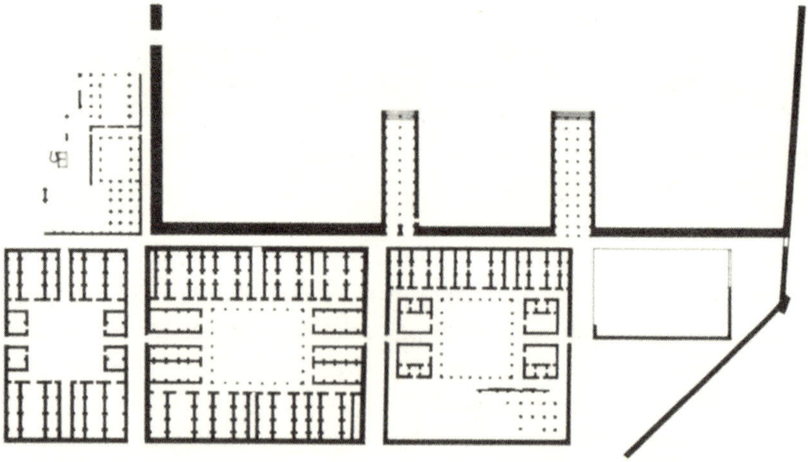

Fig. 1. Plan of the Umayyad Administrative Center (M. Ben-Dov)

that the second room within the building might have been the scene of official banquets, similar to the bathhouse of Khirbat al-Mafjar, the Jericho summer palace of the Umayyad caliph Hishām b. ʿAbd al-Malik (r. 724–43 CE).[6] Because the northern reaches of the structure are situated directly beneath the open court where throngs of Jewish worshipers congregate at present, the suggested dining hall and entertainment area has not been excavated; I would imagine there is little prospect that the dig will extend northward at any time in the foreseeable future. The remains of another building were uncovered directly south of the bathhouse and west of the purported residential-administrative complex.[7] The designated use of that building remains open to question.

Not all scholars were convinced that the four buildings were part of a large administrative complex, or that the proposed complex was built ex nihilo by the ruling house of Umayyah. Oleg Grabar, who visited the site at an early stage

6. R. Perez, "The Bathhouse from the Temple Mount Excavations," *New Studies on Jerusalem* 6 (1998), 103–16; and the brief comments of Ben-Dov in his *Shadow of the Temple Mount*, 316 ff. For Khirbat al-Mafjar, see R. W. Hamilton, *Khirbat al-Mafjar: An Arabian Mansion in the Jordan Valley* (Oxford, 1959), and his "Who Built Khirbat al-Mafjar?" *Levant* 1 (1969): 61–67 and "Khirbat al-Mafjar: The Bath Hall Reconsidered," *Levant* 10 (1978); 124–38. The use of such halls for ceremonial purposes could also apply to the Umayyad structures at Quṣayr ʿAmra and Mshatta, as noted by G. Fowden, *Quṣayr ʿAmra: Art and the Umayyad Elite in Antique Syria* (Berkeley, 2004), 162–63. For a thoughtful review of the so-called Umayyad pleasure palaces, see R. Hillenbrand, "La Dolce Vita in Early Islamic Syria: The Evidence of later Umayyad Palaces," *Art History* 5 (1982): 1–35. Brief but useful summaries of the aforementioned sites with additional bibliography can be found in *EI*, s.v. "Khirbat al-Mafdjar" and "Khirbat al-Minya."

7. See illustrations 1 and 3.

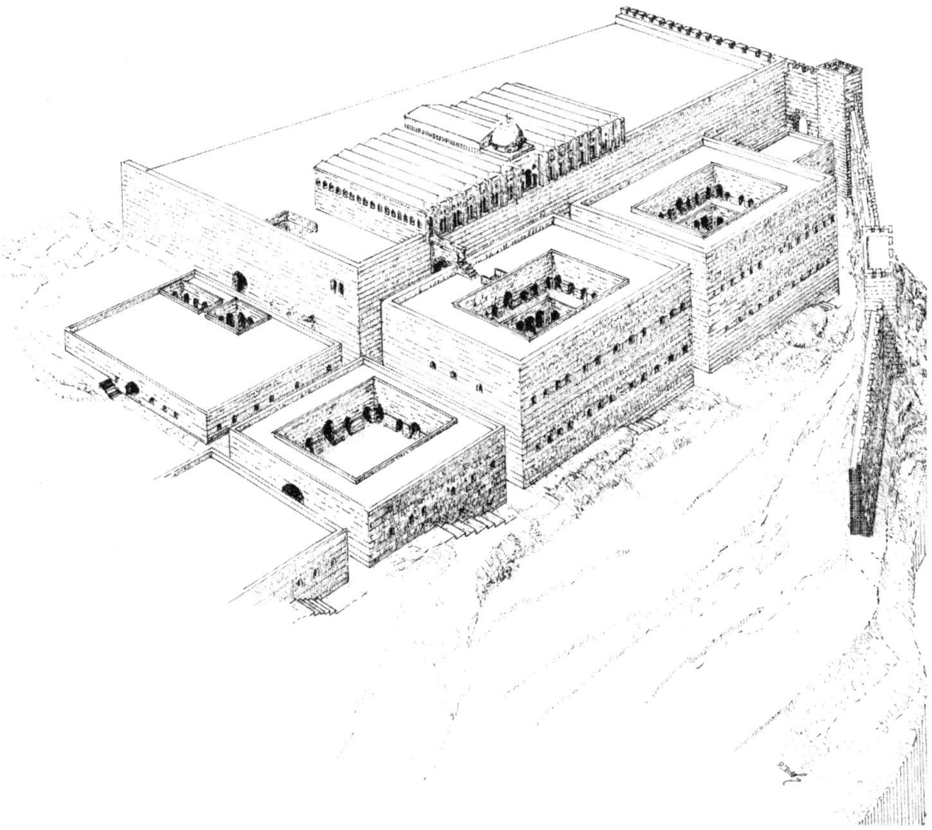

Fig. 2. Reconstruction of the Administrative Center (M. Ben Dov)

of the excavations, concluded: "Everything that has been reconstructed is hypothetical and often runs against what we know of Late Antique architectural practices." Chiding the archaeologists for excessive imagination, he dismissed their rendering of the major buildings as resembling "nineteenth century prisons or twentieth century low cost housing, at best [they resemble] motels." Grabar's appraisal of the architectural drawings may strike some readers as having fun at the expense of the archaeologists and their draftsmen, but the sum of his objections should be weighed with all seriousness. He notes that the results of the excavations had not been published in full. Accordingly, he reminds his readers they are forced to rely on somewhat romanticized descriptions and reconstructions, as well as references to documents, both published and un-

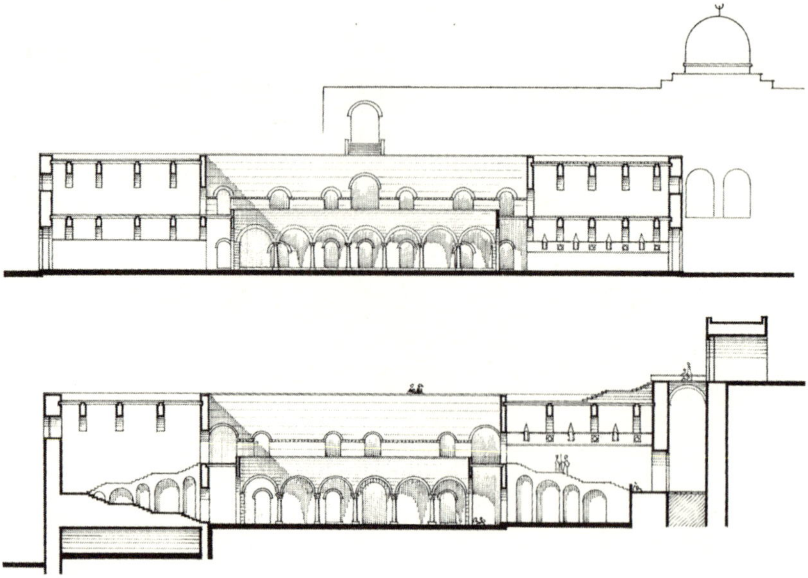

Fig. 3. Cross-section of the Umayyad Palace (M. Ben-Dov)

published, that are not always properly interpreted.[8] Add to this caveat and other reservations of Grabar the initial disparity between the different drawings. Before a consensus was reached, the various plans of the reconstructed buildings give the appearance of following somewhat different interpretations of the evidence obtained from the dig.[9] Nevertheless, there was and still remains a tendency to declare the entire building complex the administrative hub of Umayyad Jerusalem, if not the political center of Islamic rule envisioned by the founder of the dynasty. The latter view is championed by Elad, Peters, and others linking the buildings south of the Temple Wall to a grand design conceived by Muʿāwiyah b. Abī Sufyān. Add to this last claim the view of Ben-Dov, who notes in a casual remark that the later Umayyad caliphs were about to move from Damascus to Jerusalem but were prevented from doing so because of a violent earthquake that destroyed the administrative complex in 747 CE.[10]

Grabar, exercising caution, went no further than declaring the site to be of Islamic origins, a spacious area developed to serve the city's Muslim population

8. Grabar, "Notes on the Dome of the Rock," in *Jerusalem*, 222–25, volume 4 of his collected studies.

9. See illustrations 1–6.

10. Ben-Dov, *Historical Atlas of Jerusalem* (New York, 2002), 178.

Fig. 4. Plaster of Paris Model of the Administrative Center

in one way or another. Assuming that the buildings were actually completed, he imagined they could have been dwellings erected for Muslim pilgrims and immigrants (in what was presumably a vacant area of the city). He reminds us that existing Christian real estate in Jerusalem could not be confiscated because of an agreement concluded with the local authorities.[11] No doubt Grabar refers to the terms of capitulation reportedly agreed upon by the bishop Sophronius and the Muslim conquerors of the holy city, an agreement that coincides with other reported treaties of capitulation. The boilerplate treaty of capitulation between Muslims and non-Muslims guaranteed the conquered peoples of the book the right to their lives, their property, and the practice of their religion in exchange

11. Grabar, "Notes on the Dome of the Rock," 224.

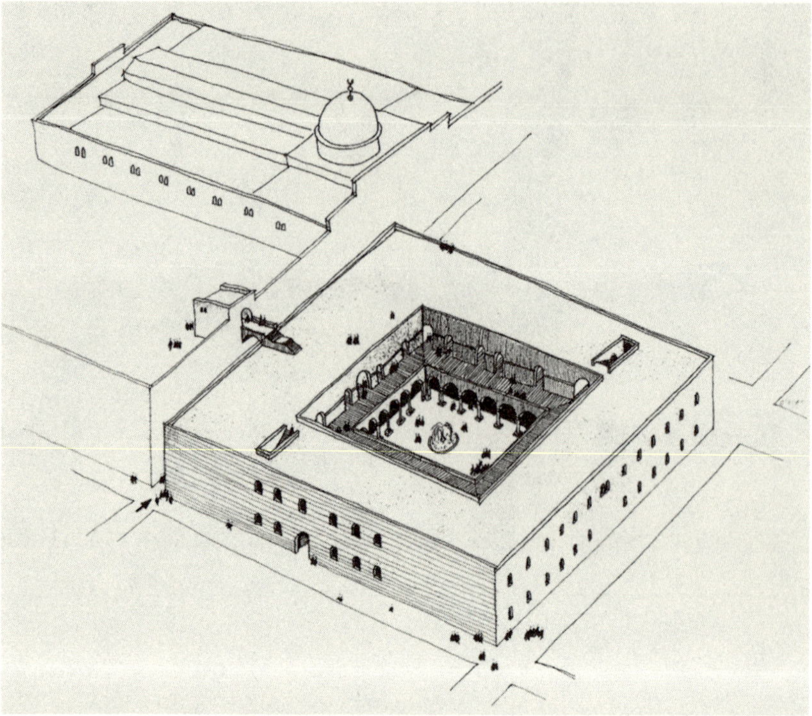

Fig. 5. Reconstruction of the Palace (E. Mazar)

for accepting of Muslim authority.[12] Assuming that reports of the agreement with Sophronius are genuine—a questionable assumption—and that the terms of the agreement were actually honored, the Muslims could have still acquired Christian properties through commercial transactions, whether these properties were occupied, left vacant, or abandoned by the original owners.[13] Grabar

12. See H. Busse, "'Omar's Image as Conqueror of Jerusalem," *JSAI* 8 (1986): 149–68.

13. Note that Muslims appropriated Christian places of worship, which they subsequently converted to mosques. See *EI*, s.v. "Masdjid." The purchase of lands on which Christian monasteries were situated in order to build monumental architecture for the ruling house is reported for Baghdad (762 CE) and Samarra (832 CE), capitals of the Abbasid caliphs, and Rafiqah, the royal city built by the caliph al-Manṣūr in 772 CE. The reported circumstances of these purchases from Christians are part and parcel of the cities' foundation lore. For the purchase of Christian property at Baghdad, see Ṭabarī, *Annales*, 3/1:272–23, 276; Ya'qūbī, *Buldān*, 238; Khaṭīb, *Ta'rīkh Baghdād*, 1:66; Yāqūt, *Mu'jam*, 1:680; Ibn Ṭabāṭabā, *Fakhrī* (Beirut), 162. For Samarra, see Ya'qūbī, *Buldān*, 257; Yāqūt, *Buldān*, 3:15; Mas'ūdī, *Murūj* (Beirut), 3:466–47. For Rafiqah, Balādhurī, *Futūḥ*, 287; Ṭabarī, *Annales*, 3/1:276; Yāqūt, *Mu'jam*, 2:734–35. Note, however, that Ya'qūbī, *Historiae*, 2:430, 445, attributes tracing the city plan of Rafiqah to al-Manṣūr's predecessor al-Saffāḥ. See also Lassner, *Topography*, 123–24, his *'Abbāsid Rule*, 164–67 (Baghdad), and his *Middle East Remembered*, 199–203 (Samarra).

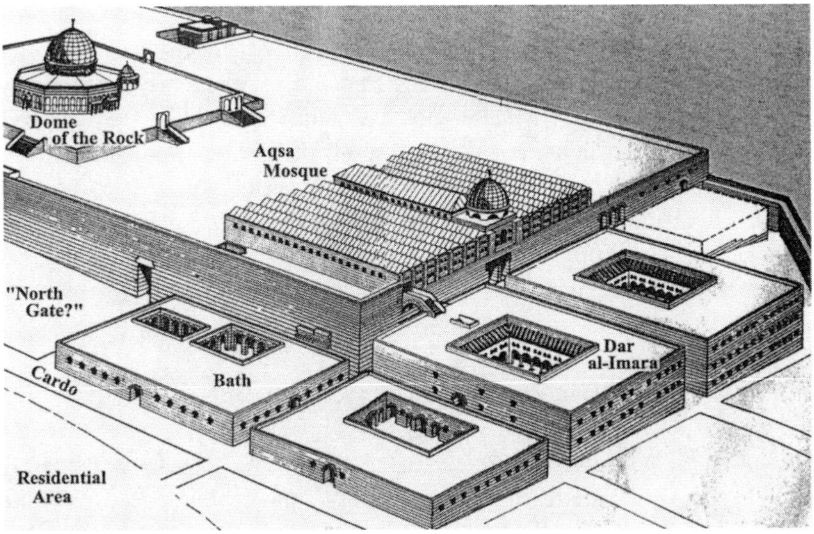

Fig. 6. Reconstruction of the Noble Sanctuary and the Administrative Center (D. Bahat)

would have been the first to admit that when it comes to the history and function of the buildings south of the Temple Mount, he and the rest of us are forced into the realm of imagination.

The data made available to Grabar during his visit to Jerusalem provide us with what is at best a rather sketchy picture of the site's history. Nor have publications since then eliminated many questions of interpretation. There are, as yet, no precise measurements for every aspect of the buildings in question; nor is there a detailed catalog of all the objects found amid the rubble. That said, one has to agree with Grabar's initial assessment, namely, that the buildings appear broadly reminiscent of Byzantine architectural design, a type of construction that continued well into the Umayyad period.[14] The proposed government complex in Jerusalem has been compared—with considerable license—to the palace-like retreats built by the Umayyads at various locations in Greater Syria, among others Qasr al-Hayr al-Sharqi, Qasr al-Hayr al-Gharbi, ʿAnjar, and most notably Khirbat al-Mafjar.[15] That still leaves us with gnawing questions: When

14. Grabar, "Notes on the Dome of the Rock," 222.

15. See M. Ben-Dov, "Umayyad Structures," 38; and in particular, D. Whitcomb, "Jerusalem and the Beginnings of the Islamic City," in *Unearthing Jerusalem*, edited by K. Galor and G. Avni (Winona Lake, IN, 2011), 399–416, esp. 408–9 (407 contains the ground plans of several Umayyad sites that he likens to the so-called Umayyad administrative complex in Jerusalem). Whitcomb is inclined to see the buildings along the south wall and the structures atop the Temple Mount as forming a distinctive Islamic city similar in many respects to the other Umayyad constructions

and in what circumstances were the buildings in Jerusalem erected? And if built at the same time, were they, from the outset, integral elements of a single project that was developed with a specific purpose in mind, namely, an immense government compound? A bathhouse is a bathhouse, but the so-called palace /dār al-imārah might have served a variety of functions at different times, perhaps going back to when Jerusalem was a Byzantine city. In the absence of epigraphic or supporting literary evidence, how confident should we be in differentiating between Byzantine style edifices erected in pre-Islamic times and those said to have been planned and built by an Umayyad caliph?

The Date and Function of the Excavated Area

Accepting the possibility that the so-called palace / dār al-imārah supposedly built by the Muslims actually dates to Byzantine times—the suggestion of the epigrapher-historian Moshe Sharon[16]—there is nothing to preclude that the pre-Islamic structure could have been renovated at some later point to serve the needs of its Muslim occupants. Nor is there any reason to deny the process of renovation was not repeated time and again before and after the onset of Islamic rule. Traces of Byzantine settlement at lower levels west of the Temple Mount's southern wall and along the eastern portion and slope leading from it are ample evidence that the city extended beyond the limits of Constantine's Heavenly Jerusalem, an expansion begun by the emperor Justinian in the sixth century.[17] Because all the aforementioned developments are at least possible, we are obliged to let our imagination wander rather than draw hard-and-fast

previously mentioned. For further amplification, see his "An Urban Structure for the Early Islamic City: An Archaeological Hypothesis," in *Cities in the Pre-modern Islamic World: The Urban Impact of Religion, State, and Society*, edited by A. K. Bennison and A. L. Gascoigne (London, 2007), 15–26. Note that, unlike other Umayyad constructions, the discrete Islamic city in Jerusalem proposed by Whitcomb lacks a protective retaining wall with or without rounded towers for defense. On the other hand, the garrison towns in Iraq founded by the Muslims initially lacked retaining walls, but they were originally isolated from the local population. Whitcomb's claim of a discrete Islamic city within the larger area of metropolitan Jerusalem occasions his acceptance of the view that Muʿāwiyah intended for Islamic Jerusalem to be his capital. To be sure, the Arab tribesmen situated in the Jerusalem area following the conquest of the city would have situated themselves in areas separate from the general population, but that need not lead us to conclude that the areas of Muslim occupation took on all the characteristics of later Muslim urban foundations. I find equally problematic Whitcomb's proposed linkage of Jerusalem and other Umayyad sites to his highly conjectural "Arabian city model." See his "Urbanism in Arabia," *Arabian Archeology and Epigraphy* 7 (1995): 38–51.

16. M. Sharon, "Shape of the Holy," *SO* 107 (2009): 283–310.

17. See *Qedem* 46 (2007), which represents volume 3 of the *Final Reports* (the Byzantine period) and 43 (2003), esp. 3–159.

conclusions about individual structures and the more inclusive site—keeping in mind that license to imagine does not mean throwing caution to the wind.

Although he accepted that the area south of the Temple Mount was the site of an early Islamic settlement, Grabar was troubled by the "imaginative reconstructions" proposed by the archaeologists and the "carelessness" of historians who, having accepted the views of the archaeologists, boldly constructed a historical context with which to give meaning to the newly discovered finds. In effect, Grabar accuses them of accepting what is problematic to promote views that are equally if not more problematic.[18] Nevertheless, he regarded as secure the data he obtained from perusing many (but not all) of the published reports, and of equal if not greater importance, he relied on impressions he gleaned from viewing the ruins in situ. Working with approximate dimensions—because he had no access to exact measurements—Grabar was willing to accept that the plans of the buildings may be broadly consistent with Umayyad construction in Syria. But he quickly pointed out that the dimensions are not. He notes that one of the buildings had been identified as a palace and considers whether it might have functioned as a temporary residence for the Umayyad caliphs whenever they visited Jerusalem. This guarded comment falls short of claims that the larger palace complex was built by Muʿāwiyah to serve as his permanent residence and the fulcrum of Islamic rule. Grabar even has serious doubts that we are dealing with a palace. He points to the absence of a prominent entrance, and long halls without light that strike him as being storage areas rather than living quarters. Moreover, he notes "a striking paucity and sobriety of ornamented architectural finds, not exactly what one would expect of the palace from which an ambitious Muslim ruler hoped to legitimize his rule."[19]

Although highly skeptical of the palace designation, Grabar is willing to concede that at one time the building was part of a government complex. Weighing the literary evidence, he cites the celebrated Aphrodito papyri, administrative documents from Egypt dating from the reign of al-Walīd I, the Umayyad caliph who, according to most authorities, built the al-Aqṣā mosque.[20] As the Greek texts mention local workers who were recruited to build a mosque and a pal-

18. Grabar, "Notes on the Dome of the Rock," 222–23.
19. Grabar, "Notes on the Dome of the Rock," 224.
20. For the text, see *The Aphrodito Papyri*, edited by H. I. Bell, with index of Coptic papyri edited by W. E. Crum; English translation by H. I. Bell in *Der Islam* 2 (1911): 269–83, 372–84; 3 (1912): 132–40, 369–73; 4 (1913): 87–96; 17 (1928): 4–8 (last segment, prepared during World War I, only appeared in 1928); also C. H. Becker, "Arabische Papyri des Aphroditofundes," *ZA* 20 (1906): 68–104. The texts relevant to our discussion were republished and translated into German by M. Küchler, "Moschee und Kalifenpaläste Jerusalems nach den Aphrodito-papyri," *ZDPV* 107 (1991): 120–43. There is no mention of these events in the Arabic papyri edited by N. Abbot in her *The Kurrah Papyri from Aphrodito in the Oriental Institute* (Chicago, 1938).

ace, understood by Grabar to be a dār al-imārah, he links the two projects with al-Walīd's construction in Jerusalem. However, unlike other scholars, Grabar does not believe that in this instance the reference to a dār al-imārah includes a palace residence. And while he accepts that some Umayyad caliphs, influenced by legends of King Solomon's palace and temple, may have toyed with the idea of building a permanent or occasional residence in Jerusalem, he finds no indication that they actually did.[21]

Moshe Sharon, Israel's foremost Arabic epigrapher and a leading historian of the Umayyads and Jerusalem, is not even willing to accept that the dār al-imārah mentioned in the papyri was situated in the holy city.[22] He notes that the documents are official letters that were sent by Qurrah b. Sharīk, the Muslim governor of Egypt, to the Christian headman of the village Aphrodito. Unlike some other Umayyad governors, Ibn Sharīk served as both *ʿāmil* and *amīr*, that is, he was responsible for taxation and other economic concerns as well as maintaining security in the province.[23] The letters, which deal with economic matters, include references to recruiting a handful of artisans to work on the mosque of the commander of the faithful and point as well to the requisitioning of undisclosed articles for his palace, a structure that was being built under the supervision of one Yaḥyā b. Ḥanḍalah. Carefully examining the text, Sharon uncouples the two projects. As did Grabar and other scholars, he identified the mosque as the al-Aqṣā in Jerusalem, but by piecing together all the references to the palace (or dār al-imārah), he contends that it was a palace being built in Babylon, the old name for what became the larger area of Arab Fusṭāṭ, the Muslim capital of Egypt.[24] Sharon's reading of the papyri is, to say the least, controversial; scholars with whom I have spoken have yet to accept his view.

21. Grabar, "Notes on the Dome of the Rock," 224, citing P. Soucek, "The Temple of Solomon in Islamic Legend and Art," in *Archeological Fact and Medieval Tradition in Christian, Islamic, and Jewish Art*, edited by J. Guttman (Missoula, 1976). For a revue of Soucek's current views, see chapter 8 Direct links between Solomon's Temple and ʿAbd al-Malik's decision to build the Dome of the Rock are also argued by M. Sharon in "Shape of the Holy," 295 ff., esp. 297, and also N. Rabbat, "The Meaning of the Umayyad Dome of the Rock," *Muqarnas* 6 (1989): 15–18, who goes so far as to argue that ʿAbd al-Malik modeled his reign after those of David and Solomon.

22. Sharon, "Shape of the Holy," 304–7.

23. For Qurrah b. Sharīk, see Abbot, *Kurrah Papyri*, 40 ff., and more briefly *EI*, s.v. "Ḳurrah b. Sharīk."

24. Sharon, "Shape of the Holy," 305–6, points to papyri other than 1403, and, piecing together the references to the palace and its builder Yaḥyā b. Ḥanḍalah in 1362 and 1378, he concludes that the building under discussion was situated at Fusṭāṭ. The text of 1378 reads: "the palace being built for . . . at Fusṭāṭ near the river by Yaḥyā b. Ḥanḍalah." The same Yaḥyā b. Ḥanḍalah was one of two clients responsible for the building of the Dome of the Rock, possibly adding to the confusion. Similarly, 1433 speaks of a laborer (to be sent to work) on the "new building of the commander of the faithful in Jerusalem [i.e., the al-Aqṣā mosque built for al-Walīd]" and of materials requisitioned for "the palace of the commander of the faithful at Fusṭāṭ." Thus Sharon uncouples the two building projects.

But if there is truth to his contention, the palace mentioned in the letters cannot refer to the massive buildings along the south wall of the Temple Mount, let alone be cited to identify one or both of the buildings as the stately residence of Jerusalem's governor or the caliph himself. In any case, because they are dated from the reign of al-Walīd I, the sixth caliph of the realm, the papyri cannot be cited to support any view that ascribes the planning and construction below the al-Aqṣā mosque to Muʿāwiyah and the outset of Umayyad rule. There is, in short, a gap of over fifty years to explain.

What date should we then assign to the buildings situated in the shadow of the great mosque? What gave rise to the massive construction, and what might have been their function over time? Sharon, who tends as a rule to be guided by Arabic literary and epigraphic data, argues that an extensive Islamic site adjacent to the al-Aqṣā mosque would surely have drawn attention from Arabic writers; if not from the earliest historians, than certainly from the tenth-century geographer Muqaddasī, the Jerusalem native who describes the city.[25] The very proximity of the buildings to the Temple Mount would have made them noteworthy. And yet there is no mention of them anywhere in the vast literature describing the times. Nor is there any inkling of their existence amid the thousands of faḍā'il traditions in praise of Jerusalem. How can it be that a complex of such impressive buildings completely escaped the attention of Muslims who venerated the holy city?

Can we assume without conclusive evidence that Jerusalem's palace / dār al-imārah was never completed, a possibility suggested by the incomplete state of the building directly to the east of the so-called palace? Or was it destroyed and never rebuilt, so that Muslims might have had neither the opportunity nor powerful memories to reflect on its existence? Sharon mockingly refers to Ben-Dov, who notes widespread evidence of structural damage suggestive of cracks caused by earth tremors in the late 740s.[26] Like Sharon, I am certainly dubious that all or some of the buildings were destroyed, or so seriously damaged by an earthquake, that they were never completed (or rebuilt), if only because our sources are absolutely mute regarding these structures. Nevertheless, we should be careful in weighing our evidence, or in this instance, lack of evidence. Many significant palace compounds and in different locations have gone unnoticed in medieval Arabic writings. These would include the residences and administrative centers of the Abbasid caliphs in Iraq before al-Manṣūr moved the capital of the realm to the Round City.[27] Still, the burden of proof is not on Sharon's

25. Muqaddasī, *Aḥsan*, 165 ff.
26. Sharon, "Shape of the Holy," 303–4.
27. See Lassner, *ʿAbbāsid Rule*, 143–62, which identifies the oft-confused early Abbasid centers

skepticism—he has good reason to question the current scholarly consensus—but on a prevailing wisdom that has proved resistant to alternative views.

Sharon also questions whether the Umayyads had the wherewithal to manage so huge a project, raising objections similar to those of Grabar, Goitein, and others regarding ʿAbd al-Malik's ability to initiate and complete building the Dome of the Rock.[28] What then might explain the massive site below the Temple Mount? Sharon suggests, albeit as a seeming afterthought, that the "colossal" structures probably date from the time of Justinian. He sees them as part of the Christian emperor's great effort to add to the Heavenly or New Jerusalem in the sixth century CE, a project that gave rise to extraordinary building activity including a great church, commonly known as the Nea.[29] At first glance, Sharon's date for the site seems plausible, certainly no less plausible than that offered by the archaeologists and the historians who follow their lead. Amid the rubble Ben-Dov noticed stones with carved crosses. These struck him as salvaged architectural members from churches destroyed during the Sasanid assault of 614, building material that Muslim rulers later considered using for their own purposes.[30] I see no overwhelming reason to endorse this view at present, especially because Ben-Dov cites no corroborating evidence that is convincing. The carved stones could have been set in any number of Byzantine buildings and then reused, including other structures originally situated on the site under consideration or nearby.

The archaeologists uncovered the remains of a Byzantine house at a level beneath the purported Islamic palace. They also discovered extensive Byzantine ruins to the east, thought to be the remains of a monastery, winery, and hospice, as well as Byzantine houses south of the dār al-imārah. It is clear that at some point, be it during Justinian's reign or that of a subsequent emperor, the built-up area within Byzantine Jerusalem extended to and beyond the later "Islamic" site adjacent the southern wall of the Temple Mount.[31] The discov-

of government, each of which was labeled al-Hāshimīyah. Nothing is known of the plans of these centers.

28. Sharon, "Shape of the Holy," 304: "It is very questionable whether the Umayyads had the ability to undertake such a project [i.e., the proposed administrative center along the southern wall of the Temple Mount] considering the financial, engineering and administrative aspects, as well as the enormous manpower needed to achieve it." For the capacity of the Umayyads to plan and execute the structures on the Temple Mount, see chapter 5.

29. Sharon, "Shape of the Holy," 308.

30. Ben-Dov in *NEAHL*, 2:793.

31. *Qedem* 46 (2007), 49–69 (Byzantine House); for the buildings further to the east and sloping south, see n. 1. For the other Byzantine houses, see *Qedem* 43 (2003), 205–45. At first, these last buildings were dated to the reign of Justinian in the sixth century. They were then said to have been destroyed during the Sasanid assault on the city in 614 some two decades before the Muslim conquest. However, a large quantity of coins and other material found in one of the houses did not

ery of this house does not mean in and of itself that the ruins above postdate the Islamic conquest. The so-called palace might have been a later Byzantine structure, whether erected by Justinian or another emperor, for example Heraclius, who was charged with rebuilding the city following the Sasanian occupation. Admittedly, Islamic coins and remnants of pottery were found amid the rubble. But why claim that the building (or rather buildings of the palace / dār al-imārah) were from the outset a project conceived and executed by Muslims? Why not a massive Byzantine structure that survived in part or whole both the Sasanid and Islamic conquests, in which case the Muslims could have utilized it for their purposes? As to the continued use of the building, the sewers beneath the floor were filled with ceramic ware similar to that found at Khirbat al-Mafjar. These finds, together with coins dating from the reign of the caliph Hishām b. ʿAbd al-Malik (r. 724–43 CE), indicate that the building was utilized in some way well into the first half of the eighth century.[32]

What purpose or changing purposes might this building have served, and what are we to make of the entire complex of buildings in the extensive site south and west of Temple Mount? Can we say for certain or even with some measure of assurance that each unit was designed from the outset to be part of a Muslim and more specifically Umayyad government center? And if some scholars are inclined to answer yes to this last question, is it necessary to conclude as did Elad and Peters that the government center was planned if not indeed begun by Muʿāwiyah when he allegedly sought to move to the holy city from Damascus? Or could the various buildings, including the large structures along the southern wall, have served a variety of changing needs at different historic moments dating back to Byzantine times?

The ruins labeled a bathhouse by the archaeologists would seem to be self-explanatory. In Graeco-Roman cities of the Near East bathhouses were in effect civic institutions, places visited for hygienic purposes but also for recreation and religious rituals. A more private space for bathing was favored by wealthy notables and leading figures in government, the most relevant example being the ornately decorated bathhouse found at Khirbat al-Mafjar, the caliph Hishām's unfinished desert place.[33] If we assume that the Jerusalem bathhouse was an integral part of a large Umayyad complex, we should consider the possibility that Hishām had a splendid residence for occasional visits to Jerusalem

date later than the third or fourth centuries. Further excavations in the general area are needed to establish the history of settlement there (243–45).

32. See n. 6.

33. Plans of several Umayyad desert palace structures are discussed in K. A. C. Creswell, *EMA*, I/2. See especially 545–77 (Khirbat al-Mafjar); 585, fig. 624 (plan); 381–89 (Khirbat al-Minya); 385, fig. 448 (plan); 578–606 (Mshatta); 592, fig. 652 (plan).

as well as a winter retreat near the Dead Sea. The discovery of coins from the time of Hishām in the Jerusalem "palace" and of Khirbat al-Mafjar ceramics in the sewage system beneath it gives cause for speculation. Could the bathhouse have been part of a residential complex for the Umayyad caliph? However, if that were the case, we would have to explain why the bathhouse was entered directly from one of the main public thoroughfares of the ancient city. Security as well as privacy would have called for restricted access. Surely, Hishām and his entourage or, if you prefer, another caliph or his appointed ruling authority in Jerusalem would have made his way to the bathhouse by using a private entrance, one directly connected to the palace complex. Keep in mind that the building of undisclosed purpose between the so-called palace and the bathhouse also opened unto the same major thoroughfare. It is unlikely that the buildings directly accessed from this road and separated by small streets from each other and also from the large structures along the southern wall represent individual units designed to be part of a single government compound. Indeed, the ruins might very well suggest a public bathhouse in what was a built-up area prior to the Muslim conquest. Given water available from nearby Pool of Siloam, it is not improbable that there is a long history of bathhouses in the area going back to when the city was called Aelia Capitolina, perhaps even earlier. Amid the debris of the building, archaeologists found bricks of the type used by the tenth Roman legion to construct their flues, an indication that material salvaged from earlier ruins was reused in the bathhouse under consideration.

That still leaves us to explain the massive ruins directly adjacent the al-Aqṣā mosque, the buildings designated palatial residence and dār al-imārah. What evidence is there that these structures were designated from the outset to serve the needs of the Umayyad caliphs or their appointed agents? The archaeologists uncovered what they believed to be traces of an open stairway leading from the flat roof of the presumed palace to the southwestern wall of the mosque. Grabar whimsically describes the archaeologists' rendering of the stairs as resembling a modern fire escape.[34] The stairway in question certainly is not the kind of structure that a figure of rank would use to move from a palace to the city's principal mosque. There is a long-established precedent for connecting palaces to communal places of worship. The model originated in Medina, where the Prophet could enter the place of Muslim prayer directly from the living quarters he shared with his wife ʿĀʾishah. Muḥammad's successors moved freely among the Muslims who had come to say their prayers, but in doing so the

34. Grabar, "Notes on the Dome of the Rock," 224.

commanders of the faithful exposed themselves to danger. The most notable example is the stabbing of ʿUmar b. al-Khaṭṭāb at the mosque in Medina, an unprecedented assault that led to his death shortly thereafter. ʿUmar may have been the first commander of the faithful to suffer such a fate, but he would not be the last. Taking stock of the situation, Muʿāwiyah reportedly introduced the *maqṣūrah*, or private prayer chamber, in the great mosque of Damascus.[35] A secure entrance way now led from the abode of the ruler to a room in which the caliph or his representative, as the case may be, participated in the prayer service without exposure to the assembled worshipers. The caliph who led prayers at his own congregational mosque, or the representatives of the ruling authority at their provincial mosques, could then safely ascend a nearby pulpit to offer a sermon, pronounce policy, or in the case of the governors also pledge allegiance to the regime.

Palace and Mosque: Comparative Musings

The existence of a stairway connecting the structure below to the al-Aqṣā mosque might tempt scholars to believe that the two buildings represent a single unit, that is, a palace-mosque. The Prophet's mosque and apartment in Medina have already been cited. In addition, there were a number of palace complexes reportedly connected to or immediately adjacent mosques beginning with the period of the Arab conquests.[36] Chroniclers report that in the reign of ʿUmar b. al-Khaṭṭāb, Saʿd b. Abī Waqqāṣ, the Muslim ruler of Iraq, shifted the mosque of Kufa so that it lay adjacent his government palace.[37] The same can be said of the palace-mosque at Basra[38] and of Muʿāwiyah's Damascus residence built during the reign of ʿUthmān b. ʿAffān.[39] Similarly, when al-Ḥajjāj b. Yūsūf, the iconic Umayyad governor of Iraq, established a new capital for himself midway between Basra and Kufa (ca. 700 CE), he built a palace-mosque and administrative complex to serve as the symbol of his authority.[40] The quint-

35. Ṭabarī, *Annales*, 1/3:2230; Muqaddasī, *Aḥsan*, 159.

36. *EI*, s.v. "Masdjid."

37. Ṭabarī, *Annales*, 1/5:2491–92; Balādhurī, *Futūḥ*, 276.

38. Ṭabarī, *Annales*, 1/5: 2489 (separated by a narrow alley); Ibn al-Faqīh, *Buldān*, 188 (adjacent "*bidūn*"); Yāqūt, *Muʿjam*, 1:240 (following Ibn al-Faqīh).

39. Muqaddasī, *Aḥsan*, 159. *EI*, s.v. "Masdjid" lists palace-mosques situated beyond the central provinces of the realm, such as Fusṭāṭ in Egypt and Qayrawan in North Africa.

40. Balādhurī, *Futūḥ*, 290; Yaʿqūbī, *Buldān*, 322; Ibn Rustah, *Aʿlāq al-nafīsah*, 187. See also F. Safar, *Wāsiṭ, the Sixth Season's Excavations* (Cairo, 1945); for Kufa, M. ʿAlī Muṣṭafā, "Al-Tanqīb fī-l-Kūfah," *Sumer* 12 (1950): 3–32, and his "Taqrīr al-awwal," *Sumer* 16 (1954): 73–85.

essential example of this type of construction was the residence and mosque of the Abbasid caliph al-Manṣūr (763 CE), conjoined buildings that were modeled after al-Ḥajjāj's palace-mosque in Wāsiṭ.[41]

The palace-mosque complex consisted of a large ensemble of units. In addition to a residential enceinte and adjacent or adjoining place of worship, it included various facilities of all sorts for the daily conduct of government: treasuries, storage rooms, registries, even prisons, and at Basra a bathhouse for the governor (*amīr*). The buildings could also be considered the visible expression of state authority, be it that of the caliph or his designated representative. As regards Wāsiṭ and Baghdad, the architectural features and dimensions of the palaces and mosques obtained from literary sources clearly indicate a remarkable linkage between the Umayyad and Abbasid complexes. The archaeological evidence from Wāsiṭ confirms the dimensions of al-Ḥajjāj's palace and mosque reported in Yāqūt's geographical dictionary: a palace four hundred cubits square connecting to a mosque two hundred cubits square.[42] The very same dimensions are listed by al-Khaṭīb al-Baghdādī for al-Manṣūr's residence and the original mosque in the great court of the Round City.[43] Moreover, the palaces of both al-Ḥajjāj and al-Manṣūr were surmounted by magnificent green domes that dominated the skyline, an architectural feature that was regarded as the visual symbol of the occupants' authority and the legitimacy of their rule. As several of the Umayyad government centers display similar green (*khaḍrā'*) domes, can we assume that they were consciously modeled after one another, beginning with Mu'āwiyah's Khaḍrā', his palace in Damascus, a building constructed during his early years as governor of al-Shām? In such fashion, later caliphs and their provincial governors would have demonstrated that they inherited the power and authority that accrued previously to their esteemed predecessors.[44]

Such demonstrations of inherited power were not limited to green domes surmounting magnificent palaces. Our sources indicate that gates installed by al-Ḥajjāj at Wāsiṭ were later removed by al-Manṣūr and placed at different points of access to the Round City. At least one of these gates was previously salvaged by the Umayyad governor from nearby al-Zandaward, a city reportedly

41. See n. 44.

42. Yāqūt, *Mu'jam*, 4:885.

43. Khaṭīb, *Ta'rīkh Baghdād*, 1:73, 107.

44. The question was first posited by O. Grabar in his "Al-Mushatta, Baghdād, and Wāsiṭ," in *The World of Islam: Studies in Honor of Phillip K. Hitti* (London, 1959), 99–108, and further elaborated on in a series of studies by J. Lassner. See his *Topography*, 128–37 esp. 133 ff. (based on his article "Some Speculative Thoughts on the search for an 'Abbāsid Capital," *MW* 55 (1965): 203–10). A somewhat more mature view of Baghdad's foundation lore and the political symbolism of the Round City is found in Lassner's *'Abbāsid Rule*, 163–83, esp. 175 ff.

built by Solomon, the mighty Israelite king and Muslim prophet.[45] The Muslim author, following long-established precedent in the Near East, would have us believe that the transfer of gates from one city to another represents more than a desire to avoid the cost of producing new gates. Like the green domes above the palaces, the reused massive iron gates came to signify the transfer of authority.[46] In this case, the Abbasid caliph could promote himself as the analogue of Israel's legendary ruler, a sovereign-prophet who was endowed by God with unique powers balanced by unusual sagacity. In addition to the legendary structure(s) removed from Wāsiṭ, al-Manṣūr installed a gate from al-Shām said to have been built by the pharaohs (a claim that identifies Abbasid rule with the imperial reach of Egypt's ancient dynasts), and another from Kufa that had been originally made for (the palace of) Khālid al-Qaṣrī. The reference is to the famed governor of Iraq appointed by the Umayyad caliph Hishām b. ʿAbd al-Malik in 724 or 725. Like al-Ḥajjāj before him, al-Qaṣrī was commissioned to bring order to the most troublesome province of the realm, and like al-Ḥajjāj he was considered an all-powerful representative of Umayyad rule.[47] Of the four major massive iron gates protecting al-Manṣūr's personal domain only one was forged expressly for the Round City. Not surprisingly, this gate lacking legendary credentials was deemed inferior to the others.[48]

There is also an account in which the caliph is advised to demolish Īwān Kisrā, the Sasanid emperor's residence at nearby Ctesiphon. The declared objective was to use the salvaged material to build the Round City, an act that would commemorate the triumph of Islam over the Persian unbelievers. However, the excessive cost of that project was said to override all other considerations. Al-Manṣūr, who had a well-earned reputation for being tight with expenditures, opted instead to produce cheaper building materials at the site of construction. The story of Īwān Kisrā and similar accounts may be encrusted with the stuff of legend,[49] but embedded therein there is a kernel of historic truth. For al-Manṣūr to build a palace complex whose architectural features

45. Ṭabarī, *Annales*, 3/1:321; Khaṭīb, op. cit., 1:75; Yāqūt, *Muʿjam*, 2:952. Note Balādhurī, *Futūḥ*, 240 for a slightly different version on the origins of the gates.

46. Note the tradition that after conquering Ctesiphon, the capital of the Sasanids, Saʿd b. Abī Waqqāṣ reportedly settled at the Muslim garrison town Kūfa, modeled his palace after the Sasanid emperor's Īwān Kisrā and fortified his own palace with iron gates transferred from the emperor's building in Ctesiphon. See Ṭabarī, *Annales*, 1/5:2491–92. The chronicler may have confused Saʿd and the building from which he ruled with Khālid al-Qaṣrī, the eighth century governor of Kufa who was more likely to have had an imposing palace. See n. 47.

47. Khaṭīb, *Taʾrīkh Baghdād*, 1:75. According to Dīnawarī, *Ṭiwāl*, 336, al-Qaṣrī was appointed governor by Yazīd II (r. 720–24 CE).

48. Khaṭīb, *Taʾrīkh Baghdād*, 1:75.

49. Ṭabarī, *Annales*, 3/1:320; Ibn Ṭabāṭabā, *Fakhrī* (Beirut), 157. For a full discussion of this account, see Lassner, *ʿAbbāsid Rule*, 169–80.

borrowed so heavily from both a real and imagined past graphically illustrates the political symbolism reflected in the architecture of the Round City and the palace-mosques that preceded it. The administrative compounds designed for the commanders of the faithful and their leading representatives were meant to signify the authority with which they were invested and the awesome power they were capable of wielding.

With these examples in mind, and allowing for reasonable doubt, I cannot quite see how the so-called palace / dār al-imārah along the south wall can be linked with any assurance to the al-Aqṣā above, let alone to the palace-mosques hitherto cited. There is no question that the jewel-like Dome of the Rock and the magnificent al-Aqṣā mosque form a single architectural unit, in all likelihood along with other elements of the Noble Sanctuary. But it seems to me that the spatial coherence of the buildings on the Temple Mount is sorely compromised if we add the proposed palace / dār al-imārah; even more so were we to consider the other buildings of what has been declared an Umayyad administrative center: the bathhouse and the structure directly north of it. By almost any standard of aesthetic appreciation, it is difficult to imagine that the two buildings of the "palace-mosque," one situated on the Temple Mount, the other on the street below, represent a single unit. Nor is the concept of the Jerusalem palace-mosque easier to accept if we consider the two major buildings along the south wall as forming a combined palace / dār al-imārah, the eastern building being the residence of the ruler, the adjacent structure to the west the seat of government. Were that so, we would expect the buildings along the south wall to be more or less mirror images of one another, at least in outward appearances. That is not abundantly clear from the drawings or plaster model. Can we even state with certitude that all the freestanding buildings below the Temple Mount are part of a single assemblage representing an Umayyad administrative center? What appears to many scholars as a discrete government compound can be seen with some justification as a collection of individual buildings, separated from one another by narrow streets, and unrelated to the permanent needs of a noteworthy occupant, be it a caliph or any of his deputies. Looking at the entire sight from aerial photos, I find the layout of the supposed Umayyad complex (including the mosque above) is jarring to aesthetic sensibilities, especially when contrasted to the remarkable symmetry of the palace-mosque of Wāsiṭ or the Round City at Baghdad.

Arguments based on aesthetic criteria can, of course, be highly subjective. There is no doubt, however, about the aesthetics of al-Manṣūr's capital in Baghdad. The Round City, actually a glorified palace compound, was the ultimate model of precise planning, a site so elegant in layout and construction that it moved a famous visitor to comment: "It is as though it had been poured into a mold and cast."[50] Even the more modest desert palaces of the Umayyads combine form and function in a manner more pleasing to the critical eye than the buildings in the shadow of the Temple Mount. Unlike the buildings in Jerusalem, they are self-contained units spatially defined by an enclosure wall with rounded towers for or designed to resemble fortifications.[51] Security was always a concern where the caliph or his governors resided and where agencies of government were situated, especially the treasury. Given the advantage of careful planning, al-Ḥajjāj's capital at Wāsiṭ and the Round City at Baghdad were designed to keep the government and public sectors at arm's length.[52] No such arrangement is apparent at the site south of the Temple Mount. To the contrary, we have already noted how two buildings that are purportedly part of a large government compound were accessed from a main thoroughfare of the city. To date, there is no evidence that any of the buildings in question denied direct access to the public, not even the palace / dār al-imārah. To be sure, if the circumstances demanded, one or both large buildings along the southern wall might have been requisitioned to house elements of local authority. A caliph visiting Jerusalem might have stayed there as well. That is a far cry, however, from the proposed Umayyad command center or the more ambitious government compound that would have made Jerusalem the hub of the Umayyad state.

So what are we to make of the site based on what we currently know? As long as we are content to speculate, I can think of any number of uses the large buildings directly below the al-Aqṣā might have served before and after the Dome of the Rock and the great mosque graced the ancient temple platform. At one time or another, the proposed palace / dār al-imārah might have been a hostel for throngs of Christian pilgrims and pietists whose visits to the holy city are well documented.[53] We already noted the building blocks with crosses that Ben-Dov thought to be the remains of churches destroyed by the Sasanids. In the absence of any real evidence to support this view, one could just as easily assume these blocks were part of a Christian hostel that might have occupied

---

50. Khaṭīb, *Ta'rīkh Baghdād*, 1:77; Lassner, *Topography*, 207 (plan of the Round City).

51. See n. 33.

52. See J. Lassner, "The Caliph's Personal Domain: The City Plan of Baghdad Reexamined," in *The Islamic City*, edited by A. H. Hourani and S. M. Stern (Oxford, 1970), 103–18 = his *Topography*, 138–54, esp. 148–49; expanding this original view see Lassner's *'Abbāsid Rule*, 184–241; F. Safar, *Wāsiṭ, the Sixth Season's Excavations* (Cairo, 1945).

53. There is an extensive literature on Christian pilgrims visiting Jerusalem in Byzantine times. Readers may wish to consult: J. Wilkinson, *Jerusalem Pilgrims before the Crusades* (Jerusalem, 1977); Y. Tsafrir, "The Maps Used by Theodosius: On the Pilgrim Maps of the Holy Land and Jerusalem in the Sixth Century C.E.," *DOP* 40 (1986): 129–45; M. E. Stone, "Holy Land Pilgrimage of Armenians before the Arab Conquest," *RB* 93 (1986): 93–110.

the site, one that had informal space set aside for personal or group devotions. Such a building could have continued to serve pilgrims in Islamic times, if not Christians, then Muslims who came to venerate Jerusalem, or who simply sought temporary lodging. That being the case, might the building south of the bathhouse have been a facility to feed visitors to the city, thus making for a configuration of buildings that accommodated what may be labeled somewhat imaginatively the tourist trade? The presence or absence of cooking utensils amid the detritus would help answer this question.

As long as we are speculating, why limit our thinking to this alternative explanation? A hostel designed for pilgrims could also have served to lodge skilled guest workers brought to Jerusalem, the likes of the craftsmen mentioned in the Aphrodito papyri and others working on pre-Islamic and Islamic projects. With a labor force of some size assembled below the Temple Mount, the large building designated a palace and possible hostel could have housed at one time storage areas for building materials, workshops, and cubicles for foremen, surveyors, engineers, and the like. We should consider Grabar's comment that the long halls seem better suited to storage than chambers of a palace residence.

Admittedly, each and every one of these suggestions is proffered without real conviction. They certainly can be questioned. Scholars will have a better idea as to the history of the site only after the entire area has been cleared and excavated, more definitive final reports have been released, and a full inventory of items found in the rubble has been published. Our most important guide thus far remains the material recovered from the alleged palace / dār al-imārah. In addition to the ceramic ware and coins already described, Ben-Dov refers to stamped roof tiles of a type used in the late Byzantine period, painted plaster fragments decorated with geometric and floral designs, and fragments of frescos and stucco work.[54] There are also reports of writing on fragmented ceramic tiles.[55] None of these items reveals definitive evidence of the building's past. They allow us to determine neither the period of original construction, whether Byzantine or Islamic, nor how the buildings were utilized at any moment in time. Ben-Dov also refers to painted pottery (mostly small bowls), wine goblets adorned with representations of animals and geometric floral motifs, and bone and glass utensils, items he labels "palace ware." The presence of luxury items suggests that the buildings designated palace / dār al-imārah were inhabited or visited at one time or another by persons of means or rank, but that still begs

54. Ben-Dov, *Shadow of the Temple*, 319 ff.

55. The existence of these tiles and their potential importance comes to me by way of a conversation with Robert Hoyland of the University of Oxford.

the question of who might they have been, when and under what circumstance they took up residence, and how long they remained.[56]

In contrast to these luxury items, the archaeologists found among the ruins fifteen small lime kilns. The kilns are an anomaly in a structure we are led to believe was a palace. Ben-Dov assumes that the Abbasids who displaced the Umayyads came across the ruins of the building after it had been destroyed by the earthquake in the waning years of the Umayyad caliphate. According to him, the new regime, having no commitment to the holy city, transformed the collapsed Umayyad government center into a quarry from which they salvaged building material.[57] Taking similar license to reconstruct the past with little if any hard evidence, one could look upon the kilns and the history of the area differently. Might the kilns be an indication of a construction site rather than an Abbasid quarry, and from a time well before Ben-Dov's earthquake, that is, much before onset of the Abbasid rule? As mentioned earlier, we might wish to consider a place containing a billet requisitioned for skilled laborers and their supervisors, with work stations nearby. Needless to say, the discovery of a wide variety of tools used in construction would narrow somewhat the odds in favor of this last suggestion, keeping in mind that it is a suggestion and no more. We would still have to explain the palace ware and coins from the period of Hishām. Readers seeking clarity should be aware that more definitive interpretations of the area south of the Temple Mount await further excavation and a published catalog of all the items recovered.

In Conclusion

The vast majority of scholars may well be correct in claiming that the ruins uncovered below and adjacent to the south wall of the Temple Mount are the remains of a palace complex built expressly for an Umayyad caliph. There is, however, no compelling reason to accept such a claim without reservation. Neither archaeology nor art-historical analyses have established beyond doubt that all the buildings are of a common construction or that they date from Islamic times. Given the large area of Byzantine settlement uncovered by the archaeologists east of the palace / dār al-imārah, Moshe Sharon could well be right in maintaining that the buildings labeled Umayyad administrative complex are Byzantine. However, scholars favoring Sharon's view may find his dat-

56. Ben-Dov, *Shadow of the Temple*, 319–20.
57. Ben-Dov, *NEAEHL*, 2:793.

ing them to the time of Justinian's New Jerusalem too precise. Accepting the Christian origins of the site still leaves unresolved the intended use of the individual structures other than the bathhouse. It also leaves unanswered whether Christians could have made use of the buildings well into Islamic times. On the other hand, even if all the ruins below the Temple Mount are Byzantine in origin, there is no reason to deny outright that they could have been adapted for use by the Muslims at various points after the Islamic conquest. Were such indeed the case, various Muslims of rank, including a commander of the faithful, might have spent time there while visiting Jerusalem for brief or extended stays. Even if that were so, there is no compelling reason to declare that the site examined in toto represents a massive Umayyad palace complex, let alone a government center erected by an Umayyad sovereign to serve the expressed needs of a Muslim ruling authority. If anything seems clear at present, it is that the remains south of the Temple Mount provide no discernible evidence that Muʿāwiyah, or for that matter any other Muslim ruler before ʿAbd al-Malik, envisioned making Jerusalem either a center of government or a sacred site for Muslims comparable in some way to the ḥaramayn of Arabia.

CHAPTER 7

The Dome of the Rock and Arabic Historiography

The Arabic historical sources devote considerable attention to ʿAbd al-Malik's lengthy reign, a twenty-year period marked by great turmoil as well as innovative projects. Acting resolutely, the caliph sustained the ruling dynasty by crushing several insurrections, most notably the one led by the counter-caliph ʿAbdallāh b. al-Zubayr in the Hijaz and that of his brother Muṣʿab in Iraq. These triumphs ensured that Damascus would remain, at least for the foreseeable future, the fulcrum of Islamic rule. After the defeat of the Zubayrids and their Iraqi allies, the Hijazis could never mount a truly serious threat to a caliphate located beyond the Arabian Peninsula, be it to the Umayyads located in Damascus or their successors, the Banū ʿAbbās, situated first at al-Hāshimīyah, and then at Baghdad and Samarra.

In addition to pacifying the Islamic realm and holding the always dangerous Byzantines at bay, ʿAbd al-Malik undertook a major language reform; stabilized the monetary system by establishing new standards for coinage; struck the first truly Islamic coins, which put an end to the widespread use of foreign currency; and constructed the famed Dome of the Rock while resurfacing the Temple Mount and shoring up its surrounding walls. Arabic thus replaced Greek as the official language of a government bureaucracy staffed to a large extent by Christian holdovers from the former Byzantine administration. Islamic coins were diminished in weight, differentiating them from the Byzantine solidi that had been circulating. Pre-Islamic issues bearing the visage of non-Muslim rulers were replaced at first by currency with the image of the Muslim caliph and then by aniconic coins featuring the name of the commander of the faithful and the Muslim doxology: "There is no God but [the One True] God and Muḥammad is His [legitimate] Messenger." The new coins thus valorized the Arabic language, caliphs of Arab stock, and Islam and the Prophet. Cleansed of pictorial representation ʿAbd al-Malik's later currency also drew attention to the pure monotheism of Islam in contrast to the ubiquitous display of graven images by Christian neighbors. The latter produced icons and wall paintings that portrayed a son of God who was at the same time God. The Muslims, having declared themselves genuine monotheists, maintained that the God of the Heavens was "neither born nor gave birth."[1] Similarly, the caliph's massive project restoring the Temple Mount transformed the topography of Jerusalem, declaring it to be an Islamic city that competed with the sacred city of its previous Christian rulers.

Although scholars of the modern West generally agree about the broad outlines of ʿAbd al-Malik's eventful reign, the circumstances surrounding particular developments are hotly contested. Narratives of a time and place far distant from us have given rise to vastly different views. Such interpretive license is hardly surprising. Western scholars tend to regard the medieval histories of the first century AH as tendentious back-projections of later times. Reflective historians who turn to the Arabic chronicles thus find themselves faced with a dilemma. In trying to recover even partial states of the early Islamic past, they are often without secure ground on which to begin their quest. Any proposed history based entirely or even partially on fragmented and unstable sources can be subjected to all sorts of criticism, not all of it rendered kindly. Reconstructing moments of the past from fragile evidence can occasion great skepticism among those critics who are apt to consider various modern histories of early Islamic times highly speculative, if not the product of unrestrained imagination. There is a minimalist school of Arabic historiography, modern scholars whose research is devoted to what we cannot possibly know, as opposed to what we might infer or deduce from admittedly difficult medieval texts.[2]

The broad historical fraternity remains committed to making sense of the Umayyad period. Its constituents have a mandate to search for a knowable history with full knowledge of how vexing that can be. Scholars, acting in good faith, agree to disagree over a wide range of issues. There is, nevertheless, general agreement that ʿAbd al-Malik's caliphate marked a significant change in the formation of the early Islamic community. As an Arab born to a distinguished Meccan family, ʿAbd al-Malik attempted to shape an Islamic ummah and civilization. On the one hand, the object of the caliph's enterprise was to create a community cleansed of undesirable cultural influences caused by intimate contacts with Jews and particularly Christians. The latter were the bearers of rich and time-honored traditions that could be both attractive and jarring to the Muslim conquerors whose primal sensibilities were shaped by an Arabian milieu. The heart of ʿAbd al-Malik's program was to promote the Arabian roots

1. Qur'ān 112:3.

2. For a reflective essay on the problems facing modern historians wishing to recover fragmented states of an imagined past, see J. Lassner, *The Middle East Remembered*, 9–59.

of Islam and its pure monotheism while at the same time forging an imperial polity that rivaled that of his Byzantine predecessors, that is, to draw a distinctive line between the Islamic community he hoped to shape and the Christian civilization Muslims encountered when they extended Islamic rule to Byzantine lands conquered by Arab tribesmen. The caliph was also mindful of his Christian rivals beyond the newly expanded frontiers of Islam, both as regards the ongoing military threat they represented and the skill with which they wielded religious symbols.

Among Orientalists, there is a consensus that the innovative fifth Umayyad caliph was one of the founding fathers of the Islamic community we have come to know: that is, the community with a clearly defined identity and established religious and political structures. This view of an emergent Islamic community in Umayyad times is also embraced by some of the most fervent minimalists. The latter maintain that a hitherto amorphous Islamic polity, which included both Arab tribesmen and monotheist sectarians of the conquered territories, morphed into what became a discrete Islamic ummah no earlier than the late seventh century. Having created this new religious polity, the Muslims gave it legitimacy by inventing, almost from whole cloth, a historical narrative that stressed its Hijazi roots in the lifetime of the Prophet.[3] On the other hand, mainstream scholars claim that Muḥammad's Hijaz was in fact the incubator of the Islamic community and faith that was to evolve, as indeed reported by the earliest Muslim chroniclers. As do the minimalists, but with an entirely different emphasis, they recognize that the conquered territories were the nursery in which the most recent Arab arrivals began to individuate by separating from their Arabian parents and adopting many local practices and beliefs of the large Christian and still vibrant Jewish populations. However, that process of assimilation had to be shaped to Muslim purposes, and so the tradi-

3. Regarding minimalist historiography, see chapter 1, nn. 37, 38. The emergence of the minimalists and A. Noth's pathbreaking work on early Arabic historiography has paved the way for a number of thought-provoking studies on Arabic historical writing. See Noth's article "Der Character der ersten grossen Sammlungen von Nachrichten zur frühen Kalifen Zeit," *Der Islam* 47 (1971): 168–99 and his later monograph *Quellenkritische Studien zur Themen, Formen, und Tendenzen früislamischer Geschichtsüberlieferung* (Bonn, 1973). This work was revised with the assistance of L. Conrad and translated into English by M. Bonner as *The Early Arabic Historical Tradition* (Princeton, 1994). Detailed works stimulated by Noth's literary analysis sources and by the challenge of revisionist history are the studies in *History and Historiography in Early Islamic Times*, edited by L. Conrad (Princeton, 1994); F. Donner, *Narratives of Islamic Origins* (Princeton, 1998); T. Khalidi, *Arabic Historical Thought in the Classical Period* (Cambridge, 1994); C. F. Robinson, *Islamic Historiography* (Cambridge, 2003). Still very valuable is 'A. 'A. Duri's *Baḥth fī nash'at 'ilm al-ta'rīkh 'ind al-'Arab* (Beirut, 1960). Note also his brief entry "The Iraq School of History to the Ninth Century—a Sketch," in *Historians of the Middle East*, edited by B. Lewis and P. M. Holt (London, 1962), 46–53. The more recent and nuanced approaches to Arabic historical writing do not seem to have altered the earlier assessment of 'Abd al-Malik's remarkable reign.

tionally minded authorities of the late seventh century CE invoked memories of the Arabian past to restore old Muslim ideals. These venerated ideals were then dressed in new garb that reflected the changing times. Circumstances dictated that ʿAbd al-Malik lay the foundations of a Muslim imperial polity strong enough and credible enough in Islamic terms to eliminate any internal challenges to the dynasty, especially from the old Muslim aristocrats of the Hijaz and their potential allies in the Islamic realm beyond Arabia. At the same time the caliph, who ruled a territorial expanse with a Christian population that still outnumbered that of the Muslims, had to create a ruling authority that could compete on all levels with a powerful Christian empire that had retreated to its heartland in Asia Minor. We are obliged to ask how ʿAbd al-Malik's decision to build the Dome of the Rock may be understood as part and parcel of these varied concerns.

Our first objective is to determine whether the project on the Temple Mount was designed to alter the recent pre-Islamic past of Jerusalem's sacred history, the city made holy by its Christian Byzantine rulers. Or, seen from a different perspective, can the Temple Mount project be judged in light of internal developments among Arab Muslim leaders contesting for political power, that is, the timeworn struggle between the old Muslims of the Hijaz and the Umayyad usurpers situated in al-Shām? Put somewhat differently, was ʿAbd al-Malik's extensive project to Islamize Jerusalem an attempt to undermine the symbolic importance of Mecca and Medina? In either case, we are forced to conjure up an explanation that is anchored in the reported history of the Umayyad regime and arrived at through a critical examination of the medieval Arabic sources, supplemented where possible from the evidence of material culture. Readers will have noted from earlier discussions that the historiographical road leading to Jerusalem's past is filled with alternate routes through an uncharted literary landscape. It is therefore best to begin at the most clearly marked road sign: the richly described opposition of the Hijazis to the rule of the Banu Umayyah and the transfer of Muslim rule to al-Shām.

The decision of consecutive Umayyad caliphs to forsake Medina, the Prophet's city and capital of the righteous caliphs, did not sit well with the Hāshimites and other aristocrats from the Hijaz. The Prophet's relatives and the descendants of his earliest followers resented the manner in which they and the ḥaramayn had been pushed aside by upstarts whose family had been, for the most part, antagonistic to Muḥammad and his mission. They were well aware that the house of Umayyah accepted Islam only when Muḥammad returned triumphantly to Mecca and offered amnesty to all his former antagonists. Responsibility for having opposed the Prophet and his followers fell hard on Mu'āwiyah's mother, Hind. The wife of Abū Sufyān bore the stigma of having violated the body of the Prophet's uncle Ḥamzah while the latter lay mortally wounded or dead on the field of battle. Licking the blood of a dead or dying enemy is an expression of revenge well known to Arab tribesmen even today. It is usually described as "eating the heart of the enemy." Hind's action earned her the sobriquet "the blood sucker"; in her case the literal expression was *ākilat al-akbād*, "the liver eater," referring to the same act of revenge but with the blood of another organ. Tradition has it that Mu'āwiyah's mother chose to remain incognito when Muḥammad returned to the city of his birth, but the anger she felt for him got the better of her and she gave away her identity. No matter, the Prophet is said to have forgiven her.[4]

Unlike his parents and the majority of his kinsmen, Mu'āwiyah had converted to Islam at a time when Muḥammad's ultimate triumph was anything but clear and served the Prophet faithfully. Difficult as it was for the Hijazis, particularly the Prophet's Hāshimite kinsmen, to accept the legitimacy of Mu'āwiyah's caliphate, there was a grudging respect for him. But his decision to appoint his son Yazīd to be his successor crossed a red line. The authority to appoint a new commander of the faithful had been invested with the larger Islamic community and not the existing ruler. With no proper precedent to guide them, the early Muslims generally relied on pre-Islamic custom and chose the early successors to the Prophet by tribal election (*shūrā*). The usual procedure called for the heads of extended family groups to elect a leader from among them. Mu'āwiyah's decision to introduce the principle of primogeniture was thus nothing less than a direct affront to still powerful tribal sensibilities and a decisive break with both pre-Islamic and Islamic precedent. Moreover, if invoking primogeniture were followed by successive rulers—as was indeed the case—the Prophet's former enemies could rule in perpetuity. Understandably, the Hijazi aristocrats, whether they were members of the Prophet's extended family or Hāshimite kinsmen linked to him by marriage, considered the Umayyad caliphs usurpers, and periodically challenged their rule.

The Revolt of the Zubayrids

The most serious confrontation of the seventh century was the aforementioned revolt led by the counter-caliph 'Abdallāh b. al-Zubayr. A two-pronged assault, the challenge to Umayyad rule was hatched in Medina and then spread to

4. See *EI*, s.v. "Hind bt. 'Utba."

Iraq, where ʿAbdallāh's brother Muṣʿab was tasked with uniting the disaffected and quarrelsome Iraqi tribesmen with the Zubayrid cause. Granted license to use a rather awkward expression, I would characterize the Medina counter-caliphate as the last serious effort of Hijazi "nationalists" to restore political power to the ḥaramayn. Can this revolt that initially rocked the foundations of Umayyad rule be linked in some manner to the construction of the Dome of the Rock? We have already dealt at great length with scholars who maintain that the challenge presented to ʿAbd al-Malik by the Zubayrids and their allies demanded so much of his attention, that taken together with other pressing concerns, he could not have possibly planned and executed the Temple Mount project as described in our sources. These scholars maintain the development of the Temple Mount must have been conceived if not indeed initiated long before ʿAbd al-Malik came to power, perhaps as early as Muʿāwiyah's reign. Hence, whatever symbolic importance one wishes to attach to the Temple Mount project, it was not ʿAbd al-Malik's conception. Thus, the initial decision to build the Dome of the Rock would not have been occasioned by the rebellion threatening his caliphate.[5]

There is, however, a second view going back to the nineteenth century, one that contends that ʿAbd al-Malik, with considerable forethought, did indeed erect the Dome of the Rock as a direct response to the Zubayrid threat. In his *Muhammedanische Studien*, Ignaz Goldziher cites Arabic chroniclers who report that various Umayyad caliphs contemplated transferring the Prophet's pulpit from Medina to al-Shām.[6] The first modern scholar to fully appreciate the linkage between Arabic historiography and political propaganda, Goldziher correctly understood that in these accounts the Umayyads are portrayed as wishing to invest themselves and the province from which they ruled with the same aura of legitimacy that accrued to the Prophet and the ḥaramayn. Similarly, Goldziher cites a brief account reported by the ninth-century historian Yaʿqūbī in which the author claims that ʿAbd al-Malik built the Dome of the Rock to divert the annual pilgrimage from Mecca to Jerusalem, an act of symbolic importance no less significant and even more provocative than the alleged scheme to relocate the Prophet's pulpit.[7] According to Yaʿqūbī, the caliph

5. See chapter 5.

6. The entirety of Goldziher's two-volume work, originally published in Halle (1895–90), was translated into English with added annotation by C. R. Barber and S. M. Stern as *Muslim Studies*, vol. 1 (Chicago, 1966) vol. 2 (London, 1971). References to this work here are cited according to the English translation with the German pagination in brackets. On the transfer of the pulpit, see *Muslim Studies*, 2:44 n. 3 [35]. For a full discussion of the accounts relating to the transfer of the pulpit (and the Prophet's staff), see chapter 4 above.

7. Goldziher, *Muslim Studies*, 2:44–45 [35–36].

became agitated because pilgrims fulfilling their religious obligation in Arabia were acknowledging the Zubayrid cause. ʿAbd al-Malik then declared that pilgrims visiting Jerusalem could emulate the *ṭawāf* (the ceremony in which pilgrims circumambulated Mecca's central shrine, the Kaʿbah) by circling the primeval rock of the Temple Mount.[8] Readers of the Arabic chronicle are thus led to believe that Jerusalem's legendary rock was the analogue of the stone situated within Mecca's Kaʿbah, the holy spot dedicated to God by Abraham and his eldest son Ishmael, the ancestor of the Prophet Muḥammad.

Stressing the holiness of Jerusalem's primeval rock and planning to build a magnificent domed structure covering it was one thing. The significance of the rock throughout history is well attested in Muslim sources.[9] However, it would have been quite another matter for the caliph to designate the site as suitable for fulfilling the ṭawāf, and still another to actually divert the pilgrimage from the ḥaramayn to Jerusalem. Yaʿqūbī' reports that people complained about the caliph's decision, asserting: "Would you prevent us from a pilgrimage to the holy house of God, an obligation (*farḍ*) that God has imposed upon us?"[10] The author thus leads us to believe that ʿAbd al-Malik exceeded the limits of his authority, or in any case was thought to have done so by an angry populace. Yaʿqūbī clearly does not expect his reader to think that the caliph could have succeeded in ordering so dramatic a change in time-honored religious behavior. More was needed than executive fiat. For the caliph to actually divert the pilgrimage to Jerusalem, he would have had to defend his decision on religious grounds, not mere political expediency. For the pilgrims, the trek to the holy cities of Arabia was a matter of *dīn*, not *dunyā*.

And so, in defense of his proposed action, ʿAbd al-Malik invokes a dictum attributed to the Prophet himself. Yaʿqūbī has the caliph referring to a well-known faḍāʾil tradition obtained from no less than the great transmitter and confidant of the Umayyads, Ibn Shihāb al-Zuhrī (d. 742 CE): "You shall prepare for a journey to three mosques: the Masjid al-Ḥaram (in Mecca); my mosque (in Medina); and the mosque in Jerusalem (Bayt al-Maqdis)."[11] In effect, Muḥammad is pictured as saying that the Temple Mount is to be the equivalent of the Prophet's mosque in Medina (*wa huwa yaqūmu lakum maqām al-Masjid al-Ḥaram*). If this statement legitimizing pilgrimage to Jerusalem were not suf-

8. Yaʿqūbī, *Historiae*, 2:311.

9. See chapter 2.

10. Yaʿqūbī, *Historiae*, 2:311.

11. For this tradition and similar traditions in praise of Jerusalem, as well as mirror image statements demeaning the importance of the holy city and its mosque, see chapter 9. The noted traditions scholar and reporter of historical accounts al-Zuhrī was closely linked to the Umayyad house from the reign of ʿAbd al-Malik to that of Hishām. See *EI*, s.v. "al-Zuhrī."

ficient to calm the anxious Muslims, the caliph points out that "the Prophet set foot on the [primeval] rock when [following his night journey (*isrā'*) to 'the furthest place of worship,'] he ascended to Heaven [a reference to his encounter (*mi'rāj*) with the Almighty]." In such fashion Muḥammad personally sanctified the already sacred rock so that it could take the place of the Ka'bah (*takūnu lakum maqām al-Ka'bah*). The caliph was thus able to mollify those Muslims who complained of his audacious plan.[12] At that point, 'Abd al-Malik built his domed structure over the rock; decorated it with brocade coverings (which resembled those of the Ka'bah); and arranged to have it staffed with attendants (*sadnah*). The Muslims then circumambulated the (primeval) rock as they had (the black stone within) the holy shrine of Mecca. The chronicler goes on to say that people continued to perform the rites of pilgrimage in Jerusalem throughout the days of the Umayyads (*wa aqāma bi-dhālika ayām Banī Umayyah*).[13]

In a footnote and without further comment, Goldziher refers to a second account found in Ya'qūbī's chronicle, one that speaks of an event taking place during the reign of 'Abd al-Malik's son Sulaymān (r. 715–17).[14] Ya'qūbī relates that Sulaymān (the former governor of Filasṭīn and presently commander of the faithful) consulted a number of legal scholars (*faqīh*) regarding the rites of pilgrimage. The author leaves the impression that at issue was the permissibility of fulfilling the obligations of the ḥajj in Jerusalem. As the assembled group of experts was hopelessly divided—no two persons were of the same opinion—the caliph sought a precedent. He asked what his father had done. Once informed of that, Sulaymān allowed the ṭawāf to be performed on the Temple Mount as did his predecessor. According to Goldziher's reading of Ya'qūbī, 'Abd al-Malik surely set a precedent in diverting the pilgrimage from the holy cities of the Hijaz to the holy city in al-Shām, an act clearly caused by a perceived threat of the Zubayrid challenge. The failure of the legal scholars to arrive at any sort of consensus allows the chronicler to accentuate the specious grounds previously used by 'Abd al-Malik to justify his action and holds the Umayyads culpable for trampling on religious tradition.

Although Goldziher was prepared to follow Ya'qūbī and accept that the caliph actually diverted the pilgrimage, he was not about to abandon his skeptical view of Arabic sources. Having introduced Orientalists to the tendentiousness

12. The traditions of a footprint on the rock of the Temple Mount is most certainly linked to Jesus's footprint on the rock surmounted by the Church of the Sepulcher as well as reflecting pro-Umayyad sentiments, as argued by J. van Ess, "'Abd al-Malik and the Dome of the Rock: An Analysis of Some Texts," in *Bayt al-Maqdis*, vol. 1, *'Abd al-Malik's Jerusalem*, edited by J. Raby and J. Johns, *OSIA* 9 (Oxford, 1992), 92 ff.

13. Ya'qūbī, *Historiae*, 2:311.

14. Goldziher, *Muslim Studies*, 2:45–46 [36–37] citing *Historiae*, 2:358–59.

of Arabic religious traditions and historiography, Goldziher did not regard as factual the legal basis presented by ʿAbd al-Malik for breaking a time-honored religious practice. The tradition attributed to the Prophet that the caliph cited in support of his decision as well as other traditions that trumpeted the praise of Jerusalem or denigrated Mecca and Medina were regarded by Goldziher as inventions of necessity (*mawḍuʿāt*) designed specifically to enhance the image of the Umayyad regime. Included among the mawḍuʿāt cited by the great Orientalist is an account that maintains that the Well of Zamzam, a celebrated religious landmark in Mecca, pays a yearly visit to the pool of Siloam in Jerusalem. That journey of the well takes place during the night of ʿArafah, the time when pilgrims leave Mecca for the plain of ʿArafah thirteen miles east of the city. There they perform the *taʿrīf*, the final rite of the ḥajj that culminates with the assembled Muslims standing in supplication before God.[15] Similarly, Goldziher cites yet another invented tradition attributed to the Prophet. Responding to a query about (the sanctuary in) Jerusalem (Bayt al-Maqdis), Muḥammad replies: "Make pilgrimages to Jerusalem and pray there"—there was then war in these lands—"and if you are unable to pray there, then send oil in order to light the lamps. [For sending oil for the lamps is the equivalent of praying there]."[16] The words set off here by dashes, *there was war then in these lands*, are presumably a gloss, perhaps a back-projection referring to the battles for Jerusalem between the Byzantines and Sasanids, a conflict mentioned obliquely in Muslim scripture and elaborated upon in Qurʾān commentary.[17] In any case, Goldziher seems to suggest that this tradition could be read as justifying ʿAbd al-Malik's decision to divert the pilgrimage from the ḥaramayn to holy city in al-Shām.

In a footnote, Goldziher lists but does not comment on a variant of this account preserved by Ibn al-Faqīh, a tenth-century author whose descriptive geography contains many faḍāʾil traditions about Jerusalem and the Temple Mount, some based on the authority of the Jewish convert Kaʿb al-Aḥbār,

15. Goldziher, *Muslim Studies*, 2:45 [36]. Goldziher indicates "Siloah." This toponym should be corrected to "Siloam," the famous Jerusalem pool (Arabic *Sulwān* or more currently *Silwān*). Goldziher cites as his source Yāqūt, *Mujʿam*, 3:726 but there is no indication of this tradition on the page cited. A brief statement about the waters of Zamzam visiting (*yazūru*, i.e., making a religious visit) to the pool in the Jerusalem suburb (*rabaḍ*) of Sulaym is found in Muqaddasī, *Aḥsan*, 171. For the *taʿrīf*, the final ceremony for Muslims at the ḥajj, see *EI*, s.v. "ʿArafa." For a description of ceremonies surrounding the well Zamzam, including recent times, see A. Ghabin, "The Zimzam well ritual in Islam and its Jerusalem connection," 116–36.

16. Goldziher, *Muslim Studies*, 2:45 [36–37], citing Abū Dāwūd, *Sunan*, 1:48. The bracketed emendation to Goldziher's remarks is based on Ibn al-Faqīh, *Buldān*, 96.

17. Qurʾān 30:2 and the extensive commentary to the verse. The seeming reference to the Qurʾānic text may also link the account, however obliquely, to the conflict between ʿAbd al-Malik and the Zubayrids controlling the holy cities in the Hijaz, a situation that called for redirecting the pilgrimage to Jerusalem. In any case, Goldziher suggests as much.

others from Kaʿb's Yemenite counterpart Wahb b. Munnabih, both legendary figures reputed to be purveyors of Israelitica. Turning to Ibn al-Faqīh, we see the Prophet is asked for a legal decision (*fatwā*) about Jerusalem, but without any inkling as to the reason for the query. In response, the Prophet launches into a familiar litany of praise for the city, and concludes with a variant of a well-known faḍāʾil expression: "Come to it [Jerusalem] and pray (*ṣallī*) in it, for a single prayer there is worth a thousand [prayers, meaning in Mecca or Medina]."[18] To be sure, the Prophet makes no explicit mention here of performing the rites of pilgrimage in Jerusalem, only of praying there, but given that the question calls for a legal judgment, it would appear Goldziher understood the two accounts in light of one another.

With an eye ever alert for the odd detail, Goldziher goes on to note that various expressions of praise for Jerusalem are complemented by statements denigrating Medina.[19] He refers to comments like that found in Ibn ʿAbd Rabibihī (d. 940 CE), where the Prophet's city is labeled "The Filthy," and in Masʿūdī's chronicle, where Muʿāwiyah's son, the hated Umayyad caliph Yazīd I, refers to Medina as "foul smelling."[20] As we shall have cause to see in the following chapter, praise for the holy city was often declared at the expense of its Arabian rivals. These random statements cited by Goldziher are in fact representative of many traditions found in works praising Jerusalem, a specific literary genre whose accounts were largely unknown to him and his generation. Indeed, Ibn al-Faqīh's geography, which Goldziher cites, contains a number of mawḍuʿāt favoring Jerusalem over the holy cities of the Hijaz. The tendentiousness of these accounts notwithstanding, with the evidence of the medieval Arabic sources then available and, not the least, the prestige of Goldziher's personal endorsement, the claim that ʿAbd al-Malik built the Dome of the Rock to divert the annual pilgrimage from the holy cities of Arabia took root and remained conventional wisdom well into the following century. Among the leading scholars of the time, only Julian Wellhausen, an older contemporary of Goldziher, expressed doubts about directing the ḥajj away from Mecca to Jerusalem, but he did so without citing any textual evidence.[21] As time progressed, Goldziher's original claim based entirely on Yaʿqūbī' was reinforced by the subsequent publication of other Arabic sources, each containing versions of ʿAbd al-Malik's decision to build the Dome of the Rock and divert the pilgrimage from Mecca to Jerusalem.

18. Goldziher, *Muslim Studies*, 2:45 [37], citing Ibn al-Faqīh, *Buldān*, 95 ff.
19. Goldziher, *Muslim Studies*, 2:46 [37].
20. Ibn ʿAbd Rabbihi, *ʿIqd al-farīd*, 7:299–300; Masʿūdī, *Murūj* (Paris), 5:161.
21. J. Wellhausen, *The Arab Kingdom and Its Fall*, 212–14.

An Alternative Explanation

In a brief article published in 1950 and later expanded into a somewhat lengthier study, S. D. Goitein rejected the accepted wisdom of some seventy years and denied that ʿAbd al-Malik diverted the ḥajj to the holy city.[22] He noted that Goldziher relies on a single source (a text whose description of events fills no more than a page or so). Goitein is only too well aware that Yaʿqūbī's account is confirmed by similar narratives found in historical works that have come to light since Goldziher's *Muhammedanische Studien*. But of these works, only the chronicle of Eutychius (d. 940) forms part of early Arabic historiography. As for the later histories that link building the Dome of the Rock with diverting the pilgrimage to Jerusalem, Goitein assumes that their version of events is ultimately derived from that of Yaʿqūbī. Because Goitein denies the historicity of the original account, it follows that the same must be said of versions found in authors whose dates range from the fourteenth to the sixteenth century CE.[23] That still leaves Eutychius, the Melkite patriarch of Alexandria, otherwise known by his Arabic name Saʿīd b. al-Biṭrīq. The Christian's chronicle, unknown to Goldziher and therefore not cited by him, contains two passing references to diverting the pilgrimage from Mecca to Jerusalem, reportedly because of the caliph's conflict with ʿAbdallāh b. al-Zubayr.[24] Neither account can be linked, however, to Yaʿqūbī or the later historians mentioned by Goitein.

What is it that moves Goitein to reject what is explicitly stated by Yaʿqūbī and Eutychius, as well as by the later historians Ibn Kathīr (d. 1373) and Ibn Taghrī Birdī (d. 1470); by Mujīr al-Dīn (d. 1521 CE), who cites the faḍāʾil of Jerusalem and Hebron; and by Diyārbakrī, the author of the *Taʾrīkh al-khamīs* (ca. sixteenth century CE)? Assessing Yaʿqūbī's foundational account, Goitein turns to the great chroniclers of the early Islamic period.[25] The Leiden edition of Ṭabarī's (d. 923 CE) massive annalistic history devotes 601 pages to ʿAbd al-Malik's reign, of which roughly two-thirds deals with the years of the Zubayrid revolt. The numerous versions of specific events often include references to many informants and written sources, and yet in all of Ṭabarī's dense descrip-

---

22. Originally as S. D. Goitein, "The Historical Background of the Erection of the Dome of the Rock," *JAOS* 70 (1950): 104–8 and then expanded into "The Sanctity of Jerusalem and Palestine in Early Islam," in his collected essays *Studies in Islamic History and Institutions* (Leiden, 1966), 135–48.

23. Goitein, "Sanctity of Jerusalem," 135–37. In addition to the early authors Yaʿqūbī and Eutychius (Saʿīd b. al-Biṭrīq), *Taʾrīkh*, 2:39–40, Goitein cites the later chroniclers Ibn Kathīr, *Bidāyah*, 8:280; Ibn Taghrī Birdī, *Nujūm*, 1:207; Diyārbakrī, *Taʾrīkh al khamīs*, 2:339; and Mujīr al-Dīn, *Uns*, 1:240–43.

24. *Taʾrīkh*, 2:39, 42.

25. Goitein, "Sanctity of Jerusalem," 136.

tion there is no mention of anything that links building the Dome of the Rock to any attempt at diverting the ḥajj. Similarly Balādhurī's (d. ca. 892 CE) *Anṣāb al-ashrāf*, a lengthy dynastic chronicle filled with details of ʿAbd al-Malik's reign, fails to report that the caliph redirected the pilgrimage away from Mecca. Nor does the geographer Muqaddasī (ca. eleventh century CE), a native of Jerusalem who devotes much attention to the city, or Ibn Aʿtham al-Kūfī (d. ca. 926 CE), a historian who focuses on the revolts of the Zubayrids and others in Iraq. The same can also be said for Masʿūdī (d. ca. 960), the author of two belletristic histories; and two shorter works: Dīnawarī's (d. ca. 895) *Akhbār al-ṭiwāl*, and the earliest extant annalistic history, the *Ta'rīkh* of Khalīfah b. Khayyāṭ (d. ca. 855). How is it then that so momentous and unprecedented an event could have gone unnoticed by so many major chroniclers, geographers, and historically informed litterateurs of the times?

Goitein notes that neither Ṭabarī nor Balādhurī can be counted as favoring the Umayyads and thus would hardly have rewritten history on their behalf by omitting from their description of ʿAbd al-Malik's reign what would have been a clear affront to Muslim sensibilities.[26] The same could be said for the geographer Muqaddasī, who relates a lengthy anecdote in which Muʿāwiyah is castigated by an Alid partisan for falsely promoting the sanctity of the Holy Land.[27] There is general agreement among modern scholars that the great Arabic historians of the ninth and tenth centuries tend to be negative toward Islam's first dynasts. They picture the Umayyads as usurping the legitimacy of Muḥammad and his earliest successors, and as being overly absorbed with the mechanics of rule and the rewards of the temporal world. If ʿAbd al-Malik did indeed divert the pilgrimage from Mecca, an unprecedented and condemnable act, there is every reason to expect that, with their customary thoroughness and anti-Umayyad bias—however mild in some instances—the great chroniclers who were closest to the event would surely have mentioned it.

That still leaves unanswered why Yaʿqūbī, unlike his contemporaries who were mute on this issue, related an invented tradition that put ʿAbd al-Malik in an unfavorable light. Goitein points to Yaʿqūbī's bias against the Umayyads, the result of the latter's sympathy for the Alid cause. Perhaps he believed that the great chroniclers of the early Middle Ages, being more responsible historians than Yaʿqūbī, did not relay a seemingly implausible tradition that was damaging to the memory of the Umayyads, however much they personally disliked the first dynasts of the Islamic world. On the other hand, historians, further

26. See n. 13 above.
27. See chapter 9.

removed from the fallout of early Alid-Umayyad relations, might have felt no constraints in reporting 'Abd al-Malik's invented break with historic precedent. Goitein notes that Ibn Kathīr lists Rajā' b. Ḥaywah as one of the officials assigned to build the Dome of the Rock, and by implication makes him a participant in diverting the pilgrimage. Goitein then reminds his reader that Rajā' was a famous theologian and intimate friend of the Umayyad caliph 'Umar b. 'Abd al-'Azīz (the latter an individual of such piety that he was the only Umayyad ruler whose grave was not desecrated following the fall of the regime). As far as Goitein is concerned, a devout Muslim such as Rajā' "could never have given his consent to such a flagrant break with the Qur'ānic ḥajj, one of the five pillars of Islam." He then adds that 'Abd al-Malik himself was "an orthodox and observant Muslim."[28] Apparently, Goitein could not conceive of seventh-century politics making strange bedfellows, at least not when such profound religious sensitivities are at issue.

There is more to Goitein's dispute with Goldziher and the seventy years of established wisdom to which the latter's view gave rise. But before returning to Goitein's brief, there is the question of the later sources cited by him. Were they indeed all dependent on Ya'qūbī as he claims? And what are we to make of the Christian Eutychius, who should also be pertinent to the Goitein-Goldziher discussion? The Melkite surely had no vested interest in Alid propaganda. What then is the relationship if any between the patriarch's brief notice in his chronicle; the account of Ya'qūbī that elicits Goitein's great skepticism; and the later historians who report that 'Abd al-Malik diverted the pilgrimage from the Hijaz to al-Shām?

The Christian chronicler from Alexandria remains somewhat of a puzzle. He notes in a passing remark that 'Abd al Malik, reacting to the Zubayrids, diverted the pilgrimage from Mecca to Jerusalem. But as he continues, he presents what seems to be a rather confusing picture. We are initially told that the caliph enlarged the mosque (*zāda fī-l-masjid*) so that the primeval rock was within it, but several pages later Eutychius informs us it was the caliph's son al-Walīd who positioned the mosque so that the rock was at its center and that al-Walīd then erected a dome over it (presumably a reference to building the Dome of the Rock). The people then celebrated the ḥajj at the rock.[29] We might think that the author, or a possibly a scribe copying a manuscript of Eutychius's work, may have inadvertently confused father and son. But al-Walīd's role in the Temple Mount project is echoed in other sources. The claim that al-Walīd

28. Goitein, "Sanctity of Jerusalem," 138, indicates "Ḥaywā," read "Ḥaywah."
29. *Ta'rīkh*, 2:39, 42.

and not ʿAbd al-Malik built the Dome of the Rock and diverted the pilgrimage from Mecca to Jerusalem is reported by the Egyptian scholar al-Ḥasan b. Aḥmad al-Muhallabī (d. 990 CE) and then repeated in the geography of Abū-l-Fidāʾ (d. 1331 CE).[30] Eutychius is also quoted by al-Makīn b. al-ʿAmīd (d. 1204 CE), whose report also comes to us in part by way of the preeminent Muslim historian Ibn Khaldūn (ca. fourteenth century CE).[31]

Eutychius's narrative thus begs for an explanation. I know of no other early source that ascribes building the Dome of the Rock to al-Walīd. My first inclination is to follow Amikam Elad, who regards Eutychius's statements as clearly confused, and leave it at that.[32] It would not be astonishing if a Christian situated in Alexandria reporting on an event that took place in another province over a hundred years before his birth might have confused two caliphs of the realm, in this instance a father and son. It is rather odd, however, that four other authorities, including the redoubtable Ibn Khaldūn, would repeat what at first glance seems to be an obvious error. Also jarring is the statement that either ʿAbd al-Malik or his son added to the mosque so that it included the rock under the dome. There is no corroborating evidence that the domed building ever served per se as a house of worship.

However, on second thought, there may be an explanation for the seeming incongruity, at least as regards the expansion of the "mosque" on the Temple Mount. It is certainly conceivable that in time the early Jerusalem mosque described by the Christian pilgrim Arculf[33] could not have accommodated all the Muslims assembling for communal prayers on Friday. The same might be said shortly after the completion of the larger al-Aqṣā mosque on the Temple Mount. That situation pertains at the Ḥaram al-Sharīf today. A similar lack of room was observed at the great Friday mosque in al-Manṣūr's Round City, even after it had been substantially enlarged in length or width.[34] Throngs of worshipers unable to enter the jammed mosque prayed in the surrounding open court. With that, the open area adjacent to the original mosque became in effect an extension of the mosque itself. The architectural historian K. A. C. Creswell seems to propose as much, regarding ʿAbd al-Malik's (or al-Walīd's) "expan-

30. Abū-l-Fidā, *Taqwīn al-buldān* (Paris, 1840), 2:227. Muhallabi's *al-ʿAzīzī*, so named because it was composed for the Fatimid Caliph al-ʿAzīz, was published in part by S. al-Munajjid as "Qiṭʿah min kitāb mafqūd al-masālik wa-l-mamālik li-l-Muhallabī," *Revue de l'insitut des manuscrits arabes* 4 (1958): 43–71, see esp. 49–51, 54. These works are cited by A. Elad, "Why Did ʿAbd al-Malik Build the Dome of the Rock," 44–45.

31. Cited by A. Elad, "Why Did ʿAbd al-Malik Build," 46, who also draws attention to Ibn Khaldūn's *K. al-ʿIbar* (Cairo, 1867), 2:226.

32. Elad, "Why Did ʿAbd al-Malik Build," 45.

33. See chapter 4.

34. Khaṭīb, *Taʾrīkh Baghdad*, 1:108 and J. Lassner, *Topography*, 189–95.

sion" of the place of worship, but draws no hard conclusions.[35] Considering the Umayyad investment in refurbishing the ancient Temple Mount, enlarging the area of prayer to include the surface of the platform seems possible, if not indeed eminently plausible. Extending the mosque to include a larger area within the platform may serve to explain the placement of the small prayer niches situated at various points on the Temple Mount. These structures might have been used originally to mark off spaces in the open court as if these spaces were part of an enclosed principal mosque (*masjid al-jāmiʿ*); that is, for legal purposes they marked a place of prayer specifically designated for communal worship on Fridays. To be sure, this interpretation of Eutychius's report is merely a suggestion, no doubt one that is likely to encounter skepticism. What is important is that the Christian author, who lived at the time of Yaʿqūbī, provides us with a direct statement that the Umayyads diverted the ḥajj and that this terse account is repeated by a number of later Muslim scholars. It is then clear that however off key the melody, we have a second early voice giving credence to Goldziher's thesis and in texts that were available to Goitein.

Amikam Elad with his usual attention to detail delves deeply into the transmission of the relevant data and attempts to identify whenever possible the earliest sources for the tradition that ʿAbd al-Malik redirected the pilgrimage to Jerusalem. His effort leads him to reject Goitein's contention that the later sources are all dependent on the anti-Umayyad account of Yaʿqūbī, an account whose historicity Goitein denies.[36] Elad provides us with a better understanding of the historiographical issue, for even a casual reading of these sources seems to reveal that we are dealing with one or several transmitted reports very different from that of the ninth-century historian-geographer. For example, the extended description found in Ibn Kathīr's *al-Bidāyah wa-l-nihāyah* includes references to the organization of labor; the handling of the payroll for the assembled workers; the lavish amount of resources made available for building the Dome of the Rock; and other details not found in Yaʿqūbī's short account, let alone the terse statement of Eutychius.[37] Reporting on the Dome of the Rock, Ibn Kathīr quotes the thirteenth-century author Sibṭ b. al-Jawzī. As distinct echoes of the latter's *Mirʾāt al-zamān* can be found in all the late sources in question, Elad draws the inescapable conclusion that these later historians relied on Sibṭ b. al-Jawzī and not Yaʿqūbī, as Goitein maintained.[38]

Sibṭ b. al-Jawzī, who died in 1256 CE, would also have to be considered

35. *EMA*, 1/2:65.
36. Elad, "Why Did ʿAbd al-Malik Build," 45–48.
37. Ibn Kathīr, *Bidāyah*, 2:280–81.
38. Elad, "Why Did ʿAbd al-Malik Build," 47–48.

a later author. Fortunately, Elad was able to consult three manuscripts of the unpublished *Mir'āt* and produced an edition and translation of the pertinent Arabic text, along with a detailed commentary.[39] It is of singular importance that the manuscripts of Sibṭ Ibn al-Jawzī draw attention to the authorities upon whom he relied. As regards the reasons for building the Dome of the Rock, that is, the need to divert the pilgrimage in response to the threat presented by the Zubayrids, the author of the *Mir'āt* refers to a tradition obtained via Muḥammad b. al-Sā'ib (d. 763 CE) and his son, the noted historian Hishām (al-Kalbī, d. 819 CE). He refers as well to a second version by way of the equally renowned al-Wāqidī (d. ca. 825 CE) and unspecified others. According to Sibṭ b. al-Jawzī, the two strands form a composite picture that he then presents his readers.[40]

Elad also refers to a sermon preached toward the end of the Umayyad regime by the Khārijite agitator Abū Ḥamzah al-Mukhtār b. 'Awf. The passage cited is found in a still unpublished manuscript of the *Kashf al-ghummah*, an eighteenth-century Khārijite tract made available to Elad by Michael Cook of Princeton University.[41] The text, in the form of a poem, accuses 'Abd al-Malik of giving the (primeval) rock the appearance (*hay'ah*) of (the rock in the Ka'bah in) Mecca (*hay'at al-maqām*). With that, the ill-behaved Syrians fulfilled the rites of pilgrimage in Jerusalem (*yaḥujju ilayhā jufāt ahl al-Shām*).[42] In his work on Muslim dogma, Cook notes that Ibn 'Awf's anti-Umayyad sermon was transmitted by al-Haytham b. 'Adī (d. ca. 822 CE), adding still another early transmitter of historical accounts to the list of those claiming that 'Abd al-Malik diverted the ḥajj from the Hijaz to Jerusalem.[43] All these well-known purveyors of historical data either predate or are contemporaries of Ya'qūbī. Leaving aside the problematic Eutychius and the later writers who relay information seemingly based on his work, there is every reason to believe that Goldziher's thesis has the support of at least two distinct lines of Muslim tradition emanating from the early period of historical activity: Ya'qūbī, whose source or sources remain unknown, and a quartet of highly visible transmitters who leave no

39. The Arabic text (53–58) and translation (33–38) serve as bookends to Elad's detailed commentary (38–52).

40. *Mir'āt* (Elad), 53.

41. Elad, "Why Did 'Abd al-Malik Build," 49–50. I have not seen the text of this manuscript.

42. Elad, following Cook, understands *maqām*, literally "place," to be the Maqām Ibrāhīm, a stone near the Ka'bah, or according to some authorities "the whole place of pilgrimage or the Ḥaram of Mecca." See p. 50, n. 83. The context clearly reveals that in building the Dome of the Rock 'Abd al-Malik was sanctifying the rock on the Temple Mount, making it the equivalent of the Ka'bah, and Jerusalem the equivalent of Mecca.

43. M. Cook, *Early Muslim Dogma: A Source Critical Study* (Cambridge, 1981), 8. For al-Haytham b. 'Adī, see *EI*, s.v. "al-Haytham b. 'Adī."

discrete written legacy, but who are often cited by the first generation of chroniclers whose works we possess.

The existence of these early accounts, statements that assert that ʿAbd al-Malik diverted the pilgrimage, does not necessarily negate the main thrust of Goitein's argument. He may have been wrong to think that Yaʿqūbī is the sole source of the later accounts, but that does not mean the tradition cited by the later authors is to be taken as fact. One could just as easily maintain that the parallel tradition found in the later sources was, like the account of Yaʿqūbī, a literary artifice to discredit ʿAbd al-Malik and the Umayyad regime. According to some modern scholars, three of the early transmitters listed by Sibṭ b. al-Jawzī held distinctively anti-Umayyad views. Hishām al-Kalbī and his father Muḥammad favored the Alids and were opposed to those who usurped the authority of the Prophet's house. Hishām's great-grandfather and grandfather both fought for ʿAlī b. Abī Ṭālib when Muʿāwiyah, then governor of Syria, rebelled against the standing caliph. Hishām's grandfather was later killed campaigning with Muṣʿab b. al-Zubayr in the unsuccessful attempt to unseat ʿAbd al-Malik and restore rule to the Hāshimites and the ḥaramayn.[44] Like Hishām, Wāqidī is thought to have inclined to the Alids, and while the evidence of this has been questioned, scholars agree that he transmitted anti-Umayyad traditions. The various offices he held at the bequest of the Abbasid caliphs could certainly explain Wāqidī's negative portrayal of the dynasty his Abbasid patrons replaced. Al-Haythm b. ʿAdī is described as anti-Umayyad but leaning to the Khārijites.[45]

Given the background of the early Muslim authorities in question, the information obtained from the *Mirʾāt al-zamān* would seem, at first notice, to strengthen Goitein's assessment, as he claims the brief against ʿAbd al-Malik is not a historic fact, but the invention of anti-Umayyad transmitters aiming to discredit the caliph. It should be clear, however, that the sentiments of the early Muslim historians are not always easy to fathom. What does it mean to label a scholar pro-Alid or anti-Umayyad, and how do such labels inform our understanding of specific passages? The great chronicle of Ṭabarī, that most detailed monument of early Arabic historical writing, contains numerous and at times contradictory versions of events. Some scholars have seen the positioning of these variants as a way Ṭabarī and other historians shape opinion without openly revealing their personal views. But if this was so, no one has yet succeeded in establishing a method that uses the positioning of variants

44. Elad, "Why Did ʿAbd al-Malik Build," 42.
45. Elad, "Why Did ʿAbd al-Malik Build," 42.

to give precise meaning to individual events. Suffice it to say, Ṭabarī cites a variety of accounts that sometimes reflect different political viewpoints, or so it would seem. His approach to assembling and recording historical material might be described as somewhat eclectic. Even Muḥammad b. Isḥāq's (d. 767 CE) biography of the Prophet, a work commissioned by the Abbasid caliphs to enhance their claims vis-à-vis their Alid cousins, contains traditions that seemingly place ʿAlī b. Abī Ṭālib in a favorable light.[46] The most partisan medieval authors occasionally insert accounts that work at cross-purposes with their overall political vision. The grudging respect given Muʿāwiyah b. Abī Sufyān by Ibn Ṭabāṭabā, the descendant of a martyred Alid namesake and an openly partisan Shiʿite historian, is a case in point.[47]

How are we to explain this phenomenon? It may be that the great chroniclers were seemingly averse to jettison all sorts of material that they or their assistants had painstakingly collected. Perhaps they feared failure to display all they knew would compromise their reputation for prodigious learning and meticulous scholarship. On the other hand, the retention of conflicting traditions seems perfectly natural in a culture that turns for guidance to sacred writings. The ongoing interpretation of scripture and other religious texts was and continues to be a huge literary endeavor in which highly diverse and often contradictory opinions are juxtaposed and/or sequentially arranged. It is worth noting that Ṭabarī was not only a great chronicler; he was also the author of a massive Qurʾān commentary and was a legal scholar of great prominence. The methods with which he approached these last disciplines surely informed his historical project.

Elad is thus right to question Goitein's claim that Yaʿqūbī's support of the Alids is compelling proof that his report of ʿAbd al-Malik diverting the ḥajj is nothing more than an anti-Umayyad invention. The same could of course be said for the other early accounts that are transmitted via Sibṭ b. al-Jawzī. Elad seems to suggest that any inclination to deny the historicity of the accounts in question would be undermined by the presence of similar anti-Umayyad traditions in what he terms undiscovered Sunni(te) sources.[48] The medieval encyclopedias mention any number of "histories" by author, title, and subject matter. The range of subjects reportedly covered in tracts that have not come to light is extraordinarily rich. Among the references to works not yet discovered

46. For a detailed treatment of Ibn Iṣḥāq's *Sīrah*, see R. Sellheim, "Prophet, Chalif und Geschichte: Die Muḥammad-Biographie des Ibn Iṣḥāq," *Oriens* 18–19 (1967): 33–91.
47. Ibn Ṭabāṭabā, *Fakhrī*, 103–9.
48. Elad, "Why Did ʿAbd al-Malik Build," 42, 43.

are histories of the caliphs and their times.[49] I doubt anyone would disagree that somewhere in that repository of lost books there might well be sources that can help modern scholars to better understand 'Abd al-Malik's activities, and more generally the Islamization of Jerusalem. As it is, we can only work with what we have. Elad's guarded statement that there may have been "'Sunnī(te)' histories which did include this [anti-Umayyad] tradition" is well taken, but it represents an argument *ex silentio* that is even weaker than that of Goitein. Moreover, there is no reason to believe that should we recover Elad's so-called "Sunnī(te)" histories, they would present us with concrete evidence that 'Abd al-Malik diverted the ḥajj in order to counter the Zubayrids.

The use of scare quotes around *Sunnī* is an indication that Elad realizes how difficult it is to apply that label to early Islamic historiography. Shi'ism and Sunnism as articulated ideological systems with well-defined and established followings had not fully crystallized in the first half of the eighth century when the assiduous collection of historical traditions first took shape. The political constellation, before and shortly after the fall of the Umayyad regime (750 CE), was very fluid. Among those wishing to restore the house of the Prophet (*ahl al-bayt*) to its rightful place at the head of the community were the early partisans (*shī'ah*) of 'Alī's progeny by way of his wife Fāṭimah, daughter of the Prophet, and those who initially followed his offspring via Muḥammad, the son of 'Alī's Ḥanafite concubine Khawlah. The early supporters of 'Alī's Faṭimid offspring were the progenitors of what was to become Shi'ism of later times. There were also proponents of Muḥammad's first cousins via his paternal uncle al-'Abbās, a heterogeneous body of adherents. These reportedly included supporters of Muḥammad b. al-Ḥanafīyah who had gone over to the Abbasids after Muḥammad died childless. The supporters of the Abbasids would eventually coalesce into what is currently referred to as the Sunnites. Opting to form a clandestine movement rather than risk premature revolt, the Abbasids bided their time, and then, literally hijacking a revolution begun by the Alids, they overthrew the Umayyad usurpers and established a dynastic order of their own. Following that, the two branches of the Prophet's clan that had shared broad political objectives and common political support during the Umayyad inter-

49. F. Rosenthal, *A History of Muslim Historiography*, 2nd edition (Leiden, 1968), esp. part 2, which contains annotated translations of segments of three unedited major works of medieval Arabic historiography. These works, Muḥammad b. Ibrāhīm al-Ījī's *Tuḥfat al-faqīr ilā ṣāḥib al-sarīr* (ca. late fourteenth century CE); Muḥammad b. Sulaymān al-Kāfiyajī's *al-Mukhtaṣar fī 'ilm al-ta'rīkh* (ca. fifteenth century CE); and Muḥammad b. 'Abd al-Raḥmān al-Sakhāwī's *al-I'lān bi-l-tawbīkh li-man dhamma ahl al-tawārīkh* (ca. fifteenth century CE) all deal with historical method and categories of historical works. Rosenthal also included Arabic fragments from other unedited texts. Note also Ibn al-Nadīm, *K. al-Fihrist*, 2 vols. (Leiden, 1871–72) (a vast medieval compendium of Muslim scholarship with brief references to authors and works).

regnum emerged as rivals. Nevertheless, it took many decades, if not several centuries, before the partisans of the Alids and the Abbasids became the Shiʿites and Sunnites we speak of today.[50] If by some chance, we manage to recover additional works that Elad terms Sunnī(te), it would not be all that surprising if some contained traditions accusing ʿAbd al-Malik of diverting the ḥajj. As did the Alids, the Abbasids and their hired pens made no formal declarations of love for the house of Umayyah, quite the opposite.[51]

Any discussion based on the supposed contents of unrecovered historical sources, some of which may or may not be labeled Sunnite (whatever that might mean to current scholars) is a matter of gross conjecture. It will not shed direct light on that which concerns us. Addressing ʿAbd al-Malik's role in the Islamization of Jerusalem, we are best served by focusing on the available sources. These may be summed up as follows: We have the tradition obtained via well-known anti-Umayyad transmitters that ʿAbd al-Malik built the Dome of the Rock and then diverted the annual ḥajj to Jerusalem. Following that, Muslim pilgrims assembling in the holy city performed the rite of ṭawāf on the Temple Mount, just as they circumambulated the Kaʿbah in Mecca. Conversely, we know for certain that other than the reportedly pro-Alid Yaʿqūbī, the Christian Eutychius, and the early anti-Umayyad purveyors of historical accounts cited in Sibṭ b. al-Jawzī's *Mirʾāt,* none of the early chroniclers makes mention of ʿAbd al-Malik tampering with the well-established Muslim ritual going back to the time of the Prophet. For Goitein, that silence is proof positive that ʿAbd al-Malik never diverted the ḥajj to Jerusalem, certainly not as told by Yaʿqūbī and the later historians Goitein pegged as relying on Yaʿqūbī's account. Some skeptics might conclude that Goitein's line of reasoning gives rise to still another argument based on silence and may therefore brook criticism from those scholars who are inclined to accept the views of Goldziher and his declared followers.

There is, however, more to Goitein's brief. He produces evidence from the very sources whose silence he notes. Discussing the events of 68 AH / 687–

50. See M. Hodgson, "How Did the Early Shīʿa Become Sectarian," *JAOS* 75 (1955): 1–13 (a reflective article proposing the gradual development of Shiʿism from its earliest Alid origins). For the development of what I would term somewhat awkwardly "early proto-Shiʿism," see the detailed study of W. Madelung, *The Succession to Muḥammad* (Cambridge, 1997), esp. 141–387. The earlier work of E. Petersen, *ʿAlī and Muʿāwiya in Early Arabic Tradition* (Copenhagen, 1964), can still be read with profit. On the development of Alid-Abbasid relations (the precursor to the Shiʿite-Sunnite division), see the studies of M. Sharon, "Ahl al-Bayt—People of the House," *JSAI* 8 (1986): 169–84; "Note on the Question of Legitimacy of Government in Islam," *IOS* 10 (1980): 116–23; and the broad historical context in *Black Banners from the East* (Jerusalem, 1983), esp. 17–48. Similarly, J. Lassner, *Islamic Revolution and Historical Memory* (New Haven, 1986), 4–38, 75–98; and F. Omar, "Aspects of ʿAbbāsid Ḥusaynid Relations," *Arabica* 22 (1976): 170–79 and his *The ʿAbbāsid Caliphate, 132/750–170/786* (Baghdad, 1969), 211–57.

51. Lassner, *Islamic Revolution*, 39–54.

88 CE, Ṭabarī mentions an incident that took place when Muslim pilgrims assembled at the plain of ʿArafāt (also referred to as ʿArafah) to perform the *wuqūf*, the final ceremony of the events marking a formal end to the annual ḥajj. The chronicler reports that four groups of pilgrims with distinctive political affiliations encamped in the vicinity. Each camp was positioned at a separate location where a standard (*liwāʾ*) was displayed to mark the camp site and the identity of the group assembled therein. The four groups were the Alids led by Muḥammad, the son born to ʿAlī b. Abī Ṭālib by his Ḥanafite concubine Khawlah; the Khārijites led by Najdah (b. ʿĀmir) al-Ḥarūrī; the Umayyads; and finally the Zubayrids. The Alids were the first to break camp, followed by the Khārijites and then Umayyads. The Zubayrids observing a pre-Islamic custom associated with the ḥajj were the last to leave the site, as they were the custodians of the sacred shrine. The peaceful withdrawal of all the factions ended an obligatory religious rite at a time of war.[52]

The chronicler goes on to explain the diplomatic maneuvers that enabled various camps, at odds, or potentially at odds with one another, to fulfill the rites of pilgrimage in 68 AH. As the Umayyads, the Khārijites, and the Zubayrids were all actively involved in the conflict, one of the faithful, fearing an outbreak of violence, visited all the camps beginning with that of the Alid Muḥammad b. al-Ḥanafīyah. The point was to obtain an agreement in which all the parties pledged to refrain from fighting on sacred ground as the pilgrimage drew to a close. Though not explicitly stated, the decision to visit the Alid camp first appears self-evident. Although Ibn al-Ḥanafīyah had been embraced by Iraqis rebelling against the Umayyads, he never showed his hand let alone encouraged action against the regime. A cautious individual by nature, he and his followers were the easiest to commit to nonviolence. However, each group, including the Alids, expressed uncertainty that the others would remain peaceful. Nevertheless, they all pledged that they would not initiate combat, thus ensuring that the end of the pilgrimage would not give rise to armed conflict on holy ground.[53]

As the ceremonies at ʿArafāt (*taʿrīf*) mark the end of the ḥajj, we can assume that until that point, the rites of pilgrimage were performed without disturbance. Apparently the bitter conflict between the caliph and his rival Ibn al-Zubayr did not disrupt the annual event in any perceptible way. That is not altogether surprising. There is ample precedent for both pre-Islamic and Islamic times of suspending combat during the season of the ḥajj. It is well known that the Prophet himself arranged for a truce allowing him and his Muslim

52. Goitein, "Sanctity of Jerusalem," 136; Ṭabarī, *Annales*, 2/2:781–83. See also Diyārbakrī, *Taʾrīkh al-Khamīs*, 2:339.

53. Ṭabarī, *Annales*, 2/2:782–83.

supporters to enter Mecca as pilgrims, after they had assembled a large fighting force outside the city with the intention of forcing its polytheist oligarchs from power. To my knowledge, the only pilgrims ever formally denied access to Mecca were the Muslim citizens of the State of Israel. Presenting Israeli documents at various border controls would have implied the very existence of the state, and recognizing passports issued by the state would have been perceived as legitimizing a Jewish polity carved out of the Islamic heartland. No such situation obtained when the four camps attended the pilgrimage of 68 AH.

Ṭabarī's account of four political parties fulfilling the rites of the ḥajj is based on Wāqidī, the pro-Alid or if you wish pro-Abbasid transmitter of historical traditions. Oddly enough, the very same authority Sibṭ b. al-Jawzī cites when he reports that ʿAbd al-Malik diverted the ḥajj to Jerusalem is invoked by Ṭabarī, who describes how it came to be that the Umayyads were present at the pilgrimage of 68 AH. Can this seeming contradiction be explained, or are we to assume that Goitein is correct in stating the pilgrimage was never diverted and the accounts claiming otherwise are anti-Umayyad inventions? If ʿAbd al-Malik diverted the pilgrimage only upon completing the Dome of the Rock, there is the possibility that both accounts are correct. The author of the *Mirʾāt al-zamān*, citing Wāqidī, refers to an action that took place after the domed building was completed. Ṭabarī, also citing Wāqidī, refers to a historic event before construction on the Temple Mount. Since the domed building and diverting the ḥajj are inextricably linked by Yaʿqūbī, Eutychius, and the later authorities previously cited, scholars supporting Goldziher vis-à-vis Goitein are obliged to demonstrate that the Umayyad caliph completed construction of the Dome of the Rock *after* the pilgrimage of 68 AH, the event that reportedly took place on the ninth day of Dhū al-Ḥijjah (July 15, 688). Were that true, we would understand why all the parties, including the Umayyads, were able to celebrate the pilgrimage of 68 AH. However, if construction was completed *before* 68 AH, Goldziher's supporters would be obliged to explain the anomaly of Umayyad loyalists participating in the pilgrimage to Mecca after the caliph had reportedly diverted the ḥajj to Jerusalem's Temple Mount.

The foundation inscription reports the domed building was completed in 72 AH / 691–92 CE. That being the case, scholars agreeing with Goldziher could argue that the pilgrimage proceeded as usual until that year and was only diverted to Jerusalem following construction of the Dome of the Rock. Is it possible that the pilgrimage was diverted with the beginning of construction? Unfortunately, we have no definitive statement to that effect, only conflicting reports of when the building project was initiated ranging from 65 AH / 684–85 CE to 69 AH / 688–89 CE. The early date indicated by Eutichius and late authorities citing him may well be confusing the building project with the onset of ʿAbd al-Malik's reign. The date 66 AH is cited by Ibn Kathīr, quoting Sibṭ b. al-Jawzī, but manuscripts of the latter's *Mirʾāt al-zamān* place the beginning of construction at 69 AH, the year following the pilgrimage under review.[54] In either case, it is not likely that the ḥajj was diverted before the completion of the Dome of the Rock. The Arabic texts describing the changed venue of the pilgrimage do not allow for such an interpretation, nor does it seem reasonable that the ṭawāf could have been performed in Jerusalem while major construction took place on the mount, especially if the pilgrims circumambulated the rock within the building and not the domed structure surmounting it.

Given the contradictory dates of the initial building effort, it is not likely that many of Goldziher's supporters will be persuaded that his case has been refuted by Ṭabarī's account of the pilgrimage *sub anno* 68 AH. Nor will they agree that the various accounts of ʿAbd al-Malik diverting the ḥajj are mere literary inventions. There is, however, a more compelling argument in Goitein's extensive brief. He points to the pilgrimage of 72 AH / 692 CE, by all accounts an event that took place well after construction on the Temple Mount had begun, perhaps even after the domed building was completed.[55] Readers will note that the earlier pilgrimage took place at a time of conflict, but the fighting had not yet spread to the vicinity of Mecca. Circumstances thus allowed for a peaceful end to the ceremonies as reported by our sources. On the other hand, when the pilgrimage season of 72 AH arrived, Mecca was besieged by a Syrian army loyal to the Umayyad caliph. The details of the siege and the oddly conducted pilgrimage of 72 AH are most fully described by Balādhurī and in a shorter version by the great chronicler Muḥammad b. Jarīr al-Ṭabarī. Both accounts are cited by Goitein. The sources indicate that the loyalist force numbered some seven to eight thousand men, an original contingent of two thousand, the rest reinforcements requested by the Syrian commander, al-Ḥajjāj b. Yūsūf. The veteran Umayyad warrior, having dreamed that he was destined to seize the rebel ʿAbdallāh b. al-Zubayr and skin him alive, requested of ʿAbd al-Malik that he be given the task of engaging the rebel in combat. With the caliph's permission, al-Ḥajjāj proceeded to the holy precinct in Arabia and defeated Ibn al-Zubayr's

54. Ibn Kathīr, *Bidāyah*, 8:280, reports 66 AH for the beginning of construction, citing Sibṭ b. al-Jawzī. See S. Blair, "What Is the Date of the Dome of the Rock?" *OSIA* 9/1:59–87, esp. 63, which refers to the Arabic sources but not to Elad's edited text of the relevant passage from Sibṭ b. al-Jawzī (see *Mirʾāt*, 53), where the date is 69 AH for the beginning of construction and 72 AH for the completion.

55. Goitein, "Sanctity of Jerusalem," 136 citing Balādhurī, *Ansāb* (Jerusalem, 1936), 5:358 ff. and Ṭabarī, *Annales*, 2/2:830–31. See also ʿA. A ʿA. Dixon, *Umayyad Caliphate*, 139, with dense annotation citing a wide range of incidental statements describing the siege of Mecca.

cavalry in a series of pitched battles. With the area surrounding Mecca secured, al-Ḥajjāj requested further permission to lay siege to the holy city. ʿAbd al-Malik gave his commander full license to do as he saw fit, whereupon al-Ḥajjāj bombarded Mecca with mangonels that inflicted great damage to persons and property. The Kaʿbah was among the buildings severely damaged.

It is then ever so clear that the fighting was intense when the pilgrimage was under way. In order to facilitate one of the five pillars of Islam, al-Ḥajjāj acceded to a request that he put a halt to the bombardment when pilgrims entered the holy territory. With the pilgrimage about to take place, the illustrious commander of the Syrian army was appointed (by the caliph) leader of the ḥajj as if Ibn al-Zubayr's presence was of no consequence. Quite understandably, performing the rituals of pilgrimage that year turned out to be a complex undertaking. Besieged in the city, Ibn al-Zubayr could not lead the ḥajj as he or his appointed agent had done throughout his counter-caliphate. He could not perform the closing ceremonies of the ḥajj because the plain of ʿArafāt was in the hands of the invading Umayyad army. We can safely assume that the counter-caliph was not about to risk entering into enemy territory while the latter held a distinct military advantage. He had reportedly turned down an offer to go to Damascus in 64 AH and be proclaimed commander of the faithful after the death of the Umayyad Yazīd b. Muʿāwiyah. The offer was proffered by the leader of a Syrian force sent by Yazid to besiege and bombard Mecca. Ever cautious, Ibn al-Zubayr refused even though the siege was lifted and the two enemies performed the ṭawāf together.[56]

The situation during the siege of 72 AH was more fraught with danger, and both the counter-caliph and al-Ḥajjāj had limited options regarding the rituals of the ḥajj. Nevertheless, as required, Ibn al-Zubayr and his men sacrificed camels in Mecca on the Day of Sacrifice and, although not explicitly mentioned in our sources, they presumably fulfilled all the obligations of the ḥajj that ordinarily took place in the city itself, including the ṭawāf. On the other hand, al-Ḥajjāj's request that his men be permitted to circumambulate the Kaʿbah was denied by Ibn al-Zubayr, no doubt because he feared what might happen if the Syrian troops were allowed to enter the holy city in the midst of a devastating campaign to crush his regime. The Syrians made this request in good faith and presumably had some expectation that the war would not interfere with the activities of the sacred season. It was clearly important to the Syrians that, as

56. Ṭabarī, *Annales*, 2/1:430–33. The account is derived largely from a report by Wāqidī, who was well connected to the Abbasids and thus not likely to portray the Umayyads in a favorable light. See also Ibn Saʿd, *Ṭabaqāt*, 5:228–29; Balādhurī, *Ansāb*, 4B: 52–53; Ibn Khayyāṭ, *Taʾrīkh* (Najaf, 1967), 1:267.

good Muslims, they honor their religious obligations despite the conflict. In the end, the situation dictated compromising established religious custom. The circumstances did not allow the Syrian army and its commanders to separate themselves from the world and be alone with God, as required of all pilgrims. Even with a truce in effect, the besieging troops forsook the required two-piece white garments of the consecrated pilgrim and instead remained dressed in full battle gear. However, with an eye to the rules of the ḥajj, al-Ḥajjāj and his second in command did not approach women (which might lead to sexual intercourse) or wear perfume, acts forbidden to pilgrims in a state of consecration. He or they continued along that path until ʿAbdallāh b. al-Zubayr was killed the following year. Most important, the pilgrims who were not combatants and who made their way to Mecca although conflict raged in the Hijaz and other regions of the Islamic world were allowed access to all the areas controlled by the rebels and the government forces. Unlike the armed belligerents, they were able to fulfill all the rites of the ḥajj.

Goitein would seem to have a point citing this tradition. It clearly refutes the claim that ʿAbd al-Malik did not allow pilgrims (in territories he controlled) to make the trip to Mecca, but instead rerouted them to Jerusalem's Temple Mount. The Syrian troops who were in the midst of a major campaign fully expected that they might be allowed to circumambulate Kaʿbah. They might have recalled a circumstances of the siege of 64 AH when ʿAbdallāh b. al-Zubayr allowed an Umayyad commander and his troops to perform the ṭawāf after they besieged Mecca and hurled stones from mangonels, causing great damage to the holy city and its great shrine.[57] Moreover, the pilgrims who had come to Mecca in 72 AH and were noncombatants were able to fulfill all the rites of the ḥajj without disturbance. In order to counter Goitein, scholars adhering to Goldziher's view would have to argue that the pilgrimage of 72 AH took place shortly before the completion of the Dome of the Rock that year. Even if that were the case, where was the great sense of urgency to do something so unusual and potentially blameworthy as diverting the pilgrimage to Jerusalem? Surely ʿAbd al-Malik had no fear that the pilgrims to Mecca witnessing the state of affairs would be swearing allegiance to the Zubayrid and joining his cause. Given ʿAbdallāh b. al-Zubayr's dire straits, besieged as he was in his own city, it boggles the imagination to think that the pilgrims who were allowed entry to Mecca would have opted to oppose al-Ḥajjāj and his patron the Umayyad caliph.

57. Dixon, *Umayyad Caliphate*, 136–38 on the damage to the Kaʿbah (maintaining that only the addition to the sacred shrine erected by Ibn al-Zubayr was slated for destruction, a symbolic act destroying his legitimacy. ʿAbd al-Malik was well aware of the sanctity of the place and the need to preserve its most sacred edifice).

Lest we forget, 72/691–92 was a memorable year. Muṣʿab b. al-Zubayr, ʿAbdallāh's talented and well-respected brother, was killed as the last vestiges of the revolt in Iraq were crushed. Within a year after the Dome of the Rock was completed, Mecca had fallen and ʿAbdallāh b. al-Zubayr was also dead. What need was there for ʿAbd al-Malik to divert the ḥajj at this point? Can Yaʿqūbī and those who attach credence to his report be correct in maintaining that the pilgrimage was diverted to Jerusalem until the end of the Umayyad regime? Common sense and all the evidence clearly point to the contrary. Following the conquest of Mecca, the caliph's appointed leader of the ḥajj was most often the governor of Medina, an obvious choice if one assumes the pilgrimage was not diverted to Jerusalem. The caliph himself led the pilgrimage to Arabia in 75 AH, and his son Sulaymān did so in 81.[58] Moreover, there is clear evidence that the Abbasids made the pilgrimage to Mecca, where they held clandestine meetings in which they plotted the overthrow of the Umayyad usurpers. These meetings took place well after ʿAbd al-Malik completed the Dome of the Rock, an indication that the pilgrimage to Mecca continued as before. The annual ḥajj was an ideal cover for intrigue because the city was bursting with pilgrims, and the authorities, already overburdened with complex arrangements, were unable to keep track of people's whereabouts.[59] Muḥammad himself established the model for such clandestine meetings, as is widely reported in medieval Arabic literature. The Prophet is said to have used the pre-Islamic ḥajj to conduct a series of secret meetings, events that paved the way for his move to Medina and the formation of the Islamic community.[60]

Above all, one has to question the logic behind rerouting the pilgrimage long after the collapse of the Zubayrid threat. One might wish to agree with some medieval authors that ʿAbd al-Malik feared pilgrims going to Mecca would incline to the rebel's cause. But what reason would there have been for the Umayyads to divert the pilgrimage for fifty-seven years after their defeat, as Yaʿqūbī maintains, or, if you prefer a more modest claim based on Eutychius and other sources, until the end of al-Walīd's reign some dozen years later? Accepting the logic of this argument forces us to maintain, or at least strongly sug-

58. For local governors leading the pilgrimage during ʿAbd al-Malik's reign after the defeat of the Zubayrids, see Ṭabarī, *Annales*, 2/2:940, 1032, 1039, 1047 and Ibn Khayyāṭ, *Taʾrīkh*, 1:268 (al-Ḥajjāj), 278, 289, 290. For ʿAbd al-Malik and his son Sulaymān leading the pilgrimage, note Ibn Khayyāṭ, *Taʾrīkh*, 270, 280.

59. Lassner, *Islamic Revolution*, 82–90 (the meeting of revolutionary agents with the Abbasid leader Ibrāhīm al-Imām during the pilgrimage of 124 or 125 AH).

60. For the Prophet's use of the pilgrimage to cover his activities, see, for example, Ibn Isḥāq, *Sīrah*, 1/1:288–89, 293–97. It is no coincidence that Abbasid propagandists stressed the relationship of their patron's clandestine activities in the construction of their revolutionary network to events in the Prophet's lifetime. Emulating the Prophet was the surest path to claiming legitimacy.

gest, that ʿAbd al-Malik never rerouted the ḥajj. That does not necessarily mean that the Umayyad caliph(s) never allowed Muslims to fulfill certain rites of the pilgrimage in Jerusalem. The accounts indicating that pilgrims performed the ṭawāf on the Temple Mount have to be taken seriously. I am not entirely convinced that Yaʿqūbī, Eutychius, and Sibṭ b. al-Jawzī and his informants invented from scratch a tradition that ʿAbd al-Malik built the Dome of the Rock as a substitute for the Kaʿbah and, following that, redirected the pilgrims to Jerusalem. The reported act, undertaken for political reasons, was meant to cast a pall on ʿAbd al-Malik's genuine achievements. Undoubtedly, the tradition can be read as it was by Goitein, who deemed it an anti-Umayyad polemic skillfully conceived by well-known anti-Umayyad transmitters. But most Muslim historians—even those given to occasional polemics—were not inclined to invent traditions out of whole cloth. They could hardly peddle sheer fantasy and persuade readers with memories of a real past. Instead, they preferred to embellish already existing accounts in answering the claims of others and making their own distinctive views trustworthy. If the general information contained within descriptions of familiar events rang true, the reader, or listener in the case of oral communication, was rendered less suspicious of the polemic that was carefully embedded in the text. We therefore have to ask whether there is a kernel of truth to Yaʿqūbī's account and those of the other authors who maintain that ʿAbd al-Malik diverted the ḥajj, and, if so, what is that truth.

Goitein himself argued that although the pilgrimage was never diverted from Mecca, as the anti-Umayyad historians claim, Muslims actually performed ceremonies linked to the annual ḥajj in Jerusalem.[61] Jurists and tradition scholars were well aware that pious individuals could be confronted by obstacles preventing them from carrying out certain religious obligations. And so legal scholars promoted the view that Islam is a flexible religion (*dīn yusr*) that allowed for exceptions (*rukhṣah*, pl. *rukhaṣ*) to general rules.[62] Examples of flexibility are the rukhaṣ concerning pilgrimage. The voice and example of the Prophet are often invoked to soften or censure practices that might have seemed excessively harsh to many pilgrims. Some of these practices were self-imposed. Men and women alike, gripped by a desire to reach a higher state of religiosity (*iḥrām*), vowed to suffer great hardship en route to Mecca. For example, they prepared to walk all the way to the holy city; the women wearing

61. Goitein, "Sanctity of Jerusalem," 137 ff.

62. M. J. Kister, "On Concessions and Conduct: A Study in Early *Ḥadīth*," in *Society and Religion from Jāhilyya to Islam* (London, 1990), chapter 13, 1–37, photo offset of his original article that appeared in *Studies of the First Century of Islamic Society*, edited by G. H. A. Juynboll Carbondale, 1982), 89–107, 214–30. The reprint contains nine additional pages of notes following the original thirty-seven pages of the study.

uncomfortable garments and observing total silence (as did some men). Vows to God are not to be trifled with, but the Prophet was made to say that God does not heed vows by which people cause harm and suffering to themselves. Discussions of meritorious and ill-advised behavior during the pilgrimage included all manner of activity, especially in the formative decades of Islam, when religious observance tended to be fluid. During that early period, there appears to have been considerable variation in practices associated with the ḥajj, including residual practices from the pre-Islamic past.[63]

Of special interest to Goitein and to us is the license granted Muslims seeking to perform the taʿrīf, the activities that initiated an end to the pilgrimage.[64] The rapid expansion of the Islamic polity created great distances between the conquered territories and the religious fulcrum of Islam in the Hijaz. Undertaking the trek to Mecca could be a financial burden for the poor; a physical hardship for the old, sick, and infirmed; and perceived as a dangerous journey for the more skittish Muslims when their native provinces were embroiled in conflict. Not surprisingly, the taʿrīf, traditionally performed on the plain of ʿArafāt, was also observed in provincial capitals and garrison towns for the benefit of Muslims unable to make the arduous journey to the Hijaz. Whereas Goitein briefly mentions some accounts of this practice, his student M. J. Kister presents us with a much fuller picture of the literature.[65] As was his wont, Kister meticulously assembled many references to Arabic sources in print and manuscript and then teased the reader to draw out the broader implications of their significance.

Like Goitein, Kister noted that the taʿrīf was first introduced in Basra by ʿAbdallāh b. ʿAbbās. A first cousin of the Prophet and one of his younger companions, ʿAbdallāh had been appointed governor of the garrison town during the caliphate of ʿAlī b. Abī Ṭālib. Hence, practicing the rites of taʿrīf beyond the Hijaz was already in evidence before the Umayyads came to power. In similar fashion, Muṣʿab b. al-Zubayr introduced the taʿrīf at Kufa when he ruled Iraq for his brother, the rebellious counter-caliph. Quite obviously, neither ʿAbdallāh, who supported ʿAlī b. Abī Ṭālib against Muʿāwiyah in the great civil war, nor Muṣʿab, who fought against the Umayyad regime on behalf of the Hijazi notables, undertook these acts to undermine the religious reputation of Mecca or the political importance of a Medina-based caliphate. At the same time, ʿAbd al-Malik's brother ʿAbd al-ʿAzīz b. Marwān, the governor of Egypt, allowed observance of the taʿrīf in Fusṭāṭ, the capital of the province. There are

63. Kister, "On Concessions and Conduct," 28–29.
64. Goitein, "Sanctity of Jerusalem," 137; and n. 62 above.
65. Kister, "On Concessions and Conduct," 31–37.

indications that the same could be said for Jerusalem, albeit at a much later time. Goitein notes that the Persian traveler Nāṣir-i-Khusraw (ca. 1047 CE) observed that throngs of pilgrims unable to journey to Mecca assembled in Jerusalem and performed the wuqūf (the act of the pilgrimage in which Muslims presented themselves before God). Similarly, the great Saladin made his way from Safad to Jerusalem in order to stand in supplication before the Almighty as did pilgrims at ʿArafāt.[66]

Reports of alternate sites in which to perform the taʿrīf beg for still another question. Might the stories of circumambulating the Dome of the Rock reflect another instance where Muslims unable to undertake the journey to Mecca performed another rite of pilgrimage at a place better suited to their circumstances? Assuming this to be so, Goitein suggests that celebrating the ṭawāf in Jerusalem would have "helped to give a semblance of truth" to the inventions of the anti-Umayyad historians.[67] Juxtaposing a historic practice with an invented tradition condemning the Umayyads would certainly have been an effective rhetorical stratagem for those criticizing the regime. Lest we forget, it was Goldziher who first alerted scholars against accepting Muslim historical traditions at face value. Goitein's suggestion that the ṭawāf was practiced in Jerusalem for the benefit of pious Muslims unable to undertake the long journey to Mecca seems at first eminently sensible, perhaps even plausible. But here, the argument *ex silentio* works against him and his supporters. If Muslims unable to reach Mecca circumambulated the Dome of the Rock during the time of pilgrimage, how is it that there is no account to that effect? The faḍāʾil literature contains reports of various ceremonies associated with the domed building and the Temple Mount, but, as far as I know, no mention of the ṭawāf.

In Conclusion

When the rabbis of the Talmud were unable to agree on a ruling, the disputants were declared deadlocked in stalemate (*teiku*) and the issue was allowed to remain unresolved. Going a step further, the great sages affirmed that two diametrically opposed positions could both reflect the words of the Living God (*eilu ve-eilu divrei Elohim Hayyim*). Unfortunately, modern historians are not always given license to evade judgment, nor are they encouraged to do so. Faced with the moot propositions before us, I find myself favoring Goitein. I

66. Goitein, "Sanctity of Jerusalem," 137. As regards Saladin's visit to Jerusalem, Goitein cites Ibn al-Athīr, *Kāmil* (Leiden, 1851–76), 12:14.

67. Goitein, "Sanctity of Jerusalem," 138.

am not persuaded that ʿAbd al-Malik diverted the annual ḥajj to Jerusalem, as claimed by Goldziher and his followers. Nor can I discern a compelling reason for subsequent Umayyad dynasts to have enforced such an unprecedented and blameworthy policy, whether until the end of the regime as Yaʿqūbī claims, or only until al-Walīd's death, the contention of Eutychius and his receptors.

Assuming Goitein is correct in rejecting any link between the domed edifice and diverting pilgrims from Mecca, we are still left with an unresolved issue. If ʿAbd al-Malik did not erect the Dome of the Rock as a substitute for the Kaʿbah, why indeed did he build it? The caliph would hardly have spent state funds so freely to construct some sort of a folly in so sacred a place. And so we return to Oleg Grabar's initial question: What is the meaning of the Dome of the Rock?

CHAPTER 8

The "Meaning" of the Dome of the Rock

Historians and art historians seeking to understand why ʿAbd al-Malik built the Dome of the Rock would be well served if they expanded their vision to look past the internal politics of Muslim society. The task of neutralizing the Hāshimites and others who challenged or might challenge Umayyad rule was only part of a far-reaching political agenda that evolved over decades. In addition to protecting the regime from Muslim rivals the likes of the Zubayrids, the Umayyad dynasts had to contend with a Byzantine Empire that remained, despite early defeats, a serious threat to Muslim rule. Having sustained the initial blows of the invading Arab armies and the loss of vast territories to the Muslim conquerors, the Byzantines were still capable of wielding powerful land and naval forces. Moreover, they made use of striking visual symbols, markers of Christian identity that appealed to the residual sentiments of Christians recently converted to Islam, newly minted Muslims who still harbored positive feelings for the religious traditions and ceremonies of their former faith. In order to legitimize their role on an expanded stage, the Umayyads were forced to employ images that spoke to diverse audiences that included Arabs attracted by the pomp of Christian religious ceremonial; Jewish and Christian converts to Islam; and non-Muslims within and beyond the borders defining the limits of Islamic rule. Given the emotions generated by the Christian loss of the Holy Land and holy city, the looming Byzantine threat was not taken lightly.

For the better part of the seventh century CE, the Byzantine emperors harbored expectations that they would soon recapture the lands lost to the Arabs, including Jerusalem. The border separating the two imperial polities remained highly volatile and marked the beginning of a drawn-out conflict that settled into ritualized combat destined to last some eight hundred years. When the snows melted and bitter winter cold gave way to balmy days, the frontier became alive with popular preachers and fighting men, many of them religiously motivated volunteers who participated in the *ṣāʾifah*, the annual summer campaign.[1] More often than not, the battles proved indecisive. The border remained more or less frozen; the only things that moved were armies probing enemy territory and Muslims and Christians who had been captured in battle and then returned for ransom.

Within their own domain, the Banu Umayyah ruled over a non-Muslim population that as yet outnumbered the Arab tribesmen in the newly conquered territories. Unfortunately, we know all too little about the social dynamics of conversion, such as it was, or the rates by which Christians embraced the newest monotheist faith.[2] One thing seems fairly certain; the indigenous inhabitants of formerly Christian lands were not about to convert to Islam en masse. The Christians under a rapidly expanded Islamic rule had been quickly swallowed but not thoroughly digested by their Muslim overlords. And yet the recalcitrant Christians were not particularly restive, let alone inclined to a general uprising like that of the Zubayrids. Oleg Grabar's likening of an "important faction" of the Christians of 'Abd al-Malik's time to a "sort of fifth column for the Byzantine state" is not supported by the Christian sources that he cites.[3] Had the caliph been seriously threatened by a large-scale Christian insurrection, the Arabic historians who write of his eventful reign would surely have registered evidence of it.

The captive Christian population represented a more subtle challenge to Muslim rule. Arab tribesmen traversing the Arabian frontier were exposed to

1. There is a vast literature dealing with Arab-Byzantine relations. A collection of important articles written over an extended period of time is reprinted in *Arab-Byzantine Relations in Early Islamic Times*, edited by M. Bonner (Aldershot, 2004). See also his "Ja'ā'il and Holy War in Early Islam," *Der Islam* 68 (1991): 45–64; "The Naming of the Frontier: 'Awāṣim, Thughūr, and the Arab Geographers," *BSOAS* 57 (1994): 17–24; "Some Observations Concerning the Early Development of Jihād along the Arab-Byzantine Frontier," *SI* 75 (1992): 5–31; and his learned monograph *Aristocratic Violence and Holy War* (New Haven, 1996), which deals largely with the Muslim-Byzantine frontier in the Abbasid period. There is also a vast literature on the theory of holy war (*jihād*) in Islam. That subject is of no direct concern to the issues discussed in this work. For studies of the subject, see among many works that deal with medieval and modern Islam: A. Morabia, *Le jihād dans l'Islam médiéval* (Paris, 1993), which deals in a detailed fashion with the development of the doctrine of jihād from its origins during the formation of Islam until the twelfth century CE; also A. Noth, *Heiliger Krieg und heiliger Kampf in Islam und Christentum* (Bonn, 1996), which is devoted largely to the period of the Crusades; and R. Firestone's imaginative formulation of jihād as it was understood in the lifetime of the Prophet, *Jihād* (Oxford, 1999).

2. The rates of conversion for different periods still defy scholars because the written sources leave hardly any evidence from which to construct a detailed picture of the processes by which a world of millions of non-Muslims conquered by tens of thousands of Arab tribesmen was transformed into an Islamic polity with a majority population of Muslims. Not dissuaded from dealing with this critical issue, R. Bulliet devised an ingenious method to trace conversion through an analysis of name patterning obtained by and large from medieval biographical dictionaries. See his *Conversion to Islam in the Medieval Period* (Cambridge, MA, 1979). Despite Bulliet's heroic effort, no clear picture of conversion to Islam has emerged, especially for the early period.

3. Grabar, *Jerusalem*, 141–42, esp. n. 129.

all sorts of foreign influences that spoke to the continuing efficacy of Christian (and Jewish) culture in the expanded abode of Islam. Early Christian (and also Jewish) converts to the new faith presumably retained many beliefs and practices that were strange but enticing to the Arabs dwelling among them. Tribesmen born and bred in the desert and oases of Arabia found their traditional values challenged in territories they had conquered by force of arms. New concepts and patterns of behavior linked to the spiritual and material life of urban and other sedentary environments eroded what had been for many Arabs time-tested and familiar responses to daily life. The physical barriers originally established between the Arab settlers and the conquered peoples, a priority of the Arab tribes crossing the frontier, were rendered porous by the pressures of new living environments and changed circumstances. Separation eventually gave way to increasing social, economic, and even cultural contact. As the Islamic state expanded, a new society was being slowly forged. The primacy of the Arabs and their worldview slowly gave way to a more inclusive outlook that complicated the tribal politics of the Umayyad dynasty.

ʿAbd al-Malik's caliphate was in many respects a historic watershed in the evolution of the Islamic state. The innovative reign of the fifth Umayyad sovereign marked a conscious decision to cloak the regime in symbols of a distinctively Islamic nature. The government bureaucracy, whose business had been conducted in Greek by former functionaries of the Byzantine regime, was now fully Arabicized. Byzantine coinage, previously prevalent throughout vast regions of the realm, was replaced, however briefly, by newly minted coins picturing the visage of the Umayyad ruler, and then by aniconic species stamped with the date of issue, the name of the caliph, and various Qurʾānic verses. By opting for aniconic currency, Muslims asserted the purity of a monotheism that prohibited graven images, in contrast to the Christians, whose art featured representation of human beings on their wall paintings, mosaic floors, and icons. Instead, the Muslim faithful cultivated their own alternative forms of artistic representation. The traditional craft of Christian artists and artisans eventually gave way to inscriptions sprinkled with quotes from the Qurʾān and elaborate geometric and floral patterns that left little if any vacant space on the surfaces they covered.[4] The new decorative forms were favored in mosques and other

4. There is evidence that in the first half of the eighth century CE, the images portrayed in various churches were defaced. See S. Griffith, *The Church in the Shadow of the Mosque*, 144–45, esp. n. 46, citing R. Schick, "The Christian Communities of Palestine from Byzantine to Islamic Rule: A Historical and Archeological Study," in *Studies in Late Antique and Early Islam* (Princeton, 1995), 2:180–219; S. Ognibene, *Umm al-Rasas: la chiesa di Santi Stefano ed il "problema iconofabico"* (Rome, 2002). It could well be that the defacement of the churches was the fallout from the iconographic controversy taking place among Christians. The account that relates the Umayyad caliph

public buildings. On the other hand, ʿAbd al-Malik's successors decorated their private compounds with familiar Byzantine themes.

Was ʿAbd al-Malik's project to develop the area of the Temple Mount part of a master plan to give visual expression to Islamic rule in what had been for centuries a thoroughly Christian land? More particularly, how did the Dome of the Rock, the signature piece of ʿAbd al-Malik's building project, fit the larger design of his historic reign? Considered by modern critics as one of the finest examples of Islamic architecture, the jewel-like Dome of the Rock has become the most recognized symbol of Islam's presence in the holy city and, beyond that, the entire Holy Land. Various medieval authorities report that ʿAbd al-Malik also built the great al-Aqṣā mosque nearby, but as regards that, there is a division of opinion. Some authorities date the mosque to the reign of the caliph's son al-Walīd, a view with which a number of modern archaeologists and historians agree. It is of course possible that the mosque was conceived together with the Dome of the Rock by ʿAbd al-Malik, but construction was not begun or completed until the reign of his successor. In any event, the two buildings and some of the adjacent smaller structures on the ancient Temple Mount formed a single unit that allowed Muslims to proclaim the city revered by Christians and Jews a sacred place of their own.[5]

Architecture and Architectural Decoration

The architectural features and decoration of the Dome of the Rock raise questions of form and function. Was there an architectural template or style that catered to ʿAbd al-Maik's aesthetic taste, and was the octagonal structure designed for a specific set of activities within its walls? Above all, was it intended

---

Yazīd II ordered the destruction of the human visages on the walls and mosaic floors of Christian churches has all the earmarks of an apocryphal tale. J. Wellhausen relates the tale as told by way of the Christian historian Theophanes, who indicates that a Jew prophesied that the caliph would remain in power for forty years if he destroyed the images in the Christian churches throughout the Umayyad realm. An edict to that effect although issued was never carried out, as the caliph died shortly thereafter (Wellhausen, *Arab Kingdom*, 324–25). Ṭabarī, *Annales*, 2/3:1463–64 indicates that a Jew did indeed predict that the caliph would reign for forty years (as opposed to the four years of his actual reign) but omits any reference to the edict, which in any case was never carried out, or so we are led to believe. The account of Theophanes might be read as a literary invention to support those who allowed pictorial representation, as it implicates both a Jew and a Muslim as well as Christians who were opposed to iconography.

5. See K. A. C. Creswell, *EMA*, 1/2:373–74 for the Arabic sources on who built the al-Aqṣā mosque. A brief description of the history of the mosque and its setting on the Temple Mount is found in *EI*, s.v. "Masdjid al-Aḳṣā."

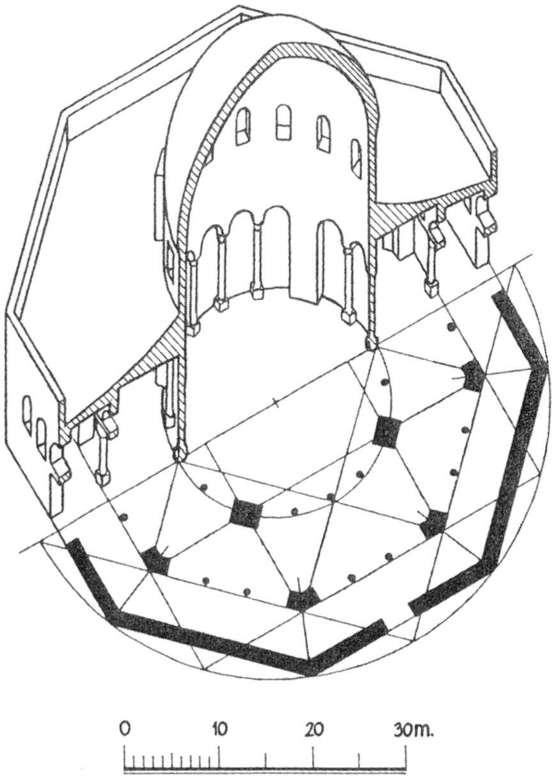

Fig. 7. The Dome of the Rock (K. A. C. Creswell)

to serve as a political symbol, and if so, for what audience or audiences? In other words, how did the caliph conceive of the edifice that was to dominate the Temple Mount? Fortunately, the architectural history of the structure is quite well known. Unlike the al-Aqṣā mosque, which was rebuilt at different times and according to different dimensions, the structure of ʿAbd al-Malik's domed building remains, more or less, as it was in the seventh century. Although repaired and redecorated on a number of occasions, the Dome of the Rock has retained its architectural form and some of its original decoration. Arguably the most-studied example of Islamic architecture from the first century AH, the building has been measured and its decoration and inscriptions carefully analyzed by scholars recruited from museums, universities, and departments of antiquities. Elements of the building have also been described by various medieval authors. And yet the Dome of the Rock remains somewhat of an enigma that gives rise to considerable controversy. Scholars continue to debate possible models that informed its conception and, as we have seen, the historic circumstances that compelled ʿAbd al-Malik to order its construction.[6]

The building is in the shape of an octagon with each of the eight segments being approximately 67.5 feet in length. The inner space is configured as an open area surmounted by a dome and framed by two concentric ambulatories, passageways that surround the sacred rock situated at the very center of the structure.[7] Seen from almost any angle, the building radiates an exquisite sense of symmetry. The Dome of the Rock was in every respect a powerful rejoinder to the visual message of monumental Christian architecture and religious iconography. As the building is the earliest surviving Islamic monument, one can only compare it to non-Muslim structures when seeking clues as to its architectural origins and original function. But must one search for parallels beyond the Near Eastern domains of the Byzantine Empire? Pointing to edifices of somewhat similar construction and decoration in areas and ages ranging from ancient Greece to Italy in Roman and later Christian times does not throw much light on the questions that are of interest to us here. Emphasis ought to be placed on buildings that might have been known to the architects who designed the Dome of the Rock, if not also to ʿAbd al-Malik, who gave their plans final approval. Common sense dictates a preference for structures in Byzantine Syria-Palaestina. By far the closest parallel, at least as regards form, is the domed octagonal Byzantine church at Caesaria, a building of comparable dimensions to the Dome of the Rock that sat on a raised platform, as did the building in Jerusalem. Moreover, the church was visible well into the eighth century CE.[8]

As for buildings in Jerusalem that might have served as template for the Muslim structure, the nearby Anastasis, or Church of the Holy Sepulcher, bears some architectural resemblance.[9] Built by the emperor Constantine in the fourth century CE, the magnificent church with its imposing dome was part of his "New Jerusalem," an extensive development that proclaimed Christianity's

---

6. For the different stages of construction, note R. W. Hamilton, *The Structural History of the Aqṣā Mosque* (Jerusalem, 1949); and for the later mosques also Creswell, *EMA*, 1/2:374–80.

7. See illustrations 3–5.

8. For a wide variety of suggested prototypes for the Dome of the Rock, see Creswell, *EMA*, 1/1:101–31. D. Whitcomb sees the inspiration for the Dome of the Rock in the octagonal Byzantine church in Caeseria. I am inclined to agree with Whitcomb that the plan of the church might very well have inspired the Muslims, though not Muʿāwiyah as he suggests, following Grabar. See Whitcomb's "Jerusalem and the Beginnings of the Islamic City," 409–13 and figures 11–12; on the church also J. Magness, "The Pottery from Area V/4 at Caesarea," *Annual of the American Schools of Oriental Research* 52 (1994): 133–45. Might the church have symbolic importance for the Muslims. as Caesarea was the seat of Christian ecclesiastical authority during the Byzantine period?

9. K. A. C. Cresell, *EMA*, 1/1:105–6.

triumph over paganism and its break with sacred Jewish geography. Instead of building on the Temple Mount venerated by Jews since the time of King Solomon, the Christian emperor looked to what had been a quarry originally situated beyond the ancient walls of the city. There he consecrated the rocky promontory where Jesus was said to have been crucified. With that, Golgotha's *lapis pertusus* replaced the Temple Mount's *even shetiyah* as the primeval rock linked to the hour of Creation. Similarly, Constantine sanctified the cave and antechamber at the alleged place of Christ's burial. The pagan temple built by the Roman emperor Hadrian that covered the site of Jesus' tomb was demolished and in its place the Byzantine ruler built the Church of the Holy Sepulcher, a striking edifice meant to signify that paganism as well as Judaism was a spent force.[10]

Like ʿAbd al-Malik's Dome of the Rock, the church consists of a central ring of supports carrying a dome and forming an ambulatory, and as in the Muslim building the dome surmounted a site identified with a sacred event of the past.[11] What better model was there for ʿAbd al-Malik and his architects to emulate than the quintessential symbol of Christianity's strength in a land recently subjected to Muslim rule? Nevertheless, the two buildings, within hailing distance of each other, could hardly be mistaken for one another. They were certainly utilized in very different ways. The size of the Dome of the Rock and the configuration of its inner space rule out that it was intended as a formal place of prayer. Oleg Grabar, following others, has likened it to a reliquary, a receptacle that contained holy relics, in this case built on a grand scale, or to a ciborium, a dome structure that surmounts an altar.[12] I know of no current scholars or medieval authorities who claim that the Dome of the Rock was specifically designed for communal worship. During the first three Islamic centuries, the obligatory Friday prayers were generally reserved for the single congregational mosque allowed any urban settlement. And so, unlike Byzantine Jerusalem, which featured many churches, the Umayyad settlements at major population centers had but a single Friday mosque. The newly erected mosques were rectangular structures with columns bracketing a large court that could accommodate a significant number of worshippers, if not all the local Muslims,

10. See chapter 2.

11. For a brief comment linking the architecture of the church and the Dome of the Rock, see K. A. C. Creswell, *EMA*, 1/1:105–6.

12. O. Grabar, in volume 4 of his collected studies, *Jerusalem*, 20 and nn. 77, 78, from the reprinted 1959 article he originally published in *Ars Orientalis*, and seemingly endorsed in a later publication reproduced in his collected studies, "The Meaning of the Dome of the Rock" in *Jerusalem*, 147, relying on Creswell, *EMA*, 1/1:105–6 (see n. 8). On p. 147, n. 10, he refers to "a more imaginative but debatable view of the same monuments" discussed by Creswell and others, namely, M. Ecochard's *Filiations de Monuments* (Paris, 1977). I have not seen this last work.

as called for by an evolving Islamic law.[13] The first mosques built by the Muslim conquerors were probably of simple construction; the later places of communal worship were grand in scope and presumably decoration. Jerusalem had a congregational (or principal mosque) going back to the early years of the Islamic conquest, a place of worship that would be later replaced by the great al-Aqṣā mosque in the time of ʿAbd al-Malik's son and successor al-Walīd. Although there is absolutely no indication that ʿAbd al-Malik ever intended the domed building to serve as a place for communal prayers on Fridays, there is no reason to deny that Muslims considered the Dome of the Rock a sacred site. Like the Kaʿbah in Mecca, the specific location of the building merited special consideration. Both the octagonal structure in Jerusalem and the square-like building in Mecca surmounted a sacred rock associated with the biblical patriarch Abraham, the first monotheist and a figure venerated by Jews and Muslims alike.[14]

This linkage between the structures in Mecca and Jerusalem prompts us to mention once more the debate between the camps of Goitein and Goldziher. At first glance the concentric ambulatories might suggest that visitors to the building were expected to circumambulate the sacred stone at its center just as they did at the Kaʿbah. K. A. C. Creswell believed that this was in fact the case and endorsed the view that ʿAbd al-Malik diverted the ḥajj to Jerusalem to stem the influence of the Hijazi counter-caliph ʿAbdallāh b. al-Zubayr. Seeing the Dome of the Rock from this perspective, one could argue that it was specifically designed to accommodate pilgrims diverted from the Hijaz. Indeed, according to Creswell, when Muslims entered the domed building and circumambulated the rock within it, they performed the rite of ṭawāf that they had hitherto celebrated at the Kaʿbah in Mecca.[15]

But pilgrims visiting Mecca did not actually enter the Kaʿbah to perform the ṭawāf. Rather, as they do today, the great throngs that had assembled in that holy city circled the structure. As for Jerusalem, the concentric ambulatories and the entrances to the Dome of the Rock are much too narrow to allow a full complement of pilgrims to perform the ceremony. There is no compel-

13. For the legal status of Friday mosques (*masjid al-Jāmiʿ*) and their relationship to urban settlements (*balad*, *miṣr*, and *madīnah*), as opposed to villages (*qaryah*), see J. Lassner, *Middle East Remembered*, 128–32. As a rule, an Islamic urban settlement such as Jerusalem was entitled to one Friday mosque during the first three Islamic centuries, that is, the period that concerns us here. In principle, the mosque was to be large enough to accommodate the entire local population, but in point of fact, even the largest mosques could not do so as the Muslim population of the individual cities expanded exponentially. At first, the overflow population prayed in areas surrounding the mosques. Beginning with the tenth century CE permission was granted in special circumstances to create additional mosques for Friday congregational prayer.

14. See chapter 2.

15. Creswell, *EMA*, 1/1:65–66.

ling reason to believe that the domed structure was created specifically to accommodate a massive influx of pilgrims that would have been diverted from Arabia. Following Goitein's suggestion, there is the possibility that the Dome of the Rock was used by pilgrims who for good reason could not make the arduous journey to the ḥaramayn and instead went to Jerusalem.[16] Still, there is no evidence that contemporaneous Muslim religious authorities made such allowances for pilgrims or that contemporaries seeking to perform the ḥajj in Jerusalem took license to do so. This is not to say the Dome of the Rock could not have served the needs of such visitors then or at some later time in history.[17] There is, however, no compelling reason to claim that ʿAbd al-Malik ordered the building's construction with that purpose in mind. Given my doubts about the historicity of the diverted pilgrimage,[18] I am inclined to look elsewhere for what has been termed the meaning of the Dome of the Rock.

The art historian Myriam Rosen-Ayalon, who conducted a meticulous study of the building's decoration, concluded that the mosaics and marble reliefs reflect an eschatological theme.[19] Drawing largely on Christian parallels, she points to the representation of precious stones, jewelry, crowns, and stylized wings and then links them directly to floral patterns and a "continuous arcade of trees." Taken together, these items represent the lushness of Paradise, where (winged) angels were said to wear crowns and where the Tree of Life (made famous by the story of Adam and Eve) was situated. She also maintains that the veined marble gives rise to a rippling effect, which signifies for her the waters that slaked the paradisiacal landscape. Having linked these decorative motifs to represent a celestial scene, the eminent art historian draws attention to pre-Islamic legends of the Temple Mount. Most telling is the reference to the sacred platform as the future site of the Day of Resurrection, the event that immediately precedes God's ascending his throne to render final judgments at the end of time. Textually oriented readers will recall the various rabbinic legends attached to the sacred area, that is, the previously cited accounts that place Paradise and God's throne and celestial court on a direct line above the *even shetiyah*, the primeval rock of Creation.[20] They might also wish to consider the various Islamic traditions that follow suit and make Jerusalem the venue of the

16. S. D. Goitein, "Sanctity of Jerusalem," 137. See also M. J. Kister, "Concessions and Conduct."

17. See Goitein, "Sanctity of Jerusalem," 137, describing the practice of *taʿrīf*, one of the rites of pilgrimage in Jerusalem as witnessed by the Persian traveler Nāṣir-i-Khusraw in the eleventh century CE and the report in Ibn al-Athīr, *Kāmil* (Leiden), 12:14 that Saladin went to the holy city for that purpose.

18. See chapter 7.

19. M. Rosen-Ayalon, *Early Islamic Monuments*, 46–69.

20. See chapter 3.

final stages of the apocalypse, a subject to be taken up in the chapter that follows. Scholars not yet persuaded by Rosen-Ayalon's analysis have still more to consider. The author points to the shape of the eight-sided building and writes that octagonal (Christian) monuments "are inherently an interpretation of the Resurrection."[21] She concludes by noting that the Qur'ānic inscriptions ringing the interior of the Dome of the Rock repeatedly refer to the resurrection of Jesus. In sum: both the architectural form and rich decoration of ʿAbd al-Malik's building refer in some manner to a coming messianic age inspired, as it were, by Christian buildings of similar design and decoration.

Another art historian, Pricilla Soucek, reads the decorative motifs of the Dome of the Rock somewhat differently. She contends that the rich decoration demonstrates that the attributes of the building were merged with memories of the Solomonic Temple, a house of worship that the early Muslims remembered as a great religious monument of the past. Soucek then turns to various Arabic literary sources that describe in detail how the ancient Israelite Temple was lavishly decorated, giving as examples the kind of objects represented on the walls of the Islamic building.[22] Soucek's proposed reading of the decoration obliges her readers to consider that ʿAbd al-Malik may have sought to declare himself heir to the great Solomon, and his jewel-like building the equivalent of one of the most celebrated symbols of the latter's religious authority. Linkage of that sort would not have been lost on Muslims; they revered Solomon and the majesty of his reign. Moreover, the pre-Islamic legends that accrued to Mount Moriah, the site of Solomon's temple, were presumably well known to any number of ʿAbd al-Malik's contemporaries and most likely the caliph as well. They were part of an evolving Muslim tradition about the ancient Israelites and their holy city, much of it based on midrashic texts that circulated freely among Jews and Jewish converts, whether in writing or in oral presentation.[23]

21. Rosen-Ayalon, *Early Islamic Monuments*, 67.

22. P. Soucek, "The Temple of Solomon in Islamic Legend and Art," 85–88, 95–98, 109, citing Dīnawarī, *Ṭiwāl*; Ibn al-Faqīh, *Buldān*; and Muhallabi, *Qiṭʿah min kitāb mafqūd: al-Masālik wa-l-Mamālik li-l-Thaʿlabī*. M. Sharon suggests that the Dome of the Rock was built to symbolize the renewal of Solomon's Temple. See his "The 'Praises' of Jerusalem," 62 and n. 38.

23. Legends of Solomon linked to rabbinic sources, including accounts of the building of the temple, are widespread in the Muslim *qiṣaṣ al-anbiyāʾ* "Tales of the Prophets." See, for example, Thaʿlabī, *ʿArāʾis*, 293–328, esp. 306–10, for the construction of the first Israelite temple. See also N. Khoury, "The Dome of the Rock, the Kaʿba, and Ghumdān: Arab Myths and Umayyad Monuments," *Muqarnas* 10 (1993): 57–65. Khoury draws a connection between the Dome of the Rock and Arabic legends linking Solomon to South Arabia, in particular Ghumdān. The Dome of the Rock is thus seen as part of an Arabian aesthetic. I leave it to readers to judge her case. Although some of the Solomonic legends were probably known to the caliph, it is not clear why Solomon would have sought a connection between his Jerusalem project and Ghumdān. Nor is it clear that all the legends of Solomon, including the detailed descriptions of his palace, entered into Muslim historical consciousness before ʿAbd al-Malik built the Dome of the Rock.

Building on Soucek's work, Raya Shani goes a step further. In a lengthy and detailed study, she suggests that specific motifs that were meant to represent implements used in Solomon's house of worship were inserted "to express contemporary prophetic concepts according to which the Islamic shrine is the actual successor to the Solomonic temple."[24] If Shani is correct in this assertion, a conscious decision to link the Israelite Temple to the Umayyad Dome of the Rock made the Umayyad caliph the analogue of the great Solomon, the all-powerful and all-wise ruler blessed by God. And so, as do Rosen-Ayalon and Soucek, Shani invests her reading of the decorative motifs with what is to all intents and purposes a religiously motivated decision, albeit a decision that can also be seen in the light contemporary politics, namely, the desire by a Muslim ruler to legitimize his rule and his faith by invoking memories of a pre-Christian Jerusalem.

As for the crowns, jewels, and other decorative motifs, I leave it for art historians to render a final judgment based on art-historical grounds. I am inclined to agree with Oleg Grabar, who calls for analyzing buildings as objects perceived by contemporaries and not bundles of influence, that is, how individuals might have felt at specific places and moments, a world far removed from modern voyeurs scanning an extended cultural horizon.[25] Needless to say, what Grabar calls for is difficult, especially when there is little if any corroborating epigraphic or literary evidence, or when what evidence that does exist creates more confusion than clarity, as is the case here. Regarding the Dome of the Rock, two questions immediately come to mind; both are suggested by Grabar's dictum that we view the building as did ʿAbd al-Malik and his subjects. The first is put to Myriam Rosen-Ayalon: What messianic expectations might have been reflected in the eschatological motifs of the Dome of the Rock? And linking her view with Soucek and Shani's Solomonic theme, did ʿAbd al-Malik and the artisans who worked on the building view the jewels, crowns, and other motifs in light of far-reaching architectural landscapes, the path of modern scholars grounded in current art-historical methods?

As for eschatology, there can be no doubt that Muslims and non-Muslims alike saw the evolving Umayyad period as rife with messianic stirrings. There

24. R. Shani, "The Iconography of the Dome of the Rock," *JSAI* 23 (1999): 158–207; see 167. Shani's lengthy article surveys in detail the opinions of M. Rosen-Ayalon and P. Soucek while calling attention to the evolving views of O. Grabar noted throughout this work and those of Sheila Blair, "Date of the Dome of the Rock."

25. Grabar, "Umayyad Dome of the Rock," in *Jerusalem*, 28–32, 40–41. I have been informed that Israeli archaeologists excavating at Zarin to the north of Jerusalem have uncovered a contemporaneous Islamic building they describe as a victory monument. I have not visited the site at Zarin, nor have I been privileged to see any evidence confirming this view.

was even a specific genre of texts describing the end of days, Muslim and Christian writings that were loosely linked to the biblical apocalypse of Daniel and the postbiblical sources to which it gave rise. We are thus given to ask how Umayyad rule might have stimulated speculation about an anticipated messianic age purportedly represented in the decoration of the Dome of the Rock. Unlike Jewish messianism, which was grounded in cries for redemption after extended periods of exile and suffering, and early Christian imaginings of the second coming of Christ—a concept born at a time when Christians were inclined to renounce the temporal world—Muslim visions of the end of days reflected a sense of triumphalism rooted in military successes of the present. It would not be surprising if this triumphal outlook was represented on the walls of the most famous Muslim edifice of the times. But as no specific picture of a transcendent Muslim future can be deduced from the decorative motifs alone, other possibilities ought to be considered, if only for argument's sake.

Umayyad Rule and Messianic Yearnings: Speculative Musings

Among Christians, whether situated in Constantinople or the provinces, the initial successes of the Arab tribesmen do not seem to have occasioned an immediate sense of foreboding. Some communities in the conquered territories viewed the onset of Muslim rule as reducing the onerous taxes imposed by the emperor or the religious pressure that was brought to bear on the nonconformist denominations of Eastern Christianity. The siege and capture of various centers of clerical authority and not the least the loss of Jerusalem, only recently restored to Christian rule, was another matter, one that caused Christians increasing concern. Still, seen from Constantinople, the nerve center of Byzantine rule, the loss of distant Christian lands to the infidels need not have implied structural flaws in the imperial polity. The onus for failing to protect the lost provinces might be placed squarely on local auxiliaries and reserve forces. Surely the mainstream contingents in the Byzantine heartland would have fared better. Moreover, with their naval strength, the Byzantines still retained the ability to land expeditionary forces along the exposed coast of Syria-Palaestina. Only when Muʿāwiyah's newly established naval force threatened the capital of the Christian realm did the emperor and his court fully grasp the enormity of the Muslim threat. The loss of Jerusalem to the unbelievers could no longer be considered a temporary aberration, but a summons to conduct warfare of metahistoric proportions. In due time, Christian writers favoring the Byzantine Empire grafted a new vision of a future messianic age onto past versions of the end of days. The new apocalyptic tradition envisioned a time leading to the defeat of Muslims; the restoration of the true faith in the holy city and Holy Land; and the second coming of Christ.[26]

How then are we to understand the eschatological themes Rosen-Ayalon posits for the decoration of the Dome of the Rock? Is it possible that the various motifs that she traces back to Christian sources might reflect pro-Byzantine notions of the end of days, bizarre as that might seem for a building commissioned by a Muslim ruler? Guided by Rosen-Ayalon's reading of the decoration, I am tempted to consider—albeit with infinite playfulness rather than any conviction—that the sentiments expressed in the Christian apocalyptic literature and the messianic stirrings to which these texts gave rise might be reflected in the mosaics and marble reliefs of the Dome of the Rock. It goes without saying that ʿAbd al-Malik would hardly have decorated his signature structure with a message he knew to signal not only the end of his regime but that of Islamic rule. But might there have been a possibility—however improbable, if not indeed implausible—that the artisans, presumably Christians, went about their work assuming that their vision of a future victory over Islam would be hidden from the unsophisticated eyes of the caliph and his advisers? Extending this thought, can we assume the message they wished to convey was carefully chosen to bolster the spirits of converts to Islam who were wavering in their allegiance to the new faith or to encourage Christians seeking deliverance from Muslim domination? If that were indeed the case, the decorative patterns would have represented a form of subversive art. I mention this extremely remote possibility to tease the reader's imagination; I think it virtually impossible that subversive art, which can be a tricky concept, is in play here. Rosen-Ayalon, using the conventional methods of art-historical analysis, is content to trace the decorative motifs back to Christian sources and for the most part leave it at that.

A favorable review of Rosen-Ayalon's 1989 study suggests that she might have cast her scholarly net further and looked with her expert eye beyond

26. One has to be careful to distinguish Christian apocalypses occasioned by an early reaction to the Muslim conquest and the many texts that circulated during the Abbasid period. As a rule, older eschatological texts were refashioned in later times to suit the circumstances and needs of contemporaneous audiences. That being the case, statements in later works might have been creations that should be dated as early as the seventh century. See P. Alexander, *The Byzantine Apocalyptic Tradition* (Berkeley, 1985), esp. 1–60 (a thorough examination of the history of Pseudo-Methodius's apocalypse of the seventh century CE with detailed references to European scholarship until the 1980s); S. Brock, "Syriac Views of Emergent Islam," in *Studies on the First Century of Islamic Society*, edited by G. H. A. Juynboll (Carbondale, 1982), 19 ff.; and more generally S. Griffith, *Byzantium and the Early Islamic Conquests* (Cambridge, 1992).

monuments of the Judeo-Christian world. The reviewer, F. B. Flood, is wont to remind us that the paradisiacal importance of bejeweled cosmic trees can be traced back as far as the Gilgamesh myth in ancient Mesopotamia.[27] That linkage may well be true, but what conclusions can be drawn therefrom? One has always to be wary of interpreting artistic representation and literary production in light of a distant past, especially when there is no perceptible line of direct influence from a past far removed in time or space from contemporaneous witnesses. Speculation about the meaning of artistic representation, however learned, may lead at times to spiraling and ever more fanciful interpretations of material culture. With that caveat in mind, let us return to the eschatological motifs suggested by Rosen-Ayalon and consider an extended and reasonable line of inquiry. We are obliged to ask how the purported representations of Paradise and a coming messianic age might be a reflection of specific historic developments, beginning with events that shaped the internal politics of the Umayyad state.

Byzantine-Muslim relations were not the only theme of apocalyptical traditions in the age of the Umayyads. There is a second Islamic tradition that stressed opposition to the house of Umayyah. Some accounts represent a back-projection seen from the vantage point of Muslims who celebrated the fall of the dynasty. However, there is reason to believe that these apocalyptic meanderings contain genuine echoes of an earlier time when the opponents of the Umayyad regime eagerly anticipated a dramatic future age. They fully expected the wheel of fortune would soon come full cycle and initiate an era when the dynasts who displaced the Prophet's family from rule would be brought to account.[28] The precise moment at which these stirrings became deeply rooted in the public imagination cannot be ascertained. In all likelihood, graphic visions of the demise of the Umayyads coincided with debilitating internal stresses that undermined the stability of the ruling order and thus served to encourage active revolts and clandestine revolutionary activity. But even if one could trace expectations of an anti-Umayyad apocalypse to the time of ʿAbd al-Malik, one would hardly expect to find visual expression of these yearnings, however disguised, in the Dome of the Rock, a building that gives every impression of trumpeting the legitimacy of the caliph and the ruling family.

In examining the messianic stirrings of Umayyad times, a second and equally prominent strand of apocalyptical imagination commands our attention—not individual anti-Umayyad traditions, some of which were shaped after the fall

27. F. B. Flood, *PEQ* 123 (1991): 133–35.

28. See J. Lassner, *Islamic Revolution*, esp. 90–97.

of the regime, but a discernable literary genre that reflected Muslim reaction to the recovery of a weakened Byzantine Empire. The Byzantines, shaken by the loss of their Near Eastern and North African domains, found the need to envision a coming age in which they would redeem their lost territories and herald the onset of their messianic era. The Muslims in turn were anything but secure about their achievements. Their failure to capture Constantinople or control the Mediterranean demonstrated the resilience of the Christian empire. In no time, the Umayyads realized that they were embroiled in an epic contest that would determine the future course of Islam. The events of the momentous seventh century CE presaged the seemingly endless conflict between Christian and Muslim polities that was to last for some eight hundred years. Faced with the ever-present threat of their powerful neighbor to the north, Muslim authors penned triumphalist texts that anticipated the conquest of Constantinople, the end of the Byzantine Empire, and the ultimate triumph of Islam over the Christian unbelievers. According to script, the time will then come when evil will be redressed and God will render final judgment from his throne on high.[29] The visual expression of this coming apocalypse might have been a project worthy of ʿAbd al-Malik's consideration—that is, if Rosen-Ayalon is correct in her reading of the decorative motifs.

With that in mind, readers are advised to take note of David Cook's detailed study of Muslim apocalyptical literature.[30] Cook observes that visions of the messianic future refer to fantastic treasures of gold, silver, and jewels, vast amounts of booty that the Muslim faithful would acquire at the end of days when they capture the very last strongholds of Christianity. In a number of sources, these treasures are said to have included relics of the Jewish Temple destroyed by the Roman general Titus, thus leading Cook to suggest that "groups circulating these kinds of traditions saw the . . . Dome of the Rock . . . as a type of Third Temple."[31] It is not clear what precise meaning Cook has in mind when he speaks of a "type of Third Temple," but his comment allows adventurous readers to stretch their imagination and link Rosen-Ayalon's eschatological

29. For a general survey, see *EI*, s.v. "Djafr" (deals broadly with Muslim apocalyptical texts known as *malāḥim* and *ḥidthān*). For details, see S. Bashear, "Muslim Apocalypses and the Hour: A Case Study in Traditional Reinterpretation," *IOS* 13 (1993): 75–99, esp. 87–92, and his "Apocalyptic and Other Materials on Early Muslim-Byzantine Wars," *JRAS* (1991): 173–207. Both of Bashear's articles draw upon a wealth of source material in manuscript and printed editions. See W. Madelung's "Apocalyptic Prophecies in Ḥims in the Umayyad Age," *JSS* 31 (1986): 141–85. Perhaps the best overall treatment of the subject is D. Cook's broad-ranging and immensely learned "Muslim Apocalyptic and *Jihād*," *JSAI* 20 (1996): 66–104, esp. 83 ff. See also M. Cook, "Eschatology and the Dating of Traditions," *Princeton Papers in Near Eastern Studies* 1 (1992): 23–47; "The Heraclian Dynasty in Muslim Eschatology," *Al-Qanṭara* 13 (1992): 3–23.

30. Cook, "Muslim Apocalyptic and *Jihād*," 93.

31. Cook, "Muslim Apocalyptic and *Jihād*," 93–94.

theme with representations of implements from the ancient Jewish temples, a view that calls to attention the argument advanced by Soucek and Shani, art historians who consider the Dome of the Rock a physical reincarnation of a celebrated biblical past. To regard the Dome of the Rock as a type of third temple built on the ruins of its predecessors would seem to combine all the aforementioned theories into a neat, if loosely tied, bundle.

As long as scholars are given to bold speculation, we might entertain still another perspective suggested by these interpretations of the crowns, jewels, and geometric and floral patterns. Rather than draw attention to an indeterminate future event, the fall of Constantinople and the end of Christian rule, the proposed eschatological theme or links to Solomon's Temple might be seen as calling attention to a historic event that had already taken place: the triumph of the Arabs that left vast territories of Byzantine imperial domains under Muslim control. A few scholars, exercising what seems a surfeit of imagination, have gone so far as to suggest that the Arab tribesmen who crossed the Byzantine frontier with Arabia were in fact motivated by an apocalyptic vision of Islam's imminent triumph over the nonbelievers. We are led to understand that the initial Arab conquest was, in essence, a religiously motivated campaign, a movement stimulated by expectations of the end of days and not, as most scholars have concluded, the result of converging political and economic forces. Assuming that the revisionists are correct, can we then assume that the eschatological themes posited by Rosen-Ayalon reflect this new vision of the Islamic conquest?[32]

One need not embrace the revisionist view to accept that there is an undeniable link between Jerusalem and the apocalypse. Moshe Sharon has observed, quite rightly, that Jerusalem breathes messianism for all the Abrahamic religions. He points to Muslim traditions that depict the caliph ʿUmar's triumphal entry into the holy city as the fulfillment of ancient Jewish prophecies, accounts that he declares charged with messianic overtones. It is clear that the accounts of the Jewish prophecies are part and parcel of a well-known Muslim literary device in which Jews (and Christians) well steeped in their prophetic traditions cite ancient sources to authenticate later events in Islamic history, legitimizing thereby the claims of Muslim persons and families and the religio-political factions aligned with them. As with the coming of the Prophet Muḥammad, the Muslim conquest of Jerusalem was the fulfillment of a long-anticipated event foretold in sacred Jewish writings.

Sharon, who is keenly sensitive to textual nuances, is aware that the prophetic narratives cited here do not stem from ʿUmar's reign but from a later

32. See chapter 2, n. 4.

moment that cannot be pinpointed. In all likelihood they are an invention of Umayyad times, a literary development that may be linked to salient expressions of praise (*faḍāʾil*) for the holy city. However, it does not necessarily follow that these Jewish prophecies said to have been invoked during ʿUmar's visit to Jerusalem are eschatological texts pointing to the central role destined for the holy city at the end of days, a well-known theme of the faḍāʾil genre. Unlike the apocalyptical literature, the statements attributed to the learned Jews witnessing the conquest of Jerusalem are not embroidered with cataclysmic events that will usher in the Messianic age. We might then consider an alternative reading that skirts the eschatological issue while still declaring the importance of the city. The Muslim stories of ʿUmar in Jerusalem may have been shaped to convey the impression that the conquest of the city, the symbol of Christianity's hegemony in the Holy Land, was preordained by God and long expected by Jews nourishing the hope that the Temple Mount, despoiled by Christians, would be restored to its previous glory.[33]

Sharon evinces no interest in art-historical methods, but like Soucek and Shani he is cognizant of the linkages between the Dome of the Rock and the ancient Temple of Solomon. He suggests that ʿAbd al-Malik himself was fully aware of the site's holy past and was intent on embracing that holiness for his own political ends. In *Bibilotheca Orientalis*, ostensibly a review journal, the Israeli epigrapher and historian takes license to produce what is in effect a challenging article occasioned by Isaac Hasson's edition of Wāsiṭī's *Faḍāʾil al-Bayt al-Muqaddas*. Wāsiṭī (ca. eleventh century CE) is explicit in acknowledging that the Dome of the Rock was situated at the very spot of the Jewish temple; he even offers a description of the site in the time of Solomon. As Sharon makes clear, Wāsiṭī's rendering of the Umayyad past is heavily laced with data ultimately based on Jewish sources.[34] The Muslim author indicates that not only did visitors (presumably Jews) enter the site to pray on Mondays and Thursdays, but Jewish attendants burned incense and washed the rock with sweet-smelling water. From another tradition we learn that Jews also lit the lamps in the Dome of the Rock. These practices reportedly continued until the reign of ʿUmar b. ʿAbd al-ʿAzīz (717–20 CE). In effect, the Muslim author is describing well-known Jewish ritual acts. On Mondays and Thursdays Jews attending synagogues engaged in communal daily prayer; read from the Torah as they did on the Sabbath and holidays; offered personal devotions; and would occasionally fast as an act of penitence.[35]

33. Sharon, "Shape of the Holy," 283 ff., esp. 286–87 and his "Praises of Jerusalem," 65–66.
34. Sharon, "Praises of Jerusalem," 61–63.
35. Sharon, "Praises of Jerusalem," 59–60.

It is not surprising that Sharon, a scholar steeped in his own tradition, could recover the Jewish memorabilia embedded in Wāsiṭī's text. But what did Wāsiṭī, an eleventh century CE author, make of these tales describing events of Umayyad times? More pertinent to our interests: What motivated ʿAbd al-Malik to allow Jews to enter and service the magnificent building that was erected on his watch, assuming that the historicity of the account bears some semblance of truth? If reports of a Jewish presence in the Dome of the Rock contain echoes of a real past, one could assume that at one point in early Islamic history, the descendants of the ancient Israelites were given license, if only briefly, to visit the most holy site of their ruined temple, even though it was enshrined within a Muslim structure. Surely, the caliph himself would have to have borne responsibility for allowing the Jews to enter the Dome of the Rock and perform pious acts within. Assuming all this to be the case, Sharon spins an intriguing scenario linking ʿAbd al-Malik's construction of the building and his political agenda with the aforementioned Jewish activity in the Dome of the Rock and their messianic yearnings.

For Jews, permission to enter the magnificent building, a visual symbol of Islamic rule, was an indication that the advent of Islam heralded the initial stage of their redemption, a sentiment given wide expression in Jewish apocalyptical literature.[36] Their ability to perform various ritual acts within it foreshadowed—or so Jews hoped—a transition to rebuilding their temple.[37] As for the Muslims, Sharon suggests that by erecting the Dome of the Rock ʿAbd al-Malik wanted to present himself as rebuilding (if only symbolically) the Temple of Solomon, thus linking himself directly with the legendary prophet and ruler of old. In such fashion, the caliph reversed in dramatic fashion the Byzantine policy of leaving the Temple Mount desolate, a policy that signaled Christianity's triumph over paganism and Judaism.[38] Following Sharon, one would then conclude that what ʿUmar began with his modest mosque on the Temple Mount, ʿAbd al-Malik completed with extensive repairs to the hallowed platform and above all the construction of the magnificent domed building.

36. See chapter 4.

37. Sharon, "Praises of Jerusalem," 65.

38. Sharon, "Praises of Jerusalem," 65–66. Similarly N. Rabbat, "The Meaning of the Umayyad Dome of the Rock," 15–18, who states, "Building a highly visible dome on a site celebrated in the past by Solomon and David . . . symbolized ʿAbd al-Malik's political aspirations and balanced his monarchial inclinations and religious convictions. The precedence of David and Solomon building the Temple in the tradition that was appropriated by Islam, combined with the Umayyads well-known symbolic and real connections with Jerusalem, emphasizes reading the Dome [of the rock] as a monument to the Islamic Umayyad rule." With that, Rabat argues that ʿAbd al-Malik built the Dome of the Rock for strictly political purposes (read the dispute with the Zubayrids). He goes on to claim that the religious importance of the building was a later development that followed on the heels of constructing the great Jerusalem mosque along the same axis.

'Abd al-Malik's vast project was then followed by another major undertaking of symbolic importance, the construction of the great al-Aqṣā mosque at the southern end of the Temple Mount, a project attributed to both 'Abd al-Malik and his son al-Walīd.

The connection between the projects on the Temple Mount and Byzantine-Muslim relations bears further comment. Whatever opinion one may hold regarding the causes of the Arab expansion and the force that drove its success, there can be no doubt that by the reign of 'Abd al-Malik the wars against the Byzantines were infused with great religious fervor. The victories were seen as epic events leading to the inevitable triumph of Islam over Christianity. How does this help us understand the decoration of the Dome of the Rock and the meanings to which it might have given rise? Oleg Grabar interpreted the jeweled crowns and diadems as representing imperial or royal symbols of Byzantine and Sasanid princes. With that interpretation he sought to establish a connection between the decorative motifs of the Dome of the Rock and "symbols of holiness, power, and sovereignty in the official art of the Byzantine and Sasanid empires."[39] The success of the Arab conquerors and the establishment of Muslim rule beyond Arabia can thus be seen as marking the onset of a new era for humankind, one in which the caliph inherits the power that had previously accrued to the great emperors of the past and in which Islam supersedes Christianity and indeed all other religions. Grabar cites various Islamic traditions of crowns and other royal objects that were placed in the Ka'bah to signify the defeated "other," imperial realia that were now paying homage to various Muslim rulers and their faith.[40] His assumption: the decoration of the archway

39. Grabar, "Umayyad Dome of the Rock," in *Jerusalem*, 22 ff. (reprint of his 1959 article in *Ars Orientalis*). Note also an essay reflecting his views on the "meaning" of the domed structure some thirty years later, also published in *Jerusalem*, 142–58. See specifically p. 147, where he states the domed building constructed by 'Abd al-Malik was a discrete visual sign that the Marwanid branch of the Umayyad family saw the polity they ruled "as a new empire continuing the old Mediterranean and even Iranian ones, but under the aegis of a new and final revelation." I should think a more apt description would be a new polity that firmly supplanted its predecessors, lest one believe the Umayyads ruled a Byzantine (or in some respects Sasanid state) dressed in Arab garb.

40. Grabar, "Umayyad Dome of the Rock," 34. N. Rabbat ("Dome of the Rock Revisited," 70 ff.), citing Wāsiṭī, *Faḍā'il*, 75–76 and variants, indicates that suspended from a chain above the rock were a magnificent pearl, the horns of the ram sacrificed by Abraham instead of his son (the binding of Isaac according to Jewish tradition took place on Mt. Moriah, the site of the Temple Mount; according to Muslim tradition at the rock situated in the Ka'bah), and most important for our purposes, the crown of (the defeated) Persian emperor. If Wāsiṭī is correct in his description of the Dome of the Rock, and not merely reflecting an imagined scene, the spolia spoken of by Grabar in the decoration of the walls were matched by actual objects, horns taken from Mecca previously held by the counter-caliph, Ibn al-Zubayr, and the crown that symbolized the defeat of the Sasanid Empire, thus giving credence to the argument that the Dome of the Rock was a kind of war memorial—if only the pearl could be linked to the defeat of the Byzantines in the Holy Land, and more particularly to the Muslim conquest of Jerusalem. For the jewel, see the text above.

in the Dome of the Rock, a building that has been compared to the sacred shrine in Mecca, served the same purpose as the acquired *spolia* hung in the Kaʿbah. In that sense, we might consider the Dome of the Rock as a kind of victory memorial similar in at least certain respects to the famed triumphal arch in Rome, the monument on which the sacred implements of the Jewish Temple are portrayed as spoils of war. That dramatic moment, represented in full relief, commemorated Titus's crushing defeat of the Jewish rebels and the destruction of their central shrine, events noted in Muslim as well as Jewish literature.

Any proposed links between the decor of the Dome of the Rock and representations of the many triumphs that dot the ancient landscape should be treated with reservation. As opposed to the readily identifiable temple implements portrayed on the Arch of Titus, the crowns and jewels configured in the decoration of the Umayyad building are not clearly marked. There is no visual narrative that specifically identifies them as objects signifying the imperial realia of the defeated Byzantines (and Sasanids). Grabar's suggestion calls, however, for further comment, especially in light of a Muslim tradition attributed to the legendary Jewish convert to Islam, the former rabbi Kaʿb al-Aḥbār. The learned Kaʿb is reported as saying: "I found in some revealed works that Almighty God said 'Rejoice O Jerusalem (*Ūrīshalam*)!'" Kaʿb goes on to say: "[That statement] is to be interpreted as 'I will send unto you my servant ʿAbd al-Malik who will reestablish your rule of old and I will adorn the [holy] sanctuary (*haykal*) with gold, silver, pearls and precious stones,' meaning [I will decorate] the [Dome of the] rock (*ṣakhrah*) 'and I shall place My throne over you as before. For I am God. There is no God but Me alone. I have no partner.'"[41]

The use of Ūrīshalam, one of several Arabic forms of the Hebrew *Yerushalayim*, is no doubt deliberately chosen to give this prophecy, allegedly derived from a revealed text of old, an air of legitimacy.[42] Another version is more explicit. It reads: "It is written in the Torah [regarding] Ūrūshalayim—which is Jerusalem (*Bayt al-Maqdis*)—and the rock (*ṣakhrah*)—which the Jews refer to as the *haykal* [holy sanctuary]: 'I will send you my servant ʿAbd al-Malik who will build you and adorn you.'"[43] Still another version adds: "For I am God, the Lord [of the Universe] and David is the King of the Israelites."[44]

41. See Elad, "Why Did ʿAbd al-Malik Build the Dome of the Rock," 38, citing an unpublished fragment of Sibṭ b. al-Jawzī's *Mirʾāt al-Zamān* that he edited (text in 57–58) and compared to variants in the faḍāʾil works of Wāsiṭī and Ibn al-Murajjā; and the more extended treatment of the tradition based on Wāsiṭī and Ibn al-Murajjā by Sharon, "Praises of Jerusalem," 59 ff.

42. For the Arabic names of Jerusalem and the Holy Land borrowed from Hebrew and Aramaic, see chapter 1.

43. Wāsiṭī, *Faḍāʾil*, 86.

44. Ibn al-Murajjā, *Faḍāʾil*, 25b, cited by Sharon in "Praises of Jerusalem," 59 and Elad, "Why Did ʿAbd al-Malik Build," 38.

It is clear that these combined reports contain echoes of well-known Jewish and Muslim traditions that situate God's throne above the primeval rock. What might not have been known to Muslims is that the last version cited reflects not only a Jewish call for the Muslim restoration of Jerusalem but also of the Davidic dynasty. Moreover, Muslims not learned in Jewish sources would have been unfamiliar with biblical verses that are most likely linked to Ka'b's dictum.[45] Decorating the sanctuary (Dome of the Rock) with gold, silver, and precious jewels of all sorts is reminiscent of Isaiah 54:11–12: "O [Jerusalem] storm tossed and uncomforted! I will lay your [rebuilt] foundations with sapphires. (11) And will make your battlements out of rubies, your gates of precious stones, and all your outer wall[46] of gems" (12). These verses are embedded in that segment of Isaiah which anthropomorphizes Jerusalem (Zion), depicting the city as a woman ravaged and living in desolation, the victim of a foreign conqueror. But the prophet foresees that all will be set right and that the city laid low will be restored to its former place and glory. Any learned Jew familiar with the Islamic tradition, particularly the version ending "David is the ruler of Israel," would have understood the messianic message embedded within the Muslim text; namely, the expected restoration of the holy city and its central shrine (*haykal*), and the return of the Davidic line to rule. By any yardstick, the words attributed to Ka'b have all the markings of an old Jewish apocalypse that was filtered by whatever means into a Muslim tradition of 'Abd al-Malik's Jerusalem.

We have then to consider whether this Muslim tradition is more or less contemporaneous with 'Abd al-Malik's reign and, that being the case, what relevance it has for determining the meaning of the domed building atop the Temple Mount. For Sharon the answer is clear: "There can hardly be any question that Ka'b's comments were composed and put into circulation in the time of 'Abd al-Malik and together with other traditions . . . [his statement] aimed at giving divine legitimacy to [the Umayyad caliph] and the building of the Dome of the Rock."[47] He concludes that the tradition (conveniently attributed here to

45. The possible connection between the Arabic text and Isa. 54:11–12 was indicated by Sharon, who adds to the mix Jer. 33:16–17 and Ezek. 37:24. Although Jeremiah and Ezekiel mention the salvation of Israel and the restoration of the Davidic line, they make no mention of jewels and precious stones. See "Praises of Jerusalem," 59. Seemingly unaware of the possible connection with the biblical text or texts, Rabbat, citing Wāsiṭī, *Faḍā'il*, 75–76 and variants, points to a chain hanging above the rock that held a celebrated pearl. He also notes that the Ka'bah and various great mosques were decorated with jewels, crowns, and other votive objects that called attention the sanctity of the buildings or the greatness or devotion of the donor. See his "The Dome of the Rock Revisited," 71 ff.

46. Hebrew *gevul*, translated here as "outer wall," might perhaps be understood as the boundary markers of the city area.

47. Sharon, "Praises of Jerusalem," 59.

Ka'b, a well-known source for accounts on the holy city) presents 'Abd al-Malik as the redeemer of Jerusalem, and declares that in building the Dome of the Rock, the caliph intended to rebuild (in a manner of speaking) the Israelite Temple of old. With that, Sharon leaves us to understand that the caliph could claim for himself a direct link to the great Solomon. Sharon is too accomplished a historian to end his comments with that assertion. Lest we misunderstand, he makes it clear that 'Abd al-Malik did not consider himself the Messiah (nor would he have claimed himself to be a prophet, a designation given Solomon in the Qur'ān and later in other Muslim sources). Nor does Sharon hint that the Dome of the Rock was built to replace Solomon's Temple as a place of extensive religious activity—certainly not for Muslims. This was not the equivalent of a third temple, a direct replica for Muslims of an ancient Jewish past. He even questions if the Umayyad caliph ever regarded Jerusalem as an Islamic sanctuary. Here he seems to be in the camp of those who follow Goitein rather than Goldziher.[48] What, then, prompted 'Abd al-Malik to build the Dome of the Rock and wrap himself in a Solomon-like robe? Sharon suggests that the caliph invited comparisons of himself to Solomon and the Dome of the Rock to the Israelite Temple to curry favor with the Jews. He sees the caliph as needing their assistance to strengthen his authority, particularly in Syria. How the meek and demographically limited Jewish communities of al-Shām could have assisted the caliph in any meaningful way is anything but clear.[49]

Despite my reservation regarding this last point, Sharon gives us much to consider. There is no denying that the aforementioned Jewish apocalyptical tradition that suggests to Jewish readers Isaiah 54:11–12 made its way into Muslim sources. Can we then assume that 'Abd al-Malik or the artisans who worked on the Dome of the Rock were aware of Isaiah's prediction of a future Jerusalem with its reference to jewels and precious stones? And how might that be connected with Grabar's suggestion that the decoration of the building should be regarded as *spolia* and the building itself some form of war memorial? I have found nothing in Jewish sources to connect Isaiah's text with the spoils of war. Nor does there seem to be any explicit evidence—at least none that I could find—to directly link the wall decoration with *spolia* or even suggest that 'Abd al-Malik or his artisans had a particular historical or metahistorical narrative in mind when choosing as a decorative motif the representation of jewels, crowns, floral designs, and the like. Grabar's reading of the decoration assumes that the

48. For the debate between Goitein and Goldziher, see chapter 5.
49. Sharon, "Praises of Jerusalem," 63.

caliph gave the same meaning to these motifs as do the modern art historians skilled in their craft, and so the caliph instructed the artisans to employ these symbols of Islam triumphant. There is much to recommend Grabar's understanding of the decoration and of the domed building in toto, but there are times when architectural forms and decoration are simply meant to be pleasing to the builder's eye. It is anything but clear whether 'Abd al-Malik or those responsible for planning and executing the fine detail of the Dome of the Rock were fully conscious of the symbolic meanings proclaimed by current specialists of Islamic art and architecture.

Scholars seeking clues to the meaning of the Dome of the Rock are best served by turning to the politically freighted inscriptions that ring the building's open space.[50] The inscriptions pertinent to our discussion are situated above and on both sides of the arches that form the inner frame of the first ambulatory. The first series of inscriptions could be seen by visitors from the center of the open space; the second by those who were moving along the octagonal passageway. As was common in virtually all major edifices, there is a dedicatory inscription; this one originally named 'Abd al-Malik as having built the Dome of the Rock in the year 72 AH.[51] Our interest focuses, however, on the inscriptions bearing statements drawn from the Qur'ān and in a script that reflects the archaic orthography of the earliest known Kufic Qur'ān manuscripts.[52] Scholars do not doubt that the Qur'ānic inscriptions, along with the dedication of the building and the geometric and floral patterns, were part of the original decoration.

Along the outer face of the arches, starting at the south and moving northwest, each of the inscriptions is introduced by the *basmala*, the Arabic formula that proclaims God "the Compassionate, the Merciful."[53] Interspersed among the Qur'ānic inscriptions are statements asserting the unicity of God, blessings of the angels for Muḥammad, and Muḥammad's role as God's messenger, including his acting as intercessor for his community on the Day of Resurrection, all themes present in scripture. The actual citations from the Qur'ān begin with the sūrah labeled *al-Ikhlāṣ*, "Asserting the unity of God":

50. A new and fully detailed treatment of the building's inscriptions awaits volume 6 of the magisterial *Corpus Inscriptionum Arabicorum Palaestinae*, prepared by M. Sharon and soon to be published by Brill (Leiden).

51. The name was effaced and replaced by that of the Abbasid caliph al-Ma'mūn in the ninth century, as can be seen from the smallish and awkward lettering that substituted the name of the Abbasid for his Umayyad predecessor.

52. C. Kessler, "'Abd al-Malik's Inscription in the Dome of the Rock: A Reconsideration," *JRAS* (1970): 2–14.

53. See *EI*, s.v. "Basmala."

1. He is God. One God, the Eternal. He begets not, nor was he begotten. There is none like him. (Qur'ān 112)
2. Indeed, God and his angels pronounce blessings upon the Prophet. O you who believe, pronounce blessings upon him and salute [him] in peace. (Qur'ān 33:54)
3. Say praise to God who begets no son and has no partner in ruling and no protector from degradation. Magnify his greatness. (Qur'ān 17:111)
4. All that is in the heavens and earth praise God. He holds dominion over all things and is due praise. (Conflates Qur'ān 57:2 and 64:1)

The inscriptions along the inner face of the arches begin by repeating the fourth and second inscriptions of the outer arches. They then add that Muḥammad is God's servant and call upon God to grant him peace and mercy. Following that, the inscriptions proceed to reaffirm a fundamental tenet of Islam: the unicity of the all-wise and all-powerful God in heaven. At the same time, they draw on verses from the Qur'ān, largely from the sūrah labeled "Mary" (*Maryam*), where the text focuses on matters of Christology:

3. O people of the Book! [can refer to Jews and Christians but intended here for Christians only] Do not exceed the bonds of your religion
4. and speak only the truth of God. The Messiah, Jesus, son of Mary, is only the messenger of God and the word he cast upon Mary and a spirit proceeding from him. So believe in God and his messengers and do not speak of the Trinity. Desist,
5. [it will be] better for you. For God [stands] One Alone. Being exulted as he is, he is above having a son. To him belongs all that is in heaven and earth. It is sufficient that God is [your] Trustee [Qur'ān 4:169 (171)]. O God! Bless your messenger and servant Jesus
6. son of Mary. Peace be upon him [Q: *'alayya*, "upon me"] the day he was born [Q: *wulidtu*, "I was born"] and the day he will die [Q: *amūtu*, "I will die"] and the day he will be resurrected [Q: *ab'athu ḥayyan*, "I will be resurrected"] [Qur'ān 19:33 (35)]. That is Jesus son of Mary—[this is] a statement of truth that they doubt [Qur'ān 19:34 (35)]. It is not fitting for God to beget a son [*ittakhadha lahu walad*, literally "take a son for himself"]. Glory to him!
7. When he decides upon a matter, he has only to say "Be!" and it is [Qur'ān 19:35 (36)]. Indeed, God is my Lord and your Lord. So serve him. This is a straight path [Qur'ān 19:36 (37)]. God has testified that

there is no God but him, as have the angels and leading men of learning who uphold justice. There is no God but him,

8. the All-Powerful and All-Wise [Qur'ān 3:16 (18)]. Indeed, Islam is the religion formulated by God. Those [people] to whom the [revealed] Book had been given [original reference to Jews or Christians or both] did not differ until they received the revelation (*al-ʿilm*) and became envious of one another. Whoever denies the [manifest] signs of God will face him who swiftly calls [deniers] to account. (Qur'ān 3:17 [19])

Oleg Grabar was quick to recognize that viewed as a whole the verses, together with Qur'ānic quotes on the gates of the building, reflect three basic themes. The fundamental principles of Islam are asserted (with special emphasis on the unicity of God). This is not unusual, as these principles appear in many inscriptions that grace monumental Islamic architecture. Grabar also notes that the inscriptions establish the legitimacy of the Prophet Muḥammad and the universal scope of his mission (that is, he was not merely a prophet sent to convert pagan Arabs to monotheism but was to bring God's message to the people of the book as well, a theme also developed in Muslim scripture). Most interesting of all are the pointed references to Jesus and Mary, both seen as revered figures, but the embrace of the two is more than balanced by a sharp polemic against the Christian concept of the Trinity. There are at present several thousand known Qur'ānic inscriptions on a wide variety of Muslim edifices, including buildings designated religious structures. But the emphasis on the sūrah "Mary" and particularly the threat to the people of the book who deny the manifest signs of God is seemingly unique and thus requires explanation. According to Grabar, the final inscription was carefully chosen with two objectives in mind: "On the one hand it has a missionary character; it is an invitation—a rather impatient one—to 'submit' to the new and final faith which accepts Christ . . . among its forerunners. At the same time it is an assertion of the superiority and of the strength of the new state and the faith based upon it."[54] His suggested reading of the final inscription surely applies to the register of inscriptions read as a whole.

With these inscriptions as our guide, the Dome of the Rock can be seen

54. Grabar, "Umayyad Dome of the Rock," in volume 4 of his collected studies, *Jerusalem*, 37. The ellipsis omits Grabar's reference to the Jews, who are included by him in the admonition of Qur'ān 4:167 [171], which begins with "O people of the book (*yā ahl al-kitāb*)." The people of the book can signify both Christians and Jews, but as the verse continues with a polemic against Muslim belief in the Trinity, it seems fairly clear that the original intention was, contra Grabar, to single out the Christians.

as giving dramatic visual expression to the ascendance of Islam in a holy land previously ruled by Christians. It also served to legitimize the ruler who built it and the ruling house into which he was born. By restoring the Temple Mount, ʿAbd al-Malik also restored the sacred geography of the holy city. The ancient platform on which the great temples of Solomon and Herod stood and where the primeval stone had been situated since Creation was returned to its former glory. In that sense, Cook's opaque phrase "type of Third Temple" could be applied to the Dome of the Rock, and the purported Jewish vision of ʿAbd al-Malik restoring Solomon's Temple might reflect a measure of historical reality.

The Symbolic Uses of Muslim Imperial Architecture: Addressing the Christians

There are, as we have already seen, instances where early Islamic architecture and decoration are designed to legitimize an Islamic regime in a specific rather than general way. The Abbasid caliph al-Manṣūr trumpeted his personal authority and that of his family by imitating features of Umayyad palace-mosques and reportedly utilizing architectural items salvaged from great dynasties of the past. The magnificent Round City that al-Manṣūr created was awe-inspiring. Visitors encountering the Abbasid palace-complex perceived that the power with which the Umayyads and others had ruled had been transferred to a new ruler and ruling authority. The perfidious behavior of the Umayyad usurpers had given way to proper governance by the Prophet's close relatives, and the political turbulence of the old regime was replaced by an era of peace and stability—hence the name of al-Manṣūr's new capital: Madīnat al-Salām, "City of Peace."[55]

The symbolic uses of imperial art and architecture could also be directed to powerful external enemies. One could argue that ʿAbd al-Malik did not build the Dome of the Rock because of the rebellious Zubayrids. A more persistent and ultimately more dangerous adversary had to be accounted for. Noting the inscriptions previously discussed, Grabar, among others, has suggested the exquisite building on the Temple Mount symbolized the strength and staying power of Islam vis-à-vis the neighboring Byzantine Empire. Despite earlier de-

55. See Lassner, ʿAbbāsid Rule," 163–83, expanding upon and correcting his earlier study "Some Speculative Thoughts on the Search for an ʿAbbāsid Capital," *MW* 55 (1965): 135–41 (part 1), 203–10 (part 2). See also O. Grabar, "Al-Mushatta, Baghdād, and Wāsiṭ," in *The World of Islam: Studies in Honor of P.K. Hitti*, edited by J. Kritzik and R. B. Winder (New York, 1959), 99–108. Grabar deals with symbolic architecture of the Umayyad administrative palaces (*dār al-imārah*) and links them to the architecture of the Round City, the great monument constructed by the Abbasid caliph al-Manṣūr in 766 CE.

feats at Muslim hands, the Christian polity remained a formidable foe. The existence of a powerful empire sharing a volatile frontier with the Abode of Islam and the large Christian population that dwelled in the lands conquered by Arab armies called not only for responses on the field of battle, but also a strategy with which to engage the Christians in an war of visual symbols.

Within the conquered territories, there was the danger that Muslims might be influenced by the rich pageantry of Christian ceremonies and the impressive churches, monasteries, and other religious buildings that dotted the landscape of the Holy Land and former Christian regions beyond. The geographer Muqaddasī (ca. tenth century CE), a native Jerusalemite and grandson of two distinguished architects (*bannā'*), records a conversation he had with his uncle about the great mosque in Damascus,[56] a spectacular edifice fashioned from a structure with a long and glorious religious history, most recently that of a Byzantine church. Arabic sources report that the Muslim conquerors first shared the Church of St. John with Christian inhabitants of the city, or, in any case, occupied part of the extended church grounds. But later, ʿAbd al-Malik's son, the caliph al-Walīd, confiscated the building and built in its stead a great mosque to serve his needs and those of the Muslim residents in the city. The historicity of the shared church has been questioned. There can be no doubt, however, of al-Walīd's intention to give the Umayyad capital a mosque worthy of his rule and that of the dynasty.[57]

Muqaddasī complained about the enormous cost of al-Walīd's Damascus mosque. The geographer suggests that the funds required to build the mosque would have been better spent restoring the roads and fortresses along the Byzantine frontier, an area that was under heavy Byzantine attack throughout the author's life. His uncle, responding sharply, reminds his nephew that the Umayyad caliph saw al-Shām as remaining (despite the Islamic conquest) a Christian land (*balad al-naṣārā*). He goes on to note the caliph's concern that the magnificent Christian architecture of the Holy Land, widely observed by the Muslims, seduced them (thus compromising their steadfast devotion to Islam).[58]

Speaking of impressive Christian edifices, the uncle included the likes of the Church of Resurrection (*al-Qiyāmah*)—that is, the Church of the Holy Sepulcher in Jerusalem. He reminds his nephew that to counteract the powerful religious imagery of Christian architecture, al-Walīd also built a great mosque (the al-Aqṣā) on the ancient Temple Mount, a house of worship that became

56. Muqaddasī, *Aḥsan*, 159.

57. The most complete study of the structure of the great mosque in Damascus remains that of K. A. C. Creswell, *EMA*, 1/1: 151–96; as regards the "shared mosque" see 180 ff.

58. Muqaddasī, *Aḥsan*, 159.

one of the wonders of the world. The uncle then adds: For similar reasons ʿAbd al-Malik built the Dome of the Rock. Like his son, he feared the grandeur of the dome of the Holy Sepulcher and the overall appearance of the church would dazzle Muslims. It is not stated what impression these words made on Muqaddasī, but elsewhere in his book the author repeats this reason for building the Dome of the Rock and adds that the al-Aqṣā mosque was also built to challenge the powerful religious imagery of the Christians. As if to reinforce this point, he notes in the former account that the Muslims refer to the Church of the Holy Sepulcher, not as "[the Church of] the Resurrection (*al-Qiyāmah*)" but as *al-Kumāmah*, "the Garbage Heap."[59]

The anecdote that appears in a tenth-century text reflects the conditions then present along the Byzantine frontier, but it also could be read as the echo of an earlier challenge to Muslim sensibilities. In erecting magnificent structures on a place rich in religious history going back to Creation itself, ʿAbd al-Malik and al-Walīd demonstrated that the message preached by the Prophet Muḥammad supplanted that of the monotheist messengers who preceded him, and that a transcendent Islam was now the religion for all humankind. Of all the buildings erected by the Muslim conquerors and their immediate successors, the Dome of the Rock can be considered the exemplar of Islam's triumph over Christian belief and power, a true marriage of the sacred and the profane. Jerusalem was never *the* religious center or political hub of the Islamic realm. Nor was it ever the capital of al-Shām or even that of a subdistrict of Greater Syria. No provincial governor or subgovernor made Jerusalem his official residence. The importance of Jerusalem derives instead from powerful resonances to a sacred history shared by all the monotheist communities past and present.

Grabar writing in 1959 intuitively grasped that the Dome of the Rock was intended as a symbol of Islamic triumphalism. I take the liberty of citing a rather lengthy passage of his, as it sums up ever so eloquently what he would call the "meaning" of the building, an understanding of the Dome of the Rock with which I heartily concur:

> In what was in the seventh century the Christian city *par excellence*, ʿAbd al-Malik wanted to affirm the superiority and the victory of Islam. This affirmation, to which was joined a missionary invitation to accept the new faith, had its expression both in the inscription [referring to the last verse quoted] and in the Byzantine and Persian crowns hanging around the sacred rock. But [the Dome of the Rock's] most immediately striking expression was the appropriation for Islam of the ancient site

59. Muqaddasī, *Aḥsan*, 168.

> of Mount Moriah. Thereby, the Christian prophecy was voided and the Jewish mount rehabilitated. But it was no longer a Jewish sanctuary; it was a sanctuary dedicated to the victorious faith. Thus the building of the Dome of the Rock implies, on the part of ʿAbd al-Malik, what might be called *prise de possession* of a hallowed area . . . [T]he Dome of the Rock should not so much be related to the [pre-Islamic] monuments whose form it took over, but to the more general practice of setting up a symbol of the conquering power or faith within the conquered land.[60]

This symbolic meaning attributed to the domed building and, more generally, the Ḥaram al-Sharīf both reinforces and is reinforced by the previous analyses of the Goldziher-Goitein debate. Following Grabar, and the weight given to Goitein's views in the preceding chapter, readers are most likely to conclude that the rededication of the Temple Mount reflects an ongoing conflict with the powerful Christian adversary Muslims forced from Jerusalem and the Holy Land, and not the caliphal pretender commanding his followers from a shaky sinecure in the holy cities of Arabia. Grabar is only too well aware that commemorating the acquisition of sacred or political space is a time-honored practice when victors boldly seek legitimacy for themselves, their dynastic order, and, where relevant, their faith. Going back to a remote past when history was first recorded and monuments first erected, rulers attempting to retain their authority or expand their dominions have sought to demonstrate through the written word and visual symbols that their rule was the manifest expression of a heavenly will. And yet, however forcefully stated, be it on the written page, in oral traditions, or through monumental architecture, such messages were contested as rulers came and went and dynasties rose and fell. New narratives of the past and present were forged and old monuments were destroyed or refashioned to suit the needs of the newly crowned. In this case, the Dome of the Rock was retained, but the dedicatory inscription was altered after the Umayyad dynasty was succeeded by the house of Abbas. During the reign of the caliph al-Maʾmūn (813–33 CE) ʿAbd al-Malik's name was removed and that of the Abbasid ruler was awkwardly inserted in its place. Oddly enough, the date of completion was retained, leaving a gap of some 120 years or more between the original dedication of the building and al-Maʾmūn's crude attempt to claim the Dome of the Rock as his own. *Sic transit gloria*.

60. Grabar, "Umayyad Dome of the Rock," in volume 4 of his collected studies, *Jerusalem*, 40–41.

CHAPTER 9

Religion and Local Politics

Praising Native Abodes

Expressions of pride in one's native abode (*ḥubb al-waṭan*) were widespread in the medieval Islamic world. In a variety of texts, including local histories, authors singing the praises of their native cities call attention to the salubrious climate, the absence of pests, the grandeur of buildings, the number of famous religious scholars, the general quality of life, and so forth. The greatest compliment was to declare a city or region "the navel of the universe" or "navel of the world (*surrat al-dunyā* or *surrat al-arḍ*)," as if all that is important in the world revolved around a particular place, and that was evident for all to see.[1]

At times, different cities are paired with rivals, whether in the same general region or in other provinces: for example, Basra versus Kufa; Mecca versus Medina; Baghdad versus Samarra and Damascus; and our concern, Jerusalem versus the holy cities of Arabia. The rivalries might be framed by foundation lore. Thus the great astrologer Nawbakht reportedly cast his horoscope and then informed the Abbasid caliph al-Manṣūr (754–74 CE) that the stars favored his establishing the capital of the realm at Baghdad. Jupiter entered the orbit of Sagittarius, a sign that portends a glorious future. With that, the city is destined for greatness, and with an added bonus—"No caliph shall die within (the city)"—a not-so-veiled reference to the murder of Abbasid rulers in Samarra, the rival capital established by the caliph's great-grandson the following century. Similarly, a Baghdādī poet muses, "Does the eye of the stranger covet sleep in al-Shām?," a slur on Damascus and the province from which the hated Umayyads ruled.[2] Basra and Kufa, old adversaries during the first Islamic civil war, and later centers of rival grammatical schools, compete in turn for scholarly recognition; Mecca and Medina vie with one another as the spiritual fulcrum of the Muslims; and regarding the subject before us, the partisans of

1. For Jerusalem, see chapter 2.
2. Khaṭīb, *Ta'rīkh Baghdād*, 1:67–69.

Jerusalem measured the holiness of their city and its historic environs against other cities and regions of the Islamic world, especially the ḥaramayn of Arabia.

The geographer Muqaddasī cites a conversation with Abū-l-Qāsim, a judge of Hijazi origins.[3] Asked by Abū-l-Qāsim about the climate of Jerusalem, Muqaddassī answered that it was neither hot nor cold, thus likening it to Paradise. The geographer's response invokes a well-known topos of the literature in praise of cities and regions, not borne out it would seem by anyone who has passed a winter in Jerusalem's dank stone buildings or experienced the combined stillness and excessively dry heat that strike the city from time to time in summer. But Muqaddasī knew he had been given an opening to praise his native city and by the son of a prominent Hijazi notable. Abū-l-Qāsim's father was the chief magistrate of Mecca and Medina. After mentioning the weather, Muqaddasī goes on to extol the fine construction of Jerusalem's stone buildings, which he declared unmatched; the ampleness of its (al-Aqṣā) mosque, than which, he claimed, there is none larger; and its markets, which he found the cleanest of all cities. He lauds as well the quality of life and the excellent and abundant victuals that feed its inhabitants, who include all means of skilled professionals (*hādhiq*) and physicians. Jerusalemites exhibit the most abstemious behavior (*a'affu*), perhaps a reference to the large numbers of ascetics who assembled there over the centuries and who are named in Jerusalem lore time and again. No wonder strangers are always flocking to Jerusalem to enjoy a way of life that cannot be duplicated elsewhere.

This bill of particulars seems an elaborate response to a question about the weather in Jerusalem. What then occasions so detailed, if not exaggerated, a reply to the seemingly offhanded inquiry of the Hijazi judge? In praising the holy city so enthusiastically, the geographer from Jerusalem seems to invite positive comparisons with the holy cities of Arabia, settlements where Abū-l-Qāsim's father was the chief judicial authority. That desire for comparison is not stated explicitly; nor is there mention of Mecca and Medina other than Muqaddasī identifying his Hijazi interlocutor and the latter's father, but the intent of the tradition is clear. Without skipping a beat, the author introduces a second narrative, a parallel account of a meeting with another judge, this time the Iraqi qāḍī, al-Mukhtār Abū Yaḥyā b. Bahram.[4] The conversation, which takes place in the judge's assembly at Basra, turned to Egypt—oddly enough, not Iraq, where the story takes place. The native Jerusalemite was asked which of the two lands was greater (his own or Egypt). He answered: "Mine [literally "ours"]."

3. Muqaddasī, *Aḥsan*, 165–66; also Yāqūt, *Mu'jam*, 4:593.
4. Muqaddasī, *Aḥsan*, 166; also Yāqūt, *Mu'jam*, 4:595.

Al-Mukhtār then raised a series of additional questions, asking Muqaddasī to compare Egypt and the latter's native land. In each instance, the geographer from Jerusalem favored his native abode. Those attending the assembly were astonished at these remarks and accused Muqaddasī of being disingenuous. His judgment thus called into question by his Iraqi hosts, Muqaddasī explained his remarks in detail, invoking the usual litany in praise of one's native land. But he then adds a series of virtues that are explicitly linked to the holiness of Jerusalem and its relationship to the ḥaramayn of Arabia. He concedes that Mecca is distinguished by the Ka'bah and Medina by the Prophet (who made it the political and religious hub of the nascent Islamic community); but the geographer from Jerusalem then points out that his city is destined to play the central role in awesome events signaling the end of time as we know it. All the world's people and its places of worship will stream to that holy city when the Messiah comes and Almighty God renders his final judgment, a theme repeated often and with evident pride in the faḍā'il al-Quds literature and Jewish sources.

Major compilations of faḍā'il make bold claims for the religious importance of the city. These claims are based on older traditions found in earlier works that are mentioned in our sources but have not yet been recovered.[5] The format of the published texts and manuscripts that have come to light vary in presentation and number of traditions, but in the end they are remarkably similar in content. The book of the eleventh-century author Abū-l-Ma'ālī al-Musharraf b. al-Murajjā, perhaps the most detailed of the sources presently known, is typical of the genre. His *Faḍā'il Bayt al-Maqdis wa-l-Khalīl wa-l-Shām* begins with the history of the site, going back to the time of Creation. He speaks of the primeval rock before there was any human settlement in Jerusalem and then discusses the antiquity of the respective sites that gave rise to historic Jerusalem and the holy cities: Mecca and Medina (pp. 8–16). Abū-l-Ma'ālī then turns to biblical history, referring to the reigns of David and Solomon, and the subsequent disasters visited upon the Israelite capital by the Babylonian monarch Nebuchadnezzar (pp. 17–41). These biblical themes are found in other Muslim sources beginning with veiled and not-so-veiled references to the Jewish past in the Qur'ān. But then, history takes a quantum leap, and without mention of Jerusalem in the all-important Graeco-Roman period we are informed of 'Umar's trip to accept the surrender of the Byzantine city (pp. 44–57). Interestingly enough, Mu'āwiyah's investiture, a subject of no small significance, is missing from Abū-l-Ma'ālī's account. The very next subject is a detailed description of the Umayyad structures on the Temple Mount (pp. 58–71).

5. See chapter 1.

Having described the historic highlights of the city as well as the major Islamic edifices gracing the ancient platform that once housed the great Temple of Solomon (and that of Herod), the author provides his readers with extensive remarks on various rituals associated with Jerusalem. Included in this discussion are references to Muḥammad changing the orientation of prayer from the city to Mecca, as well as matters related to prayer in Jerusalem's congregational mosque and whether it was permissible to fulfill the obligatory rites of pilgrimage in Jerusalem as one ordinarily did in the holy cities of the Hijaz (pp. 72–101). The largest segment of the book (pp. 103–208) is filled with numerous legends linking the site of the city with prophets of the monotheist past ranging from the mysterious al-Khiḍr, said to be a contemporary of Moses, to Jesus of Nazareth. Interspersed within this rambling section are many short traditions that could have been just as easily placed amid the initial chapters of the book: various well-known legends about the primeval rock and its surroundings, and numerous short statements referring to pietists and their religious behavior within the city and its environs (pp. 71–194).

Following that, the reader encounters a series of seemingly unrelated traditions (pp. 208–79) dealing with such diverse subjects as the role of the holy city in the Messianic Age, a point of great contention between advocates of the ḥaramayn and Jerusalem loyalists. There are traditions concerning the blessings that accrue to those who die in Jerusalem and the number of prophets buried there; the merit of giving alms to the poor and of fasting in the city; the prohibition of entering churches situated in the Valley of Gehenna, and other assorted subjects. With these wide-ranging statements, Abū-l-Maʿālī concludes his faḍā'il of Jerusalem and goes on to a general discussion of mosques that draws on familiar collections of canonical ḥadīth. He ends with a relatively short segment on the merits of al-Shām, including many statements about persons and places linked in the Hebrew Bible with the ancient land of Canaan.

The veneration of Jerusalem trumpeted throughout the Muslim literature praising the city was matched by special license given Muslims to perform pious acts of devotion there, as they did at Mecca and Medina. Jerusalem thus came to be considered by many Muslims as one of the three great holy cities of Islam. The tradition of pilgrimage to Jerusalem during the Muslim holy month of Dhū-l-Ḥijjah is epitomized by a well-known utterance attributed to the Prophet. Muḥammad allegedly said that one is allowed to fulfill the obligatory rites of pilgrimage at only three mosques: the mosques of Mecca and Medina and the mosque on the Temple Mount in Jerusalem.[6] The statement,

6. For a detailed discussion of this and related traditions, see M. J. Kister, "'You Shall Set Out

attributed to the Prophet, is clearly a back-projection designed to legitimize Jerusalem's status as one of the three holy cities of Islam. It also was meant to indicate that from almost the very outset of the faith, Jerusalem was universally proclaimed as sacred for the Muslims, as it had been and continued to be for Jews and Christians. Such claims, which appear in slightly different versions throughout the faḍā'il literature, occasioned a reaction from Muslims advocating the unique sanctity of the Hijaz and the great mosques of the ḥaramayn.[7] It also drew the ire of orthodox zealots concerned with heterodox behavior in the religious shrines of the Holy Land to the north—behavior sometimes linked to Jewish and, more particularly, Christian practices. When one takes a close look at the Arabic sources and reflects further upon them, one uncovers Muslim views that go against the accepted wisdom of Jerusalem's special status. There are texts that, at best, downplay the importance of Jerusalem as a center of pilgrimage and place of pious devotion. At worst they deny altogether that the holy city of Jews and Christians was or should have been equally sacred for observant Muslims.

Anti-Jerusalem Literature in Islam

In contrast to the many accounts listing the virtues of Jerusalem—the accepted wisdom of most Muslims—there are concurrent traditions that tend to downplay and, in certain instances, undermine completely the sanctity of the city. In some of these anti-Jerusalem traditions, the Prophet is said to declare: "The mosques which deserve most to be visited [in performing the rites of pilgrimage] . . . are the Sacred Mosque [in Mecca] and my mosque [in Medina]. A prayer in my mosque is better than a thousand in any other save that of Mecca." In this version, there is no mention whatsoever of the grand mosque erected by the Umayyads on Jerusalem's Temple Mount. In other versions of this anti-Jerusalem tradition, the al-Aqṣā mosque, though mentioned, is worth only fifty or five hundred prayers, as compared with no less than one hundred thousand at the Masjid al-Ḥaram in Mecca. Even when a single prayer in the Jerusalem

Only for Three Mosques'—a Study of an Early Tradition," *Le Muséon* 82 (1969): 173–96; see also his "Sanctity Joint and Divided: On Holy Places in Islamic Tradition," *JSAI* 20 (1996): 18–65, which takes up the way in which sanctity was extended over time to other sites in al-Shām. Kister recognizes ever so clearly the existence and importance of an anti-faḍā'il tradition, but as with many of his researches he seemingly leaves the reader to reconstruct the larger story from the myriad of detailed citations he provides.

7. Kister, "Study of an Early Tradition," 178 ff. (with numerous citations to printed texts and manuscripts).

sanctuary is the equivalent of thousands elsewhere, it always pales in comparison with Mecca's great mosque. In each and every one of these instances, the authors clearly intend to degrade the Jerusalem mosque in relation to the great houses of worship in the Hijaz.[8]

Still, partisans of Jerusalem might have discovered a silver lining in what appears, at first glance, an egregious insult to their city, whose very name in Arabic (*al-Quds* or *Bayt al-Maqdis*) designates it as a holy place whose great mosque was built where the magnificent temples of Solomon and Herod stood in ancient times. Despite the stated preference for the mosques of Mecca and Medina, there is absolutely nothing in this tradition—not even in the version that omits all mention of the al-Aqṣā mosque—that explicitly denies the sanctity of Jerusalem and its venerated house of worship. Nor does this particular version categorically state that Muslims are forbidden from fulfilling the rites of pilgrimage on the ancient platform. Quite the opposite, the expression "deserve most to be visited" with regard to the mosques of Mecca and Medina implies that at least one other mosque could be visited. The Prophet himself instructed Muslims to set out for three mosques, including the al-Aqṣā. Could we not conclude then that for those unable to make the arduous and expensive journey to the Hijaz, Jerusalem might have been an acceptable alternative? Surely, Muslims familiar with the Prophet's dictum would have seen that as a possibility. As if to leave no doubt that the mosque in Jerusalem is decidedly inferior to the great mosques of Mecca and Medina, and beyond that, ought in no way be considered a proper site of pilgrimage, the mirror image of this ambiguous tradition has the Prophet declaring: "You shall set out [on pilgrimage] for two mosques [only]; the mosque of Mecca and the mosque of Medina." Need we ask for a more explicit statement that goes against the pro-Jerusalem opinion of most Muslim scholars? Taken at face value, this second version of the Prophet's expressed view clearly excludes Jerusalem as a proper site at which to fulfill the annual pilgrimage.

Nor is this the only tradition that would lead readers to believe pilgrimage to Jerusalem was not legally permissible. Another account reports that the caliph ʿUmar b. al-Khaṭṭāb (d. 634 CE) struck two men whom he believed performed the rites of pilgrimage in Jerusalem. Fearing further punishment, the beaten men explained that they only stopped in Jerusalem to say their daily prayers. Their ultimate destination was the holy cities of the Hijaz; their goal to fulfill properly the rites of the ḥajj in the ḥaramayn. Hearing that, the caliph sent them

8. Kister, "Study of an Early Tradition," 179–80, 192 ff.

on their way.[9] In certain circumstances, merely praying in Jerusalem could and did lead to disapproval, if not outright condemnation. On the day of his triumphal entry into Mecca, the Prophet Muḥammad was reportedly approached by a man who said: "O Messenger of God! I vowed [before the Almighty] to pray in Jerusalem should you conquer Mecca." Muḥammad replied: "Pray here! [in Mecca]." Apparently, the Prophet attempted to dissuade the Muslim from acting on his vow to pray in Jerusalem. The man persisted, however, and the Prophet replied as he did earlier: "Pray here!" It was only when the man spoke a third time that the Prophet allowed him to make the decision for himself. This tradition indicates ever so clearly that Muḥammad preferred that such individual prayers be recited in Mecca, but he did not prohibit devotional prayers in Jerusalem, if reciting these prayers was meant to fulfill an earlier vow invoking God's name. The Prophet fully understood that a vow made before God is not easily contravened.[10]

Muḥammad's somewhat ambiguous response reflects a lively debate among legal scholars long after the Prophet's death. The question arises: Is one obligated to recite individual prayers and otherwise perform devotional acts in Jerusalem, if one has vowed to do so invoking God's name? Most authorities maintained that if a person had already invoked God's name, the obligation was binding; a minority said that even though God's name had been invoked, the vow was not binding. For those embracing the minority view, even a vow made to Almighty God cannot salvage Jerusalem's place as a site of very special significance for Muslims. Be that as it may, this second opinion did not go far enough to satisfy the more stringent opponents of Jerusalem's sanctity.

In his *Qā'idah fī ziyārat Bayt al-Maqdis*, a short treatise devoted to the rules governing religious visits to Jerusalem, the zealous Ibn Taymīyah (d. 1328 CE) takes issue with both the majority and the minority opinion.[11] In contrast to those scholars who generally respect, if not trumpet, the sanctity of Jerusalem, Ibn Taymīyah seriously undermines the veneration of the city and its environs. He maintains that Jerusalem cannot in any way be considered a center of pilgrimage.[12] At best, Muslims are allowed innocuous visits to Jerusalem in order

9. Kister, "Study of an Early Tradition," 181.

10. Kister, "Study of an Early Tradition," 180.

11. Text can be found in C. Matthews, "A Muslim Iconoclast (Ibn Taymīyah) on the 'Merits' of Jerusalem," *JAOS* 56 (1936): 1–21. For an account of Ibn Taymīyah's life and works, see *EI*, s.v. "Ibn Taymiyya." There are numerous traditions about prayers and rituals in Jerusalem in the faḍā'il literature. For some reflective comments, see O. Livne-Kafri, "Prayers in a Jerusalem Guide for Muslim Pilgrims [Hebrew]," *Cathedra* 66 (1992): 51–60, = his *Jerusalem in Early Islam*, 124–28 (largely citing Abū-l-Ma'ālī al-Musharraf b. al-Murajjā's, *Faḍā'il*).

12. Kister, "Study of an Early Tradition," 193–96; also the succinct statements of Ibn Taymīyah, *Qā'idah*, 8–15.

to pray there, but not as a result of having vowed to do so. In that respect Ibn Taymīyah can be seen as stricter than the Prophet, who tried to dissuade a Muslim from going to Jerusalem in order to fulfill his vow but did not prevent him from doing so. Nor, according to Ibn Taymīyah, can one even vow to spend time on a religious retreat within the city, an activity favored by many Muslim pietists and mystics. Were these prohibitions not enough to degrade the holy status of Jerusalem, Ibn Taymīyah rules that the annual pilgrimage to Mecca cannot be combined with a religious visit (*ziyārah*) to Jerusalem (lest one consider visiting Jerusalem with religious intent as fulfilling part of the sacred rites of the ḥajj). With that ruling, Ibn Taymīyah appears stricter than the "righteous" caliph ʿUmar, who released two Muslims who prayed in Jerusalem after discovering that they had not performed any rites of pilgrimage but had stopped in the holy city to say their daily prayers. Finally, Ibn Taymīyah goes on to say—and this is really startling—that the violation of any of these rules governing visits to Jerusalem is tantamount to a renunciation of Islam. To go to Jerusalem in order to fulfill a personal vow, be it to offer devotional prayers or go on a religious retreat, or even formally visit the city while en route to Mecca as a pilgrim, makes one an unbeliever. A Muslim turned infidel in this manner is then called upon to formally repent or face certain death—all that for holding Jerusalem excessively sacred. These are but a few echoes of the nuanced Muslim debate concerning the significance of historic Palestine as a holy land and of Jerusalem as a holy city.

Not all scholars who denied Jerusalem equal status with the holy cities of Arabia went as far as Ibn Taymīyah. Jamāl al-Dīn al-Isnawī (or Asnawī), an Egyptian jurist of the Shāfiʿite school (d. ca. 1370), and more or less a contemporary of Ibn Taymīyah, took a less stringent attitude toward individuals wishing to perform pious acts in the Holy City.[13] A concerned Muslim wrote to Isnawī seeking legal advice. The common people (*al-ʿawāmm*) were given to quote a tradition in which the Prophet declares: "He who visits (*zāra*) me [meaning, he who undertakes a religious visit to my grave at Medina] and to my ancestor Abraham [his burial place in Hebron] in the same year is guaranteed a lofty place in Paradise." The perturbed Muslim also reported them saying that a similar award is reserved "for the person who performs the *ḥijjah* [meaning *ḥajj*] to Jerusalem the same year [he visits my grave]."[14] Lest Isnawī misunderstand, the writer seeking advice goes on to explain that when the common people use the terms *ḥajja* and *ḥijjah* in Arabic (terms ordinarily associated

---

13. J. Sadan, "A Legal Opinion of a Muslim Jurist Regarding the Sanctity of Jerusalem," *IOS* 13 (1993): 231–45. Text is found on p. 243.

14. Follows the reading of Sadan, "Legal Opinion," 243.

with the annual pilgrimage) they [really] mean a *ziyārah* or religious visit. The question is then put to the learned Muslim jurist: "Do these [commonly held] opinions contain the truth?" That is, do visits to sacred sites in the Holy Land for religious purposes (*ziyārah*) combined with a visit to the Prophet's grave in Medina guarantee the best of Paradise? Even if one were to concede that the common people spoke the truth, we would have to conclude, based on how the question was put to Isnawī, that under no circumstances should a religious visit to Jerusalem be confused with fulfilling the rites of the yearly pilgrimage. In any case, we have the jurist's response: "This tradition is false (*bāṭil*). Neither of the two statements [one guaranteeing a lofty place in Paradise for those visiting the Prophet's grave and that of Abraham in Hebron in the same year, the other guaranteeing the same reward for a religious visit to Jerusalem] is rooted in Islamic law."[15]

The jurist concedes that "a religious visit to Jerusalem is meritorious, but that visit for pious purposes cannot be specifically linked to fulfilling the rites of pilgrimage [because such religious visits might be misunderstood by those not familiar with a certain use of *ḥajja* and *ḥijjah*]." Isnawī's response thus makes it abundantly clear that Muslims wishing to fulfill the obligation of the ḥajj can do so only at the ḥaramayn of the Hijaz. He goes on to say that pilgrims who do not visit Jerusalem while en route to Arabia do not diminish the authenticity of their pilgrimage (to the Hijaz). In sum, unlike Ibn Taymīyah, Isnawī is prepared to recognize some sacred status for Jerusalem and also Hebron (where the biblical patriarchs and matriarchs, also revered by the Muslims, are buried), but not if that limited sanctity compromises the exalted status of Arabia's holy sites.

What harm was there in vowing to perform devotional acts in Jerusalem, a place that had been sacred to monotheists from most ancient times? No doubt some Muslims believed there was something subversive about sanctifying this particular city and the land in which it was situated. Was it merely a certain form of popular pietism that offended the more rigid Muslim authorities, or could there have been an additional reason for downgrading Jerusalem after it was generally accepted as a Muslim holy city comparable in certain respects to Mecca and Medina? The canonical collections of ḥadīth do not reveal a discernible anti-Jerusalem bias. For most Muslims, Jerusalem's standing as sacred Muslim city had already taken root by the first two or three Islamic centuries. Why then were the likes of Ibn Taymīyah moved to write as sharply as they did? Addressing this issue, Suleiman Mourad proposes a significant shift in thinking about Jerusalem caused by the First Crusade (1099 CE). According to Mourad,

15. Sadan, "Legal Opinion," 243.

the occupation of Jerusalem by Christians gave Muslim scholars license to jettison the faḍā'il statements linking Jerusalem to its biblical (hence Jewish and Christian) past and favor instead various traditions that recalled the holy city's Islamic history. Mourad speaks of an increasing reliance on accounts of the *isrā'* and *mi'rāj*, and the reported visits of leading Muslims to the Temple Mount. The continuing references to the role of Jerusalem at the end of days is seen by him as referring to an eschatological turn that will bring about the "liberation" of the holy city. This reorientation of faḍā'il begins—so Mourad claims—with Diyā' al-Dīn al-Maqdisī (d. 1245 CE) and leads directly to Ibn Taymīyah.[16]

By the time of Ibn Taymīyah, the Crusaders, who were at first regarded as temporary interlopers and were accepted as actors in intra-Muslim rivalries, had come to be regarded as a dark force that had shaken Muslim self-confidence. But can that change of perceptions alone explain the hardening of the religious arteries characteristic of Ibn Taymīyah and others? Do the references to centuries' old eschatological themes speak only of restoring Islamic rule to one of Islam's three holiest cities, as Mourad seems to suggest, or should we be widening our vision of the past to include other considerations? Might we be correct in thinking that the anti-faḍā'il outlook of authors like Ibn Taymīyah stems from an internal squabble among Muslims—between the champions of Mecca and Medina and the promoters of Jerusalem's sanctity?

The more stringent protectors of the faith are well aware that traditions favoring Jerusalem are not always neutral when comparing Jerusalem to the ḥaramayn. In some faḍā'il accounts it is not enough to declare Jerusalem the equal of Mecca and Medina, that is, a place where one can perform the rites of pilgrimage as one does in the sacred precincts of the Hijaz. Pro-Jerusalem traditions, including statements attributed to the Prophet himself, go so far as to indicate a decided preference for the area of the Temple Mount and, more generally for the Holy Land over Arabia. Those who favor Jerusalem remind us of God's words in Qur'ān 21:71. Read literally, the verse indicates that God "directed Abraham and [his nephew] Lot to the land (*al-arḍ*) as a blessing for all nations." In this instance, it is clear that Muslim scripture can be linked to Genesis 12:1–4, a powerful statement in which God establishes his relationship with the progenitor of the Israelites and promises them the land of Canaan. The "land" mentioned in 21:71 is most certainly the Canaan of the Hebrew Bible. Some Muslim scholars interpret the verse as indicating that God sent Lot and Abraham to *Bayt al-Maqdis*, a term that can refer to all the Holy Land but that most often refers to Jerusalem or the Temple Mount. No wonder then that pro-

16. S. Mourad, "Jerusalem in Early Islam," 98–99.

Jerusalemites, citing God's very word, describe the Prophet as urging Muslims to emigrate (*satuhājirū*) to Jerusalem following the example of Abraham and his nephew.[17]

Mentioning Abraham's special connection with Canaan could only have jostled the sensitivity of Arabian Muslims, especially the Hijazis who claimed Abraham as one of their own. To closely identify Abraham with ancient Palestine (explicitly in the Hebrew Bible and implicitly in the Qur'ān) goes against the grain of Muslim attempts to root the origins of monotheism in the Arabian Peninsula, more particularly in Mecca where Abraham and his eldest son Ishmael established the Ka'bah, the first monotheist shrine (Qur'ān 2:125–27). A number of pro-Hijazi commentators held, against the apparent meaning of their own scripture, that the biblical patriarch was actually commanded by God to go to Arabia and to Mecca and not to Canaan or Jerusalem. Cognizant of this second and highly unlikely interpretation of Muslim scripture, some scholars attempted to harmonize the two versions, the one favoring Canaan and Jerusalem, the other favoring the Hijaz. It is true, they said, that Abraham received his marching orders to go to al-Shām, more specifically to Filasṭīn, but that was only after he and Ishmael had gone to Mecca and established the Ka'bah as its central shrine, the very shrine that was to become the holiest of all Muslim places. Seen from this perspective, there is no mistaking the sequence of events regarding monotheism's most sacred places. As it was Abraham who established the Ka'bah, the sanctity of Mecca preceded that of Jerusalem, whose first temple was built by Solomon many generations later. The primacy of the Ka'bah and Mecca is made explicit in Muslim accounts comparing the two places of worship, and, more generally, in contrasting Arabia with the holy land to the north.[18]

Linking Abraham to Arabia also goes hand in hand with traditions arabizing the patriarch's eldest son, Ishmael, the child born to Hagar, the Egyptian handmaiden of Abraham's then barren wife Sarah. Muslims believe that Ishmael was raised among Arab tribesmen after Sarah, the matriarch of the Israelites, insisted that her husband cast Hagar and her son out of his household, as in the biblical tale.[19] According to Muslim tradition, mother and son ultimately settled in Mecca, where the local Arabs accepted the boy as one of their own.

17. See *EI*, s.v. "Lūt" and s.v. "Ibrāhīm"; also S. D. Goitein, "Sanctity of Jerusalem," 144–45. The early Islamic commentary on the verse is preserved by Ṭabarī in his massive commentary, the *Jāmi' al-Bayān*, which reports a wide range of opinions when explicating the text.

18. Yāqūt, *Mu'jam*, 4:592 (among many traditions).

19. Gen. 16–17 and esp. 21.

Having become an honorary Arab of Mecca, Ishmael was destined to be the progenitor of the Prophet's clan, and by extension the ancestor of the Prophet himself. With Muḥammad's mission a success, history turned full cycle, and the link between monotheism and Mecca, first established by Abraham many generations earlier, was finally restored. Beginning with the onset of Islam, the Ka'bah, which had become a pagan shrine, was once again venerated by believers in the one true God.[20]

The Arabization of monotheism was key to Islam's debate with Jews and Christians. Abraham's progeny by way of Sarah's son Isaac also have a history, but the history of Jews and Christians runs through the Land of Israel and the Temple built by Solomon in Jerusalem. Muslims were well aware of the broad outlines of the Jewish (and also Christian) narrative with its emphasis on ancient Canaan, the land promised to Abraham's Israelite offspring. But for Muslims, the more important history is that of Abraham and the Ka'bah, which he and Ishmael established as a holy shrine for the one true God, along with the role of Ishmael's Arab progeny in the subsequent history of Mecca, with special emphasis on Muḥammad and the rise of Islam. With these declared links to Arabia, there would seem to be something subversive about Muslims stressing the sanctity of Jerusalem and historic Palestine, all the more so when those traditions seem to call for all Muslims, including the Arabs of Arabia, to emigrate to what Jews declare their promised land.

Hence, Muslims loyal to Arabia and the most genuine monotheism of all sought to degrade the sanctity of historic Palestine and Jerusalem, lest the faithful be led astray by the biblical narrative embraced by Jews and Christians. Muslims were required to embrace a more authentic narrative of the ancient past, the account of the mission and missive of God's last and quintessential messenger, the Prophet Muḥammad. Because he was a descendant of Ishmael, Muḥammad was, according to Muslim tradition, the inheritor of Abraham's patrimony. And so, in order to emphasize the break with the Israelite past and hence with contemporaneous Jews and Christians, many pro-Jerusalem traditions were consciously recast to denigrate the so-called virtues of the so-called holy city nestled amid the Judean Hills.

When pro-Jerusalem scholars declare that anyone praying in the holy city emerges sinless as on the day he was born, their opponents claim the same for Arabia's holy sanctuaries. When the Prophet reportedly says: "Prayer in [the mosque of] Jerusalem is worth a thousand prayers in any other [mosque]," the

20. See *EI*, s.v. "Ismā'īl."

anti-Jerusalem scholars mirror this statement to extol the virtues of the Arabian places of worship, while diminishing at the same time the importance of the al-Aqṣā mosque.[21] There can be little doubt that for Muslims who were offended by texts favoring Jerusalem, there was indeed a great deal with which to take issue. For the offended Muslim faithful, it is presumptuous to declare for Jerusalem's Temple Mount a status that not only equaled but even exceeded that of the holy sites in Arabia.[22] What was a pious Muslim to make of a tradition that declares that should one of the faithful enter the al-Aqṣā mosque and request a special favor of God, that favor would be granted immediately—the presumption being God would not favor such a request in any other place of worship.[23]

We should also take note of certain apocalyptic traditions, messianic texts that for Mourad signify the return of Jerusalem to Muslim control, or, as he is wont to put it, the "liberation" of city from the Crusaders. Even at first glance, the object of these texts is not to glorify the triumph of Islam over the unbelievers but to privilege Jerusalem and the Holy Land at the expense of the sacred precincts in West Arabia.[24] The End of Days will witness the destruction of Yathrib (the ancient name for Medina), a cataclysmic event that will set into motion the final Day of Judgment and the ingathering and resurrection of the dead. On that fateful day, the Kaʿbah, the holy shrine of Mecca, and all the pilgrims who ever went there in past generations will join the throngs of the living and the resurrected dead that assemble in Jerusalem, as will all the other mosques and their worshippers. On that day too, the bones of Muḥammad will be transported from his grave in Medina, to be united with those of the prominent Israelites who are buried in the Holy Land, people such as the patriarchs Abraham, Isaac, and Jacob; Jacob's son Joseph; the matriarchs Sarah, Rebecca, and Rachel; and the various kings and prophets of old. In this elaborate scenario, which is vividly descried in the faḍāʾil al-Quds literature, the holy city of Jews and Christians described as the "navel of the universe," completely upstages Mecca, the birthplace of the Prophet, and Medina, the city that served as his administrative center and the first capital of the Muslim realm.

21. Yāqūt, *Muʿjam*, 4:591 (among many traditions).

22. M. J. Kister, "An Early Islamic Tradition," 179, 184 ff.

23. See the commentaries to Qurʾān 38:35: "He [Solomon] said, 'My Lord, forgive me and bestow upon me rule not suited to anyone after me. Indeed, you are the Bestower [of munificence].'" See also Thaʿlabī, *ʿArāʾis*, 310; Ibn Kathīr, *Qiṣaṣ*, 506–7, and his *Bidāyah*, 2:26; Diyārbakrī, *Khamīs*, 1:274.

24. O. Livne-Kafri, "Jerusalem in Muslim Traditions of the End of Days [Hebrew]," *Cathedra* 86 (1998): 27–56, = his *Jerusalem in Early Islam*, 78–109. See also M. Sharon, "The Praises of Jerusalem," 62.

Polemics and Apologetics: Concerns with Judaism and Christianity

The vivid deflation of the holy sites in Arabia in these and similar accounts may explain the rather hostile reaction to the body of literature in praise of Jerusalem, but there is still more to consider as regards the anti-Jerusalem traditions. The sanctification of Jerusalem was part and parcel of a contest for legitimacy that extended beyond the community of the Muslim faithful. The debate concerning the holiness of Jerusalem was not simply a contest for bragging rights between Muslims situated in the Hijaz and Muslim rulers who moved the political center of Islam to al-Shām and then Iraq. Muslims felt obliged to fashion Jerusalem into a holy city of their own because it was revered by Jews and Christians and remained the most striking symbol of their resistance to Islam. Jews recalled the glorious reigns of David and Solomon and pointed to the central role the city was expected to play at the End of Days when the Jewish people would finally be redeemed and all humankind would stream to Jerusalem and worship the God of Israel. Christians also embraced the sanctity of Jerusalem, whose skyline was visual proof of their faith's triumph over Judaism and paganism. During the first centuries of Islam, the topography of the holy city and its surroundings testified to the resilience of Christianity under Islamic rule. The landscape was dotted with religious edifices of all sorts, monuments that were evidence of a still vibrant Christian religious culture. One can understand how the Umayyad caliphs at war with the still powerful Byzantine Empire, and facing the residual strength of Christianity in the territories conquered by the Arab tribesman, required more than large and well-equipped armies to promote Islamic objectives. There was a second conflict, the campaign to legitimize Islam and its ruling order in a new environment of great religious and cultural diversity, an environment in which Jews and Christians remained, by and large, loyal to their chosen faith communities, while exposing the Muslim settlers from Arabia to the entrapments of a new world rich in material wealth and religious pageantry.

Generations after the Islamic conquest of the Holy Land, the Muslims remained a distinct minority in the larger demographic profile of Jerusalem and its surroundings. As people of the book who shared with Muslims a sacred history and a belief in the one true God, the Jews and Christians of the expanded Islamic realm were not forced to convert. Nor does there seem to have been any massive movement of voluntary conversion. Faced with the richness of their new surroundings, Muslim tribesmen, a generation or more removed from the desert and oases of Arabia, found themselves in search of powerful symbols that spoke to the truth of their religion and their mission, be it when they confronted the Byzantine enemy across the frontier, or living amid the Jews and the vast number of Christians not yet converted to the new faith. Such conversion as there was may have been greeted by Muslims as a sign of Islam triumphant, but conversion could also result in unintended consequences. Converts retained religious baggage from a Jewish or Christian past, an intoxicating package of popular beliefs and patterns of behavior that might prove attractive to the old Muslims and compromise their commitment to a pure Islam born of an Arabian environment. According to a well-known Muslim maxim, it takes forty years, that is, an entire generation, for a convert to get rid of an earlier heritage and fully accept Islam.[25]

The Muslim authorities were thus confronted by conflicting desires. On the one hand, they valued the Jewish Land of Israel and the *Terra Sancta* of the Christians and wished to embrace the Holy Land as their own. Though not mentioned explicitly in Muslim scripture, Jerusalem and its surroundings, we can assume, were very much part of a Muslim religious heritage beginning with the biblical narratives of the Qur'ān. On the other hand, the faithful feared that specific Jewish and Christian beliefs, customs, and ceremonies linked to the Holy Land and its sacred places might influence unsuspecting Muslims. In sanctifying Jerusalem and other places, Muslims did not create holiness out of nothing. The city and the land of historic Palestine were already sacred. Among Jews, the land itself was imbued with broad religious symbolism; the same applied, but even more so, as regards the city of Jerusalem. Jewish law articulates the imperative to settle the Land of Israel and the preference for that land above all others. Merely to settle in the land is declared equal to all the other meritorious acts listed in the Torah. The holiness of the land resonates ever so clearly throughout all of Jewish tradition. The bond between Jews and that relatively small parcel of territory was at the very core of Jewish belief and observance, and so it remains for traditional Jews until this very day. Most sacred of all was the Temple Mount, upon which Jews erected the great houses of worship to their Lord. Muslims were only too well aware of the extraordinary bond between Jews and the sacred territory they call the Land of Israel. They were also well aware of the significance of the Holy Land and Jerusalem for Christians. Traditions in praise of Jerusalem and other sites of historic Palestine recalled for Muslims the various promises made by God to Abraham and his progeny in

25. There is a temptation to link this maxim with the Israelites who left Egypt and wandered in the wilderness for forty years but were unable to enter the Promised Land. Only the second generation of Israelites under Joshua who had rededicated themselves to God were allowed to enter as God's chosen people.

the book of Genesis. That biblical narrative, embraced by both Jews and Christians, was a story well known to Muḥammad and his contemporaries.

Despite their anxieties of being seduced by Jewish and Christian culture, Muslims celebrated the link between the Holy Land and the ancient Israelites, a link that remained unbroken for Jews over countless generations. As did Jews, Muslims venerated the burial places of the biblical patriarchs and matriarchs, all of which are situated in historic Palestine. In accord with the Hebrew Bible (Gen. 47:30, 48:21, 49:29, 50:7–14, 25, Exod. 13:19, Josh. 24:32), they pointed out that the bones of Jacob and Joseph were transported from Egypt to the Holy Land for burial. Elaborating on the importance of the Holy Land and Jerusalem, Muslim authorities indicated that all the prophets sent forth by God before Muḥammad made their way to the holy city where they performed religious devotions. Many of these prophets were said to be buried in Jerusalem; the figures given in Muslim tradition range upwards of four hundred.[26]

Muslim familiarity with Jewish lore and practice did not end with tales from the Bible. Jewish memorabilia in the Qur'ān and subsequent Islamic tradition reflect the vast ocean of exegesis and commentary to which the biblical text gave rise. In this case, there are seeming echoes of postbiblical Jewish tradition in Muslim praises for Jerusalem and the surrounding land. For example, interment in the Land of Israel was a custom and practice enthusiastically endorsed by Jews.[27] By the third century CE, it was common for Diaspora Jews to consider burial in the land of their forefathers. Even the bodies of the exilarchs, the leaders of the Jewish Diaspora who championed the needs and merits of their own communities, had their bodies transported to the Holy Land for burial.[28] According to the rabbis, those buried in its holy soil will not be forced to reach Jerusalem through an elaborate series of tunnels at the End of Days; they therefore will be the first to be resurrected when the Messiah comes.

Burial (anywhere) in the Land of Israel was considered the equivalent of burial in Jerusalem, and burial in Jerusalem was regarded as equal to be being buried beneath the altar of the Temple (the resting place of the primeval stone

26. Yāqūt, *Muʿjam*, 4:591–92 (among many traditions).

27. For Jewish traditions linked to reburial in the Holy Land, see I. Gafni, "Reinterment in the Land of Israel: Notes on the Origin and Development of the Custom," *Jerusalem Cathedra* 1 (1981): 96–104, who argues that the custom of burial in the Land of Israel for Jews living beyond its borders is rooted in practices of the third century CE. For some general comments on the influence of Jewish and Christian tradition on the *faḍā'il* literature and Jewish-Muslim conflicts reflected in that literature, see O. Livne-Kafri, "A Note on Some Traditions of Faḍā'il al-Quds," *JSAI* 14 (1991): 71–83; and his "Islamic Traditions on Jerusalem between Judaism and Christianity [Hebrew]," *Cathedra* 83 (1997): 45–54, = his *Jerusalem in Early Islam*, 7–16.

28. Gafni, "Reinterment in the Land of Israel," 99.

that slaked the waters of Paradise).[29] Similarly, to be buried under the altar was thought equal to being buried under the glorious throne of God, that place where the souls of Moses and the righteous are stored (awaiting resurrection and final judgment when God will sit on his throne and determine the future of all humankind). For those in Jerusalem, there will be no doubt as to their future in the world to come. The rabbis declared that being interred in the holy city (the equivalent of being buried in the Temple) guarantees the expiation of one's sins.[30] That redemptive quality of Jerusalem and the centrality of the holy city in the Messianic Age are much discussed by Muslims who report they acquired information from learned Jewish and Christian converts to the faith. Relying on these recently minted Muslims for enlightenment and guidance aroused, however, the suspicion of the more stringent defenders of the faith.

Many Muslim religious authorities were not comfortable with this acquired religious heritage, the cultural spoils, so to speak, of Muḥammad's victory over the Jewish tribes in Arabia and the Arab conquest of the Christian land to the north. At the least, some Muslim scholars were ambivalent. In any case, the faithful, whether the Arabs of old or recent converts to Islam, required distinctions between the monotheism of the Jews and Christians and the new and quintessential religion of the Prophet. Linguistic and physical markers were required the keep discrete the cultural artifacts of an early monotheism, no longer relevant, and the new faith introduced by the Prophet. *Arḍ al-ḥaram*, the Arabic term to signify the place of a holy sanctuary, is applied consistently only to the sacred precincts of Arabia. In the formative centuries of Islam, the term *ḥaramayn* referred almost exclusively to the areas of Mecca and Medina. Some authorities also included as *arḍ al-ḥaram* Wajj, a dried out riverbed in Ṭā'if, the old pagan sanctuary town several days' journey from Mecca.[31] When awarding the label sacred, some religious authorities were not comfortable with equating Jerusalem to the ḥaramayn and, more generally comparing Syria-Palestine with the Hijaz, the cradle of Islam. There were reservations about the land that had been the focus of undying Jewish allegiance since the time of Abraham and the land that had been the place of Christ's birth and death, and the anticipated place of his return at the End of Days. The strength of Jewish attachment to the Land of Israel was also reflected in Christian views of the Holy Land. Long after the defeat of the Byzantines, Jerusalem and its religious shrines remained firmly fixed in the imagination of Christians everywhere.

29. Gafni, "Reinterment in the Land of Israel," 100. For the primeval stone, see chapter 2.

30. Gafni, "Reinterment in the Land of Israel," 102–4.

31. See *EI*, s.v. "Ḥaramayn" and "al-Ṭā'if." Note that additional places were endowed with sacred credentials. See Kister, "An Early Islamic Tradition," 190–92.

However much Muslims were fascinated by the city so steeped in monotheist history, the stern religious authorities could not countenance it being made equal to the holy cities of Arabia. When asked about places of (monotheist) worship (*masjid*), Muḥammad is said to have indicated that the earliest was established (by Abraham) at Mecca, the second (by Solomon) in Jerusalem, and that forty years separated the one from the other. The tradition puzzled medieval Muslim scholars. Because their sense of chronology was based on the biblical narrative, with which they were broadly familiar, they counted generations and correctly placed Abraham "more than a thousand years prior to Solomon."[32] The point of the Muslim tradition is nevertheless clear. Given its place in monotheist history, Jerusalem was sacred, but the place of worship in Mecca, being the first monotheist sanctuary, was the most sacred of all. The primacy of Mecca is elaborated upon in any number of anti-Jerusalem traditions. Among them, one refers to building the First Temple in Jerusalem. Muḥammad reportedly said: "When [Solomon] built [the Temple in] Jerusalem (*Bayt al-Maqdis*), he asked the Lord to satisfy three needs. But the Lord, may he be exhalted, granted him [only] two. We hope that the third will be ours. Solomon asked God for wisdom to administer justice. And he granted him that. He asked God "for rule [the likes of] which would be unsuitable to any [ruler] after me" [Qur'ān 38:35]. And God granted him that. And finally, he asked for that place of worship which would be preferred by all because after leaving it, a person would be free of sin, as he was on the day he was born." Muḥammad continues: "[That last request was not granted Solomon] It is our hope that God will have granted that house of worship to us [meaning to the mosque in Mecca]."

The reference to sinless birth may have been rooted in a complex theological discussion among medieval Muslims, namely Khārijite claims that responsibility for human behavior begins with the formation of the blood clot in the womb, a view rejected by mainline Muslim communities. But the larger meaning of the text is only too clear. Muḥammad is portrayed as hoping, if not indeed expecting, that Mecca would be preferred to Jerusalem and that the Arabian sanctuary would take precedence over the Israelite temple.[33] The eleventh-century Qur'ān scholar Tha'labī (d. 1035) has much to say about Solo-

32. For example, Ibn Kathīr, *Qiṣaṣ*, 506–7 and his *Bidāyah*, 2:226; Kisā'ī, *Qiṣaṣ*, 285; and Yāqūt, *Mu'jam*, 4:592 (among many traditions); see also Diyārbakrī, *Khamīs*, 1:274.

33. Note the expressions Jerusalem was "the first [city] in whose direction Muslims prayed; the second sanctuary [after Mecca]; and the third [most important] house place of prayer," and, related to that, "I am the Seal of the Prophets and my mosque is the seal of the mosques of the prophets." See Kister, "Three Mosques," 178, quoting various authorities. For alleged Jewish objections to the change in the orientation of prayer from Mecca to Jerusalem, see Ibn al-Murajjā, *Faḍā'il*, 98 ff.

mon in his tales of the ancient prophets.[34] He reports that as soon as he finished building his temple, Solomon set off for the sacred land (*arḍ al-ḥaram*) to perform the rites of pilgrimage, by which Thaʿlabī means Solomon and his massive retinue made for Mecca. The juxtaposition of these two events—the building of the Temple in Jerusalem and Solomon's need to fulfill the obligation of pilgrimage in Arabia—is not coincidental. By going to Mecca immediately after completing the Temple in Jerusalem, the Israelite acknowledges the earlier existence of the Kaʿbah and the primacy of Muḥammad's future birthplace.[35]

Invoking the Hebrew Bible, Solomon informs his entire entourage of the Prophet's future mission, an event foretold in Jewish scripture according to the Qur'ān and subsequent Islamic writings. As did all God's messengers preceding Muḥammad, Solomon vowed before God to assist the Arab prophet by preparing the ancient Israelites and their successors for the certain arrival of the Lord and Seal of the prophets.[36] In a more extensive account, Diyārbakrī (ca. sixteenth century CE) offers a description of Muḥammad and predicts that the future prophet will be victorious against all who resist him. As does Thaʿlabī, he noted that Muḥammad will be the Lord and Seal of the prophets.[37]

On another occasion, this time a journey from Persepolis to the Yemen, Solomon is said to have stopped off in Medina. At Arabia's second holy city, the Israelite again informed his entourage of Muḥammad's coming. Anticipating the future, Solomon reveals: "This [site, namely Medina], will be the settlement of a prophet."[38] Should anyone doubt the authenticity of Solomon's prophetic vision, our source declares that God himself indicated that he would make Medina a sacred place. For it is at Medina that God will reveal an Arabic Qur'ān and send forth the most beloved of his prophets. When reading these accounts, we are asked, however indirectly, why it is that contemporaneous Jews rejected the legitimacy of Muḥammad's prophetic vocation when it was all so clearly revealed to Solomon and all the Israelites in sacred writings and oral traditions that were handed down to them and successive generations of Jews. It is then all too evident that various anti-Jerusalem traditions served as a powerful polemic

34. Thaʿlabī, *ʿArā'is*, 306–10. For Solomon's Temple in Islamic art and lore, see chapter 2.

35. Thaʿlabī, *ʿArā'is*, 311; Zamakhsharī, *Kashshāf*, 1021; Diyārbakrī, *Khamīs*, 1:274. See also Jazā'irī, *Qiṣaṣ*, 409 (describes Solomon as covering the Meccan shrine, a sign of great patronage and recognition of Mecca's superiority to Jerusalem).

36. Thaʿlabī, *ʿArā'is*, 310. The account is based on the covenant of the prophets (*mīthāq al-nabiyīn*) in Qur'ān 3:75 [81], where all the prophets swear before God that they will foretell the future coming of Muḥammad. See J. Lassner, "The Covenant of the Prophets."

37. *Khamīs*, 1:274. Note the expression "I am the Seal of the Prophet and my mosque is the seal of the mosques of the prophets." For this statement, see Kister, "An Early Islamic Tradition," 178, quoting various Muslim sources.

38. Jazā'irī, *Qiṣaṣ*, 412.

against the peoples of the book. By extension, readers of these texts are led to ask why Jews continue to venerate the site of their destroyed temples, symbols of their disobedience to God, and why they privilege their formerly sovereign land over the holy sites in the Hijaz.

However much the Jews and their rejection of Muḥammad represented a problem for Muslims, there is still another dimension to the anti-Jerusalem and anti–Holy Land traditions of the time. So many locations of historic Palestine were identified with the workings of the holy. The land was visited by all sorts of ascetics and beloved by groups of pietists both Christian and Jewish. When the Muslims conquered Byzantine Syria-Palestine, they came upon a land with an extraordinary and well-defined religious landscape. Can we then assume, as does S. D. Goitein, that local pietism might have affected the Muslims, who shared with Jews and Christians a common monotheist tradition, including the veneration of biblical persons? If so, can we also assume that after the Muslim conquest, sites held sacred by Jews and Christians became sacred to some of the Muslim conquerors, at least in the realm of popular religion?[39] Following that, may we make one more assumption, namely, that converts to Islam from among former Jews and Christians did not abandon altogether allegiances to specific places, or give up Jewish and Christian ceremonies associated with places deemed sacred for countless generations? So many studies of the veneration of saints in the Near East and elsewhere suggest an obvious answer to this series of queries. In all likelihood, Muslims who went north to conquer were intoxicated by the sanctity of that land and adopted many popular practices associated with places deemed holy, including the lore and practices associated with Jerusalem's Temple Mount.

One partisan of Jerusalem seems to have recognized the threat of lingering Jewish and Christian influence. We spoke earlier of a conversation between the geographer Muqaddasī and a circle of Basrans, a friendly chat in which the Jerusalemite favors the merits of his native city and region over those of Egypt and the holy cities of Arabia. But then his conversation with the skeptical Iraqis takes an unexpected turn. Just when we think that the author has made his point, perhaps convincing his audience of Jerusalem's merits, he suddenly launches into account of the city's shortcomings. Claiming to quote the Torah, Muqaddasī describes Jerusalem as a "golden basin filled with scorpions." He complains there is a paucity of Muslim religious scholars in the city; Muslim jurists are not (properly) consulted; scholars of broad learning are without

39. "Sanctity," 140 ff., also O. Livne-Kafri, "Early Muslim Ascetics and the World of Christian Monasticism," *JSAI* 20 (1996): 105–29.

reputation; there is no interest in scholarly lectures; mosques are empty for lack of worshippers, and courts of law are without petitioners. In contrast, the Christians are ubiquitous and behave arrogantly toward the Muslims in public (*jafā 'ala al-raḥbah*); they and the Jews have the upper hand in the city (*qad ghallabū 'alayhā*).[40]

For some Muslim authorities, there was the perceived danger that the genuine Islam of Muḥammad and his community, a system of beliefs and practices that emerged from Arabia and the world of the Arabs, was being compromised by strange and foreign elements. A proponent of strict Islamic behavior, Ibn Taymīyah is explicit in condemning the extravagant Muslim veneration of sites where the ancient Israelite prophets were said to be entombed, especially the religious sites that were also venerated by nonbelievers. Given the great popularity of celebratory visits to these and other religious shrines, the austere Muslim jurist could not prohibit them outright. But he made it clear that Muslims were not to visit these sites when graven images were displayed, an obvious reference the Christian use of icons. It seems that Ibn Taymīyah and earlier authorities worrying about religious syncretism were only too aware of the symbolic importance of the Holy Land's sacred history. It is also worth noting that concurrent with the debate on the sanctity of Jerusalem and other places that occupied the sacred landscape, there was a lively discussion of whether Muslims ought to study the traditions of the Israelites or utilize informants who had not yet converted to the faith. Those scholars who favored cultural interchange could invoke the authority of Muḥammad himself. The Prophet allegedly declared that narrating traditions about or on the authority of Jews and Christians was permissible, provided it brought no harm to the Muslim community.[41] In the end, a stricter view prevailed, and even learned converts to Islam like the former "rabbi" Ka'b al-Aḥbār were looked upon with suspicion.

Perhaps the greatest danger to a new faith comes with an attraction to that which is both shared and familiar, but not quite the same, hence a subject of possible confusion. The early Muslims appropriated the history and also customs of a more ancient monotheism as their own, but most important, they redefined the cultural artifacts of others to suit their own needs. Still, the authorities responsible for defending the Islamic faith against religious leakage remained vigilant lest popular religion lead the faithful astray and undercut their religious authority. There has always been tension between the guardians of

40. Muqaddasī, *Aḥsan*, 165–66.
41. M. J. Kister, "Ḥaddithū 'an banī Isrā'īla wa-la-ḥaraja," 215–39.

the law and those who practice religion less formally. The sanctification of the Holy Land and its holiest city should be seen in light of that tense relationship. Despite the efforts of Ibn Taymīyah and others, Muslims embraced the sanctity of the land venerated by Jews and Christians. The Holy Land became a favorite place for Muslim ascetics and pietists, and Jerusalem became a very special city comparable to Mecca and Medina.

Appendix

The Early Caliphs, 632–833 CE

The Rightly Guided Caliphs (al-Rāshidūn)

Abū Bakr al-Ṣidīq	632–34
ʿUmar b. al-Khaṭṭāb	634–44
ʿUthmān b. ʿAffān	644–56
ʿAlī b. Abī Ṭālib	656–61

The Umayyad Caliphs

Muʿāwiyah b. Abī Sufyān	661–80
Yazīd I	680–83
Muʿāwiyah II	683–84
Marwān II	684–85
ʿAbd al-Malik	685–705
al-Walīd I	705–15
Sulaymān	715–17
ʿUmar b. ʿAbd al-ʿAzīz	717–20
Yazīd II	720–24
Hishām	724–43
al-Walīd II	743–44
Yazīd III	744
Ibrāhīm	744
Marwān II	744–50

The Early Abbasid Caliphs

al-Saffāḥ	750–54
al-Manṣūr	754–75
al-Mahdī	775–85
al-Hādī	775–86

al-Rashīd	786–809
al-Ma'mūn	809–13
al-Mu'taṣim	813–33

Selected Bibliography

The bibliography is selected from among numerous sources consulted during the preparation of this work. Preference was given to the most relevant material. Sources referred to in the notes but not listed in the bibliography are fully cited in the text. The bibliography is alphabetically arranged, discounting the Arabic definite article *al-*, which is often prefixed to a given name. Thus the exegete and historian al-Ṭabarī appears as though his name were written "Ṭabarī." Works are listed under the name of the author, with the exception of compilations and editions of anonymous works, which are listed by title. Monographs that are reprinted versions of earlier editions are cited according to the edition consulted. A list of secondary sources follows.

Primary Sources

Abot deRabbi Nathan. A and B: Edited by S. Schechter. Vienna, 1887. A: Translated by J. Goldin as *The Fathers according to Rabbi Nathan.* YJS 10. New Haven, 1955. B: Translated by A. Saldarini. Leiden, 1975.

Abū-l-Fidā, Ismāʿīl b. ʿAlī. *Taqwīm al-buldān.* Edited by J. T. Reinaud and M. de Slane. 2 vols. Paris, 1840.

Abū al-Maʿālī. *See* al-Musharraf b. al-Murajjā

Aggudat Aggadot. Edited by H. Horowitz. Frankfurt am Main, 1881.

Akhbār al-dawlah al-ʿAbbāsīyah. Edited by ʿA. ʿA. Dūrī and ʿA. J. al-Muṭṭalibī. Beirut, 1971.

Anonymous. *See Tarʾīkh al-khulafāʾ*

Aphrodito Papyri. Edited by H. I. Bell with Index of Coptic Papyri edited by W. E. Crum. In *Der Islam* 2 (1911): 269–83, 372–84; 3 (1912): 132–40, 369–73; 4 (1913): 87–96; 17 (1928): 4–8.

al-Azdī, Yazīd b. Muḥammad. *Taʾrīkh al-Mawṣil.* Cairo, 1387/1967.

Al-Azraqī, Muḥammad b. ʿAbdallāh. *Akhbār Makkah al-musharrafah.* Edited by F. Wüstenfeld as *Chroniken der Stadt Mekka.* 3 vols. Leipzig, 1858.

al-Baghdādī, ʿAbd al-Muʾmin b. ʿAbd al-Ḥaqq. *Marāṣid al-iṭṭilāʿ ʿala asmāʾ al-amkinah wa-l-biqāʿ.* Edited by T. G. S. Juynboll. 6 vols. Leiden, 1852.

al-Balādhurī, Aḥmad b. Yaḥyā. *K. Anṣāb al-ashrāf.* Vol. 3. Edited by ʿA. ʿA. Duri. Beirut, 1398/1978. Vol. 4A. Edited by M. Schloessinger. Revised and annotated by M. J. Kister. Jerusalem, 1971. Vol. 5. Edited by S. D. Goitein. Jerusalem, 1936. Vol. 6. Edited by K. ʿAthamina. Jerusalem, 1993.

al-Balādhurī, Aḥmad b. Yaḥyā. *K. Futūḥ al-buldān.* Edited by M. J. De Goeje. Leiden, 1866.

Battei Midrashot. 2nd edition. Edited by S. A. Wertheimer. 2 vols. Jerusalem, 1967.

al-Bayḍāwī, ʿAbdallāh b. ʿUmar. *Anwār al-tanzīl wa asrār al-taʾwīl.* Edited by H. O. Fleischer. 2 vols. in 1. Leipzig, 1846–48.

al-Bayhaqī, Ibrāhīm b. Muḥammad. *K. al-maḥāsin wa-l-masāwī.* Edited by F. Schwally. Giessen, 1902.

Beit ha-Midrash. Edited by A. Jellinek. 6 vols. Leipzig, 1853–77.

al-Dhahabī, Muḥammad b. Aḥmad. *K. tadhkirat al-ḥuffāẓ.* 5 vols. Hyderabad, 1915–16.

al-Dīnawarī, Aḥmad b. Dāwūd. *K. al-akhbār al-ṭiwāl.* Edited by V. Guirgass. Leiden, 1888. Indexed by I. Kratchkovsky. 1912.

al-Diyārbakrī, Ḥusayn b. Muḥammad. *K. al-Khamīs.* 2 vols. Cairo, 1302/1884.

Eutychius (Saʿīd b. al-Biṭrīq). *K. al-taʾrīkh al-majmūʿ ʿala-l-taḥqīq wa-l-taṣdīq.* Edited by L. Cheikho. Louvain, 1906–9.

al-Hamadhānī, Muḥammad b. ʿAbd al-Malik. *Takmilat taʾrīkh al-Ṭabarī.* Edited by A. J. Kannan in *al-Mashriq* (1955): 21–42, 149–73; (1957): 185–216.

Ibn ʿAbd Rabbihī, Aḥmad b. Muḥammad. *al-ʿIqd al-farīd.* Edited by A. Amīn, A. al-Zayn, and I. al-Abyarī. 7 vols. Cairo, 1965.

Ibn ʿAsākir, ʿAlī b. al-Ḥasan *Taʾrīkh Dimashq.* Partial edition by S. al-Munnajid. Damascus, 1951-. Full edition by ʿU. ʿAmrawī and ʿA. Shīrī. 80 vols. Beirut, 1995–2001.

Ibn al-Athīr, ʿAlī b. Muḥammad. *al-Kāmil fi-l-taʾrīkh.* 13 vols. Beirut, 1385–87/1965–67. Edited by C. J. Tornberg. 12 vols. Leiden, 1851–76.

Ibn al-Athīr, ʿAlī b. Muḥammad. *Usd al-ghābah fi maʿrifat al-ṣaḥābah.* 4 vols. Cairo, 1285–87/1869–71.

Ibn al-Faqīh, Aḥmad b. Muḥammad. *K. al-buldān.* Edited by M. J. De Goeje. BGA 5. Leiden, 1855. A fragment appearing in the fuller Mashad MS is appended to O. K. Tsikitschvilli, *On the City of Baghdad* [Georgian]. Tiblisi, 1967.

Ibn al-Firkāḥ, ʿAbd al-Raḥmān b. Sabaʿ. *K. bāʿith al-nufūs ilā ziyārat al-Quds al-mahrūs.* Edited by C. Matthews. In *JPOS* 15 (1935): 51–87.

Ibn Ḥawqal, Abū-l-Qāsim al-Naṣībī. *K. al-Masālik wa-l-mamālik.* Edited by M. J. De Goeje. BGA 2. Leiden, 1897.

Ibn Ḥazm, ʿAlī b. Aḥmad. *K. al-faṣl fi-l-milal.* Cairo, 1317/1903. Translated and annotated by I. Friedlander as "The Heterodoxies of the Shiites." *JAOS* 28 (1907): 1–80; 29 (1908): 1–83.

Ibn Hishām, ʿAbd al-Malik. *K. Sīrah Rasūl Allah.* Edited by T. ʿAbd al-Raʾūf. 4 vols. Beirut, n.d. Edited by F. Wüstenfeld. 3 vols. Göttingen, 1858–60/Frankfurt am Main, 1961. Translated by A. Guillaume as *The Life of Muḥammad.* London, 1955.

Ibn Iṣḥāq. *See* Ibn Hishām

Ibn al-Jawzī, ʿAbd al Raḥmān b. ʿAlī. *Manāqib Baghdād.* Edited by M. M. al-Atharī. Baghdad, 1923. Partially translated and annotated by G. Makdisi in *Arabica* 6 (1959): 185–95.

Ibn al-Jawzī, 'Abd al Raḥmān b. 'Alī. *al-Muntaẓam fī ta'rīkh al-mulūk wa-l-umam*. Edited by F. Krenkow. Vols. 5/2–10. Hyderabad, 1938–39.
Ibn Kathīr, Ismā'īl b. 'Umar. *Al-Bidāyah wa-l-nihāyah*. 14 vols. Cairo, 1351–59/1932–40.
Ibn Kathīr, Ismā'īl b. 'Umar. *Qiṣaṣ al-anbiyā'*. Beirut: Dār al-Qalam, 1405/1985; Beirut: Dār wa Maktabat al-Hilāl, 1405/1985.
Ibn Kathīr, Ismā'īl b. 'Umar. *Tafsīr al-Qur'ān al-'aẓīm*. 4 vols. Beirut, 1405/1984.
Ibn Khaldūn, 'Abd al-Raḥmān b. Muḥammad. *al-Muqaddimah*. Translated and annotated by F. Rosenthal. 3 vols. New York, 1958.
Ibn Khallikān, Aḥmad b. Muḥammad. *K. wafayāt al-a'yān wa anbā' abnā' al-zamān*. Cairo, 1881. Translated and partially annotated by M. G. DeSlane as *Ibn Khallikan's Biographical Dictionary*. 4 vols. Paris, 1843–71.
Ibn Khayyāṭ al-'Uṣfurī, Khalīfah. *Ta'rīkh*. Edited by A. al-'Umarī. 2 vols. Najaf, 1967.
Ibn Khurradādhbih, 'Ubaydallāh b. 'Abdallāh. *K. al-masālik wa-l-mamālik*. Edited by M. J. de Goeje. BGA 6. Leiden, 1889.
Ibn al-Murajjā, Abu-l-Ma'ālī al-Musharraf b. Raḥmān. *Faḍā'il Bayt al-Maqdis wa-l-Khalīl wa-l Shām*. Edited by O. Livne-Kafri. Shfaram, Israel, 1995; Beirut edition edited by Naṣr al-Dīn al-Azharī as *Faḍā'il Bayt al-Maqdis*. Beirut, 2004.
Ibn al-Nadīm, Muḥammad b. Isḥāq. *K. al-Fihrist*. Edited by G. Flügel. Leipzig, 1871–72.
Ibn Qutaybah, 'Abdallāh b. Muslim. *K. al-ma'ārif*. Edited by F. Wüstenfeld. Göttingen, 1850.
Ibn Qutaybah, 'Abdallāh b. Muslim. *'Uyūn al-akhbār*. 4 vols. Cairo, 1373/1953.
Ibn Rustah, Aḥmad b. 'Umar. *K. al-a'lāq al-nafīsah*. Edited by M. J. De Goeje. BGA 7. Leiden 1892.
Ibn Sa'd, Muḥammad. *K. al-ṭabaqāt al-kabīr*. Edited by E. Sachau et al. 9 vols. Leiden, 1905–40.
Ibn Serapion. *See* Suhrāb
Ibn Sulaymān, Muqātil. *Tafsīr*. 5 vols. Cairo, 1988.
Ibn Ṭabāṭabā, Muḥammad b. 'Alī. *al-Kitāb al-fakhrī fī-l-ādāb al-sulṭānīyah wa-l-duwal al-islāmīyat*. Beirut, 1386/1966. Edited by H. Derenbourg, Paris, 1895. Translated and annotated by E. Amar as *Histoire des dynasties musulmanes depuis la mort de Mahomet jusqu' a la chute du Khalifat 'Abbāside de Baghdadz*. Paris, 1910.
Ibn Taghrī Birdī, Jamāl al-Dīn, *Nujūm al-ẓāhirah fī Mulūk Miṣr wa-l-Qāhirah*. Edited by T. Juynboll and B. Matthes. 2 vols. Leiden, 1855–61.
Ibn Taymīyah, Taqī al-Dīn. *al-Tafsīr al-kubrā*. 7 vols. Beirut, 1401/1981.
Ibn al-Ṭiqṭaqā. *See* Ibn Ṭabāṭabā
Ibn al-Zubayr, al-Rashīd. *al-Dhakhā'ir wa-l-tuḥaf*. Edited by S. al-Munajjid. Beirut, 1959.
al-Iṣfahānī, 'Alī b. Husayn. *K. al-aghānī*. Vols. 1–20. Beirut, 1390/1970. Vol. 21. Edited by R. Brünnow. Leiden, 1888.
al-Iṣfahānī, 'Alī b. Husayn. *Maqātil al-Ṭālibiyīn*. Teheran, 1365/1946.
al-Iṣfahānī, Ḥamzah b. al-Ḥasan. *Tawārīkh sinī mulūk al-arḍ wa-al-anbiyā'*. Edited by J. M. E. Gottwald. 2 vols. Leipzig, 1844–48.
al-Iṣṭakhrī, Ibrāhīm b. Muḥammad. *K. al-Masālik wa-l-mamālik*. Edited by M. J. De Goeje. BGA 1. Leiden, 1870.
al-Jazā'irī, Ni'mat Allāh. *Qiṣaṣ al-anbiyā'*. Beirut, 1398/1978.
al-Khaṭīb al-Baghdādī, Aḥmad b. 'Alī. *Ta'rīkh Baghdād*. 14 vols. Cairo, 1931. Topograph-

ical introduction edited, translated, and annotated by G. Salmon as *L'introduction topographique à l'histoire de Baghdadh.* Paris, 1904. Translated and annotated by J. Lassner as *The Topography of Baghdad in the Early Middle Ages: Text and Studies.* Detroit, 1970.

al-Khūwārizmī, Muḥammad b. Mūsā [Aḥmad?]. *K. ṣūrat al-arḍ.* Edited by H. von Mžik. BAHG 3. Leipzig, 1926.

al-Kisā'ī, Muḥammad b. 'Abdallāh. *Qiṣaṣ al-anbiyā'.* Edited by I. Eisenberg. Leiden, 1922–23.

al-Maqdisī, al-Muṭahhar b. Ṭāhir. *K. al-bad' wa-l-ta'rīkh.* Edited by C. Huart (attributed to Aḥmad b. Sahl al-Balkhī). Paris, 1899–1919.

Marāṣid. See al-Baghdādī, 'Abd al-Mu'min

al-Mas'ūdī, 'Alī b. al-Ḥusayn. *K. al-tanbīh wa-l-ishrāf.* Edited by M. J. De Goeje. BGA 8. Leiden, 1894.

al-Mas'ūdī, 'Alī b. al-Ḥusayn. *Murūj al-dhahab wa ma'ādin al-jawāhir.* Edited by Y. A. Dāghir. 4 vols. Beirut, 1385/1965. Edited and translated by C. Barbier de Meynard and P. de Courteille as *Les prairies d'or.* 9 vols. Paris, 1861–77.

Midrash Aggadah. Edited by S. Buber. Vienna, 1894.

Midrash Ekha Rabbah. Edited by S. Buber. Wilno, 1887.

Midrash Exodus Rabbah, Midrash Numbers Rabbah. Edited by S. Buber. Wilno, 1887.

Midrash Rabbah [Genesis-Deuteronomy]. 11 vols. Edited by M. Mirkin. Tel Aviv, 1986.

Midreshei Geulah. Edited by Y. Even Shemuel. Jerusalem, 1954.

Miqraot Gedolot. 10 vols. New York, 1951.

al-Mubarrad, Muḥammad b. Yazīd. *al-Kāmil.* Edited by M. A. Ibrāhīm and S. Shahatah. 3 vols. Cairo, 1956.

al-Muqaddasī, Muḥammad b. Aḥmad. *K. aḥsan al-taqāsīm fī ma'rifat al-aqālīm.* Edited by M. J. De Goeje. BGA 3. Leiden, 1877.

Mujīr al-Dīn. *See* al-'Ulaymī

Muqātil. *See* Ibn Sulaymān

al-Musharraf b. al-Murajjā. *See* Ibn al-Murajjā

al-Nasafī, 'Abdallāh b. Aḥmad. *Tafsīr al-Qur'ān al-jalīl.* 4 vols. Cairo, 1343/1925.

al-Nasā'ī, Aḥmad b. Shu'ayb. *Tafsīr.* 2 vols. Cairo, 1410/1990.

Niẓām al-Mulk. *Siyāsat Nāmeh.* Edited and translated by C. Sheffer. Paris, 1893.

Otsar ha-Aggadah. Edited by M. Gross. Jerusalem, 1954.

Pseudo-Ibn Qutaybah. *al-Imāmah wa-l-siyāsah.* Edited by T. M. al-Zarīnī. 2 vols. in 1. [Cairo?], n.d.

Qazwīnī, Ḥamdallāh Mustawfī. *Nuzhat al-qulūb.* Edited by G. Le Strange. GMS 23, pt. 1. London 1915. Translated by G. Le Strange as *The Geographical Part of the Nuzhat al-Qulūb of Qazwīnī.* GMS 23, pt. 2. London, 1919.

al-Rāzī, Muḥammad b. 'Umar Fakhr al-Dīn. *al-Tafsīr al-kabīr (mafātīḥ al-ghayb).* 6 vols. Bulaq, 1287/1870–71. 16 vols. Beirut 1485/1985.

al-Sam'ānī, 'Abd al-Karīm b. Muḥammad. *K. al-Ansāb.* Edited by D. S. Margoliouth. GMS 20. London, 1912.

Suhrāb. *'Ajā'ib al-aqālīm al-sab'ah.* Edited by H. von Mžik. BAHG 5. Leipzig, 1930. The section on hydrography equals Ibn Serapion, *Description of Mesopotamia and Baghdad,* edited and translated by G. Le Strange (London, 1895; originally published in *JRAS* [1895]).

Sa'īd b. al-Biṭrīq. *See* Eutychius

al-Suyūṭī, Jalāl al-Dīn. *Tafsīr al-Jalālayn*. Damascus, 1385/1965.

Al-Suyūṭī, Muḥammad b. Shams al-Dīn. *Itḥāf al-akhiṣṣā bi-faḍā'il al-Masjid al-Aqṣā*. 2 vols. Cairo, 1982, 1985.

al-Ṭabarī, Muḥammad b. Jarīr. *Jāmi' al-bayān 'an ta'wīl al-Qur'ān*. 30 vols. Cairo, 1954–65.

al-Ṭabarī, Muḥammad b. Jarīr. *K. akhbār al-rusul wa-l-mulūk (Annales)*. Edited by M. J. De Goeje et al. 13 vols. Leiden, 1879–1901.

al-Ṭabarsī, al-Faḍl b. al-Ḥasan. *Majma' al-bayān fī 'ulūm al-Qur'ān*. 30 vols. Beirut, 1954–57.

al-Tanūkhī, Abū 'Alī al-Muḥassin b. 'Alī. *Nishwār al-muḥāḍarah wa akhbār al-mudhākarah*. Pt. 1: Edited and translated by D. S. Margoliouth as *The Table Talk of a Mesopotamian Judge*. Oriental Translation Fund, n.s., 27 and 28. London 1921. Pt. 2: text in *RAAD* 12 (1932); 13 (1933–35); 17 (1942); translation in *IC* 5 (1931): 169–93, 352–71, 559–81; 6 (1932): 47–66,184–205, 370–96. Pt. 3: text in *RAAD* 9 (1930); translation in *IC* 3 (1929): 490–522; 4 (1930): 1–28, 223–28, 363–88, 531–57.

Targum Sheni [to Esther]. In *Miqraot Gedolot* 6. Scientific edition by D. Moritz as *Das Targum Sheni zum Buche Esther*. Kraków, 1898. Edited by L. Munk as *Targum Scheni zum Buche Esther nebst Variae Lectiones nach hand-schriftlichen Quellen*. Berlin, 1876. Edited by A. Sulzbach as *Targum Sheni zum Buche Esther: Übersetzt und mit Anmerkungen versehen*. Frankfurt am Main, 1920. Translated and annotated by B. Grossfeld in *The Two Targums of Esther*, Collegeville, MN 1991, contains full bibliography of editions, translations, and secondary sources in the Introduction, 21–22. Grossfeld's edition is his *The Targum Sheni to the Book of Esther*. Sepher-Herman Press, New York, 1994.

Ta'rīkh al-khulafā'. P. A. Gryaznevich, Moscow, 1967. Facsimile reproduction.

al-Tha'labī, Aḥmad b. Muḥammad. *'Arā'is al-majālis*. Beirut, n.d.

Al-'Ulaymī, Mujīr al-Dīn 'Abd al-Raḥmān b. Muḥammad. *al-Uns al-jalīl bi-ta'rīkh al-Quds wa-l-Khalīl*. 2 vols. Cairo, 1283 AH/ 1866–67 CE.

al-Wāqidī. *K. al-Maghāzī*. Edited by M. Jones. Cairo, 1966.

al-Wāsiṭī, Muḥammad b. Aḥmad. *Faḍā'il al-Bayt al-Muqaddas*. Edited by I. Hasson. Jerusalem, 1979.

al-Ya'qūbī, Aḥmad b. Abī Ya'qūb. *K. al-buldān*. Edited by M. J. Goeje. BGA 7. Leiden, 1892. Translated and annotated by G. Wiet as *Les Pays*. PIFAO 1. Cairo, 1937.

al-Ya'qūbī, Aḥmad b. Abī Ya'qūb. *Ta'rīkh (Historiae)*. Edited by M. Th. Houtsma. 2 vols. Leiden, 1883.

Yāqūt, Ya'qub b. 'Abdallāh. *Irshād al-'arīb ila ma'rifat al-adīb (Mu'jam al-udabā')*. Edited by D. S. Margoliouth. GMS 6. London, 1907–31.

Yāqūt, Ya'qub b. 'Abdallāh. *Mu'jam al-buldān*. Edited by F. Wüstenfeld. 6 vols. Leipzig, 1866–73.

al-Zamakhsharī, Maḥmūd b. 'Umar. *al-Kashshāf fī ḥaqā'iq al-tanzīl wa 'uyūn al-aqāwīl fī wujūh al-ta'wīl*. Edited by W. N. Lees et al. Calcutta, 1856.

al-Zubayrī, Muṣ'ab b. 'Abdallāh. *K. nasab Quraysh*. Edited by A. Levi-Provencal. Cairo, 1953.

Secondary Sources

Abbot, N. *Quranic Commentary and Tradition*. Vol. 2 of *Studies in Arabic Literary Papyri*. OIP 76. Chicago, 1967.

Abbot, N. *The Kurrah Papyri from Aphrodito in the Oriental Institute*. Chicago, 1938.

Adams, R. M. *Land beyond Baghdad*. Chicago, 1965.

Adang, C. *Muslim Writers on Judaism and the Hebrew Bible*. Leiden, 1996.

Alexander, P. *The Byzantine Apocalyptic Tradition*. Berkeley, 1985.

Alexander, P. S. "Jerusalem as the Omphalos of the World: On the History of a Geographical Concept." In *Jerusalem*, edited by L. Levine, 104–19. New York, 1999.

al-ʿAlī, S. A. *Baghdad madīnat al-salām: inshāʾuha wa tanẓīm sukkānihā fī-l-ʿuhūd al-ʿAbbāsīyah al-ūlā*. 2 vols. Baghdad, 1985.

al-ʿAlī, S. A. "The Foundation of Baghdad." In *The Islamic City*, edited by A. H. Hourani and S. M. Stern, 87–101. Oxford, 1970.

al-ʿAlī, S. A. *Khiṭaṭ al-Baṣrah wa minṭaqatuhā: Dirāsah fī aḥwālihā al-ʿimrānīyah wa-l-malīyah fī ʿuhūd al-Islāmīyah al-ūlā*. Baghdad, 1986.

al-ʿAlī, S. A. "Minṭaqat al-Ḥīrah." *Majallat kullīyat al-ādāb* (Baghdad University) 5 (1962): 17–44.

al-ʿAlī, S. A. *al-Tanẓīmāt al-ijtimāʿīyah wa-l-iqtiṣādīyah fī-l-Baṣrah fī qarn al-awwal al-ḥijrī*. Baghdad, 1953.

Ali, Y., and A. Naji. "The Sūqs of Baṣrah: Commercial Organization and Activity in a Medieval Islamic City." *JESHO* 24 (1981): 298–309.

Ashtor, E. "L'administration urbaine en Syrie médiévale." *RSO* 31 (1956): 73–128.

Ashtor, E. "L'evolution des prix dans le Proche-Orient a la basse-époque." *JESHO* 4 (1961): 15–46.

Ashtor, E. *Histoire des prix et des salaires dans l'Orient médiéval*. Paris, 1969.

Ashtor, E. "Muslim and Christian Literature in Praise of Jerusalem." *Jerusalem Cathedra* 1 (1981): 187–89.

Ashtor, E. "L'urbanisme syrien a la basse-époque." *RSO* 33 (1958): 181–209.

Avni, G. "From Hagia Polis to al-Quds: The Byzantine Islamic Transition in Jerusalem." In *Unearthing Jerusalem*, edited by K. Galor and G. Avni, 387–416. Winona Lake, IN, 2011.

Ayoub, M. *The Qurʾān and Its Interpreters*. Vol. 1. Albany, 1984.

Azami, M. M. *Studies in Early Ḥadīth Literature*. Indianapolis, 1978.

Azami, M. M. *Studies in Ḥadīth Methodology and Literature*. Indianapolis, 1977.

Azmeh, A. *Ibn Khaldun*. New York, 1990.

Azmeh, A. *Ibn Khaldun in Modern Scholarship: A Study in Modern Orientalism*. London, 1980.

Baer, F. "Eine jüdische Messiasprophetie auf das Jahr 1186 und der dritte Kreuzzug." *MGWJ* 70 (1926): 113–22, 155–65.

Bahat, D. *Carta's Historical Atlas of Jerusalem*. Jerusalem, 1973.

Bahat, D. *The Illustrated Atlas of Jerusalem*. Jerusalem, 1996.

al-Bakhit, M. A., ed. *Proceedings of the Second Symposium on the History of Bilād al-Shām during the Early Islamic Period*. 2 vols. Amman, 1987.

Baldovin, J. *The Urban Character of Christian Worship*. Rome, 1987.

Baneth, D. H. "What Did Muḥammad Mean When He Called His Religion Islām? The Original Meaning of *Aslama* and Its Derivatives." *IOS* 1 (1971): 183–90.

al-Bāqī, A. *Sāmarrā: ʿĀṣimat al-dawlat al-ʿArabīyah fī ʿahd al-ʿAbbāsīyah*. Baghdad, 1989.

Baras, Z., ed. *Meshihiyut ve-Esketalogyah*. Jerusalem, 1983.

Barkay, G. "The Divine Name Found in Jerusalem." *BAR* 9 (1983): 14–19.

Barukh, Y., and R. Reich. "Renewed Excavations at the Umayyad Building III [Hebrew]." *New Studies on Jerusalem* 5 (1997): 128–40.

Barukh, Y., and R. Reich. "The Umayyad Buildings Near the Temple Mount. Reconstruction in Light of Recent Excavation [Hebrew]." *New Studies on Jerusalem* 8 (2002): 121–32.

Bashear, S. "Qurʾān 2:114 and Jerusalem." *BSOAS* 52 (1989): 215–38.

Bashear, S. *Studies in Early Islamic Tradition*. Jerusalem, 2004.

Becker, C. H. "Arabische Papyri des Apphroditofundes." *ZA* 20 (1906): 68–104.

Becker, C. H. "The Expansion of the Saracens—the East." In the *Cambridge Medieval History*, 2:329–89. Last reprint with corrections, Cambridge, 1987.

Becker, C. H. *Islamstudien*. Leipzig, 1924–32.

Beckwith, C. "The Plan of the City of Peace: Central Iranian Factors in Early Abbasid Design." *AO* 38 (1984): 143–64.

Bell, R. *A Commentary on the Qurʾān*. Edited by C. E. Bosworth and M. E. J. Richardson. 2 vols. *JSS* Monograph 14 (1991).

Bell, R., and W. M. Watt. *Introduction to the Qurʾān*. Edinburgh, 1970.

Bell, R. *The Origin of Islam in Its Christian Environment*. London, 1926.

Bell, R. *The Qurʾān*. 2 vols. Edinburgh, 1937.

Beltz, W. "Über den Ur-Qurʾān." *Zeitschrift für Religions- und Geistgeschichte* 27 (1975): 169–71.

Ben-Dov, M. "Building Techniques in the Omayyad Palace Near the Temple Mount in Jerusalem [Hebrew]." *Eretz Israel* 11 (1973): 75–91.

Ben-Dov, M. *The Historical Atlas of Jerusalem*. New York, 2002.

Ben-Dov, M. *In the Shadow of the Temple*. New York, 1985.

Ben-Dov, M. "The Omayyad Structures Near the Temple Mount [Hebrew]." *Eretz Israel* 10 (1971): 35–40.

Bitton-Ashkenazi, B. "The Attitudes of the Church Fathers towards Pilgrimage to Jerusalem in the Fourth and Fifth Centuries." In *Jerusalem,* edited by L. Levine, 188–203. New York, 1999.

Blachere, R. *Introduction au Coran*. Paris, 1947.

Blair, S. "What Is the Date of the Dome of the Rock?" *OSIA* 9/1 (1992): 59–88.

Bligh-Abramski, I. "Evolution versus Revolution: Umayyad Elements in the ʿAbbāsid Regime 133/750–320/932." *Der Islam* 65 (1988): 226–43.

Bonner, M., ed. *Arab Byzantine Relations in Early Islamic Times*. Aldershot, 2000.

Bonner, M. *Aristocratic Violence and Holy War*. New Haven, 1996.

Bonner, M. "Jalāʾil and Holy War in Early Islam." *Der Islam* 68 (1991): 45–64.

Bonner, M. *Jihād in Islamic History*. Princeton, 2006.

Bonner, M. "The Naming of the Frontier: ʿAwāṣim, Thughūr, and the Arab Geographers." *BSOAS* 57 (1994): 17–24.

Bonner, M. "Some Observations Concerning the Early Development of Jihād along the Arab-Byzantine Frontier." *SI* 76 (1992): 5–31.

Bowker, J. "Intercession in the Qur'ān and the Jewish Tradition." *JSS* 4 (1968): 183–202.

Bowman, J. "Banū Isrā'īl in the Qur'ān." *IS* 2 (1963): 447–55.

Bravmann, M. *The Spiritual Background of Early Islam*. Leiden, 1972.

Brett, G. "The Automata in the Byzantine Throne of Solomon." *Speculum* 29 (1954): 477–87.

Brockelmann, C. *Geschichte der arabischen Literattur.* 2 vols. and 3 supplemental vols. Leiden, 1937–49.

Brown, L. Carl, ed. *From Medina to Metropolis: Heritage and Change in the Near Eastern City.* Princeton, 1973.

Brunschvig, R. "Urbanisme médiéval et droit musulman." *REI* 15 (1947): 127–55.

Bukharin, M. "Mecca and the Caravan Routes in Pre-Islamic Arabia." In *The Qur'ān in Context,* edited by A. Neuwirth et al., 115–34. Boston, 2011.

Bulliet, R. *Conversion to Islam in the Medieval Period.* Cambridge, MA, 1979.

Burton, J. *The Collection of the Qur'ān.* Cambridge, 1977.

Busse, H. "*Bab Ḥiṭṭa*: Qur'ān 2:58 and the Entry into Jerusalem." *JSAI* 22 (1998): 1–17.

Busse, H. "The Destruction of the Temple in Jerusalem and Its Reconstruction in Light of Sūra 17:2–8." *JSAI* 20 (1996): 1–17.

Busse, H. "'Omar b. al-Ḫaṭṭāb in Jerusalem." *JSAI* 5 (1984): 73–119.

Busse, H. "'Omar's Image as Conqueror of Jerusalem." *JSAI* 8 (1986): 149–68.

Busse, H. "The Sanctity of Jerusalem in Islam." *Judaism* 17 (1968): 441–68.

Busse, H. "The Tower of David / *Miḥrāb Dāwūd*: Remarks on the History of a Sanctuary in Jerusalem in Christian and Islamic Times." *JSAI* 17 (1994): 108–41.

Cameron, A., and L. Conrad, eds., *The Byzantine and Early Islamic Near East: Papers of the First Workshop on Late Antiquity and Early Islam*. Princeton, 1992.

Cameron, A., and G. D. R. King, eds. *The Byzantine and Early Islamic Near East: Papers of the Second Workshop on Late Antiquity and Early Islam*. Princeton, 1995.

Cassel, P. *An Explanatory Commentary on Esther.* Edinburgh, 1888.

Cassel, P. *Zweites Targum zum Buche Esther.* Leipzig, 1885.

Chabbi, J. "Histoire et tradition sacrée: La biographie impossible de Mahomet." *Arabica* 43 (1996): 189–205.

Cohen, M. "Islam and the Jews: Myth, Counter-myth, History." *Jerusalem Quarterly* 38 (1986): 125–37.

Cohen, M. *Under Crescent and Cross.* Princeton, 1993.

Conrad, L. "Abraham and Muḥammad: Some Observations Apropos of Chronology and Literary Topois in Early Arabic Historical Tradition." *BSOAS* 50 (1987): 225–40.

Conrad, L. *History and Historiography in Early Islamic Times.* Princeton, 1994.

Cook, D. "Muslim Apocalyptic and *Jihād*." *JSAI* 20 (1996): 66–104.

Cook, M. *Early Muslim Dogma*: *A Source Critical Study*. Cambridge, 1981.

Cook, M. "Eschatology and the Dating of Traditions." *Princeton Papers in Near Eastern Studies* 1 (1992): 23–47.

Cook, M. "The Heraclian Dynasty in Muslim Eschatology." *Al-Qanṭara* 13 (1992): 3–23.

Cook, M., and P. Crone. *Hagarism.* Cambridge, 1977.

Creswell, K. A. C. *Early Muslim Architecture.* 2 vols. Oxford, 1940. 2nd edition. Vol. 1 in 2 parts. Oxford, 1969.

Crone, P. *Meccan Trade and the Rise of Islam.* Oxford, 1987.

Crone, P. *Slaves on Horses*. Cambridge, 1977.

Crone, P., and M. Hinds. *God's Caliph*. Cambridge, 1986.

de Planhol, X. "The Geographical Setting." In *Cambridge History of Islam*, edited by A. Lambton et al., 1:443–69. Cambridge, 1970.

de Planhol, X. *The World of Islam*. Ithaca, 1959.

Dixon, 'A. A. 'A. *The Umayyad Caliphate, 65–86/684–705*. London, 1971.

Djait, H. *Al-Kufa: Naissance de la ville islamique*. Paris, 1986.

Donner, F. *The Early Islamic Conquests*. Princeton, 1981.

Donner, F. *Narratives of Islamic Origins: The Beginning of Arabic Historical Writing*. Princeton, 1998.

Donner, F. "The Origins of the Islamic State." *JAOS* 106 (1986): 283–96.

Drijvers, H. "The Gospel of the Twelve Apostles: A Syriac Apocalypse from the Early Islamic Period." In *The Byzantine and Early Islamic Near East: Papers of the First Workshop on Late Antiquity and Early Islam*, edited by A. Cameron and L. Conrad, 189–213. Princeton, 1992.

Duri, 'A. 'A. *Baḥth fī nash'at 'ilm al-ta'rīkh 'ind al-'Arab*. Beirut, 1960. Translated with expanded bibliography and footnotes by L. Conrad as A. A. Duri. *The Rise of Historical Writing among the Arabs*. Princeton, 1983.

Duri, 'A. 'A. "The Iraq School of History to the Ninth Century—a Sketch." In *Historians of the Middle East*, edited by B. Lewis and P. Holt, 46–53. London, 1962.

Duri, 'A. 'A. *The Historical Formation of the Arab Nation: A Study in Identity and Consciousness*. Translated from Arabic by L. Conrad. London, 1987. Originally published as *al-Takwīn al-ta'rīkhī li-l-ummah al-'arabīyah*. Beirut, 1984.

Elad, A. *Medieval Jerusalem and Islamic Worship*. Leiden, 1995.

Elad, A. "Why Did 'Abd al-Malik Build the Dome of the Rock? A Re-examination of the Muslim Sources." *OSIA* 9/1 (1992): 33–58.

Ephal, I. *The Ancient Arabs*. Jerusalem, 1982.

Even Shemuel, Y. *Midreshei Geulah*. Jerusalem, 1944.

Fahd, T. "The Dream in Medieval Islamic Society." In *The Dream and Human Societies*, edited by G. von Grunebaum. Berkeley, 1966.

Faruqi, N. *Early Muslim Historiography*. Delhi, 1979.

Firestone, R. *Jihād*. Oxford, 1999.

Firestone, R. *Journeys in Holy Lands*. Albany, 1990.

Fishbein, M. *Inner Biblical Exegesis*. Oxford, 1985.

Fowden, G. *Quṣayr 'Amra: Art and the Umayyad Elite in Antique Syria*. Berkeley, 2004.

Fraenkel, S. *Die armäischen Fremdwörter im Arabischen*. Leiden, 1886.

Friedlander, I. "Jewish-Arabic Studies." *JQR*, n.s., 1 (1910–11): 183–215; 2 (1911–12): 481–516; 3 (1912–13): 235–300.

Fritsch, E. *Islam und Christentum im Mittelalter*. Breslau, 1930.

Fück, J. *Muhammad ibn Ishaq*. Frankfurt am Main, 1925.

Gafni, I. "Reinterment in the Land of Israel: Notes on the Origin and Development of the Custom." *Jerusalem Cathedra* 1 (1981): 96–104.

Galor, K., and G. Avni, eds. *Unearthing Jerusalem*. Winona Lake, IN, 2011.

Geiger, A. *Was hat Mohammed aus dem Judenthume aufgenommen?* Bonn, 1833. Translated by F. M. Young as *Judaism in Islam*. Madras, 1898.

Gelbhaus, S. *Das Targum Scheni zum Buche Esther*. Frankfurt am Main, 1893.

Gil, M. *Be-Malchut Yishmaeil be-Tekufat ha-Geonim*. 4 vols. Tel Aviv, 1997. Vol. 1 translated into English by D. Srassler as *Jews in Islamic Countries in the Middle Ages*. Leiden, 2004.

Gil, M. *Erets Yisrael ba-Tekufah ha-Muslimit ha-Rishonah*. 3 vols. Jerusalem, 1983. Volume 1 translated into English by E. Broido as *A History of Palestine, 634–1099*. Cambridge, 1992.

Gilliot, C. "Coran 17, isrā' dans la recherche occidantale: De la critique des traditions au Coran comme texte." In *Le Voyage initiatique en terre d'Islam: Ascensions célestes et itineraires spirituels*, edited by M. A. Moezzi, 1–26. Louvain, 1996.

Gilliot, C. "Les informateurs Juifs et Chrétiens de Muḥammad." *JSAI* 23 (1988): 84–126.

Ginzberg, L. *The Legends of the Jews*. 7 vols. New York, 1928.

Goitein, S. D. "Benei Yisrael u-Mahloktam." *Tarbiz* 3 (1932): 410–22.

Goitein, S. D. "Did Omar Prohibit the Stay of Jews in Jerusalem [Hebrew]." In *Palestinian Jewry in Early and Islamic and Crusader Times in Light of the Geniza Documents*, edited by J. Hacker, 36–41. Jerusalem, 1980.

Goitein, S. D. *Ha-Islam shel Muḥammad*. Jerusalem, n.d.

Goitein, S. D. "The Historical Background of the Erection of the Dome of the Rock." *JAOS* 70 (1950): 104–8. Expanded as "The Sanctity of Jerusalem and Palestine" in his *Studies*, 135–48.

Goitein, S. D. "Isra'iliyat [Hebrew]." *Tarbiz* 6 (1936): 89–101.

Goitein, S. D. *A Mediterranean Society*. 6 vols. Berkeley, 1967–93. (The cumulative indices in vol. 6 were arranged by P. Sanders following Goitein's death.)

Goitein, S. D. "Messianic Troubles in Baghdad." In *Essential Papers on Messianic Movements and Personalities in Jewish History*, ed. M. Saperstein, 189–201. New York, 1992.

Goitein, S. D. *Minhah li-Yehudah*. Jerusalem, 1950.

Goitein, S. D. "The Origin and Nature of the Muslim Friday Worship." *MW* 50 (1960): 23–29. Reprinted in his *Studies*, 126–34.

Goitein, S. D. "Prayer in Islam." Reprinted in his *Studies*, 73–89.

Goitein, S. D., ed. *Religion in a Religious Age*. Cambridge, MA, 1974.

Goitein, S. D. "Sanctity of Jerusalem and Palestine." In his *Studies*, 135–48.

Goitein, S. D. "The Spiritual World of Eastern Judaism at the Time of Its Efflorescence [Hebrew]." *Yedion Yad Ben Zvi* 2 (1973): 13–20.

Goitein, S. D. *Studies in Islamic History and Institutions*. Leiden, 1966.

Goitein, S. D. "Who Were Muḥammad's Notable Teachers [Hebrew]." *Tarbiz* 23 (1953): 146–59.

Goldziher, I. *Muhammedanische Studien*. 2 vols. Halle, 1895–90. Translated into French by L. Bercher as *Études sur la tradition islamique*. Paris, 1952. Translated into English and annotated by C. R. Barber and S. M. Stern as *Muslim Studies*. 2 vols. Chicago, 1966 (1) and London, 1971 (2).

Goldziher, I. *Oriental Diary*, edited and translated by R. Patai in *Ignaz Goldziher and His Oriental Diary*. Detroit, 1987.

Goldziher, I. *Tagebuch*. Edited by S. Scheiber. Leiden, 1978.

Goldziher, I. "Über muḥammedanische Polemik gegen Ahl al-Kitāb." *ZDMG* 32 (1878): 341–87.

Goldziher, I. *Vorlesungen über den Islam*. Translated into English with additional annotation by A. Hamori and R. Hamori as *Introduction to Islamic Theology and Law*. Princeton, 1981.

Gottheil, R. "A Christian Baḥīrā Legend." *ZA* 13 (1898): 189–242; 14 (1989) 203–68; 15 (1900): 56–102; 17 (1903): 125–66.

Grabar, A. "Le Success des arts orientaux a la cour byzantine sous les Macedoniens." *Münchner Jahrbuch der bildenen Kunst*, 3rd ser. (1951): 56.

Grabar, O. "The Architecture of the Middle Eastern City from Past to Present: The Case of the Mosque." In *Middle Eastern Cities*, edited by I. M. Lapidus, 26–46. Berkeley, 1969.

Grabar, O. *Constructing the Study of Islamic Art*. 4 vols. Aldershot, 2005. (Reprint of several of his collected studies.)

Grabar, O. "Ceremonial Art at the Umayyad Court." Ph.D. diss., Princeton University, 1955.

Grabar, O. *Jerusalem*. Vol. 4 of his collected studies, *Constructing the Study of Islamic Art*.

Grabar, O. "The Meaning of the Dome of the Rock in Jerusalem." In his collected essays *Jerusalem*, 143–58.

Grabar, O. "Al-Mushatta Baghdād and Wāsiṭ." In *The World of Islam: Studies in Honor of P. K. Hitti*, edited by J. Kritzek and R. B. Winder, 99–108. New York, 1959.

Graff, C. *Geschichte der christlichen-arabishen Literatur*. 5 vols. Vatican City, 1940–53.

Grayson, A. K. "History and Historians of the Ancient Near East: Assyria and Babylonia." *Orientalia*, n.s., 49 (1980): 140–94.

Griffith, S. *The Church in the Shadow of the Mosque*. Princeton, 1908. (Bibliography contains an extensive list of Griffith's important studies.)

Griffith, S. "Jews and Muslims in Christian Syriac and Arabic Texts of the Ninth Century." *Jewish History* 3 (1988): 65–94.

Griffith, S. "The Monk in the Emir's *Majlis*: Reflections on a Popular Genre of Christian Literary Apologetics in Arabic in the Early Islamic Period." In *The Majlis: Interreligious Encounters in the Early Islamic Period*, edited by H. Lazarus-Yafeh et al., 13–65. Wiesbaden, 1999.

Griffith, S. "Muḥammad and the Monk Baḥīrā: Reflections on a Syriac and Arabic Text from Early Abbasid Times." *Oriens Christianus* 79 (1995): 146–74.

Grohmann, A. *Einführung und Chrestomathie zur arabischen Papyruskunde*. Prague, 1955.

Grossfeld, B. *The Targum Sheni to the Book of Esther*. New York, 1994.

Grossfeld, B. *The Two Targums to Esther*. Collegeville, 1991.

Gruber, E. *Verdienst und Rang: Die Faḍā'il als literarisches und gesellschaftliches Problem im Islam*. Frieburg im Brisgau, 1975.

Guillaume, W. "A Note on the Sira of Ibn Isḥāq." *BSOAS* 18 (1956): 1–4.

Guillaume, W. *The Life of Muḥammad*. London, 1955. Trans. of Ibn Iṣḥāq's *Sīrah*.

Guillaume, W. "Where Was the Masjid al-Aqṣā?" *A1-Andalus* 18 (1953): 323–36.

Guttman, J. *Archeological Fact and Medieval Tradition in Christian, Islamic, and Jewish Art*. Missoula, 1976.

Hamilton, R. W. *Khirbet al-Mafjar: An Arabian Mansion in the Jordan Valley*. Oxford, 1959.

Hamilton, R. W. "Khirbet al-Mafjar: The Bath Hall Reconsidered." *Levant* 10 (1978): 124–38.

Hamilton, R. W. "Who Built Khirbet al-Mafjar?" *Levant* 1 (1969): 61–67.
Haneda, M., and T. Miura, eds. *Islamic Urban Studies.* New York, 1994.
Hasson, I. "Muslim Literature in Praise of Jerusalem." *Jerusalem Cathedra* 1 (1981): 168–84.
Hawting, G. R. *The First Dynasty of Islam.* London, 1986.
Hayman, P. "Monotheism—a Misused Word in Jewish Studies." *JJS* 42 (1990): 1–16.
Heller, B. "Récits et personnages bibliques dans la légende mahometane." *REJ* 85 (1928): 113–36.
Herzfeld, E. *Die Ausgrabungen von Samarra.* 8 vols. Berlin, 1921–48.
Herzfeld, E. *Erster vorlaufiger Bericht über die Ausgrabungen von Samarra.* Berlin, 1912.
Herzfeld, E. "Die Genesis der islamischen Kunst und das Mshatta-Problem." *Der Islam* 1 (1910): 60–63.
Herzfeld, E. *Geschichte der Stadt Samarra.* Vol. 6 of *Ausgrabungen.* Berlin, 1948.
Herzfeld, E. "Mitteilungen über die Arbeiten der zweiten Kampagne von Samarra." *Der Islam* 5 (1914): 196–204.
Herzfeld, E. *Samarra, Aufnahmen und Untersuchungen zur islamischen Archäologie.* Berlin, 1907.
Herzfeld, E., and F. Sarre. *Archäologische Reise im Euphrat und Tigris Gebiet.* 4 vols. Berlin, 1911–20.
Hillebrand, R. "La Dolce Vita in Early Islamic Syria: The Evidence of Later Umayyad Palaces." *Art History* 5 (1982): 1–35.
Hinds, M. "Kufan Political Alignments and Their Backgrounds in the Mid-7th Century A.D." *IJMES* 2 (1971): 346–67.
Hirschberg, H. Z. *Jüdische und christliche Lehren im vor- und frühislamischen Arabien.* Kraków, 1939.
Hirschberg, H. Z. *Yisrael ba-'Arav.* Tel Aviv, 1946.
Hirschfeld, H. *Beiträge zur Erklärung des Koran.* Leipzig, 1886.
Hirschfeld, H. "Historical and Legendary Controversies between Muḥammad and the Rabbis." *JQR* 10 (1897–98): 100–116.
Hirschfeld, H. *Jüdische Elemente im Koran.* Berlin, 1878.
Hodgson, M. "How Did the Early Shī'a Become Sectarian?" *JAOS* 75 (1955): 1–13.
Horovitz, J. "The Earliest Biographies of the Prophet and Their Authors." *IC* 2 (1928): 22–50, 164–82, 492–526.
Horovitz, J. "Jewish Proper Names and Their Derivatives in the Koran." *HUCA* 2 (1925): 145–227. Reprinted as a separate monograph with cross-pagination. Hildesheim, 1964.
Horovitz, J. *Koranische Untersuchungen.* Berlin, 1926.
Horovitz, J. "Muhammeds Himmelfahrt." *Der Islam* 9 (1918): 159–83.
Hourani, A. H. "The Islamic City in Light of Recent Research." In *The Islamic City,* edited by A. H. Hourani and S. M. Stern, 9–14. Oxford, 1970.
Hourani, A. H., and S. M. Stern, eds. *The Islamic City.* Oxford, 1970.
Humphreys, R. S. "Qur'ānic Myth and Narrative Structure in Early Islamic Historiography." In *Tradition and Innovation in Late Antiquity,* edited by F. Clover and R. S. Humphreys, 271–90. Madison, 1988.
Jacobs, I. "Elements of Near Eastern Mythology in Rabbinic Aggadah." *JJS* 28 (1977): 1–11.

Jawād, M., and A. Sūsah. *Baghdād.* Baghdad, 1969.
Jeffery, A. *The Foreign Vocabulary of the Qur'an.* Baroda, 1938.
Jeffery, A., ed. *Materials for the History of the Text of the Qur'an.* Leiden, 1937. Index, Leiden, 1951.
Juynboll, G. H. A. *Authenticity of Tradition Literature.* Leiden, 1969.
Juynboll, G. H. A., ed. *Studies on the First Century of Islamic Society.* Carbondale, 1982.
Juynboll, T. W. *Handbuch des islamischen Gesetzes.* Leiden, 1910.
Kaegi, W. *Byzantium and the Early Islamic Conquests.* Cambridge, 1992.
Kaegi, W. "Initial Byzantine Reactions to the Arab Invasions." *Church History* 10 (1969): 139–49.
Kahle, P. "Arabic Readers of the Qur'ān." *JNES* 8 (1949): 65–71.
Katsh, A. *Judaism in Islam.* New York, 1980.
Katzenelbogen, I. "The Seventy Names of Jerusalem [Hebrew]." *Sinai* 16 (1995): 141–59.
Kennedy, H. *The Early Abbasid Caliphate.* London, 1981.
Kennedy, H. *Prophet and the Age of the Caliphates.* New York, 1986.
Kessler, C. "'Abd al-Malik's Inscription in the Dome of the Rock: A Reconsideration." *JRAS* (1970): 2–14.
Khalidi, T. *Arabic Historical Thought in the Classical Period.* Cambridge, 1994.
Khoury, N. N. "The Dome of the Rock, the Ka'ba, and Ghumdān: Arab Myths and Umayyad Monuments." *Muqarnas* 10 (1993): 57–65.
Khoury, R. G. *Wahb b. Munabbih.* Wiesbaden, 1972.
Kister, M. "The Battle of Ḥarra, Some Socio-economic Aspects." In *Studies in Memory of Gaston Wiet*, edited by M. Rosen-Ayalon, 33–49. Jerusalem, 1997.
Kister, M. "A Comment on the Traditions Praising Jerusalem." *Jerusalem Cathedra* 1 (1981): 185–86.
Kister, M. *Concepts and Ideas at the Dawn of Islam.* London, 1997.
Kister, M. "Ḥaddithū 'an bānī Isrā'īla wa-la-ḥaraja." *IOS* 2 (1972): 215–39.
Kister, M. "The Interpretation of Dreams." *IOS* 4 (1974): 67–103.
Kister, M. "Mecca and the Tribes of Arabia." In *Studies in Honor of David Ayalon*, edited by M. Sharon, 33–57. Leiden, 1986.
Kister, M. "On 'Concessions' and Conduct: A Study in Early *Ḥadīth*." In his *Society and Religion in Early Islam*. Study 13, 1–37. Additional Notes, 1–9.
Kister, M. "Sanctity Joint and Divided: On Holy Places in Islamic Tradition." *JSAI* 20 (1996): 18–65.
Kister, M. *Society and Religion from Jāhiliyya to Islam.* London, 1990.
Kister, M. *Studies in Jāhiliyya and Early Islam.* London, 1980.
Kister, M. "'You Shall Set Out Only for Three Mosques"—a Study of an Early Tradition." *Le Muséon* 82 (1969): 173–96.
Kritzeck, J., and R. B. Winder, eds. *The World of Islam: Studies in Honor of P. K. Hitti.* New York, 1959.
al-Kubaysī, H. *Aswāq Baghdād ḥatta bidāyat al-'aṣr al-Buwayhī.* Baghdad, 1979.
Küchler, M. "Moschee in Kalifenpaläste Jerusalems nach den Aphrodito-Papayri." *ZDVP* 107 (1991): 120–43.
Lambton, A., et al., eds. *Cambridge History of Islam.* 2 vols. Cambridge, 1970.
Lammens, H. *La Mecque a la veille de l'hégire.* Beirut, 1924.

Lammens, H. "La republique marchande de la Mecque vers l'an 600 de notre ére." *BIE,* 5th ser., 4 (1910): 23–54.

Landau-Tesseron, E. "Sayf b. 'Umar in Medieval and Modern Scholarship." *Der Islam* 67 (1950): 1–26.

Lapidus, I. M. "Muslim Cities and Islamic Societies." In his edited work *Middle Eastern Cities*, 47–79.

Lapidus, I. M., ed. *Middle Eastern Cities.* Berkeley, 1969.

Lassner, J. "The Caliph's Personal Domain: The City Plan of Baghdad Reexamined." In *The Islamic City.* edited by A. H. Hourani and S. M. Stern, 103–18. Oxford, 1970.

Lassner, J. "The Covenant of the Prophets: Muslim Text, Jewish Subtext." *AJSR* 15 (1990): 207–38.

Lassner, J. *Demonizing the Queen of Sheba.* Chicago, 1993.

Lassner, J. *Islamic Revolution and Historical Memory.* AOS 66. New Haven, 1986.

Lassner, J. "Massignon and Baghdad: The Complexities of Growth in an Imperial City." *JESHO* 9 (1966): 1–27.

Lassner, J. "Municipal Entities and Mosques: More on the Imperial City." *JESHO* 10 (1967): 53–63.

Lassner, J. "Notes on the Topography of Baghdad: The Systematic Description of the City and the Khaṭīb. al-Baghdādī." *JAOS* 83 (1963): 458–69.

Lassner, J. "The 'One Who Had Knowledge of the Book' and the Mightiest Name of God: Qur'ānic Exegesis and Jewish Cultural Artifacts." *Studies in Jewish-Muslim Relations* 1 (1993): 59–74.

Lassner, J. "The Origins of Muslim Attitudes towards Jews and Judaism." *Judaism* 39 (1990): 498–507.

Lassner, J. *The Shaping of 'Abbāsid Rule.* Princeton, 1980.

Lassner, J. "Some Speculative Thoughts on the Search for an 'Abbāsid Capital." *MW* 55 (1965): 135–41, 203–10.

Lassner, J. *The Topography of Baghdad in the Early Middle Ages: Text and Studies.* Detroit, 1970.

Lassner, J. "Why Did the Caliph al-Manṣūr Build ar-Ruṣāfah—a Historical Note." *JNES* 24 (1965): 95–99.

Lazarus-Yafeh, H. *Intertwined Worlds: Medieval Islam and Biblical Criticism.* Princeton, 1992.

Lazarus-Yafeh, H. *Some Religious Aspects of Islam.* Leiden, 1981.

Leder, S. "The Literary Use of the *Khabar:* A Basic Form of Historical Writing." In *The Byzantine and Early Islamic Near East: Papers of the First Workshop on Late Antiquity and Early Islam*, edited by A. Cameron and L. Conrad, 277–316. Princeton, 1992.

Le Strange, G. *Baghdad during the Abbasid Caliphate.* London, 1900.

Le Strange, G. "Description of Mesopotamia and Baghdad." *JRAS* (1895): 14–26.

Le Strange, G. *Lands of the Eastern Caliphate.* Cambridge, 1905.

Le Strange, G. *Palestine under the Moslems.* London, 1890.

Levine, L., ed. *Jerusalem.* New York, 1999.

Levy-Rubin, M. *Non-Muslims in the Early Islamic Empire.* New York, 2011.

Lewis, B. "An Apocalyptic Vision of Islamic History." *BSOAS* 13 (1950): 308–38.

Lewis, B. *History—Remembered, Recovered, Invented.* Princeton, 1975.

Lewis, B. *Islam in History.* London, 1973.

Lewis, B. *The Jews of Islam.* Princeton, 1984.

Lewis, B. *Semites and Anti-Semites.* New York, 1986.

Lewis, B., and P. Holt, eds. *Historians of the Middle East.* London, 1962.

Lieberman, S. *Tosefta ke-Fishutah.* Vols. 1–8 New York, 1955–73. Vols. 9–10 Jerusalem, 1988.

Livne-Kafri, O. "Early Muslim Ascetics and the World of Christian Monasticism." *JSAI* 20 (1996): 105–29.

Livne-Kafri, O. "Islamic Traditions on Jerusalem between Judaism and Christianity [Hebrew]." *Cathedra* 83 (1997): 45–54 = his *Jerusalem in Early Islam*, 7–16.

Livne-Kafri, O. *Jerusalem in Early Islam* [Hebrew]. Jerusalem, 2000.

Livne-Kafri, O. "Jerusalem in Muslim Traditions of the End of Days [Hebrew]." *Cathedra* 62 (1986): 27–50 = his *Jerusalem in Early Islam*, 78–109.

Livne-Kafri, O. "Jerusalem—Navel of the Earth in Muslim Tradition [Hebrew]." *Cathedra* 69 (1993): 79–105. English version in *Der Islam* 84 (2007).

Livne-Kafri, O. "A Note on Some Traditions of Faḍā'il al-Quds." *JSAI* 14 (1991): 71–83.

Livne-Kafri, O. "Prayers in a Jerusalem Guide for Muslim Pilgrims [Hebrew]." *Cathedra* 66 (1992): 51–60 = his *Jerusalem in Early Islam*, 124–28.

Livne-Kafri, O. "The Sanctity of Jerusalem in Islam [Hebrew]." Ph.D. diss., Hebrew University, Jerusalem, 1985.

L'Orange, H. P. *Studies in the Iconography of Cosmic Kingship in the Ancient Near Eastern World.* Cambridge, 1953.

Maas, M. *Bibel und Koran.* Leipzig, 1893.

Madelung, W. "Apocalyptic Prophecies in Ḥims in the Umayyad Age." *JSS* 31(1986): 141–85.

Mango, C. "The Temple Mount AD 614–638," *OSIA* 9/1 (1992): 1–16.

Marçais, G. "La conception des villes dans l'Islam." *Revue d'Alger* 2 (1945): 517–33.

Marçais, G. "Consideration sur les villes musulmanes et notament sur le role du mohtasib." *La Ville: Recueil de la Société Jean Bodin* 6 (1954): 245–62.

Marçais, W. "L'islamisme et la vie urbaine." *Comptes Rendus, Academie des Inscriptions et Belles Lettres* (1928): 86–100.

Margoliouth, D. S. *Lectures on Arabian Historians.* Oxford, 1930.

Massignon, L. "Explication du plan de Basrah." In *Westöstliche Abhandlungen R. Tschudi*, edited by F. Meier, 154–74. Wiesbaden, 1954.

Massignon, L. "Explication du plan de Kufa." In his *Opera Minora*, edited by Y. Moubarac, 3:35–60. Beirut, 1963.

Masson, D. *Monotheisme coranique et monothéisme biblique.* Paris, 1976.

Matthews, C. "A Muslim Iconoclast (Ibn Taymīyah) on the Merits of Jerusalem." *JAOS* 56 (1936): 1–21.

Mayer, T., and S. Mourad, eds. *Jerusalem, Ideal and Reality*. New York, 2008.

Mazar, B. "The Era of David and Solomon." *WHJP*, 4.1:76–79.

Mazar, E. *The Complete Guide to the Temple Mount Excavations.* Jerusalem, 2000.

Mazar, E. "The 'Jewish Beth Ha-Menorot' in the Temple Mount Excavations in Jerusalem [Hebrew]." In *New Studies on Jerusalem: Proceedings of the Fourth Conference*, edited by E. Baruch and A. Faust, 64–80. Ramat Gan, 1996.

Mazar, E. *Temple Mount Excavations II*. As *Qedem* 43 (2003)
Mazar, E. *Temple Mount Excavations III*. As *Qedem* 46 (2007).
Mazar, E., and B. Mazar. *Excavations in the South of the Temple Mount, Jerusalem*. As *Qedem* 29 (1989).
McAuliffe, J. *Qur'ānic Christians*. Cambridge, 1991.
Montgomery, J. A. *Arabia and the Bible*. New York, 1969.
Morabia, A. *Le Ǧihād dans l'Islam médiéval*. Paris, 1993.
Morabia, A. "Ibn Taimiya, les juifs et la tora." *SI* 49 (1978): 91–122; 50 (1979): 77–107.
Moubarac, Y. *Abraham dans le Coran*. Paris, 1958.
Mourad, S. "Did the Crusades Change Jerusalem's Religious Symbolism in Islam." *Bulletin of Middle East Medievalists* 22 (2014): 3–8.
Mourad, S. "Jerusalem in Early Islam." In *Jerusalem Ideal and Reality*, edited by T. Mayer and S. Mourad, 86–102. New York, 2008.
Müller, D. H. *Die Propheten in ihrer ursprünglichen Form*. Vol. 1. Vienna, 1896.
Müller, H. P. "Der Begriff 'Ratsel' im Alten Testament." *VT* 20 (1970): 465–89.
Munajjid, S. "*Qiṭ'ah min kitāb mafqūd. al-Masālik wa-l-mamālik li-l-Muhallabī*." *RIMA* 4 (1958): 43–71.
Muṣṭafā, M. A. "*al-Tanqīb fī-l-Kūfah*." *Sumer* 12 (1950): 3–32.
Nagel, T. *Die Qiṣaṣ al-anbiyā'*. Bonn, 1967.
Neuwirth, A. "Erste Qibla—Fernstes Masgid? Jerusalem im horizont des historischen Muḥammad." In *Zion—Ort der Begenung. Festschrift für Laurentius Klein*, edited by F. Hahn et al., 227–70. Hanstein, 1993.
Neuwirth, A. "Jerusalem and the Genesis of Islamic Scripture." In *Jerusalem*, edited by L. Levine, 315–26. New York, 1999.
Neuwirth, A. *Studien zur Komposition der mekkanischen Suren*. Berlin, 1981.
Neuwirth, A., et al., eds. *The Qur'ān in Context*. Boston, 2011.
Newby, G. "Abraha and Sennacherib: A Talmudic Parallel to the *Tafsīr* on *Sūrat al-Fīl*." *JAOS* 94 (1974): 431–37.
Newby, G. *A History of the Jews of Arabia*. Columbia, SC, 1988.
Newby, G. *The Making of the Last Prophet*. Columbia, SC, 1989.
Newby, G. "Tafsīr Isrā'ilīyāt." In *Studies in Qur'ān and Tafsīr. JAAR* Thematic Issue 47 (1979): 685–97.
Nöldeke, T. *Neue Beiträge zur semitischen Sprachwissenschaft*. Strasbourg, 1910.
Nöldeke, T, et al. *Geschichte des Qorans*. 2nd edition. 3 vols. Vols. 1 and 2 revised by F. Schwally. Vol. 3 revised by G. Bergstrasser and O. Pretzl. Leipzig, 1909–26.
Northedge, A. "Archeology and New Urban Settlement in Syria and Iraq." In *The Byzantine and Early Islamic Near East: Papers of the Second Workshop on Late Antiquity and Early Islam*, edited by A. Cameron and G. R. D. King, 231–65. Princeton, 1994.
Northedge, A. "Herzfeld, Creswell, and Samarra." *Muqarnas* 8 (1991): 74–93.
Noth, A. "Der Character der ersten grossen Sammlungen von Nachrichten zur frühen Kalifenzeit." *Der Islam* 47 (1971): 168–99.
Noth, A. *Heiliger Krieg und heiliger Kampf in Islam und Christentum*. Bonn, 1996.
Noth, A. *Quellenkritische Studien zur Themen, Formen und Tendenzen frühislamischer Geschichtsüberlieferung*. Bonn, 1973. Edited by L. Conrad and translated by M. Bonner as *The Early Arabic Historical Tradition*. Princeton, 1994.

Obermann, J. "Islamic Origins: A Study in the Background and Foundation." In *The Arab Heritage*, edited by N. A. Faris, 58–120. Princeton, 1944.
Omar, F. *The ʿAbbāsid Caliphate, 132/750–170/786.* Baghdad, 1969. (A slightly shortened version of his *al-ʿAbbāsīyūn.*)
Omar, F. *ʾAbbāsīyāt: Studies in the History of the Early ʿAbbāsids.* Baghdad, 1976.
Omar, F. *al-ʿAbbāsīyūn al-awāʾil: 132–70/750–86.* 2 vols. Beirut, 1380/1970–73.
Omar, F. "Aspects of ʿAbbāsid Ḥusaynid Relations." *Arabica* 22 (1976): 170–79.
Paret, R. *Grenzen der Koranforschung.* Stuttgart, 1950.
Paret, R. "Der Koran als Geschichtsquelle." *Islamica* 27 (1961): 26–42.
Paret, R. *Der Koran: Kommentar und Konkordanz.* Stuttgart, 1971, 1977.
Paret, R. "Toleranz und Intoleranz im Islam." *Saeculum* 21 (1970): 344–65.
Pauliny, J. "Islamische Legend über Bukht-Nassar (Nebukadnezar)." *GO* 4 (1972): 161–83.
Pauliny, J. "Zur Rolle der Quṣṣaṣ bei der Entstehung und Überlieferung der popularen Prophetenlegenden." *Asian and African Studies* (Bratislava) 10 (1974): 125–41.
Pauty, E. "Villes spontaneés et villes crées en Islam." *AIEO* 9 (1951): 52–75.
Perez, R. "The Bathhouse from the Temple Mount Excavations [Hebrew]." *New Studies on Jerusalem* 6 (1998): 103–16.
Perlmann, M. "Another Kaʿb al-Aḥbār Story." *JQR* 45 (1954): 48–51.
Perlmann, M. "A Legendary Story of Kaʿb al-Aḥbār's Conversion to Islam." In *The Joshua Starr Memorial Volume*, 85–99. New York, 1953.
Perlmann, M. "The Medieval Polemics between Islam and Judaism." In *Religion in a Religious Age,* edited by S. D. Goitein, 103–29. Cambridge, MA, 1974.
Peters, F. S. *Jerusalem and Mecca.* New York, 1986.
Petersen, E. *ʿAlī and Muʿāwiyah in Early Arabic Tradition.* Copenhagen, 1964.
Prawer J., and H. Ben-Shammai, eds. *The History of Jerusalem, 638–1099.* Jerusalem, 1996.
Prior, M., ed. *Western Scholarship and the History of Palestine.* London, 1998.
Qedem. Monographs of the Institute of Archeology. Hebrew University, Jerusalem.
Rabbat, N. "The Dome of the Rock Revisited." *Muqarnas* 10 (1993): 67–75.
Rabbat, N. "The Umayyad Meaning of the Dome of the Rock." *Muqarnas* 6 (1989): 12–21.
Rabbat, N. "The Religious Situation of Mecca from the Eve of Islam up to the Ḥijra." *IS* 16 (1977): 289–301.
Rahman, F. "Pre-foundations of the Muslim Community in Mecca." *SI* 43 44–66.
Reinink, G. "Ps.-Methodius: A Concept of History in Response to the Rise of Islam." In *The Byzantine and Early Islamic Near East: Papers of the First Workshop on Late Antiquity and Early Islam*, edited by A. Cameron and L. Conrad, 149–88. Princeton, 1992.
Reinink, G. *Die Syrische Apokolypse des Pseudo Methodios.* Louvain, 1993.
Reitemeyer, E. *Die Städtegrundungen der Araber im Islam.* Leipzig, 1912.
Rheuter, O. "Sassanian Architecture: A History." In *Survey of Persian Art,* edited by A. U. Pope, 1:491–578. New York, 1964.
Richter, G. *Das Geschichtsbild der arabischen Historiker des Mittelalters.* Tübingen, 1933.
Richter, G. *Studien zur Geschichte der älteren arabischen Fürstenspiegel.* Berlin, 1932.

Ringgren, H. *Islam, Aslama, and Muslim*. Lund, 1949.
Roberts, J. J. "Myth versus History: Relaying the Comparative Foundations." *CBQ* 38 (1976): 1–13.
Robinson, C. F. *Islamic Historiography*. Cambridge, 2003.
Robson, J. "Ibn Isḥāq's Use of the Isnād." *Bulletin of the John Rowlands Library* 38 (1955–56): 449–65.
Rogers, J. M. "Sāmarrā." In *The Islamic City*, edited A. H. Hourani and S. M. Stern, 119–56. Oxford, 1970.
Rosen-Ayalon, M. *Art et archéologie islamiques en Palestine*. Paris, 2002.
Rosen-Ayalon, M. *The Early Islamic Monuments of al-Ḥaram al-Sharīf*. As *Qedem* 28 (1989).
Rosenthal, F. *A History of Muslim Historiography*. Leiden, 1952. 2nd edition, 1968.
Rosenthal, F. "The Influence of the Biblical Tradition on Muslim Historiography." In *Historians of the Middle East*, edited by B. Lewis and P. M. Holt, 35–45. London, 1962.
Rothstein, G. *Die Dynastie der Lakhmiden in al-Ḥira*. Berlin, 1895.
Rubin, U. "Between Arabia and the Holy Land: A Mecca-Jerusalem Axis of Sanctity." *JSAI* 34 (2008): 345–62.
Rubin, U. "Prophets and Progenitors in the Early Shīʿa Tradition." *JSAI* 1 (1979): 41–65.
Rubin, U. "Muḥammad's Night Journey (*Isrā'*) to al-Masjid al-Aqṣā: Aspects of the Earliest Origins of the Islamic Sanctity of Jerusalem." *Al-Qanṭara* 29 (2008): 147–64.
Rubin, Z. "The Church and the Holy Sepulcher and the Beginning of the Conflict between the Sees of Caesarea and Jerusalem." *Jerusalem Cathedra* 2 (1982): 76–106.
Rudolph, W. *Die Abhängigkeit des Korans von Judentum und Christentum*. Stuttgart, 1922.
Sachedina, A. A. *Islamic Messianism*. Albany, 1981.
Sadan, J. "A Legal Opinion of a Muslim Jurist Regarding the Sanctity of Jerusalem." *IOS* 13 (1993): 231–45.
Safar, F. *Wāsiṭ, the Sixth Season's Excavations*. Cairo, 1945.
Salmon, G. *L'introduction topographique à l'histoire de Baghdadh*. Paris, 1904.
Sāmmarā'ī, Y. *Ta'rīkh madīnat Sāmarrā*. 3 vols. Baghdad, 1968–73.
Sanders, P. *Ritual Politics and the City in Fatimid Cairo*. Albany, 1994.
Saperstein, M., ed. *Essential Papers on Messianic Movements*. New York, 1992.
Schacht, J. "A Revaluation of Islamic Traditions." *JRAS* (1949): 143–54.
Schapiro, I. *Die haggadischen Elemente im erzählenden Teil des Korans*. Berlin, 1907.
Schick, R. "The Christian Communities of Palestine from Byzantine to Islamic Rule: A Historical and Archeological Study." In *Studies in Late Antique and Early Islam*, edited by A. Cameron and G. R. D. King, 2:180–219. Princeton, 1995.
Schoeler, G. "Die Frage der schritlichen oder mundlichen Überlieferung der Wissenschaften im früen Islam." *Der Islam* 62 (1985): 2011–30.
Schoeler, G. "Mundliche Thora und Ḥadīt: Überlieferung, Shreibverbot, Redaktion." *Der Islam* 66 (1989): 213–51.
Schoeler, G. "Schreiben und Veröffentlichen zur Verwendung und Function der Schrift in den ersten islamischen Jahrhunderten." *Der Islam* 69 (1992): 1–43.
Schoeler, G. "Weiteres zur Frage der schriftlichen oder mundlichen Überlieferung der Wissenschaften im Islam." *Der Islam* 66 (1989): 38–67.

Scholem, G. *The Messianic Idea in Judaism.* New York, 1971.
Schützinger, H. "Die arabische Legende von Nebukadnezar und Johannes dem Teufer." *Der Islam* 40 (1965): 113–41.
Seeligman, J. "The Hinterland of Jerusalem during the Byzantine Period." In *Unearthing Jerusalem*, edited by K. Galor and G. Avni, 361–83. Winona Lake, IN, 2011.
Sellheim, R. "Prophet, Chalif, und Geschichte: Die Muḥammad-Biographie des Ibn Isḥāq." *Oriens* 18–19 (1967): 33–91.
Sezgin, F. *Geschichte des arabischen Schrifttums.* Vol. 1. Leiden, 1967.
Sezgin, U. *Abū Miḫnaf: Ein Beitrag zur Historiographie der umaiyadischen Zeit.* Leiden, 1971.
Sharon, M. "The ʿAbbāsid Daʿwa Re-examined on the Basis of the Discovery of a New Source." *Arabic and Islamic Studies* (Bar-Ilan University) 1 (1973): 21–41.
Sharon, M. "Ahl al-Bayt—People of the House." *JSAI* 8 (1986): 169–84.
Sharon, M. *Black Banners from the East.* Jerusalem, 1983.
Sharon, M. *Corpus Inscriptionum Arabicorum Palaestinae.* 5 vols. Leiden, 1997–.
Sharon, M. "Notes on the Question of Legitimacy of Government in Islam." *IOS* 10 (1980): 116–23.
Sharon, M. "The 'Praises' of Jerusalem as a Source for the Early History of Islam." *BO* 49 (1992): 56–80.
Sharon, M. "Shape of the Holy." *SO* 107 (2009): 38–51.
Sharon, M. *Social and Military Aspects of the ʿAbbāsid Revolution.* Jerusalem, 1990.
Sharon, M., ed. *Studies in Honor of David Ayalon.* Leiden, 1986.
Shinan, A. "The Many Names of Jerusalem." In *Jerusalem,* edited by L. Levine, 120–32. New York, 1999.
Shoemaker, S. *The Death of a Prophet.* Philadelphia, 2012.
Siddiqi, M. Z. *Ḥadīth Literature.* Cambridge, 1993.
Sidersky, D. *Les origines des légendes musulmanes dans le Coran.* Paris, 1933.
Silver, A. H. *A History of Messianic Speculation in Israel.* New York, 1927.
Sivan, E. "Beginnings of the Faḍā'il al-Quds Literature." *IOS* 1 (1971): 263–71.
Sivan, E. "Le Caractere sacré de Jerusalem dans l'Islam aux xiie–xiiie siècle." *SI* 27 (1967): 49–82.
Sivan, E. *L'Islam et la Croisade.* Paris, 1967.
Smith, J. *An Historical and Semantic Study of the Term "Islām" as Seen in a Sequence of Qur'ān Commentaries.* Missoula, 1975.
Smith, J. "The Meaning of Islām in Ḥadīth Literature." *IC* 48 (1974): 139–48.
Soggin, J. A. "The Davidic-Solomonic Kingdom." In *Israelite and Judean History*, edited by J. H. Hayes and I. M. Miller, 332–80. London, 1977.
Sommer, B. *A Prophet Reads Scripture.* Stanford, 1998.
Soucek, P. "The Temple of Solomon in Islamic Legend and Art." In *Archeological Fact and Medieval Tradition in Christian, Islamic and Jewish Art*, edited by J. Guttman, 73–123, 184–93. Missoula, 1976.
Sousah, A. *See* Susa, A.
Speiser, E. A. *Genesis.* Anchor Bible Series. New York, 1964.
Speyer, H. *Die biblischen Erzälungen im Qoran.* Hildesheim, 1961.
Steinberg, M. *The Poetics of Biblical Narrative.* Bloomington, 1987.

Steinschneider, M. *Polemische und apologetische Literatur in arabischer Sprache.* Hildesheim, 1966.

Stemberger, G. "Jerusalem in the Early Seventh Century: Hopes and Aspirations of Christians and Jews." In *Jerusalem*, edited by L. Levine, 260–74. New York, 1999.

Stemberger, G. *Juden und Christen in Heiligen Land.* Munich, 1987.

Stern, S. M. "The Constitution of the Islamic City." In *The Islamic City,* edited by A. H. Hourani and S. M. Stern, 25–50. Oxford, 1970.

Stillman, N. A. "The Story of Cain and Abel in the Qur'ān and Muslim Commentaries." *JSS* 19 (1974): 231–39.

Stone, M. E. "Holy Land Pilgrimage of Armenians before the Arab Conquest." *RB* 93 (1986): 129–45.

Streck, M. *Die alte Landschaft Babylonien.* Leiden, 1900.

Strousma, G. *The Making of the Arbrahamic Religions in Late Antiquity.* Oxford, 2015.

Sulzbach, A. *Targum Scheni zum Buche Esther.* Frankfurt am Main, 1920.

Susa, A. *Rayy Sāmarrā fī 'ahd al-khilāfat al-'Abbāsiyah.* 2 vols. Baghdad, 1948–49.

Taeschner, F. "Die alttestamentlichen Bibelzitate vor allem aus dem Pentateuch in Aṭ-Ṭabarīs Kitāb ad-dīn wad-daula und ihre Bedeutung für die Frage nach der Echtheit dieser Schrift." *OC*, 3d ser., 9 (1934): 23–39.

Thackston, W. M., Jr. *The Tales of the Prophets.* Boston, 1978.

Torrey, C. C. *The Jewish Foundations of Islam.* New York, 1967.

Tritton, A. S. *The Caliphs and Their Non-Muslim Subjects.* London, 1970.

Tritton, A. S. "Islam and the Protected Religions." *JRAS* (1931): 311–38.

Tsafrir, Y. "Byzantine Jerusalem: The Configuration of a Christian City." In *Jerusalem,* edited by L. Levine, 133–50. New York, 1999.

Tsafrir, Y. "The Maps Used by Theodosius: On the Pilgrim Maps of the Holy Land and Jerusalem in the Sixth Century C.E." *DOP* 40 (1986): 93–110.

Urbach, E. "A Midrash of Redemption from Late Crusader Times." *Eretz Israel* 10 (1971): 58–63.

Vajda, G. "Juifs et Musulmans selon le ḥadīt." *JA* 229 (1939): 57–127.

van Ess, J. "Vision and Ascension: Sūrat al-Najm and Its Relationship with Muḥammad's Mi'rāj." *JQS* 1 (1999): 47–62.

van Seters, J. *In Search of History.* New Haven, 1983.

van Vloten, G. *Recherches sur la domination arabe, le chiitisme et la croyances messianiques sous le khalifat des Omayydes.* Amsterdam, 1894.

Vecca Vaglieri, L. "The Patriarchal and Umayyad Caliphates." In the *Cambridge History of Islam*, edited by A. Lambton et al., 1:57–103. Cambridge, 1970.

Vilnai, Z. *Jerusalem the Capital of Israel* [Hebrew]. 2 vols. Jerusalem, 1970.

von Grunebaum, G. "The Cultural Function of the Dream as Illustrated in Classical Islam." In his *Dream and Human Societies.*

von Grunebaum, G., ed. *The Dream and Human Societies.* Berkeley, 1966.

von Grunebaum, G. "Die islamische Stadt." *Saeculum* 6 (1955): 138–53.

von Grunebaum, G. "The Muslim Town and the Hellenistic Town." *Scienta* (1955): 304–70.

von Grunebaum, G. "The Structure of the Muslim Town." In *Islam: Essays in the Growth and Nature of a Cultural Tradition*, 141–55. Chicago, 1955.

Waldman, M. "Semiotics and Historical Narrative." *Papers in Comparative Studies* 1 (1981): 167–85.

Waldman, M. *Toward a Theory of Historical Narrative: A Close Study in Perso-Islamicate Historiography.* Columbus, OH, 1980.

Walker, P. *Holy Cities, Holy Places.* Oxford, 1990.

Wansbrough, J. *Quranic Studies.* LOS 31. Oxford, 1977.

Wansbrough, J. *The Sectarian Milieu.* LOS 34. Oxford, 1978.

Wasserstrom, S. *Between Muslim and Jew.* Princeton, 1995.

Watt, W. M. *Bell's Introduction to the Qur'ān: Completely Revised and Enlarged.* Edinburgh, 1970.

Watt, W. M. "The Dating of the Qur'ān: A Review of Richard Bell's Theories." *JRAS* (1957): 46–56.

Watt, W. M. "The Early Development of Muslim Attitudes towards the Bible." In his *Early Islam,* 77–85, 195–97.

Watt, W. M. "Early Discussions about the Qur'ān." *MW* 40 (1950): 27–40.

Watt, W. M. *Early Islam.* Edinburgh, 1990.

Watt, W. M. "The Materials Used by Ibn Isḥāq." In *Historians of the Middle East,* edited by B. Lewis and P. M. Holt, 23–34. London, 1962.

Watt, W. M. *Muhammad at Mecca.* Oxford, 1953.

Watt, W. M. *Muhammad at Medina.* Oxford, 1956.

Weil, G. *The Bible, the Koran, and the Talmud.* New York, 1846.

Weil, G. *Biblische Legenden der Muselmänner.* Leipzig, 1886.

Wellhausen, J. *Das arabische Reich und sein Sturz.* Berlin, 1902. Translated by M. G. Weir as *The Arab Kingdom and Its Fall.* Calcutta, 1927.

Wellhausen, J. *Reste arabischen Heidentums.* Berlin. 1961.

Wendell, C. "Baghdad: *Imago Mundi* and Other Foundation Lore." *IJMES 2* (1971): 99–128.

Wensinck, A. J. *Mohammad en de Joden te Medina.* Leiden, 1908. Translated and edited by W. Behn as *Muḥammad and the Jews of Medina.* Freiburg, 1975.

Whitcomb, D. "An Urban Structure for the Early Islamic City: An Archaeological Hypothesis." In *Cities in the Pre-modern Islamic World: The Urban Impact of Religion, State and Society,* edited by A. K. Bennison and A. L. Gascoigne, 15–26. London, 2007.

Whitcomb, D. "Jerusalem and the Beginnings of the Islamic City." In *Unearthing Jerusalem,* edited by K. Galor and G. Avni, 399–416. Winona Lake, IN, 2011.

Whitcomb, D. "The *Miṣr* of Ayla: Settlement at al-ʿAqaba in the Early Islamic Period." In *The Byzantine and Early Islamic Near East: Papers of the Second Workshop on Late Antiquity and Early Islam,* edited by A. Cameron and G. R. D. King, 155–70. Princeton, 1995.

Whitcomb, D. "Urbanism in Arabia," *Arabian Archeology and Epigraphy* 7 (1995): 38–51.

Whitelam, K. *The Invention of Ancient Israel.* New York, 1996.

Wilkin, R. *The Land Called Holy.* New Haven, 1992.

Wilkinson, J. *Pilgrims before the Crusades.* Jerusalem, 1997.

Wolfensohn, I. *Kaʿb al-Aḥbār und seine Stellung in Ḥadīt und der islamischen Legendenliteratur.* Frankfurt am Main, 1933.

Wüstenfeld, F. *Chroniken der Stadt Mekka.* 2 vols. Hildesheim, 1981.
Wüstenfeld, F. *Die Geschichtschreiber der Araber und ihre Werke.* Gottingen, 1882.
Yusuf Ali, A. *The Meaning of the Glorious Qur'ān*. London, 1983.
Zambauer, E. *Manuel de généalogie et de chronologie pour I'histoire de l'Islam.* Hanover, 1927.
Zwettler, M. *The Oral Tradition of Classical Arabic Poetry.* Columbus, OH, 1978.

Index

al-ʿAbbas ibn ʿAbd al-Muṭṭalib, 139
Abbasids, 86–88, 91–93; 68 AH pilgrimage and, 142; administrative centers in, 109; Arabic historiography and, 137; Ben Yochai cycle and, 1875; imperialism and, 176, 179; al-Maʾmūn and, 173n51; messianism and, 163–64; palace-mosques and, 114–15, 119; Samarra murders and, 180; siege of Mecca and, 146; Sunnis and, 140; Temple Mount excavations and, 98; Umayyads and, 63; unrecovered historical sources and, 139
ʿAbdallāh b. ʿAbbās, 148
ʿAbdallāh b. al-Zubayr, 70, 83, 85, 121, 126–31, 143–46, 158
ʿAbd al-ʿAzīz b. Marwān, 148
ʿAbd al-Malik b. Marwān, 83–87, 147, 150; 68 AH pilgrimage and, 143; Alids and, 133; apocalyptic literature and, 78–79; Arabic historiography and, 121–22, 124, 131–32, 134, 136–37; Arab tribes and, 152–53; architectural symbolism and, 155–57; Christianity and, 176; construction practices compared and, 87–91; decorative motifs and, 159–61; Dome of the Rock's meaning and, 151; *faḍāʾil* and, 11; Friday mosques and, 135; imperialism and, 177–79; Jewish traditions and, 168; messianism and, 163–65, 167, 171–72; Muʿāwiyah and, 77, 95; non-Muslim sites for mosque building and, 59; palace-mosques and, 115; rebellions against, 91–94; siege of Mecca and, 144–46; site of Islamic rule and, 65, 68–70, 72, 80; Sunnis and, 140; *Sūrah* 17:2–8 and, 54; Temple Mount excavations and, 100, 110–11; triumphalism and, 169–70; Umayyad administrative complex and, 120; unicity of God and, 173; unrecovered historical sources and, 138–39; visual symbolism and, 154; Zubayrid rebellion and, 92–94, 126–30
Abraham, 1, 3, 6; anti-Jerusalem literature and, 189–91; blessed lands and, 45; God's promise to, 21, 194; holy sites and, 196–97; messianism and, 166; monotheism and, 28; Mount Moriah and, 35; New Jerusalem and, 52; primeval rock, 158; *Sūrah* 5 and, 22; vows to visit Jerusalem and, 187–88; Wāsiṭī and, 169n39; Zubayrid rebellion and, 127
Abū Bakr, 60, 70
Abū Ḥamzah al-Mukhtār b. ʿAwf, 136
Abū-l-Fidāʾ, 134
Abū-l-Maʿālī, 182–83. *See also* Ibn al-Murajjā
Abū-l-Qāsim and, 181
Abū Sufyān, 125
Abū ʿUbaydah b. al-Jarrāḥ, 57
Acre, siege of, 75n41

and, 74; cosmogony in, 36–37; decorative motifs and, 159–60; New Jerusalem and, 50; *Sūrah* 2:114 and, 30; *Sūrah* 5 and, 22–23; *Sūrah* 17:2–8 and, 49
Rafiqah, 104
Rajā' b. Ḥaywah, 12, 89–90, 133
Ramle, 61
al-Rāzī, Muḥammad, 29n18, 48, 48n22, 52
Resurrection, 63, 160, 192
revisionist historians, 17–19, 43–46, 84, 166
Rhineland, 76n42
righteous caliphs, 17, 60, 124
rock of Creation. *See* primeval rock (Temple Mount)
Romans, 2, 25, 72–74; architectural symbolism and, 156; Christian-pagan alliance and, 31; *faḍā'il* literature and, 9; name of Jerusalem and, 6n14; New Jerusalem and, 50; palace complexes and, 112; Palestine and, 4n6; *Sūrah* 17:2–8 and, 48; Temple Mount and, 38
Rosen-Ayalon, Myriam, 159–61, 163–66
Rosenthal, Franz, 139n49
Round City, 91–94, 114–17, 134, 176; construction practices and, 86–88. *See also* al-Manṣūr
Rubin, Uri, 43–46, 50, 52; messianism and, 48n22; *Sūrah* 17:2–8 and, 49, 53–55
rukhaṣ (exceptions to rules of Islam), *147*
Rūm (Rome), 30. *See also* Byzantines; Romans

Sabaeans, 45
Sa'd b. Abī Waqqāṣ, 113, 115n46
al-Sā'ib, Muḥammad b., 136
Sa'īd b. 'Abd al-'Azīz, 13
ṣā'ifah (summer campaign), 151
Saint Catherine's Monastery, 16
Saladin, 149, 159n17
Saljuqs, 75
salvation history (*Heilsgeschichte*), 18n37
al-Sām, 4. *See also* al-Shām; Shem
Samaria (Shomron), 5
Samarra, 104, 121, 180
Sarah, 1, 190–91
Ṣa'ṣa'ah b. Ṣuḥān al-'Abdī, 63–64
Sasanids, 40n4, 47, 87, 99, 115, 169–70; Byzantine war and, 24; churches destroyed by, 110, 117; occupation by, 111; Palestine and, 26n10; Zubayrid rebellion and, 129
Seal of the Prophets, 197n33, 198
Seleucids, 30
self-identity, 41n4
Sennacherib, 4, 47
Shāfi'ite school, 187
al-Shām, 2–5, 16, 45, 193; administrative centers of, 69; anti-Jerusalem literature and, 190; Arabic historiography and, 124, 136; Christian rule and, 25; concentric circles of holiness and, 36; construction practices and, 89; diverting the *ḥajj* and, 133; *faḍā'il* and, 9–10, 184n6; historical sources for, 7; imperialism and, 177–78; messianism and, 172; modern nations in, 5; Mu'āwiyah and, 60; Mu'āwiyah and, 61; Muslim conquest and, 56; non-Muslim sites for mosque building and, 59; palace-mosques and, 115; praise for native abodes and, 180, 183; site of Islamic rule and, 64, 66–68, 80; *Sūrah* 2:114 and, 33; Zubayrid rebellion and, 126, 128–29
Shāmīn, 4–5
Shani, Raya, 166–67
Sharon, Moshe, 106, 108–10, 119, 168; messianism and, 166–67, 171–72
Sheba, Queen of, 68
Shechem, 5n10
Shem, 3. *See also* al-Shām
Shi'ites, 138–40
Shiloh, 47
Shoemaker, Stephen, 18–19; *The Death of a Prophet*, 41n4
Shomron. *See* Samaria

Umayyads (*continued*)
symbolic transfers of authority and, 114–15; Temple Mount excavations and, 96–98, 102–6, 110–13, 119–20; Temple Mount functions and, 106–10; triumphalism and, 169–70; unicity of God and, 173–75; Zubayrid rebellion and, 91–94, 126–29. *See also* Arabia
ummah (community), 122–23, 146
unicity of God, 173–75. *See also* monotheism
United Israelite Monarchy, 4
al-Urdunn (Jordan), 3; blessed lands and, 45n15; *faḍā'il* transmission chains and, 12. *See also* Jordan
Ūrīshalam (Jerusalem), 56n33, 170
'Uthmān b. 'Affān, 60, 67, 78–79, 113

Vaglieri, L. Vecca, 41n4
Via Dolorosa, 51
visual symbolism, 123, 154–58; Arabic historiography and, 124; Christianity and, 176–79; decorative motifs and, 159–62; Dome of the Rock and, 151, 154, 159–62; Jewish memorabilia and, 167–68; messianism and, 162–66, 171–72; unicity of God and, 173–75

Wadi al-Arish (river of Egypt), 5–6
Wādī-l-Qurā, 45n15
Wahb b. Munnabih, 130
al-Walīd, 65, 68, 70, 72; *Aphrodito papyri* and, 109; Arabic historiography and, 133, 150; architectural symbolism and, 158; diverting the *ḥajj* and, 134; *ḥajj* and, 146; imperialism and, 177–78; non-Muslim sites for mosque building and, 59; palace complexes and, 107–8; *Sūrah* 17:2–8 and, 54–55; triumphalism and, 169; visual symbolism and, 154
Wansbrough, John, 18n37
al-Wāqidī, 136–37, 142, 144n56
Wāsiṭ, 114–17
al-Wāsiṭī, Muḥammad b. Aḥmad, 167–68, 169n39, 171n45; *Faḍā'il al-Bayt al-Muqaddas*, 11
Wellhausen, Julian, 66–68, 130, 154n4
West Bank, naming of, 5n10
Whitcomb, Donald, 105n15, 106n15, 156n8
wuqūf ceremony, 141, 149

Yaḥyā b. 'Amr al-Shaybānī al-Ramlī, 12
Yaḥyā b. Ḥanḍalah, 108
al-Ya'qūbī, Aḥmad b. Abī Ya'qub: 68 AH pilgrimage and, 142; Alids and, 140; anti-Umayyad bias of, 132; Arabic historiography and, 131, 133, 136–37, 147, 150; *faḍā'il* and, 11; *faḍā'il* transmission chains and, 13; Friday mosques and, 135; *ḥajj* and, 146; siege of Mecca and, 146; unrecovered historical sources and, 138; Zubayrid rebellion and, 126–28, 130
Yāqūt al-Ḥamawī, 4, 86n8; *faḍā'il* transmission chains and, 13; Muqaddasī and, 129n15; palace-mosques and, 114; al-Shām and, 5
Yathrib (Medina), 192
Yazīd b. Mu'āwiyah, 79–80, 125, 130, 144
Yazīd II, 154n4
Yazīd b. Salām, 89–90
Yemen, 45, 198
Yerushalayim (Jerusalem), 61, 170

Zamzam, Well of, 129
al-Zandaward, 114
Zeus, 30
Zion, 6n13. *See also* Holy Land
ziyārah (religious visit), 188
Zoroastrians, 25
Zubayrids, 91–94, 130, 141–42; 'Abd al-Malik and, 85; Arabic historiography and, 125–29, 132, 136; Arab tribes and, 152; diverting the *ḥajj* and, 133; Dome of the Rock's meaning and, 151; imperialism and, 176; Rabbat on, 168n38; siege of Mecca and, 145–46; unrecovered historical sources and, 139
al-Zuhrī, Ibn Shihāb, 127